CLOSED DOORS, OPPORTUNITIES LOST

CLOSED DOORS, OPPORTUNITIES LOST

The Continuing Costs of Housing Discrimination

John Yinger

Russell Sage Foundation • New York

The Russell Sage Foundation

The Russell Sage Foundation, one of the oldest of America's general purpose foundations, was established in 1907 by Mrs. Margaret Olivia Sage for "the improvement of
social and living conditions in the United States." The Foundation seeks to fulfill this
mandate by fostering the development and dissemination of knowledge about the
country's political, social, and economic problems. While the Foundation endeavors
to assure the accuracy and objectivity of each book it publishes, the conclusions and
interpretations in Russell Sage Foundation publications are those of the authors and
not of the Foundation, its Trustees, or its staff. Publication by Russell Sage, therefore,
does not imply Foundation endorsement.

Library of Congress Cataloging-in-Publication Data

Yinger, John, 1947–
    Closed doors, opportunities lost: the continuing costs of housing
discrimination / John Yinger.
      p. cm.
    Includes bibliographical references and index.
    ISBN 0-87154-967-0
    1. Discrimination in mortgage loans—United States. I. Title.
HG2040.5.U5Y56 1995
332.7'22'0973—dc20   95-30260
                                        CIP

RUSSELL SAGE FOUNDATION
112 East 64th Street, New York, New York 10021

10 9 8 7 6 5 4 3 2 1

To Mary and Cara with all my love

CONTENTS

PREFACE
AND
ACKNOWLEDGMENTS

Events in the 1960s brought housing discrimination and other civil rights issues onto the national stage. Following up on a campaign promise, President John F. Kennedy signed, in November 1962, an executive order banning discrimination in new housing financed by the federal government. The next June, he proposed a civil rights bill that outlawed discrimination in employment and public accommodations and promoted school desegregation, but which was silent on the more controversial issue of housing discrimination. President Kennedy supported this bill with remarkably clear, strong language:

> "We are confronted primarily with a moral issue. It is as old as the Scriptures and is as clear as the American Constitution. The heart of the question is whether all Americans are to be afforded equal rights and equal opportunities, whether we are going to treat our fellow Americans as we want to be treated." [Branch, 1988, pp. 823–824]

That August one-quarter of a million people marched on Washington to urge the strengthening and passage of this civil rights bill and an end to racial segregation in all aspects of American life, including housing. Although this bill did not become law, its direct descendant, the Civil Rights Act of 1964, was passed, followed a few years later by the Civil Rights Act of 1968. Title VIII of the 1968 Act, which is known as the Fair Housing Act, forbids racial and ethnic discrimination in housing.

This civil rights legislation brought some significant changes to this country, including a decline in the most aggressive forms of housing discrimination. Unfortunately, however, neither this legislation nor any of the civil rights legislation that came later has been sufficient to eliminate housing discrimination or the huge cost that it imposes on African American and Hispanic American households—and indeed on us all. The purpose of this book is to document this continuing discrimination and its high costs and to propose remedies. Attacking racial and ethnic discrimination remains one of this country's greatest challenges—and greatest opportunities.

As I look back over this project, I am amazed by the quantity and quality of assistance I have received from colleagues around the country. I take this as a sign that the topic of this book is current and important (and reject the alternative interpretation that so many of my colleagues believe I need help). I am grateful for all this assistance, but the reader should not assume that any of these helpful people agrees with what I have to say.

All my life I have been learning about race relations from my parents. My mother Winnie Yinger and my father J. Milton Yinger taught me by their example how to treat all people with dignity and respect. My intellectual debt to my father also is beyond words. When, as a high school student, I was fascinated by the March on Washington and the struggle for civil rights, he gave me his textbook written with George Simpson, *Racial and Cultural Minorities,* then in its second edition, and *Dark Ghetto,* by Kenneth Clark. This was a high-quality, and obviously influential, introduction to social science! In June 1965, just after I graduated from high school, he introduced me to Dr. Martin Luther King, Jr., who gave the commencement address at Oberlin College, where my father was a professor of sociology and Dr. King's official host. What a memorable encounter for an eighteen-year-old kid! Since then I have had countless conversations with my father about racial and ethnic relations and have read many of his books and articles on the subject. I have observed his broad approach to problems, his ability to cross disciplinary boundaries, and his meticulous approach to scholarship and language. I can only hope that some of it has rubbed off on me. Anyone who knows his work (or for that matter who reads the endnotes to Chapter 1) can see how strongly it has influenced my own. On top of all this, he gave me many helpful comments on drafts of this book. Thanks, Mom. Thanks, Dad.

This book draws heavily on data and results from the Housing Discrimination Study (HDS), a $2 million research project sponsored by the U.S. Department of Housing and Urban Development (HUD). I was the study's research director. In writing this book, I build on the work of the hundreds of other people who contributed to this study at the Urban Institute, at Syracuse University, and in the many urban areas where data were collected. For their contributions to my understanding of the issues in HDS, I would particularly like to thank Raymond Struyk, the project director; Margery Turner, the deputy research director; and Cliff Schrupp, the director of field operations. In addition, Lauria Grant and Nigel M. Grant, my research assistants, played a crucial role in helping me to prepare the HDS data set for detailed analysis.

The Russell Sage Foundation gave me a grant in the fall of 1991 to begin work on this book, and the Foundation's president Eric Wanner has patiently encouraged me throughout the process and given me several helpful suggestions. Charlotte Shelby provided valuable editorial advice.

Margery Turner participated in my original proposal to Russell Sage and in particular planned to be the author of what is now Chapter 4. But my portion of the book had a long gestation, and by the time I was up to speed, she had taken on new responsibilities that precluded her involvement. Nevertheless, Chapter 4 draws heavily on Marge's research and has benefited greatly from conversations with her. In addition, she made helpful comments on several other chapters and was a key part of the HDS team.

George Galster and I have discussed housing discrimination and related topics ever since we were both hired to participate in writing a literature review for HUD in 1979. George also played an important role in HDS as a member of the advisory board, has written extensively on housing discrimination, and gave me a great deal of helpful material as well as extensive comments on drafts of this book. Overall, George has influenced my thinking so much and I have cited him so often that I can't help but think of him as a silent co-author of several chapters — without assuming he agrees with any of my conclusions.

John Goering made numerous contributions to this project. He invited me to present a survey paper at the HUD-sponsored conference on discrimination and mortgage lending. Not only did this invitation give me an opportunity to immerse myself in the literature on discrimination in mortgage lending, the topic of Chapter 5, it also brought me many contacts that proved valuable in learning about current developments in research and enforcement. In the fall of 1993 John also arranged a series of interviews for me with policy and enforcement officials at HUD and the Justice Department and arranged for me to give a seminar at HUD on some of my preliminary findings. These interviews provided me with crucial information, and I received some helpful feedback at my presentation. In addition,

John has responded cheerfully to my numerous requests for specific material or information.

Steve Ross was my research assistant when I began work on this project, but he quickly moved to the role of a colleague and made many valuable contributions to the book. Steve helped me prepare the HDS data for the new analysis in this book, he put together the data set used to estimate the cost of discrimination in Chapter 6, and he provided valuable comments on many topics as I was drafting the book. Meanwhile, Steve was completing his doctoral dissertation on the spatial mismatch hypothesis (Ross, 1994), a key topic in Chapter 8. His observations on the spatial mismatch literature and his own work on the topic were both extremely helpful to me as I prepared this chapter.

Jan Ondrich, one of my colleagues at Syracuse, signed up to be on the original HDS team and has patiently answered my questions about statistics ever since. His expertise and advice have been very valuable. Jim Follain (who sits in the office next to me) and I have had several helpful conversations about issues in the book, especially in Chapters 1 and 9. Doug Massey gave me extensive comments on the entire manuscript and sent me many helpful papers. Harriet Newburger and Maris Mickelsons each provided detailed information to help me write Chapter 4.

Other colleagues who have provided helpful comments and/or material include Robert Avery, Katharine Bradbury, Richard Burkhauser, Paul Courant, Amy Crews, Reynolds Farley, Ron Ferguson, Paul Fischer, Keith Ihlanfeldt, Helen Ladd, Patrick Mason, Samuel Myers, Jr., Leonard Nakamura, Gary Orfield, Marianne Page, Robert Plotnick, William Rodgers, III, Juliet Saltman, Dave Sjoquist, Tim Smeeding, James Smith, Gary Solon, Geoffrey Tootell, Robert Van Order, Michael White, Ron Wienk, Tony Yezer, and Peter Zorn. Several federal officials were kind enough to grant me an interview and/or to send me helpful material. These officials include Goldia D. Hodgdon, Diane L. Houk, Peter M. Kaplan, Laurence Pearl, Alexander C. Ross, and James P. Turner. While writing this book, I gave seminars on the topic at Brown University, Cornell University, and the Center for Policy Research at Syracuse University and received helpful comments from the seminar participants. Esther Gray helped me produce dozens (hundreds?) of drafts, and Jodi Woodson helped me produce the final version of this book and provided secretarial assistance. In addition, I have received valuable help tracking down data and publications and other research assistance from Marc Tomlinson, Alex Striker, and Coleman McMahon.

Finally, I thank my family, Mary and Cara, for their endless support and inspiration.

P A R T

INTRODUCTION

Race and Ethnicity, Prejudice and Discrimination

In July 1989 a 42-year-old African American woman, married with children, visited a real estate office in the suburbs of Washington, D.C., to inquire about a house that had been advertised in *The Washington Post*. Her family's income of $125,000 was more than enough to qualify for a mortgage on this $189,900 house. The real estate broker told her that the advertised house had been sold and that no similar units were available at that time. The agent, an older white woman, did not invite this customer to call again.

Later that same afternoon, a somewhat younger white woman, also married with children and with a family income slightly below $125,000, visited the same real estate broker to inquire about the same house. Her search was considerably more successful. She too was informed that the advertised unit had been sold, but the broker then took her to inspect four similar houses in the same price range, all of which were still on the market. Moreover, this white customer was invited to call back later for more information and the broker offered to help her find a mortgage.

Across the country in the suburbs of Tucson, a 36-year-old Hispanic man visited a real estate office one morning in June 1989 to ask about another advertised house. The house was just the right size for himself, his wife, and his children, and with a family income of $64,000, he could afford the $89,000 sale price. The real estate broker, who was a middle-aged woman, showed him the advertised house, which was in a neighborhood where half of the residents were Hispanic, and told him that it was still available. She went on to tell him, however, that she knew of no other houses currently for sale in the same price range.

This same agent had told quite a different story to a non-Hispanic white customer the previous afternoon. This 35-year-old white man, also married with children and with a family income somewhat below $64,000, not only was shown the house in the advertisement but also was shown six similar houses in the same price range, all available to be purchased.

These true stories illustrate the unfavorable treatment that African American and Hispanic American households often encounter when they search for a place to live.[1] The problem is not confined to Washington, D.C., and Tucson; it appears in apartment rentals and condominium purchases, as well as in the sale of single-family houses; it shows up in many different types of actions by both housing agents and lenders; and it imposes high costs both on minority households and on society at large. This book documents the extent of racial and ethnic discrimination in housing and mortgage markets, explores the social and economic consequences of this discrimination, and designs a comprehensive set of antidiscrimination policies for the federal government.

Housing discrimination plays a crucial role in a complex social system that produces racial and ethnic animosity and economic disparities. Unfortunately, this role has often been neglected by scholars and policy analysts. For example, an otherwise excellent textbook on poverty and discrimination, now in its fifth edition, does not even mention discrimination in housing.[2] In addition, a supposedly comprehensive exploration of social and economic conditions facing African Americans, commissioned by the National Academy of Sciences, devotes only two paragraphs to discrimination in housing and only eight pages to housing attitudes and residental segregation in a 550-page report issued in 1989.[3] Recently, a few scholars have begun to redress this balance, but the importance of housing discrimination is still not widely known.

This book will show not only that housing discrimination continues to be widespread but also that it makes a powerful contribution to the racial and ethnic disparities that cause this nation so much pain.[4] The book's foundation is evidence from a recent national study of housing discrimination, a study based on new research techniques that make it possible to compare the treatment that equally qualified minority and white households receive when they inquire about available housing. The results are striking. Compared to their white counterparts, African American and Hispanic homeseekers are shown far fewer houses and apartments (and indeed sometimes excluded from available housing altogether), given far less assistance in finding the house or apartment that best fits their needs and in finding a mortgage, and are steered to neighborhoods with minority concentrations or low house values.

Other recent research reveals that real estate agents discriminate in the marketing of housing in largely minority neighborhoods, that lenders discriminate against minorities in pre-application procedures, that black and Hispanic mortgage applicants are more likely than comparable white applicants to be turned down, and that both mortgages and home insurance are difficult to obtain in many minority neighborhoods. All this discrimination drastically restricts the choices of African American and Hispanic households who want to move, contributes directly to large racial and ethnic disparities in homeownership and housing quality, and helps to maintain extensive residential segregation in most urban areas.

This book also documents the fact that continuing housing discrimination has an influence far beyond the costs it imposes on individual minority households. Through its impact on residential segregation, for example, housing discrimination is a key cause of extensive segregation in elementary and secondary schools. Despite decades of federal desegregation efforts, minority children are still heavily concentrated in largely minority schools in which most of the students come from disadvantaged backgrounds, and significant racial and ethnic disparities in dropout rates and educational achievement continue to exist.

Housing discrimination also contributes to minority–white disparities in labor market outcomes. The lines of influence flow not only through housing discrimination's impact on educational disparities, which translate into lower wages and employment rates for minorities, but also through the spatial mismatch that arises when housing discrimination restricts minority households' access to suburban neighborhoods and job opportunities. Thus, a full explanation of minority–white disparities in employment, income, and poverty must recognize the important role played by housing discrimination.

The social costs of this discrimination are very high, not only for the minority households who encounter it, but also for the nation as a whole. Intergroup hostility and distrust place a clear drain on our time and resources, and in today's competitive international economy, we can hardly afford a system that undermines the productivity of so many of our citizens.

■ RACE AND ETHNICITY

Because the topic of this book carries so much emotional power, it is crucial to begin with careful definitions of the terms *race* and *eth-*

nicity. These definitions contain something of a surprise: Despite its focus on racial and ethnic divisions, this book is not, in one important sense, about race or ethnicity at all. As we will see, race and ethnicity are important symbols that influence social and economic outcomes, but neither term in its literal meaning is connected to the system of discrimination.

Race

Strictly speaking, the term *race* refers to a group whose members share certain inherited physiological characteristics. Many of these characteristics, including skin color, hair texture, and the shape of facial features, are easily observed, but scholars have also identified other less obvious characteristics that differ across races. However, none of the physiological characteristics associated with different racial groups have anything to do with a person's abilities or skills in meaningful human endeavor.

Many people balk at this claim. Racial differences are perceived as important because some racial groups achieve more success, on average, than others, or are more likely than others to engage in socially productive activities. A recent book, for example, draws on intelligence test results to feed the perception that blacks are inherently less intelligent than whites.[5] But if one carefully untangles the role of race itself from the role of the environment in which a person grew up and of the external constraints he or she faces, the evidence to support this claim is overwhelming. Despite lower test scores for blacks than for whites, there is no scientific basis for the claim that some races are inherently less intelligent than others.[6]

The strongest evidence comes from the study of human genetics. No two individuals, except identical twins, have the same genes, but the frequency of some genetic features varies systematically from one location to another.[7] The gene frequencies in the people born in a particular location are the product of two offsetting processes.[8] The first process is genetic differentiation. Going back far enough in time, all human beings are descended from Africans. Different racial groups evolved; that is, genetic differences across people arose, as some people migrated within or outside of Africa and became isolated from those who stayed behind. Isolation made it possible for genetic differences to arise due to "genetic drift or natural selection to different environmental conditions."[9] Skin color is an example of an adaptation to environmental conditions, and in particular it is a "good indicator of past climate."[10]

The second process, which to some degree offsets the first, is genetic mixing, which occurs as the people from one location, who draw on one pool of genes, expand into other locations and mix with people who draw on another pool of genes. Although some genetic differentiation can still be observed across people, there have been so many human expansions in so many directions that currently recognized racial groups represent centuries of genetic mixing, with a large share of the remaining genetic variation associated with differences in climate. Indeed, recent sophisticated research into human genetic patterns reveals that "All races and ethnic groups now seem to be a bewildering array of overlapping sets and subsets that are in a constant state of flux."[11] According to some leading scholars, widespread understanding of this genetic research would "undercut conventional notions of race and underscore the common bonds between all humans."[12]

To be more specific, population movement within Africa produced three of the six primordial racial groups identified by some scholars.[13] Although all three of these groups have dark skins, two of them, the Pygmies and the Khoisan (represented by the Bushmen), have very small populations today, and most African people around the world are drawn from the third, called blacks.[14] The first great migration of "anatomically modern" humans out of Africa began about 100,000 years ago.[15] This migration took people to Europe; to Asia, where Asians, another one of the six broad racial categories, evolved; and eventually to Australia and the Americas.[16]

Recent genetic research reveals that Europeans, who fall into the broad racial group usually called whites, did not begin to emerge until about 30,000 years ago and that their immediate ancestors were roughly 65 percent Asian and 35 percent African.[17] Moreover, this reseach makes it possible to observe the genetic legacy of some of the human expansions that ultimately produced Europeans.[18] The first of these expansions began about 10,000 years ago, as people from the Middle East migrated to Europe after they had developed the farming of cereals and the domestication of animals. A second expansion started about 5,000 years ago, as pastoral nomads from the Russian Steppes, who learned how to raise horses and developed new modes of warfare, spread in several directions, including into Europe. Between 4,000 and 2,400 years ago, Greeks, who had developed new methods of navigation and trade, also expanded into Europe. The genetic makeup of modern Europeans reflects the influence of all these expansions, and perhaps others.

Human migration and genetic mixing have not, of course, been confined to prehistoric times, and events in more recent years reinforce the claim that genetic differences across races, as such, are insignificant. Although anthropologists have developed various schemes for identifying racial groups, each group inevitably is diverse, and the boundary lines between the groups are arbitrary.[19] Moreover, just as the genetic makeup of currently identified racial groups was produced by the mixing of different groups in the distant past, the racial ancestry of the people in any given location today typically is mixed through sexual contact between people from different racial groups.

In the United States, for example, scholars have estimated that at least 80 percent of African Americans have some European ancestors.[20] Most of this mixing occurred in the past because of sexual contact, often forced no doubt, between white slave owners and their African American slaves.[21] A smaller, but growing source, is interracial marriage.[22] Most people with this type of mixed ancestry have dark skin and are considered to be African Americans, but the fact is that many of them have a genetic makeup that is virtually indistinguishable from that of someone whose ancestors all came from Europe.

The racial ancestry of so-called white Americans is not as homogeneous as many people believe. Some scholars estimate that as many as one-quarter of Americans classified as "white" may have at least one African ancestor.[23] Moreover, some people whose ancestors lived in northern Africa before Europeans colonized the continent have very fair skin and are classified by scholars as whites, as are many people who live in the Middle East.[24] Thus, not all whites or even all white Americans have European ancestry.

Overall, the concept of race is elusive: because of the ongoing and widespread mixing of human genes, human beings around the world draw on virtually the same genetic pool. A few physiological differences, most of which arose as adaptations to different climates, can be associated with broad racial groups, but "racial differences are minor biological variations in an essentially homogeneous species."[25] To put it another way, "despite the obvious physical differences between people from different areas, the vast majority of human genetic variation occurs *within* populations, not *between* them."[26]

Ethnicity

Ethnicity has to do with cultural differences among people, such as differences in language, religion, dress, or customs.[27] In many cases, these traits are associated with the country from which a person's ancestors originated.[28] This book examines the treatment of one major ethnic group, namely, Hispanic Americans. "Hispanic" is an ethnic, not a racial designation. In fact, Hispanic Americans have a diverse racial makeup.[29] Some of them have European ancestors, some Native American ancestors, some African ancestors, and others ancestors from more than one of these racial groups.[30] Instead, the term *Hispanic* is intended to identify people who can trace at least some of their ancestors back to "Hispania," a name for the Iberian peninsula on which Spain and Portugal are located,[31] usually through South America, Central America, or the Caribbean, and who retain some connection with the language, religion, or customs of their ancestors. Because it encompasses the cultures of so many countries, twenty-three by one count, the Hispanic designation masks great cultural variety.[32]

A person's ethnic identity may influence his or her preferences or choices or training, but it has no connection with inherent abilities. All ethnic groups draw on essentially the same human genetic pool. Moreover, this country has long gained strength from its diverse ethnic heritage and the resulting variety of approaches to the challenges of human existence. Just as race, as such, proves to be unimportant, ethnicity, as such, cannot explain why some people are the victims of prejudice and discrimination.

The Social Reality of Race and Ethnicity

In another important sense, this book is about race and ethnicity. Even though race and ethnicity in their most literal sense cannot explain deep divisions among people, race and ethnicity both provide means for distinguishing among people and can become powerful symbols for a history of conflict, oppression, and mistrust. These symbols have power whenever they influence the way people are treated, that is, when they have social reality.[33] This book could be thought of as testimony about the power of race and ethnicity as symbols in the United States.

Few places on earth have escaped some sort of conflict along racial or ethnic lines, and the newspapers are full these days of tragic examples of this type of conflict.[34] Many human beings appear to have a need to feel superior to people who somehow differ from themselves and, if possible, to translate this feeling into economic and social domination.[35] Because skin color and other visible physiological differences are easily observed, they often provide a way to identify a group that is believed to be inferior. Ethnic distinctions, such as language or mode of dress, sometimes serve the same purpose. Of course, different racial and ethnic designations gain power in different societies.

Millions of Africans were brought to the United States as slaves, and their descendants have experienced centuries of mistreatment and relative deprivation. The legacy of this oppression is an African American population with far fewer skills and resources, on average, than those of the average American of European descent and sometimes with self-destructive or socially unacceptable behavioral responses to mistreatment, actual or anticipated.[36] This legacy gives great power to skin color as a symbol. Many whites perceive the relatively low success of the average African American, conclude that African Americans are inferior, develop an anti-black prejudice, and sometimes discriminate against them. Most African Americans perceive that they are treated unfairly, at least some of the time, because of their race, and must develop coping mechanisms.[37]

Behavioral responses by some African Americans to their past and current mistreatment, which include turning to drugs or to violence, also serve to reinforce this cycle. There is no reason to believe that African Americans are any more likely than members of other groups to respond to a history of deprivation or mistreatment by engaging in self-destructive or antisocial behavior.[38] However, responses of this type by whites do not have the same symbolic power as those of blacks because they do not feed the stereotypes that are at the heart of our racial divisions. This troubling asymmetry is part of the legacy of our racist past.

The power of race as a symbol in the United States is also demonstrated by the fact that individuals with any visible physical traits that appear to be African, primarily dark skin, are treated as black, regardless of their overall genetic makeup.[39] Individuals with three white grandparents and one black grandparent, for example, often have brown or light brown skin and are treated as blacks. This has been called " 'the one-drop rule,' which defines as black a person with as little as a single drop of 'black blood.' "[40] Other societies, which have different histories, do not define "black" so broadly. For example, "race in the Caribbean is perceived as a spectrum running from white to black"[41]; and in South Africa during apartheid, clear legal and social distinctions were made between "blacks," whose ancestors are all African, and "coloureds," whose ancestors are a mix of Africans and Europeans.[42]

The history of the United States has also given power to the "Hispanic" ethnic identity as a symbol. Although the so-called Hispanic population is diverse, both racially and culturally, many Hispanic Americans can be identified by their accent or surname or by an appearance revealing that some of their ancestors were Native Americans or Africans. The power of Hispanic ethnicity as a symbol draws not only on the nation's history of oppressing Native American and

African American people but also on the history of conflicts between European American workers and immigrants from Mexico and other parts of Latin America.[43] The diversity of the Hispanic population ensures that Hispanic identity plays a more important role for some Hispanic groups than for others; nevertheless, our society has given enough power to this symbol to justify a focus on "Hispanics" as a whole.[44]

Terminology, or Talking about Race and Ethnicity

The power of race and ethnicity as symbols is demonstrated by the ongoing debate about the right terms to use. Terms themselves sometimes become symbols of oppression, and the debate about terms sometimes seems as heated as the debate about public policy to combat discrimination. During the late 1960s, the term *Negro* came to be a symbol of oppression to many African Americans and was gradually replaced in public discussion by the term *black*.[45] Many scholars and commentators now use the term *African American* instead of or in addition to *black*.[46] This book uses *African American* and *black* as synonyms.

Given the mixed racial ancestry of most African Americans, and indeed of many groups in the United States, the Census Bureau recently has been debating whether to add a "multiracial" category on decennial census forms and other government documents.[47] It may seem that those who favor a multiracial category are emphasizing the biological definition of race whereas those who oppose it are emphasizing the social definition. After all, many people in this country do have multiracial backgrounds in the biological sense, but thanks to the "one-drop rule," people whose multiracial background includes African ancestors usually are treated as black. Since any set of racial categories exaggerates the biological differences among people, this debate is really about whether official labels magnify existing social divisions by giving them more credibility or help eliminate these divisions by bringing attention to the economic and social disadvantages some groups face.[48] For many purposes, it is valuable to acknowledge the growing number of people in this country with diverse racial backgrounds, but I believe that adding a multiracial category to the census at this time would obscure the severe social and economic disparities that continue to exist in this country between blacks and whites as traditionally defined.

Hispanic is a term used by the U.S. Bureau of the Census to identify people in the many groups with ancestry that traces back to *Hispania,* including Mexican Americans (also called Chicanos), Puerto Ricans, Cubans, and immigrants from Central and South America. Some people called Hispanic by the census object to *Hispanic* as a term invented by the oppressor and prefer the term *Latino*.[49] One author calls Hispanic "a repulsive slave name."[50] Others believe that Latino should be limited to people who were born in Latin America or that Latino is even more removed from their experience than is Hispanic because it refers to "an even older empire."[51] Still other people with a Spanish surname, indeed a majority according to a recent survey, prefer to be identified by their own subgroup, such as Cuban, Mexican, or Puerto Rican.[52] No single term can possibly reflect this diversity of views, let alone the diversity in country of origin, among people called Hispanic by the census. This book therefore retains the census usage and makes reference to the experience of specific subgroups under this label where appropriate.

A discussion of the relative position of Hispanics requires a term for the comparison group, namely non-Hispanic whites. In some of my earlier writing, I used the term *Anglo* for this comparison group to emphasize the role of language in this particular ethnic distinction. In retrospect, this usage appears to place too much weight on language and to imply, incorrectly, that non-Hispanic whites all share an Anglo or English background. To remove this implication and to preserve conciseness, this book uses the term *white* to mean non-Hispanic white. The reader should remember, however, that in terms of their racial background, many Hispanics are white themselves.

■ PREJUDICE AND DISCRIMINATION

Racial and ethnic divisions among people are most directly observed in the form of prejudice and discrimination. Because these concepts play such an important role in the analysis that follows, we must define both terms carefully.

Prejudice

Prejudice is "an emotional, rigid attitude (a predisposition to respond to a certain stimulus in a certain way) toward a group of people."[53] This book explores the troubling consequences of widespread white prejudice against having blacks or Hispanics as neighbors or as classmates for one's children.

In the words of the song, "you have to be taught to hate," and prejudice is a sad inheritance that some children receive from their parents, often reinforced by perceptions and experience. People who observe that one racial or ethnic group tends to live in poorer neighborhoods or to be more likely to receive welfare or commit crimes may assume, incorrectly, that these outcomes reflect some inherent characteristic of this group.[54] Over time, specific stereotypes (that is, stylized negative images) of a particular group may develop and help reinforce the misperceptions on which prejudice feeds.[55]

Surveys of the racial attitudes of whites have been conducted for many decades.[56] For our purposes, the evidence about whites' racial attitudes concerning the racial and ethnic integration of neighborhoods is particularly relevant.[57] Although this evidence must be interpreted with care, because attitudes about surveys, as well as attitudes about race, may have changed over time, virtually all studies find that white aversion to black neighbors persists but is less severe than it once was.[58] Surveys by the National Opinion Research Center (NORC) and Gallup polls, for example, find a steady decline in the share of white people who care whether a black person with the same income and education moves into their neighborhood, who would move if a black family moved in next door, who believe whites have the right to keep blacks out of white neighborhoods, or who oppose fair housing legislation.[59]

Particularly detailed surveys of white attitudes toward neighborhood racial integration were conducted in Detroit in 1976 and 1992. In 1976, half of whites said they would not move into a neighborhood that was 20 percent black, and almost three-quarters said they would not consider moving into a neighborhood that was 33 percent black. Comparing the 1992 and 1996 results reveals that

> white attitudes about racial integration have become more liberal. Whites, in the 1990s, were, apparently, more willing to move into areas which had a few black residents. However, there was considerable resistance to living in neighborhoods that were one-third or more black. For example, 45 percent of Detroit area whites felt uncomfortable in a neighborhood in which five of fifteen homes were occupied by blacks, 28 percent said they would try to move away if their neighborhood came to have such a composition and 56 percent would not consider moving into such a location if they found an attractive house they could afford there.[60]

Similar conclusions are provided by 1990 data from NORC, which found that almost half of whites were somewhat or strongly opposed to living in a neighborhood that was either half black or half Hispanic.[61] A 1991 Cleveland area survey uncovered somewhat less white prejudice: 68 percent of whites said they would prefer their neighborhood to be racially mixed (defined by most whites as about one-quarter black), 22 percent of whites said they would be willing to move into a neighborhood where most of the residents were black, and only 16 percent of whites chose an all-white neighborhood.[62]

Discrimination

Racial and ethnic discrimination is adverse treatment of an individual solely on the basis of his or her membership in a particular racial or ethnic group. An employer who hires a highly qualified white applicant instead of a poorly qualified Hispanic applicant is not discriminating because his decision is based at least in part on the relative skill of the two applicants, which is a legitimate component in his decision. However, an employer who consistently hires white applicants instead of Hispanic or black applicants who are equally qualified based on all legitimate, observable criteria is guilty of discrimination.[63] In the housing market, it is discrimination when a real estate broker shows four houses to a white couple but nothing to a black couple with the same income, housing needs, and credit qualifications. Thus, the examples that begin this chapter clearly involve discrimination. And a lender is discriminating if he gives equal credit ratings to a white and an Hispanic applicant for the same type of mortgage but approves the loan only for the white.

Discrimination can take many forms as well as have many causes.[64] Discrimination and prejudice are mutually reinforcing, but each can, and sometimes does, exist without the other.[65] Prejudice sometimes leads a real estate broker or lender to discriminate, and some people develop prejudice as a rationalization for discriminatory behavior, but unprejudiced brokers and lenders sometimes decide to practice discrimination whereas others obey laws against discrimination in spite of their own personal prejudice.

Together, prejudice and discrimination have a powerful impact on American society. They greatly restrict the housing choices of many black and Hispanic households, and they are among the key causes of racial and ethnic residential segregation, which is the physical separation of the residential areas of different racial and ethnic groups. One of the key objectives of this book is to untangle the complicated connections between—and the powerful consequences of—prejudice and discrimination based on race and ethnicity.

■ PLAN OF THE BOOK

The rest of this book is divided into three parts. The first part presents recent evidence about the extent and nature of discrimination in housing and mortgage markets in the United States. The second part explores the consequences of this discrimination in terms of the costs imposed on minority households in addition to the implications for broader social and economic outcomes. The third part presents the history of federal antidiscrimination policy and develops a program of federal actions to combat discrimination today.

Historically, discrimination has been difficult to document because people conceal behavior, such as discrimination, that is illegal. However, recent innovations in research methods have made it possible to obtain direct measures of discrimination in both housing and mortgage markets. Extensive evidence about racial and ethnic discrimination in housing markets comes from the 1989 Housing Discrimination Study (HDS), a nationwide study of discriminatory practices. Chapter 2 describes HDS and its methodology; Chapter 3 presents the HDS results on racial and ethnic discrimination in housing availability; and Chapter 4 presents the HDS results about racial and ethnic steering. Chapters 3 and 4 also review recent evidence from studies other than HDS. The final chapter in the first part of the book, Chapter 5, presents recent evidence concerning racial and ethnic discrimination and redlining in mortgage markets and explains why this evidence has led to a recent rediscovery of discrimination in mortgage lending.

Part Two explores the consequences of discrimination in housing and mortgage markets, both for the affected individuals and for society as a whole. Chapter 6 describes a new method for estimating the direct costs that current discrimination imposes on black and Hispanic households who want to find new places to live. The resulting cost estimates are disturbingly high. Past and current discrimination also have impacts on a wide range of outcomes in the housing market, including racial and ethnic residential segregation as well as racial and ethnic disparities in homeownership rates, in housing wealth, and in housing quality. Chapter 7 reviews recent evidence about the magnitude of these impacts. Finally, discrimination in housing and mortgage markets is one part of a broader system that includes the labor market and public services, such as education. Chapter 8 explores the role of housing discrimination in this broader system. For example, several recent studies, which are reviewed in this chapter, provide evidence that discrimination in housing contributes to relatively high unemployment and poverty rates for black and Hispanic households.

The last part of the book examines cures for discrimination in housing and mortgage markets. To help inform the policy debate, this part begins with an exploration of the causes of discrimination, based largely on the HDS results. The second chapter in the part,

Chapter 10, then reviews the history of fair housing and fair lending policy, starting with U.S. Supreme Court cases in the early 1900s and ending with the extensive legislative changes and court decisions of the last few years. These two chapters set the stage for Chapter 11, which presents several principles for fair housing and fair lending policy and then develops a comprehensive plan to combat discrimination in housing and mortgage markets. The basic premise of this chapter is that simple enforcement of antidiscrimination legislation, no matter how effective, is necessary but incomplete as a strategy for eliminating discrimination and all its costs. Additional policies, some of which are now being attempted on a small scale, to provide education on matters of race and ethnicity and to undo the market outcomes that perpetuate the discriminatory system, are also required. The final chapter, Chapter 12, summarizes the book's findings and policy recommendations and explores the feasibility of these policies in today's political environment.

CLOSED DOORS:
THE EXTENT
OF DISCRIMINATION

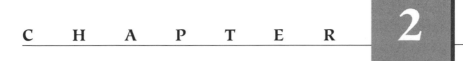

C H A P T E R   2

The Housing Discrimination Study

The stories that begin this book, in which the treatment of comparable white and minority homeseekers is compared, illustrate the technique called a fair housing audit. The power of such an audit to shed light on the discriminatory practices of landlords and real estate brokers was recognized long ago by people running fair housing agencies. During the 1970s this power was discovered by researchers. By the time the U.S. Department of Housing and Urban Development sponsored its second national audit study, called the Housing Discrimination Study (HDS), audits were widely recognized as a refined and reliable research tool. This chapter presents a brief history of audit research, outlines the key features of a fair housing audit, and describes the audit methodology employed by HDS. The following two chapters explore the HDS results in detail.

▌ A BRIEF HISTORY OF FAIR HOUSING AUDITS

Before fair housing audits were developed, researchers studied discrimination in urban housing markets indirectly by looking for the impacts of discrimination on housing market outcomes, such as housing prices, housing quality, homeownership, and the pattern of racial residential segregation.[1] Several studies documented, for example, that black households lived in lower quality housing and were far less likely to be homeowners than were white households with the same income and family characteristics.[2] These findings were consistent with the view that discrimination restricts the opportunities of black households, but they did not measure discrimination directly.

Indirect connections and abstract arguments are common currency for researchers, but they are not marketable in public debate. As a result, these studies did not have a major impact on public policy, even though most of them found evidence of discrimination.

Fair housing audits were developed by fair housing groups as a way to determine whether discrimination complaints had validity.[3] Most agency actions begin with a complaint, that is, by the appearance of a black or Hispanic person who claims that he or she has been unfairly denied access to a house or an apartment. Agencies learned that they could establish whether a house or an apartment was indeed available and whether the complainant had indeed been unfairly denied access to it by sending a comparable white person to inquire about the same unit. When the white person was offered the unit that the black or Hispanic person was denied, the agency had powerful evidence of discrimination, for both administrative and legal purposes. By the early 1970s, many fair housing groups had gained experience in bringing audit evidence into court, and how-to manuals for conducting audits were widely available.[4]

Researchers then discovered that they could measure discrimination by conducting fair housing audits for a sample of housing agents or of advertised housing units.[5] The first examples of audits research in the United States were small-scale studies conducted in Southern California in 1955 and 1971, followed by a large audit study in Detroit in 1974–1975.[6] A large audit study was also conducted in Great Britain in 1967.[7] Audits became a highly visible research tool when, in 1977, the U.S. Department of Housing and Urban Development sponsored the Housing Market Practices Survey (HMPS), which was a national study of housing discrimination against African Americans.[8] HMPS conducted 3,264 audits in 40 metropolitan areas and found evidence of significant discrimination against blacks in both the sales and rental markets.[9] A follow-up study in Dallas found high levels of discrimination against Hispanics, particularly those with dark skin.[10]

The pioneering HMPS report made it clear that fair housing audits are an appropriate and feasible method for studying discrimination in housing. Unlike indirect methods found in earlier research on the topic, fair housing audits provide direct, easy-to-interpret evidence about the extent of discrimination. An audit literally catches a discriminator in the act of discriminating, and it furnishes a compelling narrative about the discriminatory actions encountered by many black and Hispanic homeseekers. Moreover, the strong HMPS results played a major role, albeit after a 9-year lag, in the passage of the 1988 amendments to the Fair Housing Act.[11]

It did not take long before many fair housing agencies and researchers conducted additional audit studies. Between 1977 and 1990, at least seventy-two other audit studies were done in individual cities, with well-publicized studies in Boston and Denver.[12] Virtually all of these studies provided further evidence of discrimination.[13]

Thanks to the power of the HMPS results and the mounting evidence of continuing discrimination, the U.S. Department of Housing and Urban Development decided to sponsor a second national audit study. A request for proposals was sent out in the spring of 1988, and that fall the project, the Housing Discrimination Study (HDS), was awarded to a team consisting of researchers at the Urban Institute, a nonprofit research organization in Washington, D.C., and at the Metropolitan Studies Program, a research center in the Maxwell School of Citizenship and Public Affairs at Syracuse University. HDS conducted about 3,800 audits in twenty-five metropolitan areas in the spring and early summer of 1989, and the final HDS reports were issued in September 1991.[14]

HDS was designed to build on the foundation laid by HMPS and to achieve four main objectives:

Provide a current national estimate of the level of discrimination against blacks in urban areas.

Provide, for the first time, a comparable national estimate of the level of discrimination against Hispanics.

Effectively measure racial and ethnic steering, whereby minorities may be shown or recommended housing units but are "steered" away from majority neighborhoods.

Advance the state-of-the-art in the methodology of systematic housing audits, providing researchers and fair housing enforcement officials with more reliable tools for measuring patterns of discrimination.[15]

◼ WHAT IS A FAIR HOUSING AUDIT?

A fair housing audit is a survey technique designed to isolate the impact of a person's minority status on the way she is treated when asking a landlord or real estate agent about available housing.[16] An audit consists of successive visits to the same housing agent by two audit teammates who are equally qualified for housing but who differ in minority status.[17] Each teammate then independently completes a detailed audit survey form to describe what she was told and how she was treated. An audit study, which consists of a sample of audits, makes it possible to isolate discrimination, which exists whenever, according to the information on the survey forms, housing agents systematically treat minority auditors less favorably than their white teammates.

The key objective of audit design is to make the members of an audit team as comparable as possible on all characteristics, except for minority status, that might influence their ability to rent an apartment or buy a house. Without this comparability, researchers cannot be confident that differences in the treatment of minority and white auditors are due solely to discrimination.[18] If the minority auditor is always older than her white teammate, for example, researchers cannot definitively rule out the possibility that minority auditors are treated less favorably because of their age.

Researchers cannot make audit teammates exactly comparable, but they have four tools to build comparability: matching, assignment, training, and timing.[19] The careful use of these four tools produces audits in which teammate comparability is sufficiently high so that systematically less favorable treatment of minority auditors can be interpreted as discrimination.

The use of audits raises some ethical issues because they are an imposition on the audited housing agents, some of whom have never practiced racial or ethnic discrimination.[20] In effect, an audited agent involuntarily donates about one hour of his time for a sales audit and about 20 minutes for a rental audit, regardless of his discriminatory practices.[21] However, given the long history of discrimination in the housing market, the strong evidence of continuing discrimination, and the lack of alternative investigative tools, audits are widely regarded as an appropriate technique for measuring discrimination and identifying discriminators. The case for fair housing audits is similar to the case for income tax audits, from which honest taxpayers are not exempt.

Moreover, the U.S. Supreme Court ruled unanimously, in the 1982 *Havens* case, that auditing is a legitimate investigative tool to combat discrimination in housing.[22] In fact, the *Havens* decision even stated that an auditor who encounters discrimination has standing to sue the offending housing agent even though she is not a bona fide housing seeker. This ruling created a potential conflict of interest for auditors, who are hired to collect information but who might gain from information that suggests discrimination. To avoid this conflict of interest, many audit studies, including HDS, have required all auditors to relinquish their rights to sue housing agents who treat them unfavorably.

◼ THE HDS AUDIT METHODOLOGY

The HDS audit methodology builds heavily on earlier audit studies, especially HMPS. The key methodological issues include audit design, sampling, and administrative procedures. Interpretation of the HDS results requires a clear understanding of the HDS choices on each of these issues.

Audit Design

To isolate discrimination, HDS carefully employed the four tools of audit design—matching, assignment, training, and timing.

The first tool, matching, involves the selection of audit teammates with the same fixed characteristics of sex, age, and general appearance. People with different fixed characteristics may be treated differently by housing agents, so all HDS audit teams consisted of two people, one black or Hispanic and the other white, of the same sex and approximately the same age. Individuals with an unusual appearance or manner were not selected as auditors.

The Hispanic population in the United States is very diverse, both racially and culturally.[23] A previous audit study found that the shade of an Hispanic homeseeker's skin may affect whether she experiences unfavorable treatment by a housing agent.[24] Her treatment might also be affected by the strength of her Spanish accent. As a result, HDS recruited as auditors both light- and dark-skinned Hispanics, with and without noticeable accents, all with Hispanic surnames.

The second tool for enhancing teammates' comparability is assignment. Since a household's ability to rent an apartment or buy a house depends on its income and family composition, audit teammates are assigned similar economic and family characteristics for the purposes of each audit. These characteristics include income, assets available for a down payment, occupation, martial status, and number of children.[25] Each audit was based on a specific advertised housing unit and the two teammates were assigned characteristics that made them fully qualified for that unit. Their given incomes were high enough to afford the rent or price of the advertised unit, and they were assigned a family composition that was appropriate for the number of bedrooms that unit contained. To help keep an agent from figuring out that he was being audited, minority and white teammates were not assigned exactly the same income. Moreover, to make certain that minority auditors were never treated less favorably because of their income, a slightly higher income was always assigned to the minority teammate.

The third tool, training, helps to minimize differences in team-mates' queries and in the way they behave. All HDS auditors were trained to begin the audit by asking whether the advertised unit or similar units were available;[26] to behave in a serious, professional manner during the interview; to avoid trying to elicit any particular behavior from the agent; to express an interest in all available hous-ing units that meet their price and size requirements; to keep track of information, with informal notes if necessary, and to fill out the survey as completely and accurately as possible; to refrain from indi-cating community or neighborhood preferences; and to try to inspect several housing units.[27]

Two themes of this training are worth highlighting. First, the train-ing did not conceal the purpose of the study but instead emphasized the need for accurate, complete reporting and taught each auditor not to communicate with her teammate. The decision not to run a fully "blind" study in which auditors were not aware of the existence of their teammate or the purpose of the study was deliberate.[28] Some early audit studies discovered that minority auditors who encoun-tered blatant unfavorable treatment became upset and were unable to complete their audit forms in an accurate manner, thereby inval-idating some audits in which discrimination was the most severe. To avoid this possibility, auditors were told that they should behave in a professional manner no matter how they were treated, and they were debriefed after each audit.

Moreover, to minimize differences in their behavior, audit team-mates received exactly the same training. Since they can observe that half of the people in a training session are black or Hispanic and the other half are white, it is better to tell them the purpose of the study and to emphasize the need for accurate reporting than to leave them guessing.

Second, each auditor was instructed to be interested in all housing that was offered but to ask for the housing agent's opinion instead of giving clear preferences of her own. This approach ensured that the agent, not the auditor, determined which units were recommended or shown to each auditor.

Finally, a person's experience at a housing agency depends in part on the circumstances she encounters there. Is the market active that day or that week? Has the advertised unit already been sold or rented? And so on. The fourth tool, therefore, is to manipulate the timing of the two teammates' visits to make the circumstances they encounter as similar as possible. In the case of HDS, teammates initiated their visits within a short time of each other.[29]

Advertisements identify a housing agency but often do not mention the housing agent. Thus, audit teammates inquire about the advertised unit but speak to whomever they encounter at the housing agency. The possibility that audit teammates may deal with different agents within an agency in no way compromises the audit design. The matching of customers to agents may be a random process, in which case it cannot systematically influence the treatment of minority auditors relative to white auditors, or it may itself be a means of discriminating, in which case its effects on the treatment of auditors are reflected, as they should be, in measures of discrimination.[30]

One final aspect of timing concerns the order of visit. An auditor's treatment may depend on whether she preceded or followed her teammate. If a rental agent believes that the first auditor will rent the advertised apartment, for example, he may not show this apartment to the second auditor. To ensure that the order of visit did not influence treatment, HDS randomized order; it determined at random the order in which two teammates contacted the housing agent targeted by each audit.[31]

Sampling Plan

The HDS sampling plan, like that of HMPS, contained two stages. In the first stage, a sample of metropolitan areas was selected to yield nationally representative estimates of differential treatment of minority homeseekers in major urban areas.[32] In the second stage, a sample of newspaper advertisements was selected to yield a representative sample of available housing units in each metropolitan area.

HDS audits were conducted in twenty-five metropolitan areas, selected from the set of large urban areas with significant minority populations.[33] The 105 metropolitan areas in this set all had central city populations greater than 100,000 and were more than 12 percent black or more than 7 percent Hispanic, the average shares of blacks and Hispanics in the U.S. population as of 1980.[34] A relatively large number of audits was conducted in five sites where a large share of the nation's black and Hispanic citizens live. These five sites are New York, Chicago, and Los Angeles, where both black–white and Hispanic–white audits were conducted; Atlanta, where only black–white audits were conducted; and San Antonio, where only Hispanic–white audits were conducted. The remaining twenty sites range from small metropolitan areas, such as Pueblo, Colorado, and Macon-Warner-Robins, Georgia, to large urban areas, such as Detroit, Miami, Philadelphia, and Washington, D.C. The complete list of sites, which is presented in Table 2.1, is geographically diverse, with representatives

TABLE 2.1 **HDS SITES AND SAMPLE SIZES**

Site	Black–White Audits		Hispanic–White Audits	
	Sales	*Rental*	*Sales*	*Rental*
Atlanta	94	66	—	—
Austin	43	32	63	55
Bergen County	36	28	64	47
Birmingham	48	34	—	—
Chicago	103	65	122	81
Cincinnati	25	34	—	—
Dayton	25	33	—	—
Denver	47	42	73	59
Detroit	51	33	—	—
Houston	48	42	53	51
Lansing	43	35	—	—
Los Angeles	104	75	120	81
Macon	45	33	—	—
Miami	39	32	60	58
New Orleans	44	33	—	—
New York	87	52	118	62
Orlando	43	32	—	—
Philadelphia	44	30	—	—
Phoenix	—	—	72	56
Pittsburgh	46	38	—	—
Pueblo	—	—	68	50
San Antonio	—	—	116	67
San Diego	—	—	76	61
Tucson	—	—	71	59
Washington	43	32	—	—
Total	1,081	801	1,076	787

from all four census regions and from fourteen states plus the District of Columbia.

In the second stage of the HDS sampling plan, newspaper advertisements for available housing units were randomly selected from the major newspaper in each sampled metropolitan area.[35] In the sales audits, housing units for sale by the owner were excluded from the sample, but condominiums were included.[36] A sample of available units was drawn each weekend in each site until the desired number of audits was completed.

Administrative Procedures

A national audit study cannot be conducted without a large, complex administrative structure. HDS was administered by the Urban Institute, following administrative procedures similar to those pioneered by HMPS. Local fair housing organizations were hired to conduct the audits and to hire and train local auditors, using procedures developed by the central research staff. The people selected as auditors were judged to be capable of role-playing and not to have any unusual personality or physical characteristic that might influence their treatment by housing agents. The local administrator's responsibilities included preserving confidentiality and debriefing each auditor after each audit to maintain high standards of completeness and accuracy on the survey forms. Regional supervisors, working under the direction of a central audit manager, monitored the activities at each audit site, to ensure that the audits were conducted according to the standard procedures, and they provided a second review of the audit survey forms.

The central research staff selected the random samples of advertisements and randomly determined the order of the teammates' visits for each advertisement. Because advertisements were selected from a weekend newspaper for audits that began on Monday, there was a flurry of sampling activity and fax transmissions at the central office each weekend. The central research staff also gave the audit survey forms a final review for completeness and consistency. The completed audit survey forms were then compiled into final data sets by the central research staff, with extensive efforts to check the data, to find information for completing missing entries, and to resolve any inconsistencies. The final data sets were analyzed by researchers at the Urban Institute and Syracuse University.

Interpretation

The audit design and sampling procedures employed by HDS lead to a specific interpretation of the HDS results.

To begin, the HDS results cannot be generalized to all housing transactions because they are based on a sample of newspaper advertisements. In fact, some housing is not advertised in major metropolitan newspapers, some real estate or rental agents do not use this means to attract customers, and some minority homeseekers do not use newspaper advertisements in their housing search.[37] In other words, the HDS results reveal something about discrimination associated with housing units advertised in major newspapers, but not about housing discrimination in general. The focus on advertised units probably means that HDS understates discrimination in the housing market as a whole. After all, many owners sell their houses through word of mouth precisely because they want to avoid selling to certain types of people. Moreover, some landlords employ apartment referral services that will send them the type of tenants they want.[38]

In addition, the income, assets, debt, and household size assigned to each audit team were matched to the cost and size of the advertised housing unit; that is, the auditors were qualified for the sample of advertised units. This sample is quite different from the set of housing units for which the actual population of black and Hispanic households is qualified or in which it lives. The HDS results do not necessarily reflect, therefore, the experience of the average black or Hispanic homeseeker. Instead, they reflect the treatment that can be expected by black or Hispanic homeseekers who search for housing using newspaper ads and who are qualified to rent or buy the average housing unit advertised in a major metropolitan newspaper.[39]

In short, HDS measures discrimination in a major segment of the metropolitan housing market—a segment that is accessible through the newspaper to every homeseeker, regardless of race or ethnicity—but the HDS results do not necessarily apply to the housing market as a whole.

One could argue that the housing advertised in the major metropolitan newspaper is fairly representative of the housing available for white households. One recent study in Boston, for example, found that three-quarters of the whites looking to buy a house consulted *The Boston Globe*.[40] Consequently, the HDS results reveal the discrimination to be expected by black or Hispanic households with characteristics similar to those of whites. With no past discrimination, black and Hispanic households presumably would have economic and social characteristics very similar to those of white households, so HDS can be interpreted as measuring the discrimination that black and Hispanic households could expect to encounter if past discrimination had not placed them at a disadvantage in the housing market. This approach probably makes HDS somewhat conservative; the available evidence indicates that discrimination is higher against the average black or Hispanic household than against the black or Hispanic household qualified for the average advertised housing unit.[41]

■ CONCLUSIONS

Fair housing audits have been widely used by private fair housing organizations, researchers, and civil rights enforcement officials.

Thanks to the tools of matching, assignment, training, and timing, an audit can isolate the impact of minority status on the treatment a person receives from a housing agent, and a sample of audits can provide a direct measure of discrimination in housing.

The Housing Discrimination Study built on the experience of previous audit studies to obtain data on the treatment of African American and Hispanic American homeseekers in a nationally representative sample of metropolitan areas. The HDS audits are tied to randomly selected newspaper advertisements, and the HDS results describe the treatment black and Hispanic households who are qualified for advertised housing units can expect to encounter when they ask housing agents whether those units are available.

C H A P T E R   3

Discrimination in Housing

■ ACCESS DENIED, ACCESS CONSTRAINED

When an auditor or an actual customer arrives at the office of a real estate broker or rental agent, the first thing she does is to inquire about the advertised unit that brought her there. She then proceeds to ask whether any similar units are available. These questions, and the agent's responses to them, constitute the first stage of a housing market transaction, and bring out the first signs of discrimination.

As illustrated in Figure 3.1, an agent may withhold all information about available housing from a minority customer, who is thereby denied access to the housing market, at least by that agent. Even if a minority customer is not literally denied access to housing, her access may be constrained, perhaps severely, by an agent who shows her fewer units than he shows her white counterpart.

Agents not only provide information about available housing, they also take many actions to facilitate a potential housing transaction: they indicate the terms and conditions of sale or rental; they help a potential buyer learn about mortgage possibilities; and they inform customers about the features of available units and the steps required to complete a transaction. Although these actions may not literally take place after the exchange of information about available housing, it is convenient to place these steps in stage 2 of a housing market transaction. Discrimination in this stage further constrains minority customers' access to housing.

A final important aspect of a housing transaction is the geographic location of the housing units the agent makes available, which, for

31

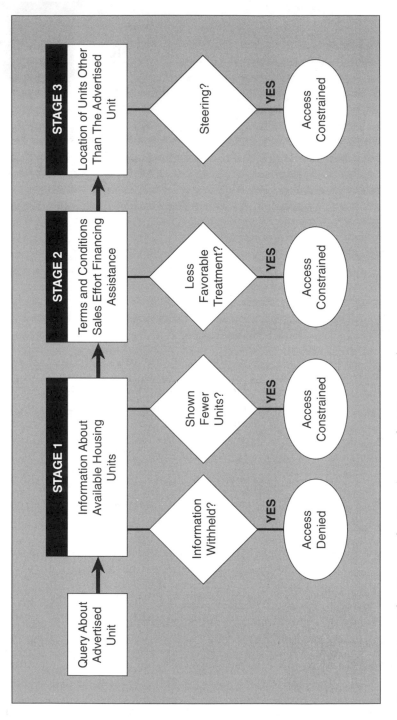

FIGURE 3.1. The Stages of a Housing Market Transaction

32

convenience, is called stage 3. A customer's access to housing is constrained if she does not state any preference for a certain type of neighborhood but is nevertheless only shown housing in neighborhoods with a particular racial or ethnic composition. This type of agent behavior is called steering.

This chapter presents the HDS evidence on discrimination in stage 1 of a housing market transaction and in all aspects of stage 2 except the provision of information about mortgages. It also summarizes the evidence from other audit studies concerning discrimination in these stages. Racial and ethnic steering are considered in Chapter 4, and real estate brokers' role in the mortgage market is discussed in Chapter 5.

In an audit study, discrimination is defined as systematically less favorable treatment of minority auditors than of their white teammates. Several different methods of calculating discrimination are consistent with this definition, however. This chapter focuses on two simple measures, the *net incidence of discrimination* and the *severity of discrimination,* both of which indicate the unfavorable treatment of minority auditors relative to the unfavorable treatment of their white teammates. Alternative ways of measuring discrimination are briefly considered later in the chapter.

For any particular type of agent behavior, such as denying an auditor access to all available housing, the net incidence of discrimination equals the share of audits in which the minority auditor was treated less favorably than her white teammate minus the share of audits in which the white auditor was treated less favorably. The severity of discrimination only applies to agent behavior that can take different values, such as the total number of housing units an agent shows to an auditor. In this example, the severity of discrimination equals the average number of units shown to white auditors minus the average number of units shown to minority auditors.[1]

■ DISCRIMINATION IN STAGE 1: HOUSING AVAILABILITY

The Net Incidence of Discrimination

Most of the time the housing agent tells both the minority and white auditors that the advertised unit is still available, but the first signs of discrimination can appear in the responses to the query regarding availability. The HDS survey forms reveal whether the auditor was told that the advertised unit was available and whether the auditor

TABLE 3.1 THE NET INCIDENCE OF DISCRIMINATION
          IN HOUSING AVAILABILITY

	Black–White %	Hispanic–White %
Sales Audits		
Advertised unit available	5.45*	4.51*
Advertised unit inspected	5.63*	4.20*
Similar units inspected	9.04*	6.26*
Excluded	6.34*	4.51*
Number of units recommended	11.09*	13.12*
Number of units shown	14.00*	9.68*
Number of units available	19.44*	16.50*
Rental Audits		
Advertised unit available	5.48	8.37
Advertised unit inspected	12.50*	5.09
Similar units inspected	2.47*	1.61
Excluded	10.66*	6.52*
Number of units recommended	11.09*	5.36
Number of units shown	17.16*	7.94
Number of units available	23.25*	9.76

NOTE: Entries marked with an asterisk are statistically significant at the 5 percent level
or above (two-tailed test) based on a fixed-effects logit model.

was able to inspect the advertised unit. The net incidence of discrimination in the availability of the advertised unit was 5.5 percent for blacks in both the sales and rental markets, 4.2 percent for Hispanics in the sales market, and 8.4 percent for Hispanics in the rental market.[2] These results are in the first sales and rentals rows of Table 3.1.

After asking about the advertised unit, auditors, as well as most actual customers, ask whether any similar units are available. In the sales market, agents are able to discriminate in response to this question because similar units often are available but unknown to the customer. Thus, the net incidence of discrimination in the inspection of units similar to the advertised unit is 9 percent in the black–white sales audits and 6.3 percent in the Hispanic–white sales audits. In the rental market, however, agents often do not have similar units for inspection, and the net incidence of discrimination for this variable is very low: 2.5 percent in the black–white audits and 1.6 percent in the Hispanic–white audits (see Table 3.1).

Auditors, like many actual customers, then proceed to find out about and to inspect as many housing units as possible. Housing agents have a great deal of leeway in deciding what units to make available to each customer, and they frequently recommend or show fewer units to minority than to white auditors. As shown in Table 3.1, the net incidence of discrimination is particularly dramatic for the total number of units available, which is the sum of the units recommended and shown. The net incidence of discrimination against black auditors on this variable is 19.4 percent in the sales market and 23.4 percent in the rental market. About one-fifth of the time, in other words, blacks learn about fewer housing units than do comparable whites.[3] In the Hispanic–white audits, the net incidence of discrimination in the total number of units available is 16.5 percent in the sales audits and 9.8 percent in the rental audits. Although somewhat lower than those for the black–white audits, these figures are still disturbingly high. Moreover, these results are the same for all Hispanics; the incidence of discrimination is not lower against Hispanics with light skins or without Spanish accents.[4]

Perhaps the most dramatic form of discrimination is exclusion, which is the complete withholding from minority customers of all information about available housing. Before the Fair Housing Act of 1968, this type of discrimination was the norm, as black and Hispanic customers were simply told that nothing was available—if indeed they could get an appointment in the first place.[5] In the HDS audits, exclusion is said to exist when an auditor is told that nothing is available while her teammate is recommended or shown at least one unit. The fourth row of Table 3.1 reveals that minority homeseekers still encounter exclusion: the net incidence of exclusion ranges from 4.5 percent in the Hispanic–white sales audits to 10.7 percent in the black–white rental audits.

The Severity of Discrimination

These results reveal how often minority auditors are recommended or shown fewer housing units than their white teammates, but they do not reveal the magnitude of the differences in the number of units shown. In other words, these results indicate the incidence of discrimination in housing availability, but they do not reveal its severity.

As shown in Table 3.2, the severity of discrimination in housing availability is quite high: minority auditors are recommended or shown significantly fewer housing units than are their white teammates.[6] Again focusing on the total number of units available, Table 3.2 reveals that blacks are shown 23.7 percent fewer units in the sales market and 24.5 percent fewer units in the rental market. For Hispanics, the differences are 25.6 percent in the sales market and 10.9 percent in the rental market.[7] With the exception of Hispanic renters,

Table 3.2 **THE SEVERITY OF DISCRIMINATION**
         IN HOUSING AVAILABILITY

	Black–White	*Hispanic–White*
Sales Audits		
Number of units recommended		
Number of units	0.316*	0.534*
Percentage of white units	32.22%	50.78%
Number of units shown		
Number of units	0.302*	0.167*
Percentage of white units	18.55%	9.92%
Number of units available		
Number of units	0.619*	0.701*
Percentage of white units	23.69%	25.63%
Rental Audits		
Number of units recommended		
Number of units	0.171*	0.078
Percentage of white units	48.26%	24.50%
Number of units shown		
Number of units	0.233*	0.099*
Percentage of white units	18.01%	7.58%
Number of units available		
Number of units	0.404*	0.177*
Percentage of white units	24.50%	10.90%

Notes: Entries marked with an asterisk are statistically significant at the 5 percent level or above (two-tailed test) using a weighted, paired difference-of-means test. The percentage figures simply scale the units figures and require no additional statistical test.

therefore, minority homeseekers can expect to learn about almost one-quarter fewer housing units than comparable whites: they must visit four housing agents to learn about the same number of housing units that whites learn about in three visits.

Withholding some units from minority customers has about the same quantitative impact on the number of units they learn about as simply excluding them from all information about available housing. When minorities are excluded, they are denied access to all the housing recommended or shown to their white teammates in those audits, which equals about 2.5 houses in the sales audits and 1.6 apartments in the rental audits, on average. These figures are very similar to the severity of discrimination in Table 3.2; on average, both outright exclusion and the withholding of some available units deny minorities access to over 2 housing units in the sales audits and 1.6 units in the rental audits. Exclusion is a more dramatic type of discrimination with a single visit to a housing agent because it cuts minorities off from all information about available housing. If minority homeseekers visit several housing agents, however, a minority homeseeker who encounters exclusion by one agent loses access to approximately the same number of housing units, at least on average, as another minority homeseeker who encounters one agent who withholds some available units.

Taking Advantage
of the Opportunity to Discriminate

Housing agents do not always have the opportunity to discriminate. An agent with no housing units to show, for example, cannot show fewer units to a minority than to a white customer. Moreover, the severity of an agent's discriminatory behavior is limited by his opportunity; the severity of discrimination by an agent with only one housing unit to show, for example, cannot exceed one unit. The question is: To what extent do housing agents take advantage of the opportunity to discriminate when it arises?

The opportunity to discriminate is difficult to measure, but it can be measured for one aspect of housing availability in the sales audits; namely, the number of units inspected. In this case the opportunity to discriminate equals the total number of housing units available to be inspected, which equals, in turn, the number of housing units inspected by either the minority or the white auditor.[8]

The question becomes, therefore, whether the severity of discrimination in the number of units shown increases with the opportunity to discriminate. The answer, which is illustrated in Figure 3.2, is affirmative.[9] The greater the number of units other than the advertised unit that are available to be inspected, the greater the severity of discrimination against minorities. This relationship is particularly striking for blacks. With a single unit available to be inspected, the severity of discrimination is only 0.11 houses or 0.08 apartments, but with fifteen additional units available, which is about the maximum found by HDS, the severity of discrimination rises to 2.26 houses or 1.07 apartments. If a real estate agent has fifteen houses ready to be inspected, for example, a black customer can expect to inspect two fewer houses than her white counterpart.[10] The maximum severity of discrimination is about 1.4 apartments for black renters and 1.0 units for Hispanics in either market.

Figure 3.3 expresses the severity of discrimination as a percentage of the number of units available to whites. When only one unit is open for inspection, the severity of discrimination against blacks in

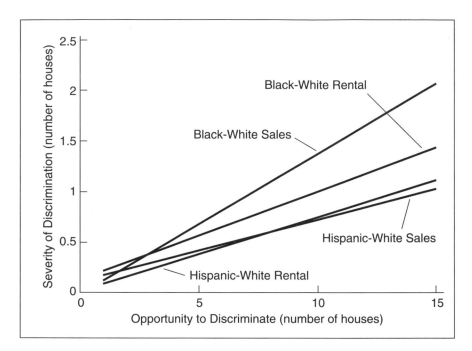

FIGURE 3.2.   The Severity of Discrimination and the Opportunity to Discriminate I

the sales market equals 11 percent of the number of houses seen by whites, but it increases to 23 percent when ten additional houses are available. With eleven or more houses, including the advertised unit, available to be inspected, in other words, a black can expect to inspect only three houses for every four inspected by a white. In the case of Hispanics, however, the severity of discrimination in the sales market declines slightly, from 17 to 12 percent, as the number of units open for inspection increases. Black renters face a pattern similar to the one for Hispanic buyers, whereas for Hispanic renters the severity of discrimination remains constant at about 9 percent of the units seen by whites, regardless of the number of units open for inspection.

Examining the opportunity to discriminate provides some perspective on the meaning of the basic HDS results. When a homeseeker responds to a newspaper advertisement, a typical housing agent has only the advertised unit, and perhaps one more, available to sell or rent and therefore does not have much opportunity to practice discrimination. It is not surprising, therefore, that the average severity of discrimination, measured in numbers of units denied, is not very

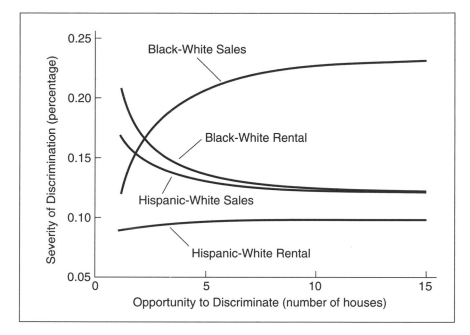

FIGURE 3.3.   The Severity of Discrimination and the Opportunity to Discriminate II

large. Agents who have many units to sell, however, have a much greater opportunity to discriminate and tend to take advantage of it. This clear relationship underscores the conclusion that the HDS results do not reflect isolated behavior by a few wayward housing agents, but instead reveal that many housing agents are willing to discriminate when the circumstances are "right."[11]

■ DISCRIMINATION IN STAGE 2: COMPLETING THE TRANSACTION

While an auditor or actual customer is trying to obtain information about available housing units, a housing agent can take a variety of actions to facilitate the completion of a potential housing transaction. As illustrated in Figure 3.1, these actions constitute stage 2 of a housing market transaction. HDS discovered discrimination in many of these actions, in the sense that they were taken for white but not for minority customers.

Some of the discrimination in these agent actions is annoying and

TABLE 3.3 DISCRIMINATION IN AGENT EFFORTS
TO COMPLETE A TRANSACTION

	Black-White	*Hispanic-White*
Sales Audits		
Net incidence measures (percent)		
Auditor asked to call back	3.34**	11.45*
Follow-up call	7.74**	5.51**
Ask about income[a]	8.08**	1.96**
Ask about housing needs	6.46	3.65**
Waiting time[a]	8.71	4.92**
Positive comments on house	12.47**	7.52**
Severity measures		
Waiting time[a,b]	0.67**	0.37
Positive comments on house[c]	0.29*	0.16
Rental Audits		
Net incidence measures (percent)		
Auditor offered special rental incentives	5.37**	5.06**
Auditor asked to call back	15.78**	8.57**
Rent for advertised unit[a]	11.29**	8.61**
Waiting time[a]	5.09	16.42**
Positive comments on apt.	16.80**	14.59**
Positive comments on apt. complex	12.93**	11.92**
Severity measures		
Rent for advertised unit[a,d]	12.16**	7.08*
Waiting time[a,b]	0.46*	0.97**
Positive comments on apt.[c]	0.41**	0.30**
Positive comments on apt. complex[c]	0.32**	0.37**

NOTES: An * indicates statistical significance at the 5 percent (10 percent) level with a one-tailed (two-tailed) test; ** indicates significance at the 2.5 percent (5 percent) level with a one-tailed (two-tailed) test. For the incidence measures, statistical significance is determined with a fixed-effects logit model; for the severity measures it is determined with a weighted, paired difference-of-means test.

[a]For this type of agent behavior, a higher value is considered less favorable treatment.
[b]Severity measured in minutes.
[c]Severity measured in average comments per unit inspected.
[d]Severity measured in dollars per month.

degrading to minority customers but does not seriously constrain their access to housing. As shown in Table 3.3, for example, minority auditors must wait longer than their white teammates until they are served by the agent, and in the sales market they are less likely to be asked about their housing needs and more likely to be queried about their income.[12] Agents' comments may encourage customers to pursue certain housing units, and minority auditors also are less likely to hear positive comments by the agent about the houses they inspect, the apartments they inspect, or the complexes in which these apartments are located.

Some other types of discrimination have more substantive impacts on housing access. In the sales market, minority auditors are less likely than white auditors to be invited to call the agent back and less likely to receive a follow-up call the next day. In the rental market, minority auditors are less likely than their white teammates to be offered special rental incentives, which include reduced rent, a free month's rent, a rebate at the end of the year, or a reduced or waived security deposit. Minority rental auditors are also less likely to be asked to call back.

The quoted rent for the advertised unit tends to be higher for minority than for white auditors, but this difference disappears when audits with a longer lease for minority auditors are excluded. A longer lease may be an advantage because it locks in the starting rent for a longer time, but it also limits a tenant's flexibility. Hence, landlords may simply be offering minorities a different, but comparable, combination of rent and lease length, or they may be stating higher rents and longer lease lengths in an attempt to discourage minority customers.

Overall, discrimination in housing availability is accompanied by discrimination in housing agents' efforts to complete a transaction. Black and Hispanic homeseekers not only must put up with petty mistreatment but also must put forth greater effort than their white counterparts to ensure that their own housing market transactions are completed.

◼ DISCRIMINATION DURING HOUSING SEARCH

All these results apply to the discrimination that a minority homeseeker can expect to encounter during a visit to a single housing agent. But many homeseekers visit more than one agent, and a minority homeseeker visiting several agents will probably encounter at least one act of discrimination.[13]

A recent study in Boston found that white households searching for a house to buy visited 2.1 real estate brokers, on average, whereas minority households visited 1.9.[14] Some particularly diligent households visited four or five brokers. Households searching for an apartment undoubtedly visit even more housing agents, on average, because an individual rental agent tends to have access to fewer housing

TABLE 3.4 THE INCIDENCE OF DISCRIMINATION
         DURING HOUSING SEARCH

	Black–White Number of Visits %			Hispanic–White Number of Visits %		
	2	4	6	2	4	6
Sales Audits						
Advertised unit available	10.60	20.08	28.56	8.22	15.77	22.70
Advertised unit inspected	10.94	20.69	29.37	10.41	19.74	28.10
Similar units inspected	17.28	31.58	43.40	12.13	22.79	32.15
Excluded	12.28	23.05	32.50	8.82	16.86	24.19
Number of units recommended	20.95	37.51	50.60	24.52	43.03	57.00
Number of units shown	26.04	45.30	59.54	18.42	33.45	45.71
Number of units available	35.10	57.88	72.67	30.28	51.39	66.11
Rental Audits						
Advertised unit available	10.66	20.18	28.69	16.04	29.51	40.81
Advertised unit inspected	23.44	41.38	55.12	9.92	18.86	26.91
Similar units inspected	4.88	9.52	13.93	3.19	6.29	9.28
Excluded	20.18	36.29	49.15	12.61	23.64	33.27
Number of units recommended	20.95	37.51	50.60	10.43	19.78	28.15
Number of units shown	31.38	52.91	67.68	15.25	28.17	39.13
Number of units available	41.25	65.48	79.72	18.57	33.69	46.00

NOTE: These figures are calculated from the results in Table 3.1 using the formula in footnote 15.

units than does a real estate broker, who is likely to use a multiple listing service. Consequently, apartment seekers often visit four, five, or even more rental agents.

The incidence of at least one act of discrimination in several visits to a housing agent is far greater than the incidence during one visit, which was presented in Table 3.1.[15] For example, as shown in Table 3.4, black home buyers who visit four housing agents can expect to be totally excluded from all available housing by at least one agent 23 percent of the time. The comparable figures for black renters, Hispanic home buyers, and Hispanic renters are 36 percent, 17 percent, and 24 percent, respectively. It seems that even outright exclusion is not an uncommon occurrence for minority homeseekers—at least not for diligent ones. Moreover, except in the case of Hispanic renters, *most* minority households who visit four or more agents will encounter at least one agent who withholds some housing from them.

■ OTHER WAYS
TO MEASURE DISCRIMINATION

So far, the discussion has focused on the net incidence of discrimination using a simple measure drawn from audit data. Alternative concepts of discrimination and alternative measurement techniques appear in the literature. In fact, the literature contains a lively debate about the strengths and weaknesses of various ways to conceptualize and measure discrimination.[16]

The most important distinction to make is between the concepts of net and gross incidence. The *gross incidence of discrimination* is the probability that a minority homeseeker will encounter unfavorable treatment because of her minority status. Since unfavorable treatment of minorities is explicitly outlawed by the Fair Housing Act of 1968, this approach measures the incidence of behavior that is, at least in spirit, illegal.[17]

The *net incidence of discrimination,* which is the concept employed in the preceding sections, focuses on the relative treatment of minority and white homeseekers. In contrast, the gross incidence concept is based on the view that discrimination should be measured by the absolute treatment of minority customers, not their treatment relative to whites. In a courtroom, a discrimination case is decided on the evidence about whether a single housing agent has denied a black or Hispanic customer access to the same housing made available to a white customer, regardless of whether or not another broker on the other side of town has treated a minority customer more favorably than a comparable white.

This book focuses on net incidence — the relative disadvantage imposed on minority households by discrimination. For some purposes, such as determining the extent to which additional law enforcement is needed, gross incidence may be a more appropriate concept. Thus, estimates of the gross incidence of discrimination are presented here to complement the estimates of net incidence presented earlier.

The key problem in exploring the gross incidence of discrimination is that the appropriate measurement technique is not clear. One possible measure, called the simple gross measure, is the share of audits in which an agent treats the minority auditor less favorably than the white. The simple net measure presented earlier begins with this gross measure and nets out cases in which minority auditors are favored.

Simple gross measures for the housing availability variables are

TABLE 3.5 **THE GROSS INCIDENCE OF DISCRIMINATION**

	Black–White %	*Hispanic–White* %
Sales Audits		
Advertised unit available	11.09	9.53
Advertised unit inspected	13.35	13.23
Similar units inspected	19.74	17.08
Excluded	7.59	7.50
Number of units recommended	31.34	34.30
Number of units shown	30.38	29.62
Number of units available	44.07	43.59
Rental Audits		
Advertised unit available	17.23	15.51
Advertised unit inspected	23.03	17.64
Similar units inspected	13.74	15.16
Excluded	15.12	12.09
Number of units recommended	22.28	18.55
Number of units shown	31.72	26.87
Number of units available	41.35	34.60

NOTE: All entries in this table are statistically significant at the 5 percent level (two-tailed) using a weighted t-test. See footnote 18.

presented in Table 3.5.[18] For some variables, such as exclusion, the gross measure is not much larger than the net measure in Table 3.1. For the variables indicating whether the two auditors saw the same number of units, however, the gross measures are much larger. In fact, the gross measure for the number of units recommended or shown exceeds 40 percent, except in the case of Hispanic renters, for whom it is 35 percent. About two-fifths of the time, minority home-seekers can expect to learn about fewer housing units than their white counterparts.

Some scholars have argued that the simple gross measure is inappropriate because it includes cases in which a minority auditor is favored for purely random reasons — not because of her minority status. It includes, for example, an audit in which the minority auditor cannot inspect an apartment because it was rented after it was shown to the white auditor. These scholars argue that minority auditors are unlikely to be favored except for random reasons, so the share of audits in which minority auditors are favored provides a reasonable estimate of the extent to which random factors are at work.[19] Subtracting this share from the share of audits in which the white auditor was favored, which yields the simple net measure, can be seen as a correction for random events. In short, some people argue that the simple net *measure* provides a reasonable estimate for the gross incidence *concept*.

This assumption is too extreme. Agents sometimes take systematic actions that favor minority customers. One important example is racial or ethnic steering. When steering occurs, an agent may show more houses to a minority customer, appearing to be favoring her according to standard measures, but the agent may show her houses only in largely minority neighborhoods, thereby limiting her housing options (as well as the options of her white counterparts). In calculating the gross incidence of discrimination, it makes no sense to "net out" cases like these.[20]

This type of agent behavior is not just hypothetical: 24.0 percent of the sales audits in which blacks are recommended or shown more houses than their white teammates and 25.9 percent of those in which Hispanics are so "favored" involve the steering of the minority auditor to neighborhoods that have a larger minority population or lower-valued houses than those offered to whites.[21]

An alternative assumption, which is at the opposite extreme from the assumption behind the simple net measure, is that all audits in which minority auditors appear to be favored involve some form of steering or other agent behavior that works against both minority and white households. In this case it makes no sense to net out minority "favored" audits when calculating a measure of relative disadvantage; in fact, the relative disadvantage faced by minority auditors equals the simple gross measure of discrimination.

The alternative assumption also goes too far: both minority and white auditors are sometimes favored because of random events. But it is difficult to determine which assumption is right or, to be more precise, how often minority auditors are favored for purely random reasons. The simple net and gross measures appear to provide lower and upper bounds on the gross incidence of discrimination, but these bounds are far apart and therefore not very helpful guides.

No consensus has emerged among scholars on the best way to measure the gross incidence of discrimination, but a recent paper provides one possible approach.[22] It develops a more elaborate estimating technique that makes it possible to isolate, within bounds, the impact of random factors. This technique is applied to several types of agent behavior in the HDS black–white sales audits. For the first three types of agent behavior in Tables 3.1 and 3.5, the estimated upper bounds are very close to the simple gross measures in Table 3.5, and the estimated lower bounds are about twice as large as the simple net measures.[23] For the first four types of agent behavior in Table 3.3, the estimated upper bounds also are very close to the simple gross measures, which range from 20 to 26 percent, and the lower bounds are from 50 to 300 percent larger than the simple net measures.[24] In short, this work indicates that the simple net measure understates, often dramatically, the gross incidence of discrimination, whereas the simple gross measure provides a reasonable upper bound.

The simple net measure is plausible and easy to understand, but it is not the only way to measure discrimination. For those interested in the gross incidence of discrimination, that is, in the likelihood that a minority will encounter presumptively illegal treatment, the simple net measure is based on an extreme assumption about agent behavior and greatly understates the true gross incidence of discrimination. The story told by the simple net measure is bleak enough: it should give us pause to recognize that in some ways the story may be even worse.

■ HAS DISCRIMINATION DECLINED OVER TIME?

A 1970 report by the National Committee Against Discrimination in Housing concluded that blacks occasionally encounter real estate brokers who refuse to deal with them, but that "more frequently, non-white customers meet with efforts to discourage them, with evasion or misrepresentation, with withholding of information or with delaying tactics."[25] Among the broker tactics listed in this report are the following: telling the buyer that no houses meeting his specifications currently are available when such houses actually are available; not making the follow-up calls that would be made for a white buyer; advising blacks they cannot afford a house under circumstances in which whites would be advised otherwise; misrepresenting the price or other terms of the transaction; and refusing to help black buyers find a mortgage. Although two of these tactics (differences in advice about affordability and misrepresentations of the price and terms) are no longer used very often, this list could almost serve as a summary of the HDS results.[26]

A more formal look at changes in discrimination over time can be obtained by comparing the HDS results with those of the first national audit study, HMPS, which was conducted in 1977.[27] In fact, one of the objectives of HDS was to determine, through just such a comparison, whether the incidence of discrimination had declined. But the HDS audit methodology differed from that of HMPS in one important respect, and the results of the two studies are difficult to compare with precision.[28]

The change in audit methodology concerns the use of the advertised unit that is the starting point of an audit. HMPS drew a single sample of advertisements at the beginning of the study. The audits sometimes took place several weeks after the sample was drawn, so asking about the advertised unit specifically would not have been appropriate. Instead, each audit team was told to ask about a housing unit that was similar in price, size, and location to the unit mentioned in the ad. HDS drew a separate sample each weekend, so it made sense to ask about the advertised unit itself. Moreover, this procedure provided a more precise "anchor" to the audit, in which audit teammates gave identical initial signals to the housing agent.

This difference in audit methodology implies that the housing agent had more leeway to practice discrimination in response to the initial request by a HMPS auditor than to that by a HDS auditor. After all, it is difficult to deny the existence of a unit you have advertised in the newspaper. Even with no change in the discriminatory behavior of housing agents, one would expect to find less discrimination in information about the "advertised unit" in HDS than in HMPS. This turns out to be the case. In the sales audits, the net incidence of discrimination in the availability of the advertised unit is 10 percent in HMPS and 4.4 percent in HDS.[29] The comparable figures for the rental audits are 19 percent and 10.2 percent for HMPS and HDS, respectively. Given the difference in methodology between the two studies, this difference obviously cannot be interpreted as a decline in the incidence of discrimination.

This issue does not arise for some other types of agent behavior, however. There is no reason to believe, for example, that the differences in methodology between the two studies would significantly impact their estimates of discrimination in the number of housing units inspected or made available. Consider first the net incidence of discrimination in the number of housing units inspected. In both the sales and rental audits, this measure of discrimination is higher in HDS than in HMPS. The sales audit results are 10 percent in HMPS and 13.3 percent in HDS, and the rental audit results are 6 percent in HMPS and 24.4 percent in HDS. Not all comparisons reveal higher discrimination for HDS than for HMPS, however. In the case of the total number of units volunteered or inspected, to use the HMPS terms, the net incidence of discrimination is 30 percent in HMPS and 20 percent in HDS for the sales audits and 24 percent in HMPS and 23.5 percent in HDS for the rental audits.

Overall, a comparison of the HDS and HMPS results does not reveal any clear trend in discrimination between 1977 and 1989. Both studies find widespread discrimination. For some types of agent behavior, the estimated net incidence of discrimination is higher for HDS than for HMPS, but for other types of agent behavior the HMPS estimates are higher. In most cases that are not influenced by differences in methodology, however, the estimated incidence of discrimination is similar for the two studies.

At least seventy-two other audit studies were conducted during the late 1970s or the 1980s.[30] These studies covered all regions of the country, both sales and rental markets, and both African Americans and Hispanics.[31] The evidence from these studies overwhelmingly supports the conclusion that minority homeseekers have faced and continue to face widespread discrimination in housing.

Twenty-nine of these audit studies present summary measures of the incidence of discrimination.[32] The average incidence for these studies is 47 percent, ranging from 4 percent to 90 percent, and every study except one concludes that the incidence of discrimination is statistically significant. Moreover, many of these studies find discrimination in the number of houses or apartments made available; in the terms or conditions of sale or rental; in the extent and quality of the information auditors were given about available housing; in the stated application procedures or waiting times for apartments; in the quality of the apartments shown to auditors; or in the courtesy with which the auditors were treated. No section of the country is immune from these types of discriminatory behavior, and the studies do not reveal any clear downward trend in the incidence of discrimination.[33]

A few of these audit studies estimate the severity of discrimination. The 1981 Boston study provides estimates of discrimination against blacks that are comparable to those in Table 3.2.[34] For the number of units inspected, the severity of discrimination relative to the number of units inspected by whites is 23.8 percent in the sales audits and 32.9 percent in the rental audits. These figures are somewhat higher than the comparable figures from HDS.[35] The Boston severity results for the total number of units "suggested as serious possibilities" are 26.2 percent in the sales market and 28.6 percent in the rental market. These results are similar to the HDS results for the total number of units available, namely, 23.7 percent (sales) and 24.5 percent (rental). Twenty-seven other audit studies conducted between 1980 and 1985 estimate the severity of discrimination in housing availability against blacks or Hispanics.[36] All but two of these studies find statistically significant discrimination.[37]

■ CONCLUSIONS

African American and Hispanic households are very likely to encounter discrimination when they search for housing. This discrimination occurs throughout the country; it severely limits the information minority households receive about available housing; and it adds annoyance, complexity, and expense to their housing search process.

The evidence to back up these claims is overwhelming. The 1989 Housing Discrimination Study, which directly observed discrimination nationwide using fair housing audits, found that between 5 and 10 percent of the time, all information about available housing units was withheld from black and Hispanic customers; that black and Hispanic home buyers and black renters were informed about 25 percent fewer housing units than comparable whites; and that whites were significantly more likely than blacks or Hispanics to receive follow-up calls from the housing agent or to hear positive comments about an available house, apartment, or apartment complex. An earlier large national study and dozens of studies in individual cities during the 1980s came to the same conclusion. Despite the 1968 Fair Housing Act, discrimination in housing shows no signs of going away.

Racial and Ethnic Steering

In July 1989 a 31-year-old black man entered a real estate office in Atlanta to see if a $110,000 house advertised in *The* Sunday *Atlanta Journal and Constitution,* or anything similar, was still available. With an annual income of $75,000, he and his wife could readily afford this house, which was just the right size for them and their children. The real estate agent recommended two other houses far to the south of her office. Shortly thereafter, a 27-year-old white man went to the same agency to inquire about the same house. His income, down payment capability, and family characteristics were virtually identical to those of the black man, but he was told about two available houses only slightly north of the real estate office and was not told about the houses to the south.[1]

This difference in treatment was not simply random variation in the location of available houses. As shown in Figure 4.1, all four houses were in largely white areas of Atlanta, but the two southern houses were close to neighborhoods where blacks were in the majority, whereas the two northern houses were relatively isolated from largely black areas and bordered on a large region in which virtually no blacks lived. Moreover, the two southern houses were separated from the agent's office by the largely black parts of Atlanta, whereas the two northern houses and the agent's office were in similar, almost contiguous, neighborhoods.

This example from HDS illustrates racial and ethnic steering, which is defined as behavior that directs a customer toward neighborhoods in which people of his or her racial or ethnic group are concen-

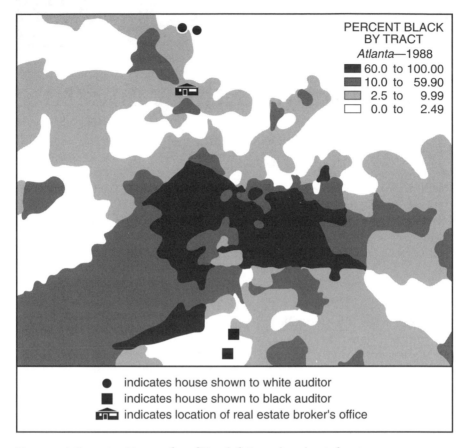

FIGURE **4.1.** An Example of Racial Steering in Atlanta

trated. In the most dramatic cases of steering, a minority customer is shown houses only in largely minority neighborhoods even though other houses are available. Steering also can involve agent behavior that discourages or makes difficult the purchase or rental of housing in certain locations without withholding all information about available housing there.

Racial and ethnic steering is important for two reasons. First, it represents another constraint on the housing choices of minority households. Even when a minority homeseeker is shown at least as many housing units as a white homeseeker, her choices may be constrained because the housing agent decides not to show her housing in some or all largely white areas.[2] To find the total impact of housing discrimination on minorities, therefore, the impact of steering must be added to the impact of other forms of discrimination.

Second, steering restricts the choices of white households in a way that promotes racial and ethnic residential segregation.[3] Many white families would no doubt decide not to buy or rent housing in an integrated neighborhood even if it were shown to them, but white families that would consider or even prefer living in an integrated neighborhood may not learn about available housing there or may be discouraged from selecting it. As illustrated by the example from Atlanta, even housing in white neighborhoods near integrated or largely black neighborhoods may be withheld from white customers.

■ THE INCIDENCE OF RACIAL AND ETHNIC STEERING

Racial and ethnic steering is a particularly elusive type of discrimination because it involves complicated geographic patterns that vary from one urban area to another in addition to involving comments and subtle actions that are difficult to record and quantify. Nevertheless, both HDS and several other audit studies have been able to document steering's continued existence.

Steering Results from HDS

To obtain information on steering, HDS required each auditor to record the address of each house that was recommended or shown to her. The resulting address information was used to place each house into a census tract, thereby identifying the characteristics of the tract in which each house was located.[4] Address information was collected for both the sales and rental audits, but the HDS researchers carried out a detailed analysis of steering only for house sales.[5] This analysis revealed some clear differences between the locations of the houses recommended or shown to minority and white auditors.

As indicated in Table 4.1, the houses recommended or shown to black auditors tended to be in neighborhoods with greater minority populations, lower incomes, and lower house values than the houses recommended or shown to their white teammates. The net incidence of cases in which the minority auditor was steered to census tracts with a greater minority concentration than was her white teammate was 6.2 percent for blacks and 4.8 percent for Hispanics.[6] Moreover, at least one type of steering occurred in 9.3 percent of the black–white audits and 4.3 percent of the Hispanic–white audits in which

TABLE 4.1 **THE NET INCIDENCE OF RACIAL AND ETHNIC STEERING**

	Black–White Audits		*Hispanic–White Audits*	
Tract Characteristic	*All Units* %	*Excluding Advertised Unit %*	*All Units* %	*Excluding Advertised Unit %*
Minority Concentration[a]	6.2	11.8	4.8	0.5
Per Capita Income[b]	3.7	2.0	3.3	7.7
Median House Value[c]	5.1	5.4	1.3	6.0
Composite Index[d]	9.3	11.9	4.6	7.9

SOURCE: Turner, Mickelsons, and Edwards (1991), Tables 3, 4, 7, 12, 13, and 16.

[a]Share of audits in which the houses recommended or shown to minority auditor were in census tracts with greater minority concentration than those recommended or shown to their teammate minus the same share for white auditors.
[b]Share of audits in which the houses recommended or shown to minority auditor were in census tracts with lower per capita income than those recommended or shown to their teammate minus the same share for white auditors.
[c]Share of audits in which the houses recommended or shown to minority auditor were in census tracts with lower median house value than those recommended or shown to their teammate minus the same share for white auditors.
[d]Share of audits in which the houses recommended or shown the minority auditor were in census tracts with greater minority concentration, lower per capita income, or lower median house value than those recommended or shown to their teammate (and not the reverse for any of these characteristics) minus the same share for white auditors.

each auditor saw at least one house.[7] Small differences in census tract characteristics do not have a substantive meaning, so these steering calculations do not count differences in tract characteristics unless one auditor's average value exceeds her teammate's by 5 percentage points for racial composition, $2,500 for per capita income, and $5,000 for median house value.

The advertised house is included in these calculations, but real estate brokers may have a difficult time steering customers away from this house because the customer may already have seen the advertisement. Moreover, auditors reveal their interest in this house by making an explicit request to see it. A more reasonable procedure, therefore, is to exclude the advertised unit in calculating the net incidence of steering. As shown in the second and fourth columns of Table 4.1, this step boosts the net incidence of steering to 11.9 percent for blacks and 7.9 percent for Hispanics.[8]

The figures in Table 4.1 give the net incidence of steering during a single visit to a real estate broker. Homeseekers who visit more than one broker have a correspondingly higher chance of encountering at least one act of steering. Following the logic presented earlier, a black homeseeker who visits four real estate brokers has a 39.8 percent chance of encountering some steering.[9] The comparable figure for an Hispanic homeseeker visiting four agents is 28.0 percent. Thus, racial or ethnic steering is a common experience for black and Hispanic households looking for a house to buy.

A follow-up study using the HDS data revealed that the pattern of steering is not the same in every metropolitan area.[10] This study, which focused on Chicago and Atlanta, compared the characteristics of the census tracts in which the houses made available to white and black auditors were concentrated.[11] In Chicago, the houses shown to blacks were in areas with significantly higher black populations, lower incomes, lower property values, fewer new houses, and fewer occupied units. By contrast, the most striking feature of steering in Atlanta was that the houses shown to blacks were significantly closer to largely black tracts than were the houses shown to whites.[12]

The HDS data also show that in some cases real estate brokers' comments serve to steer white customers away from black neighborhoods, thereby helping to perpetuate segregation. Brokers tend to make more comments, both positive and negative, to white than to minority customers.[13] There is no difference in the average number of negative comments about the neighborhood made to black and white auditors when the advertised house is in a largely white neighborhood, but whites hear significantly more negative comments about the neighborhood than do their black teammates when the advertised house's neighborhood is largely black. To be specific, the expected difference in negative comments increases from zero in an all-white neighborhood to about 0.25 when the neighborhood is 50 percent black and to 0.5 when it is 100 percent black.[14] Because negative comments about a neighborhood are relatively rare, a rough summary of these results is to say that blacks almost never hear negative comments about a neighborhood, but one in four white customers will hear such a negative comment when the advertised unit is in a neighborhood that is 50 percent black, even though they specifically asked to see the house, and half of all white customers will hear such a comment in an all-black neighborhood.

An audit study cannot determine, of course, the impact of real estate brokers' comments on households' decisions. In fact, HDS and most other audit studies train auditors to attempt to visit as many houses as possible, regardless of any comments the agent might make. If agents' discouraging comments have a powerful impact on actual customers, then HDS and other audit studies may understate the differences in the racial composition of neighborhoods surrounding the houses visited by actual minority and white customers.[15]

A full analysis of steering in the rental market was not attempted by the HDS researchers, but an analysis of rental agents' comments provides one hint about possible steering. In particular, agents do not make more negative comments about the complex in which an apartment is located to either white or black customers when the advertised unit is located in a largely white neighborhood. As the black representation in this neighborhood increases, however, white customers hear significantly more negative comments than do comparable blacks.[16] This type of steering does not arise for Hispanic renters.

Previous Studies of Steering

At least 36 other audit studies, including the first large audit study in the United States, have explored some aspect of racial steering in either the sales or rental market between 1974 and 1987.[17] These studies, which focus almost exclusively on steering of blacks and whites, vary widely in their methodology and address a variety of questions about steering, but the vast majority of them find some evidence of steering that is consistent with the HDS results.[18] Somewhat ironically, several of these studies of steering were conducted in places with aggressive antidiscrimination programs, so that their results probably understate the extent of steering in the nation as a whole.[19]

These studies do not support the conclusion that blacks are excluded entirely from largely white neighborhoods nor do they indicate that blacks are shown houses in fewer areas (defined as municipalities, school districts, or neighborhoods) than are whites. Many of the studies find, however, that the houses shown to blacks are in neighborhoods with a higher percentage of black residents or are closer to largely black neighborhoods than are the houses shown to whites. Moreover, studies in Chicago (1979–1980), Grand Rapids (1981–1982), Cincinnati (1983), and Boston (1983–1984) provide evidence that agents make comments to discourage whites, but not blacks, from living in integrated areas.[20]

Only a few audit studies have investigated racial steering in rental housing, but evidence of this type of steering has been found. Studies in Baltimore (1981–1982), Cambridge-Somerville (1983), Wisconsin (1984–1985), Kentucky (1985), Lexington (1987), Louisville (1987), and South Bend (1987) all find that black apartment seekers are shown different apartments or different sections of a building or different buildings in a complex than are comparable whites.

▉ THE GREAT HDS PUZZLE AND STEERING THROUGH MARKETING PRACTICES

While investigating racial steering, the HDS researchers discovered that the vast majority of the houses recommended or shown to both minority and white auditors were in largely white neighborhoods.[21,22] Despite the fact that HDS was conducted in metropolitan areas with relatively large minority populations, 68.1 percent of the houses made available to auditors in the black–white audits and 67.3 percent of those made available to auditors in the Hispanic–white audits were in census tracts that were over 90 percent white.[23] Moreover, the average available house in the black–white audits was in a census tract that was 8.8 percent black, which is far below the average for all tracts in the sampled metropolitan areas, namely 19.9 percent.[24] The same contrast appears in the Hispanic–white audits, for which the census tract of the average available unit was 15.6 percent Hispanic compared to 23.8 percent for all tracts in the sampled metropolitan areas.

This concentration of available housing in largely white tracts leads to an important puzzle: How are houses in largely minority and integrated neighborhoods marketed and sold? For the most part, these houses are not advertised in newspapers and not shown to customers who inquire about advertised units. Because reading newspaper advertisements and contacting real estate brokers are the most common housing search procedures, this feature of real estate marketing practices dramatically limits the access of all customers to housing in largely minority and integrated neighborhoods and therefore constitutes an important form of steering.[25]

Three recent studies, two of them directly inspired by the HDS puzzle, have explored real estate marketing practices and found strong evidence of this type of steering.[26] The first study monitored the advertising practices of one large real estate firm in Milwaukee over a 3-year period. This firm's listings in largely black and integrated neighborhoods were only half as likely to be advertised in *The Milwaukee Journal* and only one-quarter as likely to have an open house as were its listings in largely white neighborhoods with comparable housing.

These findings were confirmed by the two post–HDS studies conducted in Boston and Washington, D.C. Both of these studies investigated the marketing of houses with for sale signs in largely black, integrated, and largely white census tracts with similar incomes, house values, and homeownership rates. In both cases, houses for sale in largely black and integrated tracts were less likely to have open houses than were houses in largely white tracts. The share of houses with an open house in largely black tracts was 1.8 percent in Boston and 14 percent in Washington, D.C., and the shares in integrated neighborhoods were 17.5 and 26 percent, whereas the shares in largely white tracts were 27.5 and 40 percent, respectively.

Moreover, in Boston, the houses for sale in largely black and integrated tracts were less likely to be listed by a broker who advertised in *The Boston Globe*. Similarly, houses for sale in largely black and integrated tracts in Washington, D.C., were less likely to be advertised in *The Washington Post* than the houses in largely white tracts. To be specific, only 14 percent of the houses in largely black tracts and 32 percent of the houses in integrated tracts were advertised, compared to 53 percent of the houses in largely white tracts. Furthermore, houses for sale in largely black or integrated areas were not advertised in community or alternative metropolitanwide newspapers.[27]

The Boston study also finds that different types of real estate firms sell houses in largely black and integrated areas than in largely white areas. Firms that sell in a largely black tract (and to a lesser extent in an integrated tract), unlike firms that sell in a largely white tract, tend to have few other listings in that tract. Moreover, firms operating in largely black tracts were less likely than other firms to belong to a multiple listing service (MLS).[28] In short, real estate firms in Boston avoid specializing in the sale of houses in largely black neighborhoods, and many firms with access to an MLS appear to avoid listing houses in black neighborhoods altogether.

The relatively low access to an MLS in largely minority neighborhoods is confirmed by the HDS data. HDS auditors could not literally identify firms that belonged to an MLS, but they did record whether an MLS directory was used to identify houses.[29] Real estate firms that did not use an MLS directory for either auditor either did not belong to an MLS or else did not turn to MLS listings in response to inquiries about the advertised unit. The probability that at least one auditor was shown houses from an MLS directory was lower in largely minority than in largely white neighborhoods for both the black–white and Hispanic–white audits.[30] To account for the fact that an MLS is more widely used in some metropolitan areas, these results statistically control for the audit site.[31]

The effect of neighborhood is large. Moving from an all-white to an all-black neighborhood reduces the probability that an MLS directory will be used from 50 to 28 percent. A somewhat smaller reduction, from 57 to 40 percent, occurs in moving from an all-white to an all-Hispanic neighborhood. Because HDS excludes real estate firms that do not advertise in major metropolitan newspapers, which appear to be overrepresented in largely minority neighborhoods and relatively unlikely to use an MLS, these results probably understate the lack of access to an MLS in these areas.

Although different cities appear to have somewhat different marketing conventions, these findings reveal that real estate agencies often practice steering through their marketing practices. Houses for sale in largely black neighborhoods are advertised less often, have fewer open houses, and are more likely to be sold by a real estate firm that does not belong to an MLS than are houses in largely white neighborhoods. More limited information from HDS indicates that this type of steering also may affect Hispanics searching to buy a house. This type of steering implies not only that housing for sale in a largely minority or integrated area is marketed less actively and advertised less widely than housing elsewhere,[32] but also that people who search for housing in largely minority or integrated areas often will not gain access to information about the housing that is available in largely white areas.

To some degree, this type of steering involves discriminatory practices by individual real estate firms, such as limiting advertising or open houses for houses in black and white neighborhoods or refusing to accept listings in largely black or integrated neighborhoods. Discriminatory actions by individual firms are not the whole story, however. No real estate firm is required to actively seek listings in a particular neighborhood or to belong to a multiple listing service. Thus, the bifurcation of the market into firms that do not list houses in largely minority neighborhoods and firms that do (and which may not advertise heavily or belong to an MLS) reflects in part perfectly legal business decisions. The cumulative impact of these decisions is to limit the access to housing in all-white areas of people who begin their housing search in largely minority neighborhoods, most of whom belong to a minority group themselves, and to limit the access to housing in largely minority and integrated areas of people who begin their housing search in largely white areas, most of whom are themselves whites.[33] Even though they are legal, these actions by real estate firms direct customers to neighborhoods in which people of their own racial or ethnic group are concentrated—which is the definition of steering.

Existing studies establish that houses in largely minority and integrated neighborhoods are not advertised as often or marketed as aggressively as houses in largely white neighborhoods, but they do not reveal the relative importance in causing these outcomes of discriminatory practices versus legal business decisions. Discriminatory behavior clearly plays some role, but currently legal business practices also appear to contribute. Consequently, policy makers cannot eliminate differences in marketing between largely minority and largely white neighborhoods without either expanding their set of tools beyond antidiscrimination measures or expanding the definition of illegal behavior.[34]

The fact that houses for sale in largely black neighborhoods are marketed by real estate firms that are relatively unlikely to advertise, to use open houses, to sell many houses in those neighborhoods, or to belong to an MLS also contributes to differences in housing availability between minority and white homeseekers. Even if these firms do not make fewer houses available to minority than to white customers, the people who visit them, most of whom belong to a minority group, will learn about fewer housing units than the people, mostly white, who visit firms in largely white areas. The cumulative effect of certain legal behavior by individual firms, therefore, not only contributes to steering but also contributes to the disparity between white and minority households in information about the number of available houses.

▌CONCLUSIONS

Clear evidence from HDS and numerous other audit studies reveals that racial and ethnic steering continue to be widely practiced by housing agents. These studies demonstrate that the houses made available to minority homeseekers tend to be in neighborhoods with greater minority representation than are the houses made available to white customers, and that real estate brokers often discourage white customers from buying houses in largely black or integrated neighborhoods. The existing evidence indicates that Hispanic homeseekers do not encounter as much steering as black homeseekers, but far less evidence about the steering of Hispanics has been collected. Steering in the rental market has not been widely studied, but the limited evidence that is available indicates that black households who are searching for an apartment also encounter steering in some cases.

This steering of individual customers is accompanied by equally powerful steering in the marketing practices of real estate firms. Houses for sale in largely minority and integrated neighborhoods are less likely to be advertised in the major metropolitan newspaper, less likely to have an open house, and less likely to be sold by a firm that belongs to a multiple listing service than are houses in largely white neighborhoods. This type of steering reflects both the direct effect of discriminatory actions, such as a decision to hold open houses in largely white but not in largely black areas, and the cumulative effect of legal actions, such as a decision by real estate firms that advertise heavily to specialize in houses in largely white areas.

These two forms of steering, in the treatment of individual homeseekers and in the marketing of available houses, restrict the housing options of all homeseekers and help to preserve racial and ethnic residential segregation. As we will see, this segregation is a key pillar of the system that promotes discriminatory behavior by landlords and real estate brokers.

Discrimination and Redlining in Mortgage Lending

In Chicago in 1990, a black customer entered a lending institution to inquire about a mortgage and was told that he could not meet with a loan officer until he had completed an application and paid an application fee. An identically qualified white customer who entered the same institution on the same day was immediately given an appointment with a loan officer.

Equally egregious acts of discrimination occurred at other lending institutions. One black customer was told that the institution did not make loans to first-time home buyers and another was told that it was illegal for the lender to provide mortgages for under $40,000. Both statements were untrue and were not made to white customers who visited the same lender on the same day. These lender actions, which were discovered by a pilot audit study of lender behavior conducted by the Chicago Fair Housing Alliance, illustrate the kind of discriminatory treatment that many minorities encounter when they apply for a mortgage loan.[1]

Discrimination in mortgage lending is important because most families must obtain a mortgage before they can afford to buy a house.[2] Minority families' access to housing is limited, therefore, not only by the discriminatory acts of real estate brokers but also by the discriminatory acts of lenders.

This chapter explores what is known about discrimination against mortgage loan applicants and about redlining, which is discrimination against people trying to buy houses in minority neighborhoods. The chapter begins by explaining why discrimination in mortgage

63

lending recently has become, after a long period of neglect, the subject of renewed debate and policy attention. The following sections provide precise definitions of mortgage discrimination and redlining, present the evidence on discrimination in the approval of loans, discuss discrimination in other actions by lenders and discrimination by other actors in mortgage markets, and review what is known about redlining.

■ THE REDISCOVERY OF DISCRIMINATION IN MORTGAGE LENDING

Despite its potential importance, discrimination in mortgage lending received relatively little attention during most the 1980s. A few academic studies provided evidence that this type of discrimination existed, but these studies were not widely recognized. Private fair housing groups processed complaints from minority loan applicants, conducted some investigations of lender behavior, and negotiated a few settlements with lenders.[3] The occasional investigations into discrimination complaints by government enforcement agencies typically concluded that discrimination in loan approvals did not exist, and policy makers were not convinced that this type of discrimination was problematic.

Enforcement agencies concluded that there was no lending discrimination because most minority applicants had some flaw in their credit history that appeared to justify a lender's decision to deny them a loan. Although this conclusion proved to be incorrect, the source of their error was not apparent until recently.

The lack of attention to mortgage discrimination started to change in 1988 when *The Atlanta Journal and Constitution* published a series of articles titled "The Color of Money."[4] This series, which won a Pulitzer Prize, documented the limited flow of mortgage funds to black neighborhoods in Atlanta and described some of the seemingly discriminatory policies of Atlanta's lending institutions.

Attention grew with the 1991 release of data required by the Home Mortgage Disclosure Act (HMDA). This act was passed in 1975 to provide information about the location of loan origins. Because the information proved useful to policy makers and community groups, HMDA was renewed in 1980, made permanent in 1987, and amended by the Financial Institutions Reform, Recovery, and Enforcement Act of 1989.[5] The 1989 amendments expanded HMDA reporting requirements and required lenders to provide detailed information on all loan applications.[6]

The resulting 1990 HMDA data described the outcome of all home purchase, refinancing, and home improvement loan applications submitted to the vast majority of lending institutions in the country.[7] Moreover, the data identified the race and ethnicity of each applicant, as well as the name of the lender, the census tract in which the associated house was located, and the income of the applicant. These data revealed striking differences in loan denial rates for minority and white applicants. In fact, the overall denial rate was 33.9 percent for blacks and 22.4 percent for Hispanics, compared to only 14.4 percent for whites. Not surprisingly, these results received a great deal of publicity, with featured articles in *The New York Times* and *The Wall Street Journal.*[8]

These dramatic results cannot be interpreted as an indication of discrimination in mortgage lending because the HMDA data are incomplete. In particular, the HMDA data do not include the applicants' credit histories, so one cannot rule out the possibility that the higher denial rate for blacks and Hispanics exists because they have poorer credit histories than whites. Nevertheless, the differences between minority and white denial rates are so large that they make the possibility of extensive discrimination seem plausible and identify a serious social problem, even if it is not entirely, or even largely, caused by discrimination in loan approval.

The "Color of Money" series and the release of the 1990 HMDA data gave rise to two more events that brought mortgage discrimination into active public debate. First, the series caught the attention of the Justice Department, which in 1989 began an investigation into the practices of one large lending institution in Atlanta, Decatur Federal Savings and Loan, which appeared to be discriminating. This investigation might have ended on the same inconclusive note as earlier ones except that it was still in progress when the 1990 HMDA data were released. The dramatic racial differences in loan denial rates revealed by these data induced the Justice Department to redouble its efforts. Ironically, the investigation was aided by the full cooperation of Decatur Federal, which apparently believed that its procedures were not discriminatory. By the time the Justice Department and Decatur Federal signed a consent decree in the fall of 1992, this investigation had uncovered extensive discrimination and set a new standard for investigation in mortgage discrimination cases.[9]

Moreover, the investigation revealed why enforcement agencies, and even the owners of lending institutions, might not find existing discrimination. As it turns out, most loan applicants, both minority and majority, have some flaw in their credit histories, to which the intake workers who process loan applications and the underwriters who make final loan decisions must respond. Loan processors are in a position to help an applicant resolve any deficiencies in his or her credit history by soliciting an explanation from the applicant, for example, or by encouraging the applicant to pay off existing credit card debt. But these discretionary extra steps by loan processors are not provided at the same rate to minority and white applicants. The Decatur investigation revealed that loan processors tend to give white applicants complete information and to coach them about ways to make their applications look stronger. However, they generally do not even tell minority applicants that it is possible to resolve deficiencies in their applications. In addition, underwriters tend to give white applicants the benefit of the doubt, whereas they focus on flaws in the minority applications and even exaggerate these flaws by using inappropriate information, such as after-tax income instead of gross income. Some of this disparate treatment may not have been intentional, but its effect was unambiguous.

Before the Decatur case, enforcement officials observed the flaws in most minority applications and concluded that lenders were legitimately denying them loans; the Decatur investigation established that the real issue is whether lenders provide equal treatment to minority and majority applicants with the same credit flaws. The Decatur case could not resolve, however, whether this type of discrimination was widespread or limited to a few lenders, such as Decatur Federal.

Meanwhile, the 1990 HMDA data caught the attention of many officials in the Federal Reserve System, and researchers at the Boston Federal Reserve Bank undertook a study to obtain information on borrowers' credit histories and to determine whether relatively high rejection rates for minorities were due to discrimination.[10] Lenders in Boston cooperated fully with this effort, and extensive data on credit history and other variables were collected. This study, widely called the Boston Fed Study, provides strong evidence of discrimination and shows that the problem is, in fact, widespread.[11]

Thanks to these four events, the problem of discrimination in mortgage lending is now widely recognized. Not only has it been actively discussed in the press, it has become a major policy priority of the Department of Housing and Urban Development, the Justice Department, and the Office of the Comptroller of the Currency.[12]

▮ DEFINITIONS: MORTGAGE DISCRIMINATION AND REDLINING

The most dramatic type of discrimination by lenders with the most obvious consequences for minority access to housing is discrimination in the approval of mortgage loan applications. This is also the type of behavior highlighted by the HMDA data and emphasized by the Boston Fed Study and earlier academic research.

The Decision to Lend

Lenders are in the business of making money. Mortgage loans are a good investment for lenders because these loans can yield a relatively high rate of return in the form of interest payments. In deciding whether to act favorably on a particular loan application, a lender must determine the rate of return he expects to earn on that loan. The higher the expected return, the higher the likelihood that the loan will be granted. In formal terms, therefore, the probability that a loan will be approved depends on the expected rate of return for that loan.

Although the expected rate of return is difficult to observe, it depends on the terms of the loan, such as the interest rate and the loan-to-value ratio; the probability that the loan will go into default; and the impact of default on the return. Moreover, the probability of default depends on the characteristics of the applicant, the characteristics of the property and its neighborhood, and the terms of the loan; and the expected cost of default depends on the difference between the expected value of the property and the amount of the loan. An applicant with regular payments on a previous mortgage, for example, is less likely to default, and either rapid expected housing appreciation or a low loan to value ratio strengthens a borrower's incentive not to default by raising her equity in the house. In addition, lenders are more likely to lose money if a house's value is expected to decline and the loan-to-value ratio is high.

Therefore, the expected rate of return on a loan depends on the characteristics of the applicant, the property, and the loan itself. The basic loan decision can be restated as follows: *The probability that a loan application will be accepted depends on applicant, property, and loan characteristics, with a higher probability of acceptance associated with those characteristics that lower the likelihood and costs of default.*

Definitions of Discrimination and Redlining

This framework leads directly to definitions of discrimination in mortgage lending and of redlining. These definitions are based on individual lender decisions and will therefore be called process-based, as distinct from the outcome-based definition to be discussed below. Specifically, *discrimination exists if minority applicants are more likely to be rejected for a mortgage than are white applicants, after accounting for the applicant, property, and loan characteristics on which the loan's return depends.* The term *redlining* comes from the imagined lender practice of drawing a line on a map, presumably in red ink, around sections of the city where loans will not be made. In our framework, *redlining exists whenever a mortgage with a given set of applicant, property, and loan characteristics is more likely to be turned down in a minority than in a white neighborhood.*[13]

Several studies put these definitions into practice by determining whether the probability that a mortgage application will be denied is higher for minority than for white applicants (or for loans in minority than in white neighborhoods), statistically controlling for applicant, property, and loan characteristics.

These definitions refer to applicant and property characteristics that can be observed by a lender. In fact, lenders may not be able to observe some characteristics that influence the return on a loan (or the risk or cost of default). To give one example, lenders are unlikely to know whether an applicant has friends or relatives who will loan her money if she runs into financial trouble. The above definitions of discrimination and redlining do not allow an agent to make guesses about these characteristics; loan decisions must be based on characteristics that a lender can observe and document for each applicant.

Lenders may believe, based on past experience or biased perceptions, that minority applicants have poorer unobserved qualifications than whites on average, and may therefore believe that at any given level of observed characteristics the expected loan return is smaller for a minority than for a white borrower. Nevertheless, denying a loan to a minority applicant on the basis of this belief is a form of discrimination, called statistical discrimination.[14] An agent is practicing discrimination when he turns down a loan to a minority applicant on the basis of information that is valid for minorities on average but which may not be valid for that individual. This decision may be economically rational, but it still is illegal discrimination.

Several scholars employ an alternative definition of redlining that focuses on the flow of funds into the minority neighborhoods served by a lender, not simply on the loan decisions a lender makes.[15] According to this outcome-based definition, redlining exists if the flow of funds into minority neighborhoods lags behind the flow of funds into white neighborhoods with comparable risk characteristics. A lender who treats comparable minority and white applicants exactly the same may still be guilty of redlining by this definition.

This definition implicitly recognizes that lenders may discriminate in many actions other than the decision to grant or deny loans.

Some lenders discriminate in the placement of their branch offices, in their advertising, and in their pre-application procedures. These actions, which are difficult to observe, all deny credit to minority households without showing up in the actual loan decision. This outcome-based definition of redlining avoids the problem of measuring individual acts of discrimination by focusing on the outcome of all lender decisions, namely, the flow of funds to minority neighborhoods. Of course, a lack of mortgage loans in minority neighborhoods could also be influenced by discrimination in housing markets or by actors in mortgage markets other than lenders, such as insurers or appraisers, and by the decisions of potential loan applicants.[16] Strictly speaking, the outcome-based definition of redlining cannot isolate the role of lenders.

■ DISCRIMINATION IN LOAN APPROVAL

During the 1990s the HMDA data have continued to bring bad news about the high denial rates faced by minorities. In 1993 the denial rate was 34.0 percent for blacks, 25.1 percent for Hispanics, and 15.3 percent for whites.[17] These figures are virtually the same as in 1990. Moreover, minorities continue to face significantly higher denial rates than whites at all income levels.[18] These racial and ethnic gaps in loan denial exist in all regions, for all types of loans, and for all types of lenders. Many of the lenders with the highest disparities between minority and white denial rates are large mortgage bankers, although many thrifts and commercial banks also have much higher denial rates for minorities than for whites.[19] In many minority neighborhoods, mortgages are most likely to be provided by small mortgage bankers, who often charge higher fees and higher rates of interest than larger lenders do.[20]

The differences among black, Hispanic, and white denial rates are particularly dramatic for home purchase loans.[21] The 1991 national denial rate was 29.0 percent for blacks, 24.3 percent for Hispanics, and 14.0 percent for whites. Blacks were turned down for mortgage loans over twice as often (and Hispanics almost twice as often) as whites. Even after accounting for the applicant economic characteristics in the HMDA data, for the location of the property, and for the lender, the denial rate for blacks was still 10.6 percentage points higher than the denial rate for whites. Black applicants who applied to the same lenders, had the same economic characteristics, and purchased the same types of properties as white applicants would be turned down at a 24.6 percent rate compared to the 14.0 percent rate for whites. Even with controls, in other words, blacks were still almost twice as likely as whites to be turned down for mortgage loans. The denial rate with controls was 4.5 percentage points higher for Hispanics than for whites.

Although the HMDA data cannot be used to obtain formal estimates of discrimination, they do reveal several patterns that are unlikely to be caused by minority–white differences in credit history.[22] One such pattern is that the minority–white differences in loan denial rates, even after accounting for all the variables in the HMDA data, are remarkably similar across income classes and across neighborhood types. The 1991 denial rate for blacks was about 11 percentage points higher than the denial rate for whites, for example, in both high-income largely white neighborhoods and in low-income largely black neighborhoods, again controlling for all the variables in the HMDA data.[23] Another such pattern is that the denial rate for blacks is over 8.5 percentage points higher than the denial rate for whites (after available controls) for both refinancing and home-improvement loans, even though minority homeowners who apply for these loans had a good enough credit history to get a mortgage in the first place and have further enhanced their creditworthiness by not defaulting on that loan. This pattern is even stronger for Hispanics, as the Hispanic–white denial rate difference is larger for refinancing (5.7 percentage points) and home improvement (9.2 points) than for home purchase loans (4.5 points).

These patterns from the HMDA data are consistent with earlier research that attempted to determine whether minority applicants are more likely than white applicants to be denied a loan, after accounting for applicant, property, and loan characteristics.[24] Although virtually all of these early studies found evidence of discrimination, the impact of this evidence was limited by the fact that these studies, like the HMDA data, did not have information on all relevant applicant characteristics.[25] Most of the studies lacked information on wealth, for example, and they all lacked full information on an applicant's credit history. It was impossible, therefore, for these studies to rule out the hypothesis that higher loan denial rates for minority applicants are due to their lower wealth or poorer credit history, not to discrimination. The power of the Boston Fed Study is that it is based on an unusually complete data set, with information on an applicant's wealth, credit history, and many other things.

The Boston Fed Study

The Boston Fed Study compares minority and white loan denial rates using a sample of over 3,000 loan applications for conventional mort-

TABLE 5.1 CONTROL VARIABLES USED BY THE BOSTON FED STUDY

Risk of Default	*Loan Characteristics*
Housing Expense/Income	Two- to Four-Family House
Total Debt Payments/Income	Fixed-Rate Loan
Net Wealth	30-Year Loan
Monthly Income	Special Loan Program
Liquid Assets	
Poor Credit History	
Probability of Unemployment	
Self-Employed	

Cost of Default	*Personal Characteristics*
Loan/Appraisal Value	Age
Rent/Value in Tract	Married
Received Private Mortgage Insurance	Dependents
Denied Private Mortgage Insurance	

SOURCE: Munnell et al. (1992, Table 1).

gages in the Boston area during 1990.[26] This sample includes all applications by blacks and Hispanics in that year, about 1,200, and a random sample of white applications, and it covers all types of lenders.

The study begins with the HMDA data but supplements them with thirty-eight additional variables. These additional variables were selected on the basis of extensive conversations with lenders and other people knowledgeable about underwriting decisions. The researcher attempted to identify and collect information on every factor that lenders consider in making a loan decision. The final list of variables covered aspects of the risk of default, the cost of a default when it occurs, the nature of the loan, and the characteristics of the applicant. To give a sense for the range of information the study explored, Table 5.1 presents the variables that were accounted for in the study's preferred estimates.

The variety of the variables on this list reveals how complex a loan decision can be. The consumer and mortgage credit variables measure the seriousness of previous problems, ranging from "slow pay" accounts or late payments to serious delinquencies or extensive late payments. One version of the unemployment variable measures the likelihood, based on industry, occupation, and personal characteristics, that an applicant will be unemployed in the next 5 years. Overall, the Boston Fed data set was assembled with thoroughness and care and provides the most comprehensive set of credit characteristics ever assembled for a study of mortgage discrimination.[27]

The Boston Fed researchers use these data to determine whether minority applicants are more likely to be turned down for a loan than are comparable white applicants with comparable properties to buy. In their preferred specification, the probability of loan denial is 56 percent higher for blacks and Hispanics than for whites, controlling for the risk and cost of default and for loan and personal characteristics.[28] The white denial rate is 11 percent, so this result implies that minority applicants with the same credit and property characteristics as the average white applicant would face a denial rate of 17 percent. In my judgment, this 6 percentage point disparity provides strong evidence that lenders discriminate against blacks and Hispanics.

The Boston Fed researchers were not content to follow a single procedure and conclude that they had identified discrimination. They explored a dozen variations on their central theme to determine whether their result depends on the precise form of their estimating procedure. It clearly does not. Whether they include additional variables, use alternative functional forms, identify individual neighborhoods, or exclude applicants who were denied private mortgage insurance, the result is the same: Minority applicants are turned down for loans far more often than are comparable white applicants.[29]

The Boston Fed Study has been intensely scrutinized by academics and columnists. Despite a few extreme claims about data errors or omitted control variables, the results of the study have held up very well.[30] Indeed, two thorough reexaminations of the Boston Fed data, which use data cleaning techniques and explore many alternative control variables, clearly support the Boston Fed Study's conclusions. One of these reexaminations even found somewhat higher levels of discrimination than did the original study.[31]

The Conservative Nature of Existing Studies

The approach to estimating discrimination in loan approval that is used by all studies of the topic, including the Boston Fed Study, is conservative and almost certainly understates the extent of discrimination. This likely understatement exists because the studies do not consider four important aspects of lender behavior.[32]

First, all of the studies assume that mortgage terms, including the down payment requirement or loan-to-value ratio, are determined entirely by the borrower and are not influenced by the lender. The available evidence indicates that this assumption is not correct. In fact, black borrowers receive higher loan-to-value ratios than similarly qualified white borrowers.[33]

This lower down payment requirement may be an advantage for people with limited savings,[34] but from a methodological point of view, it implies that the standard approach understates discrimination in loan denial. If loan-to-value ratios were assigned on an equal basis to all customers, the loan-to-value ratio for minority applicants would decline. A decline in the loan-to-value ratio is associated with an increase in the rate of return, so the expected return on mortgages for minority borrowers would rise. Thus, the share of the minority–white difference in denial rates that could be explained by differences in loan-to-value ratios would fall, and the share left over to be explained by discrimination would rise.[35]

Second, existing studies make the assumption that all the applicant, property, and loan characteristics used as control variables are in fact related to loan returns. However, anecdotal evidence indicates that some of these characteristics are used as screens to shut out minority applicants. Four of the ten banks investigated as part of the New York State Banking Study, for example, used underwriting standards that were not in line with industry standards and which had a disproportionately severe impact on minority and female applicants.[36] One bank refused to make loans under $75,000 in certain areas, another refused to make fixed-rate loans with a maturity over 15 years or any loans with a loan-to-value ratio above 80 percent.[37] Moreover, a majority of the conventional loan applications in Boston in 1990 failed to meet at least one of the underwriting standards used by the secondary mortgage market.[38] Since most applicants receive loans and do not default, this fact constitutes prima facie evidence that underwriting criteria often do not correspond to creditworthiness.

When an applicant, property, or loan characteristic is used to screen out minority applicants, the standard procedure hides some discrimination in the impact of that characteristic on loan denial.[39] If banks deny loans below a certain amount in order to exclude most minorities, for example, it is inappropriate to "control" for loan amount in a statistical procedure, because the impact of loan amount on loan denial is itself a type of discrimination. No existing study of loan denial considers this issue.

This type of screening could occur consciously, as lenders who want to discriminate but do not want to get caught try to avoid a direct connection between their decisions and the minority status of an applicant, or it might occur unconsciously as lenders use underwriting criteria or rules of thumb that are not related to loan returns. Lenders may honestly believe that loans below a certain amount are riskier, but if this is not true and if refusing loans below that amount has a disproportionate impact on minority applicants, then the lender's actions constitute discrimination as defined above.[40] As it turns out, the relationship between loan returns and the applicant, property, and loan characteristics that are observable at the time of application is poorly understood, so many underwriting criteria may be needlessly conservative and have a disproportionate impact on minorities.

Because the link between underwriting criteria and loan returns is difficult to study, direct evidence that existing criteria have a disparate impact on minorities is not yet available. Nevertheless, indirect evidence suggests that this is the case. Recent in-depth interviews discovered that "lenders who have been active in the inner city" believe that inner-city neighborhoods contain "investment quality borrowers who defy the neighborhood stereotypes."[41] Moreover, lenders around the country appear to be having success with mortgage programs that employ nontraditional underwriting criteria.[42] For example, a recent examination of loans by seven lenders in low-income neighborhoods around the country concluded: "By and large, the community reinvestment loans in our sample performed very well in comparison with much larger national samples of loans not directed at low and moderate income neighborhoods."[43]

Third, the limited available evidence suggests that lenders have considerable influence over "defaults." The quotation marks here indicate that a default, which is defined as nonpayment by the borrower, typically is not observed until it becomes a foreclosure, which is defined as the lender claiming legal rights to a property. As a result, many studies treat the terms *default* and *foreclosure* as synonyms, which they are not, and estimate models of "default" using data on foreclosures.

Default *is* heavily influenced by the borrower since borrowers who have little or no equity in their house and who are in financial trouble may decide to stop making payments on their mortgage. Nevertheless, it is the lender who turns this behavior into an observable default. As one study puts it, "although it is the borrower who stops payments, it is the lender who decides if default has occurred by choosing whether to work with the borrower or to foreclose."[44]

In fact, lenders have a great deal of discretion in how to treat people who have missed payments. They can be content to accept penalties for several months, they can negotiate a repayment schedule to bring the borrower back up to date, or they can start foreclosure proceedings. Even in the case of mortgages in the secondary market, for which default and foreclosure procedures are explicitly spelled out, loan administrators may have considerable discretion in the timing of their actions.

This issue is relevant here because some lenders may take a harsher stance against minority than against white customers. This harsher stance implies that defaults will be more quickly resolved, and therefore be less costly, with minority than with white customers. Moreover, in extreme cases lenders may be able to increase their returns by giving loans that encourage defaults, such as loans with high loan-to-value ratios, initiating foreclosure proceedings if any payment is late, and selling the property for a profit.[45] This type of aggressive posture toward defaults, primarily on home equity loans held by blacks, was featured by CBS News in "A Matter of Interest," *60 Minutes,* November 15, 1992.[46]

Lender influence on defaults causes conceptual difficulties for loan denial studies because some minority applicants may be accepted only because a loan officer knows that he is more likely to foreclose on their property than on the property of equally qualified white applicants, and he will therefore face relatively low costs if minority borrowers default. This type of behavior is another source of downward bias in estimates of discrimination because it implies that lenders' acceptances of minority loans are boosted by this higher probability of foreclosure.[47]

Fourth, the Decatur investigation revealed that loan officers may help white applicants make their applications look stronger, by paying off credit card debt, for example, and not even tell black applicants that deficiencies in applications could be resolved.[48] This type of counseling has not been considered in any study of loan denial. If it is common, however, then the applicant "control" variables are themselves contaminated by discrimination, and the standard approach underestimates discrimination because it does not account for the fact that the characteristics of white but not minority applicants have been "improved" through coaching.[49]

Default Rates
as an Indicator of Discrimination

Several recent columns in popular journals have proposed an alternative way to test for discrimination in mortgage markets by examining defaults.[50] This approach has also appeared, with far more qualifications, in the academic literature.[51]

The basic idea is simple. Assuming that lenders rank applicants by their creditworthiness, discrimination in the form of a higher standard for minority applicants implies that the last white applicants whose loans are approved are less qualified than the last minority applicants whose loans are approved. As a result, the argument goes, the probability of default should be higher for the least-qualified whites than for the least-qualified minorities.

As it turns out, black loan recipients have higher default rates than white applicants on average. On the basis of this argument, the columns mentioned above all conclude that there must not be any discrimination against blacks. In fact, these columns go further: They claim that the Boston Fed Study was "flawed" or "invalid" because it did not look at defaults. This claim does not make sense. An analysis of defaults may be an alternative way to test for discrimination, but the existence of this alternative does not invalidate the more direct approach used by the Boston Fed Study.

Moreover, for three fundamental reasons, the default approach is not a legitimate alternative to the standard approach to estimating discrimination.[52] Ironically, these three weaknesses are all acknowledged, if not emphasized, in a recent default study that has been incorrectly interpreted by some commentators as proof that lending discrimination no longer exists.[53]

The first flaw in the default approach is that the average white applicant may be a very low credit risk while the average minority applicant is a moderate credit risk; if so, the average creditworthiness of minority loan recipients could be below that of whites even if minorities must meet a higher hurdle to get a loan. The leap to average default rates makes sense only if majority and minority loan applicants have similar distributions of creditworthiness, which is clearly not the case.[54]

Some scholars have recognized this point, but argued that the problem can be solved by controlling for credit characteristics.[55] These scholars agree that minority–white differences in average default rates cannot be an indication of discrimination; however, they also claim that discrimination will show up in the minority–white difference in default rates at any given level of creditworthiness. Because minority borrowers tend to have higher default rates than white borrowers even after controlling for credit characteristics, such as income and credit history, these scholars conclude that discrimination must not be at work.[56]

The problem with this argument is that it forgets that many credit characteristics are not observed by the lender.[57] The lender cannot determine, for example, whether a borrower has friends or relatives who will bail her out if she has trouble meeting her mortgage payments. If, as is likely, minority borrowers have less favorable *unobserved* credit characteristics than do white borrowers, then they also may have higher default rates, even when discrimination exists and *observed* credit characteristics have been taken into account.[58] In other words, higher default rates for minority borrowers may be an indication of relatively poor unobserved credit characteristics for minorities instead of evidence that discrimination does not exist.

The default approach's implicit dismissal of a minority–white disparity in unobserved credit characteristics is particularly troubling because such a disparity could itself be a cause of lender discrimination. When such a disparity exists, lenders can lower their risk by using minority status as a signal that an applicant has relatively poor unobserved credit characteristics; that is, by extending loans to whites but not to minorities with the same observed credit characteristics. As noted earlier, this type of behavior is called statistical discrimination.[59] Thus, it is quite plausible that many lenders, perceiving the higher default rate for minorities than for whites at any given level of observable credit characteristics, infer that minorities have less favorable unobserved credit characteristics, and, as a result, discriminate against minority applicants. Assuming no difference in the unobserved credit characteristics of minority and white borrowers is equivalent to dismissing this possibility. This comes dangerously close to assuming what one is trying to prove.[60] Ultimately, the default approach fails because it cannot rule out the possibility that lenders discriminate precisely because minority borrowers have higher default rates than whites whose applications are comparable.

A second reason why the default approach cannot shed light on discrimination is that default studies are based on foreclosures, not defaults. A default by a borrower, which involves protracted failure to make mortgage payments, is not observed until it becomes a foreclosure, which is the decision by a lender to claim the loan collateral, namely, the house. As explained earlier, lenders have leeway in making foreclosure decisions, and anecdotal evidence indicates that some lenders try to work things out with white borrowers who have late payments but move to foreclose on minority borrowers who fall behind. Thus, relatively high "default" rates for minorities may be a symptom of discrimination in foreclosure proceedings instead of a sign that there is no discrimination in loan approval.[61]

Finally, the risk of default is not the same thing as the expected loss on a mortgage, which is ultimately what lenders care about. The expected loss on a mortgage equals the probability of default multiplied by the expected loss if a default occurs. Although extensive evidence on default losses is not available, one study finds that the expected loss given default is lower for blacks than for whites.[62] Moreover, to the extent that lenders foreclose more aggressively on minority than on white loans, white "defaults" will be observed only in the worst cases, those cases with the highest losses. Thus, the expected return on loans to minority borrowers could be higher than the expected return for whites even if minority borrowers have a higher default rate.[63] "Default" rates for minorities and whites may be easy to observe, but they are not easy to interpret and may provide a misleading picture of the relative returns on loans to these two groups.

Overall, therefore, the default approach is a fatally flawed method for studying discrimination in mortgage lending. Evidence that default rates are higher for minority than for comparable white borrowers provides no support whatsoever for the claim that there is no discrimination in mortgage lending, let alone for the claim that the Boston Fed Study is invalid. In fact, the Boston Fed Study and other recent research provide compelling evidence that racial and ethnic discrimination in mortgage lending have not disappeared.

▚ DISCRIMINATION IN OTHER LENDER ACTIONS

The process of obtaining a loan involves more than the lender's decision to accept or reject an application. In addition to evaluating loan applications and administering loans, lenders also advertise their loans, decide on office locations, counsel prospective applicants, and set loan terms. Although limited, the available evidence suggests that these types of lender actions may also involve discrimination.

Discrimination in Outreach and Application Procedures

Existing information about lenders' pre-application behavior comes primarily from three pilot audit studies, which are the first applications of the audit technique to mortgage lending.[64] These studies, which took place in Pontiac, Louisville, and Chicago, provide some intriguing hints about lender behavior at this stage. Lenders often appear to be less interested in giving information to black than to white customers; they urge black customers, but not whites, to go to other lenders; or they emphasize to black customers, but not whites, that the application procedures are long and complicated. In many cases, lenders also appear to be more helpful to white than to black customers; white customers are told about more options and, as in the Decatur investigation, are the only ones given tips on how to meet the lender's underwriting standards. Moreover, blacks are more likely than equally qualified whites to be told that they do not qualify for a mortgage.

This type of agent behavior potentially could have a large impact on the access of minority households to loans. By putting up extra barriers for minority customers, lenders may also be able to discriminate in the provision of mortgage loans in a way that does not show up in the behavior researchers can best observe; namely, the loan approval decision.

To some extent, lenders use traditional means for advertising loans, such as newspapers and television, but they also advertise by posting signs in their windows. Thus, the location of their branch offices is an important element of their advertising program, and lender decisions about the location of their branches also affect the access of minorities to information about loans. An example of lender branching decisions that appears to involve discrimination was uncovered by the Decatur investigation.[65] Decatur Federal Savings and Loan opened 43 branches in the Atlanta metropolitan area after its founding in 1927. Only one of those branches was placed in a largely black neighborhood. Moreover, the only two branches that were closed over this period were the one originally placed in a largely black neighborhood and one in a neighborhood that had become largely black.

Discrimination in Loan Terms

Lenders decide not only whether to grant a loan; they also decide on the loan terms, including the interest rate, the maturity, the loan-to-value ratio, and the loan type (conventional, adjustable rate, government-insured, and so on). Several researchers have argued that lenders do not select the interest rate for an individual loan.[66] The interest rate is posted in the window, the argument goes, and any borrower who comes in on a given day can borrow at that rate. In fact, however, different interest rates are charged on different types of loans and some customers may be encouraged to take the higher-rate alternatives. Moreover, interest rates change from day to day, and some customers may be encouraged to lock in a rate when rates are rising or to wait for a lower rate when they are falling. In addition, banks may have different branches with different rates to which different types of customers are steered (either by branch location or by explicit lender recommendation). Thus, discrimination in interest rates may occur despite the fact that rates are posted.

A few studies, now somewhat out of date, explore this issue and find that minority borrowers are indeed charged higher interest rates, on average, than comparable white borrowers.[67] These studies also find evidence of discrimination in loan fees but not in loan maturities. No recent study reveals whether these types of discrimination persist.[68]

Even without discrimination in loan terms by individual lenders, minority borrowers may face less favorable terms if the lenders that operate in minority neighborhoods offer less favorable terms to all their customers. The available evidence indicates, for example, that thrifts, commercial banks, and large mortgage companies tend to leave the business in minority neighborhoods for small mortgage companies, which often charge higher fees or interest rates.[69] Ironically, some of these small mortgage companies are backed by large lenders. Hence the geographic dimension of lender behavior, which takes the form of decisions about branches and advertising, may result in less favorable terms for minority borrowers than for comparable white borrowers with comparable properties.

Another interesting question is whether minority borrowers are more likely than white borrowers to receive a Federal Housing Administration (FHA) loan instead of a conventional loan. The type of loan is significant because FHA loans are insured by the government, which protects the lender, but cost more than comparable loans with private mortgage insurance, which raises the cost to the borrower. Moreover, FHA loans have relatively low down payment requirements, which makes them more accessible to many low-income borrowers.

Heavy reliance of minority borrowers on FHA loans is also important because the FHA program has occasionally contributed to rapid racial or ethnic transition and to housing deterioration in some neighborhoods.[70] Steering minorities to FHA loans, in other words, has consequences, including racial and ethnic segregation of neighborhoods, beyond the direct costs to the individual borrowers.

The evidence clearly shows that minority borrowers, particularly blacks, rely far more heavily on FHA loans than do white borrowers. In 1990, for example, 27 percent of qualifying loans to whites were FHA loans, whereas the comparable shares for blacks and Hispanics were 57 percent and 31 percent.[71]

Because of their low down payment requirements, FHA loans may be particularly appealing to borrowers with limited wealth. The heavy reliance of black borrowers on FHA loans is only partially explained, however, by the fact that their wealth tends to be relatively low. In fact, several studies show that minority borrowers are far more likely to receive FHA loans than are comparable white borrowers at all levels of income or wealth and for all types of property.[72]

One study finds that white households are 2½ to 3 times as likely to get a conventional loan as are comparable blacks with comparable properties.[73] These results suggest that minorities are, to some degree, excluded from access to conventional mortgages and therefore turn to mortgages insured by FHA. Ironically, however, minorities still face a higher denial rate for FHA loans than do comparable whites, just as they do for conventional loans.[74]

■ DISCRIMINATION BY OTHER ACTORS IN MORTGAGE MARKETS

Mortgage lenders are by no means the only actors in the mortgage market. Outcomes in this market are also influenced by the actions of real estate brokers, appraisers, insurers, and loan repurchasers.[75]

Real Estate Brokers

For many homebuyers, real estate brokers are the primary source of information about available mortgages, and "lending institutions rely heavily on real estate brokers for referrals."[76] Discrimination in the provision of this information therefore could have a large impact on the ability of minority homebuyers to obtain the mortgage funds they need.

Evidence from fair housing audit studies indicates that this type of discrimination exists. One early study found that real estate brokers were far more likely to tell white than black customers about both conventional mortgages and opportunities for creative financing.[77] More recently, the Housing Discrimination Study found large differences in the willingness of brokers to help white and minority customers find financing.[78] In the black–white audits, 24.4 of the white auditors were offered assistance finding a loan compared to 13.3 percent of the black auditors. The comparable figures for the Hispanic–white audits are 22.1 and 18.1 percent.[79]

Moreover, white auditors were far more likely to be told about both fixed rate and variable rate mortgages, whereas minority auditors were more likely to be told about FHA loans. To be specific, the difference in the probability that white and black auditors were told about loans was 21.5 percentage points for fixed rate mortgages and 15.1 points for adjustable rate mortgages. The comparable figures for the Hispanic–white audits are 14.7 percent and 10.9 percent. In addition, blacks were 6.7 percentage points more likely than whites (and Hispanics 3.4 percentage points more likely than whites) to be told about FHA loans.[80]

Appraisers

Appraisers play a role in the mortgage market because lenders base the value of a house, and hence of the loan collateral, on an appraisal and tie the amount of the loan to the appraised value. The borrower must pay the market value of the house, not the appraisal. Thus, if the ratio of appraised-to-market value is systematically lower for minorities than for whites, minorities will be forced to make higher down payments than comparable whites and may be unable to afford a house at all.

The history of appraisal practices suggests that appraisal bias may occur. Until 1977, appraisal texts approved by the American Institute of Real Estate Appraisers (AIREA), the main trade organization for appraisers, explicitly called for lower appraised values in racially mixed neighborhoods. This practice was eliminated after a successful Justice Department suit against AIREA.[81]

Despite this history, the limited research on this topic does not uncover a great deal of discrimination in appraisals. One study finds that appraisals were systematically lower for Hispanic loan applicants in some metropolitan areas in California in the late 1970s.[82] The Hispanic–white differences in appraisals were not large, however, with a maximum of 3.6 percent in one metropolitan area.

Insurers

In 1987 an insurance salesman in Milwaukee used a hidden microphone to record his supervisor's orders to "stop selling blacks insurance. . . . You gotta have good, solid premium-paying white people." The same supervisor also wrote down his view with the words: "Quit writing all those blacks!" A few years later, in 1993, an insurance conglomerate in San Francisco was fined $500,000 by the state insurance commissioner for practicing insurance redlining. In fact, this conglomerate literally had a map designating (with a yellow pen as it turns out) black and Hispanic neighborhoods as "keep out areas."[83]

Insurers play two roles in the mortgage market. They provide home insurance, which lenders generally require before they will issue a mortgage, and they provide mortgage insurance, which is required by the secondary mortgage market institutions when the loan-to-value ratio is above 80 percent. The government serves as insurer for FHA and Veterans' Administration mortgages.

Discrimination and redlining in insurance can deny minorities access to housing. If a minority household is denied home insurance, it may not be able to obtain a mortgage and therefore may not be able to buy a house at all. Moreover, a minority household that cannot obtain private mortgage insurance faces severely restricted access to a conventional mortgage.

A growing body of scientific evidence reveals that the above examples are not isolated incidents.[84] The authors of the Boston Fed Study, for example, found clear evidence of discrimination in private mortgage insurance in Boston. After accounting for all the factors in Table 5.1, minority applicants were more likely to be turned down for this insurance than were whites.[85] Moreover, a pilot audit study of redlining in home insurance in Milwaukee found that insurance agents stated more stringent inspection standards for houses in black than in white neighborhoods.[86] Another recent audit study uncovered extensive redlining by two large home insurance companies in Louisville, Atlanta, and Milwaukee (against black neighborhoods) and in Chicago (against Hispanic neighborhoods).[87]

Secondary Mortgage Market Institutions

Most home mortgages are no longer held by the lenders that issue them but instead are sold to institutions in the secondary mortgage market. In fact, about half the home loans originated in 1990 were sold on the secondary market that same year.[88] The institutions in the secondary market include the federally chartered private corporations Fannie Mae and Freddie Mac. Moreover, another government-chartered institution, GNMA, participates in this market by supporting government-backed mortgages. Overall, these three government-sponsored enterprises (GSEs) were involved in over two-thirds of the loans purchased in the secondary mortgage market in 1990. Many private firms, including thrifts, commercial banks, pension funds, and insurance companies, also participate in this market. The GSEs will not purchase mortgages that do not meet certain standardized underwriting criteria. Because many if not most lenders now plan to sell their loans on the secondary mortgage market, the criteria established by these institutions have an enormous influence on mortgage market outcomes.

Because they do not deal directly with borrowers, secondary mortgage market institutions are not in a position to discriminate directly, but the underwriting criteria they set clearly could have a discriminatory impact. As explained earlier, using underwriting criteria that are not related to a loan's profitability and that have a disproportionate impact on minorities is a form of discrimination. Because the link between criteria and profitability is not known with precision, the possibility of some discrimination in secondary-market underwriting criteria cannot be ruled out.[89] Fannie Mae and Freddie Mac are aware of this issue and have introduced several programs that employ nontraditional underwriting criteria.[90] In addition, these two GSEs have revised their forms to ensure that the instructions cannot "be misinterpreted in a discriminatory way."[91]

◼ REDLINING

As noted earlier, two different definitions of mortgage redlining have appeared in the scholarly literature: process-based and outcome-based. The process-based definition focuses on the geographic dimension of lenders' loan approval decisions, whereas the outcome-based definition focuses on credit flows to minority neighborhoods. Redlining according to the outcome-based definition can be caused by the discriminatory actions of any actor in the mortgage market, not just those of lenders.[92]

Most of the studies that have pursued the process-based definition have failed to find strong evidence of redlining.[93] The Boston Fed Study, for example, found that the racial composition of a neighborhood had no impact on the probability of loan denial, controlling for the characteristics of the applicant (including minority status), the property, and the loan.[94]

In contrast, several studies that pursue the outcome-based definition have concluded that redlining exists.[95] Because they use different methodologies, these studies are difficult to compare, but most of them determine whether the number of mortgage loans per separately owned housing unit in a neighborhood is negatively associated with the minority share of the neighborhood's population, after accounting for other factors that might influence the number of loans. One careful study of Boston, for example, showed that during the 1982–1987 period, largely black neighborhoods received far fewer loans per housing unit than did largely white neighborhoods, controlling for a wide range of neighborhood attributes, such as average income and wealth, rents and house values, housing construction, and the presence of commercial property.[96]

Studies of redlining by the outcome-based definition face severe methodological difficulties that have not been entirely resolved, but the results from some of these studies are quite striking and establish, in my view, a presumption that something limits the flow of loans to minority neighborhoods compared to white neighborhoods. These studies cannot pin down the exact causes of this loan deficit, but the obvious suspects are past discrimination, which limits the creditworthiness of minority potential borrowers; current discrimination by lending institutions in advertising, pre-application procedures, and loan acceptance (on the basis of the race of the applicant); discrimination by real estate brokers, which limits the number of minority homebuyers; and limited minority pursuit of loans due to anticipated discrimination.[97]

■ CONCLUSIONS

As if discrimination by real estate brokers were not enough, minority households searching for a house to buy also must confront discrimination by lending institutions and other actors in mortgage markets. The evidence for discrimination against blacks and Hispanics in the loan approval decision is strong, recent, and compelling. Although many minority applicants who are turned down for loans have problems in their credit history that make the loan denials look legitimate, lenders readily grant loans to white applicants with the same problems. After accounting for all the applicant, property, and loan characteristics that lenders say they consider, minority applicants are turned down at a rate that is over 50 percent higher than the rate for comparable whites.

Additional evidence indicates that lenders also discriminate in advertising and outreach, in pre-application procedures, and in loan terms, and that their discrimination is reinforced by the discriminatory actions of real estate brokers, insurers, and perhaps appraisers. The net effects of all this discrimination are severe constraints on the ability of many minority households to buy houses and a lack of access to credit in many minority neighborhoods.

THREE

OPPORTUNITIES LOST:
THE CONSEQUENCES
OF DISCRIMINATION

The Direct Cost of Current Discrimination

The evidence of continuing discrimination in housing and mortgage markets implies that minority households face severe barriers in trying to find housing, but it does not reveal the magnitude of the cost that these barriers impose. This chapter presents one way to measure this cost: It calculates how much minority households would be willing to pay to avoid current housing discrimination.

This approach to the cost of discrimination is not intended to be comprehensive. It does not consider, for example, the benefits to the nation as a whole that would accrue from equal treatment of all citizens, nor does it explore the indirect costs of discrimination, such as separation and distrust among groups or poor access of minority children to good schools and of minority workers to good jobs. These indirect costs are explored in Chapters 7 and 8. Instead, this approach is designed to give a rough idea of the immediate, direct cost imposed by current discrimination.

The results in this chapter build on an analysis of the process by which households search for housing. The outcome of this process, called a consumer surplus in the literature, or surplus for short, is the household's valuation of the housing it obtains relative to what it has to pay.[1] The analytical tools in the literature make it possible to obtain an estimate of a household's surplus as a function of its search costs and the nature of the available housing.

Discrimination in both housing and credit markets makes the search process more costly and more difficult for minority than for white households, so that minority households end up with a lower surplus, net of search costs. The direct cost of discrimination can be measured, therefore, by its impact on the net surplus obtained by minority households. Because the surplus is measured in terms of what a household is willing to pay, this approach yields an estimate of what minority households would be willing to pay to remove the discriminatory barriers they face. Measuring the cost of discrimination in this manner does not imply, of course, that minority households should be required to pay for the removal of discrimination. Instead, it expresses the cost of discrimination in a way that is directly related to the restrictions that discrimination imposes on minority households as they search for housing.

■ AN ANALYSIS OF THE SEARCH FOR HOUSING

Many types of change induce households to think about looking for a new place to live, including a significant change in income or wealth (which could occur suddenly or gradually), a job change, and a change in family size or composition. Once a household begins to think about moving, it enters a search process such as the one described in Figure 6.1.[2]

The household's first step in this process, illustrated in the top branch of Figure 6.1, is to decide whether searching for new housing is likely to pay off. It must weigh the costs of searching for housing, applying for credit, and moving against the likely benefits from finding housing better suited to its needs, that is, housing that yields a higher surplus. Figure 6.1 focuses on the search for a house to buy, but the same concepts apply to the search for an apartment.

The key idea in this analysis is that most houses or apartments of the type that a household prefers cannot be evaluated by the household without a visit. Many housing units can be eliminated from consideration, of course, simply on the basis of their price or the number of bedrooms they contain or their description in a newspaper advertisement, but houses in the right price range with the right number of bedrooms are difficult to evaluate unless they are actually inspected. Even at a given price, the houses or apartments on the market at a given time often have very different characteristics, and a homeseeker in that price range might receive a large positive surplus from some of those houses and perhaps a negative surplus from others. A household might be willing to pay $5,000 more than the asking price for one house, for example, but it would not buy another house unless it could be purchased for $5,000 less than the asking price—a

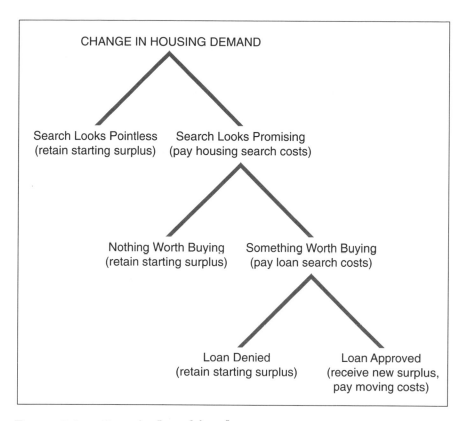

FIGURE 6.1.   Steps in Searching for a House

difference in surplus of $10,000.[3] A household considering new hous-
ing must think about the likely range of surpluses among the housing
units it will have to visit to fully evaluate. The larger this range, the
larger the potential benefits from housing search.

If a household decides to search, its must then select a search strategy. The analysis in this chapter is based on a one-stop strategy,
which calls for visiting a real estate broker or rental agent and looking at all the houses that the agent makes available.[4] With this strategy, a household must consider both the number of housing units it
expects to see and the likely distribution of surpluses among those
units. This strategy is a particularly realistic depiction of household
search behavior in the sales market when a broker has access to all,
or virtually all, available houses through a multiple listing service.
In this case, visiting a second broker would not result in any new
houses to look at. The one-stop strategy makes it possible that a house-

hold will see more than one house that it is willing to buy, but it does not guarantee that the household will find anything better than its current house, because the number of houses inspected is limited to the number provided by the broker.

At the end of the housing search process, the household faces another decision, namely, whether to pursue the transaction on the best housing unit it has found, that is, on the housing with the highest surplus. This decision is illustrated by the second branch in Figure 6.1. If the improvement in surplus that this house represents compensates the household for moving costs and the costs of either applying for a loan (in the sales market) or going through a credit check (in the rental market), then the household will make an offer on the house or apply for the apartment. In some cases, however, the best housing the household is able to find may not provide enough improvement in surplus to justify a move, and the household will end its search and stay in its current housing.

Once a household's offer or application is accepted, perhaps after some negotiation, it will apply for a mortgage or go through a credit check. The outcome of this step, which is illustrated by the third branch of Figure 6.1, is determined by the lender or the credit agency, not the household. If the loan is granted or the credit check passed, the household actually will move, and the net surplus it obtains equals the surplus from its new house minus its moving costs and the costs of housing and lender search.[5]

To calculate a household's expected net surplus from search, one must make assumptions about housing search costs, loan or credit application costs, moving costs, the probability of being denied a loan (or of not passing a credit check), and the range of surpluses among the housing units a household might inspect.[6] Here are some illustrative calculations for the sales market. A household might spend $10 in driving and parking costs to reach a house and 30 minutes valued at $10 per hour actually inspecting it. In this case housing search costs equal $15 per house. Obtaining a loan requires at least two trips to a lender's office, several hours of filling out forms, and perhaps the payment of various fees. A typical value for all these costs might be $250. Moving costs involve both the cost of hiring a mover and the value of the time the household spends packing, lugging, and unpacking, plus the mortgage fees that are paid after the mortgage is approved. These costs might be something like $2,000. Moreover, the Boston Fed Study estimated the probability that an average white household will be denied a mortgage to be 11 percent.[7]

The expected range in surplus among the houses the household might inspect is perhaps the most crucial parameter. To determine

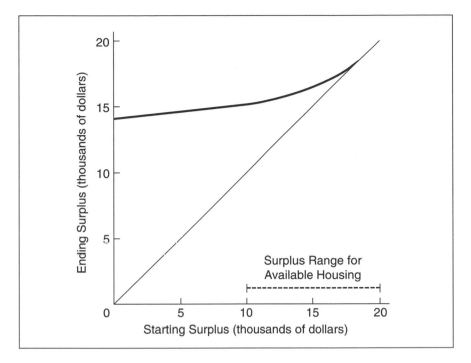

FIGURE **6.2.**   The Outcome of Housing Search

a value for this range, we must start with the range in a household's monthly surplus among these houses. This monthly amount corresponds to the range in a household's willingness to pay a monthly mortgage payment.[8] Suppose the household is willing to pay $80 more per month for the house with the highest surplus than for the available house with the lowest surplus. This $80 per month corresponds to $960 per year. Now suppose the household expects to stay in its house for 15 years then, with a real interest rate of 5 percent, the $80 per month corresponds to a total of $10,000 over their expected stay.[9]

The outcome of housing search based on these assumptions is illustrated in Figure 6.2.[10] This figure shows the surplus a household obtains after search as a function of the surplus it starts out with before search.[11] The diagonal line indicates points at which starting and ending surplus are the same. In this figure, a household's surplus after search is greater than its surplus before search as long as its starting surplus is lower than about $17,000. Above this point, the possibility of finding a house with a higher surplus is so low that the household decides not to search. In other words, houses with starting surpluses above $17,000, in this example, take the left branch of the first choice in Figure 6.1.

The range of surpluses in available houses also is indicated in Figure 6.2. Households whose starting surplus is far below the range of surpluses among houses that are available obviously stand to gain the most from search. In fact, the households whose starting surplus is the farthest from the surplus range for available houses can expect to gain over $14,000 in surplus from housing search. The gains from search are much smaller if a household's current surplus already falls into the range for available houses, and the gains drop to zero when the household's current surplus is well above the average surplus for houses it might discover from a search. If the expected gain is zero or less, the household obviously will not undertake a search.

■ THE IMPACT OF DISCRIMINATION ON HOUSING SEARCH

By restricting the options of minority households, discrimination lowers the surplus they can attain from housing searches relative to that of comparable white households. As explained earlier, the difference in the post-search surpluses of minority and white households is a measure of the cost of discrimination.

Discrimination affects the housing search process in at least five distinct ways. First, discrimination restricts minority households' access to housing. With a one-stop strategy, discrimination changes the number of housing units minority households can expect to encounter when they visit a housing agent.[12] Table 6.1 shows the distribution of housing units made available to minority and white auditors in the HDS sales audits. One can see that minority house seekers are far more likely than are comparable whites not to learn about any available housing units and are far less likely to learn about more than two units. As a result, a minority household can expect a significantly smaller improvement in its housing surplus from search than can a white household.

Second, discrimination makes housing search more unpleasant for minority than for white households and forces minority households to take more responsibility for ensuring that a transaction is completed.[13] Minority households are less likely than white households to be asked to call the agent back, for example, or to receive a follow-up call from the housing agent the next day. These types of discrimination raise the cost of search for minority households, measured

TABLE 6.1 **THE PROBABILITY OF SEEING DIFFERENT NUMBERS OF HOUSES**

Number of Houses Recommended or Shown	Black–White Audits		Hispanic–White Audits	
	Black (%)	White (%)	Hispanic (%)	White (%)
0	8.42	3.03	8.67	2.59
1	39.30	32.86	36.05	31.55
2	19.36	16.09	18.55	15.91
3	11.86	19.44	16.24	18.48
4	9.33	11.42	11.61	14.22
5	4.28	6.89	4.67	5.83
6	3.85	4.17	2.19	4.61
7	1.72	1.93	0.60	2.42
8	0.43	1.24	0.35	1.61
9	0.76	0.51	0.21	0.23
10	0.25	0.83	0.07	1.11
11	0.06	0.06	0.31	0.17
12 or more	0.40	1.55	0.46	1.27
Average Number of Houses Recommended or Shown	2.26	2.84	2.23	2.93

both in terms of the annoyances they must endure and the effort they must personally put forth to complete a transaction.

Third, minority households receive far less assistance from lenders than do white households when applying for a mortgage.[14] White applicants are told how to resolve problems in their credit history and how to fill out the application forms, whereas minority applicants often are discouraged from applying and are not even told that it is possible to resolve credit history problems. This added difficulty for minority households begins even before they visit a lender; real estate brokers provide far more information and assistance concerning financing to white than to minority customers. In addition, minority households may have more trouble getting house insurance or private mortgage insurance than do comparable white households.

Fourth, minority applicants are more likely than comparable white applicants to be turned down for a mortgage.[15] To be specific, the Boston Fed Study found that the denial rate for white households was 11 percent whereas the denial rate for comparable minority households was 17 percent. This 6 percentage point differential in denial rates, which remains after applicant, property, and loan characteristics are accounted for, measures current discrimination in mortgage lending. It is important here because minority households have a 6 percentage point higher chance of not being able to purchase the house they select after search and therefore of not being able to realize the associated gain in surplus.

In principle, households who are turned down for a mortgage by one lender can apply to another. Hence, the ultimate denial rates for white and minority households may be less than 11 and 17 percent, respectively. The ultimate denial rates are not likely to be much lower, however, because lenders may be aware, through credit checks or other means, when a household is applying for a second time, and because many people whose application is denied have a credit problem that will make them ineligible for a loan wherever they apply. Moreover, the extensive evidence that white applicants are more likely to be given both assistance and the benefit of the doubt implies that minority households who reapply are less likely to meet with success than are whites.[16] Bringing reapplications into the analysis, therefore, probably would increase the differential in denial rates between comparable minority and white households, and limiting the analysis to a single lender probably yields a conservative estimate of the cost of discrimination.

Finally, discrimination in the moving business makes it more difficult for minority than for white households to find housing with a surplus that is large enough to compensate them for moving and credit costs. To the best of my knowledge, no study has investigated discrimination in the moving business. Given the pervasiveness of discrimination in other aspects of economic life, however, it seems likely that some moving companies are reluctant to deal with minority customers or to work in minority neighborhoods. Moreover, a few studies have found that loan fees for approved loans, which are part of moving costs as defined here, are higher for minority than for white borrowers.[17] As a result, some of the calculations that follow include a small discriminatory premium; namely, 5 or 10 percent, in the moving costs of minority households.

The net result of these various types of discrimination is that minority households gain less from search and are therefore less likely to move than are comparable white households. Moreover, minority households are less likely than comparable white households to find houses worth moving to, and when they do move, the houses they move into provide a lower surplus than do those purchased by whites. All these possibilities are summarized by a lower expected post-search surplus for minority than for white households.

This analysis of housing search recognizes that minority households respond to discriminatory behavior. For example, minority households respond to anticipated discrimination by being less likely to search at all than are comparable whites and by being more likely to cut a search short by not applying for a loan.[18] In general, minority households cannot escape discrimination or avoid its costs, but they may be able to lower these costs by taking evasive measures. These measures illustrate the complexity of housing search behavior and show why a comprehensive measure of the cost of discrimination must compare the net post-search surplus of minority and white households.

These so-called evasive measures can themselves become a problem for minority households if they are based on an overestimate of discrimination or continue even after discrimination has disappeared. Minority households who cut their search short expecting discrimination that is not there, for example, will end up with a lower surplus, on average, than comparable whites. The effects of past discrimination can linger, in other words, in the perceptions of its victims. The limited available evidence suggests that minority households perceive that discrimination is at least as high as the levels found by HDS and the Boston Fed Study.[19] This chapter builds, therefore, on the assumption that minority households' perceptions about discrimination are accurate.[20]

▪ ILLUSTRATIVE CALCULATIONS OF THE COST OF DISCRIMINATION

Before turning to actual calculations of the cost of discrimination, it may prove useful to illustrate how this cost can be calculated. The HDS black–white sales audits imply that black households face the probabilities in the first column of Table 6.1. Moreover, the HDS audits reveal that it takes about 30 minutes to inspect a house, on average. Based on the Boston Fed Study, the probability that an applicant will be denied a mortgage loan can be set at 11 percent for whites and 17 percent for minorities.[21] In addition, suppose the fixed cost of visiting a house or broker is $10, the value of time is $10 per hour, and the range of surpluses among available houses is $10,000. Finally, assume that minorities face a discriminatory premium of 10 percent in both their housing and loan application costs and of 5 percent in their moving costs.

The costs of discrimination that result from these assumptions are presented in Figure 6.3. These costs are strikingly high. A black household with a current surplus well below the range of surpluses from available houses faces a cost of up to $2,231. This cost drops to

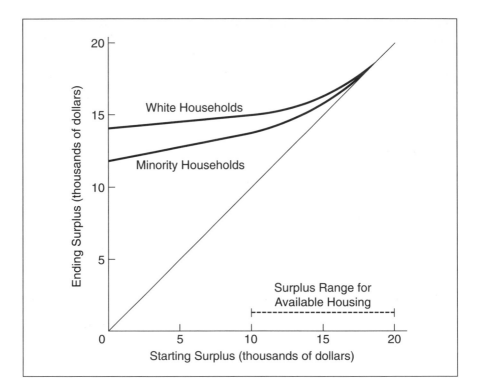

FIGURE 6.3.   Illustrative Calculations of the Cost
of Discrimination: One-Stop Strategy

$508 for a household whose current surplus is at the midpoint of the
range for available houses.[22]

The cost of discrimination declines steadily as the starting surplus
increases up to the point at which minority households are discouraged from searching. At this starting surplus, which is $17,500, the
cost of discrimination starts to decline more rapidly until it reaches
zero at the starting surplus at which white households are discouraged
from searching, which is only $300 higher.

▪ THE COST OF DISCRIMINATION

The key to estimating the cost of discrimination is determining the
surplus a household must fall back on if its housing search fails to
turn up a house worth buying. Some standard tools of economic anal-

ysis make it possible to calculate this surplus as a function of a household's income.[23]

Central to this analysis is the concept that there is an ideal size and quality of house for each income level, a size and quality that maximize a household's surplus.[24] Low-income households maximize their surplus by selecting relatively modest houses, whereas high-income households maximize their surplus by selecting relatively large houses with many amenities. A low-income household would benefit from more square footage and more amenities, but because of the many other things it must buy with its limited budget, it is not willing to pay what these housing improvements cost. In contrast, a high-income household would not maximize its surplus with a modest house because it is willing to pay more than the cost for increments to size and quality.

For any household that is searching for a house to buy, the appropriate starting surplus is the surplus it would receive if it stayed in the house it previously purchased.[25] Consider a household whose income has increased since its last move. The house it previously purchased may have been ideal (or as ideal as possible in light of search costs) given its previous income, but it is not ideal at its new higher income. The household is now willing to pay the cost for more square footage and amenities, so staying in its current house does not maximize its surplus. The argument is similar for a household whose income has declined between moves. At its old income, this household was willing to pay the cost for above-average square footage and amenities, but at its new income these extras are no longer worth the cost.

Changes in income are not, of course, the only reason that households move and not the only reason why moving might lead to a higher housing surplus. Changes in number of children, in number of adults, and in jobs also affect housing demand. When a baby is born, a family is likely to be willing to pay for another bedroom even without an increase in its income. A recent study estimates the impact of these other types of household change on the surplus associated with moving.[26] This study finds that for homeowners the addition of one child has the same impact on the surplus from moving as does an income increase of $3,437, and the addition of an adult to the household has the same impact as an income increase of $11,260.

Data on changes between moves in income, household composition, and the job of household head and spouse for a representative sample of households can be obtained from the well-known Panel Study of Income Dynamics (PSID).[27] In particular, the following calculations draw on white households that moved during the 1984–1986 period in a sample of households selected to be representative of the white population in the United States.[28] The data set is restricted to white households because the calculations are intended to focus on the cost of current—not past—discrimination.[29] Blacks and Hispanics presumably would have socioeconomic characteristics similar to those of whites were it not for discrimination in the past.[30] Another way to put it is that the calculations determine the costs that would be imposed on white households if they were treated like blacks or Hispanics.

Most of the calculations also exclude the 48 percent of mover households who end up renting an apartment, because less is known about some key elements in renter search, such as credit checks.[31] No study indicates, for example, whether potential minority tenants are more likely to fail a credit check than are comparable whites. Although, as shown in Table 3.2, discrimination in housing availability is equally severe against black renters as against black homeowners, the cost of discrimination probably is lower for renters, primarily because the search process is less costly and because the impact of credit discrimination is unlikely to be as large. In addition, the severity of discrimination is lower against Hispanic renters than Hispanic owners. As a result, one of the calculations presented below finds the total cost of discrimination on all minority households based on the assumption that the cost per renter household is one-third the cost per owner for blacks and one-quarter the cost per owner for Hispanics.

As explained earlier, the surplus a household can gain from moving depends on its change in income and on the changes in its composition and in the jobs held by the household head and (if present) his or her spouse. Moreover, these nonincome changes can be translated into income equivalents; that is, into the income change that would have an equivalent impact on the surplus from moving as does each nonincome change, such as the addition of a child.[32] These income equivalents, along with some assumptions about housing demand, make it possible to estimate the starting surplus and the surplus gained by searching for each household in the PSID sample of white movers.[33]

The cost of discrimination obviously depends on the assumptions one makes about those aspects of discrimination that have not or cannot be precisely measured. These aspects include the impact of discrimination on minority households' housing search, lender search, and moving costs. In addition, the cost of discrimination depends on the assumption one makes about the range of surpluses a household might encounter during a housing search. To show the effect of all these assumptions, this chapter carries out calculations for three dif-

TABLE 6.2 **THE DIRECT COST OF CURRENT DISCRIMINATION IN HOUSING AND MORTGAGE MARKETS**

	Black Households			*Hispanic Households*		
	Low[a]	*Base[b]*	*High[c]*	*Low[a]*	*Base[b]*	*High[c]*
Mean Cost Per Move	$3,050	$3,238	$ 4,190	$3,234	$3,435	$4,429
Median Cost Per Move	851	1,036	1,589	899	1,102	1,723
Cost Per Household that Moves During a 3-Year Period	3,579	3,800	4,918	3,794	4,031	5,197
Share of Minority Moves Discouraged by Discrimination	1%	10%	14%	2%	15%	16%
Total Cost to All Minority Homebuyers Over a 3-Year Period (in millions)	5,665	6,013	7,781	3,398	3,610	4,654
Total Cost to All Minority Households Over a 3-Year Period (in millions)[d]	7,415	7,872	10,186	4,186	4,446	5,733

NOTES: All calculations are based on the one-stop strategy, the extent of discrimination in housing estimated by HDS, the incidence of mortgage discrimination estimated by the Boston Fed Study, and the characteristics of a representative sample of households. Other assumptions are detailed in endnote 34.

[a]Based on a relatively low assumed degree of discrimination.

[b]Based on best-guess assumptions about discrimination.

[c]Based on a relatively high assumed degree of discrimination.

[d]Assumes the cost per renter household equals one-third the cost per owner household for blacks and one-fourth the cost per owner household for Hispanics.

ferent cases: a base case, predicated on realistic, but somewhat conservative, guesses as to the values of the parameters; a low-discrimination case, which sets the impacts of discrimination and the range of surpluses at relatively low values; and a high-discrimination case, which sets the impacts of discrimination and the range of surpluses at relatively high, but not inconceivable, values.[34]

The estimated direct cost imposed on minority homebuyers of current discrimination in housing and mortgage markets is presented in Table 6.2. The table reveals that the average cost per move for blacks ranges from $3,050 to $4,190 and the cost per household from $3,579 to $4,917.[35] The median costs are considerably lower, which indicates that the cost of discrimination is particularly high for the relatively few households with relatively large changes in income or household composition; that is, for the households with the most to gain from moving. Corresponding costs for Hispanics are slightly higher because the distribution of number of units shown, presented in Table 6.1, is slightly less favorable for Hispanics than for blacks.

The fourth row in Table 6.2 reveals the share of moves by minority households that do not take place because of anticipated discrimination. In the base case, this share is 10 percent (for blacks) and 15 percent (for Hispanics).[36] These shares are somewhat higher in the high-discrimination case, but in the low-discrimination case virtually no minority households are discouraged from moving.

In 1990 there were 10,485,000 black households, as defined by the U.S. Census.[37] According to the PSID data, 29.1 percent of white households move during a 3-year period and 51.9 percent of these moving households end up buying a house. Without past discrimination, therefore, one would expect $(0.291)(0.519)(10,485,000) = 1,583,539$ black households to buy a house during a 3-year period. Multiplying this number by the average cost per household gives the total cost of current discrimination on presumptive black homeowners. As shown in Table 6.2, with the base-case assumptions the total cost of discrimination on presumptive black owners comes to $6.013 billion. Assuming that the cost that discrimination imposes on renters is one-third the cost on owners, the total base-case cost of discrimination for all black households over a 3-year period is almost $8 billion. In the high-discrimination case, this figure rises to over $10 billion.

The number of Hispanic households in 1990, again as defined by the U.S. Census, was 5,933,000.[38] Following the same procedure, we find that the base-case cost of discrimination on presumptive Hispanic homeowners over a 3-year period is $3.6 billion. Bringing in renters, at one-quarter the cost imposed on owners, raises this figure to $4.4 billion.

■ CONCLUSIONS

The calculations in this chapter reveal that black and Hispanic households pay a discrimination "tax" of about $3,000, on average, every time they search for a house to buy. This tax applies to all minority houseseekers, not just those who actually encounter discrimination. It summarizes the expected cost imposed by discrimination itself as well as by the losses in consumer surplus that occur when, in anticipation of discrimination, minority households cut short their housing search, decide not to apply for a loan, or decide not to search at all. The cumulative impact of this "tax" is staggering; every 3 years the black community implicitly pays out $7.9 billion and the Hispanic community another $4.4 billion in the form of higher search costs and lost housing opportunities. In other words, the cost imposed on blacks and Hispanics by current housing discrimination comes to $4.1 billion per year.

These results are estimates of the direct cost of current discrimination and do not include either the indirect costs of current discrimination or the direct and indirect costs of past discrimination. In fact, society as a whole pays a high cost for the distrust, hostility, and lost productivity that are the products of a discriminatory system (and the subjects of the next two chapters). Nevertheless, the direct cost of current discrimination estimated here is disturbingly high, and the results in this chapter give no comfort to those who say that racial and ethnic discrimination are no longer significant phenomena in the United States.

The Impact
of Housing Discrimination
on Housing Quality,
Racial Segregation,
and Neighborhood Change

■ SEPARATE AND UNEQUAL

The Sherman Park neighborhood in Milwaukee appeared to demonstrate the promise of stable racial integration. Thanks to an active community organization that was committed to integration, Sherman Park had grown from less than 1 percent black in 1970 to about one-quarter black in 1980. Moreover, Sherman Park was an island of integration in a sea of separateness, as half of the blacks in Milwaukee lived in neighborhoods that were at least 90 percent black. By 1990, however, almost half of Sherman Park's residents were black, and its white population had declined by over 60 percent since 1970.[1] Prospects for continued stable racial integration were poor, indeed.

This pattern has been repeated throughout our history in neighborhoods across the country. Despite the civil rights movement, fair housing laws, and a softening of white prejudice, blacks and whites, and to a lesser extent Hispanics and whites, tend not to live in the same places. Islands of integration occasionally arise, and, with concerted effort, a few remain stable for long periods of time, but the forces that produce residential segregation are powerful and persistent. Not surprisingly, racial and ethnic discrimination makes a key contribution to the power these forces retain.

Housing market outcomes of blacks and whites, or of Hispanics and whites, are not only geographically separate, but profoundly unequal, with housing discrimination again playing a major role. This chapter examines racial and ethnic disparities in homeownership

105

and housing quality as well as racial and ethnic segregation and explores what is known about the success of private and local government actions to promote and maintain integration.

■ HOMEOWNERSHIP AND HOUSING QUALITY

Current discrimination in housing and mortgage markets combined with centuries of past discrimination in all aspects of economic life have left their mark on housing outcomes for black and Hispanic households. Current discrimination shuts off housing opportunities and induces many minority households to cut short their housing searches, that is, to settle for less desirable housing than that obtained by their white counterparts. Past discrimination has resulted in lower incomes, less wealth, more central residential locations, and less information about owner-occupied housing for minority than for white households. Thus, blacks and Hispanics are far less likely than whites to be homeowners and far more likely to live in deficient or overcrowded housing.

Homeownership

The stark facts are these: In 1990, 69.1 percent of white households owned their own homes, compared to 43.4 percent of black households and 42.4 percent of Hispanic households.[2] This large difference between white and minority homeownership rates has not narrowed for at least two decades.[3] Moreover, minorities are not only less likely to own homes, the values of the homes they do own are far lower than the values of the homes owned by whites. To be specific, the average house value in 1990 was $116,570 for white homeowners, $73,145 for black homeowners, and $111,376 for Hispanic homeowners.[4]

A household's expected housing wealth equals its probability of owning a house multiplied by the expected value of a house if it does own. These numbers imply, therefore, that white households have an expected housing wealth of $(0.691)($116,570) = $80,550$, whereas the expected wealth of black households is less than half as much, namely $(0.434)($73,145) = $31,745$. Without any past or current discrimination, black households could expect to have the same housing wealth as whites, so the difference between these two figures, $48,805, is a measure of the impact of racial discrimination on housing wealth.[5] In 1990 there were 9.976 million housing units with a black householder (to use the census term for the head of the household), so the aggregate impact of discrimination on the housing wealth of blacks is $48,805 multiplied by 9.976 million, which comes to $487 billion.[6] To put it another way, without any past and current discrimination to prevent blacks from accumulating housing at the same rate as whites, the housing wealth of blacks in the United States would be $487 billion higher than it actually is.

The expected housing wealth of Hispanic households is their homeownership rate, 0.424, multiplied by their average house value, $111,376, or $47,223. Hence, the impact of past and current discrimination on Hispanic housing wealth is $33,327 per household. In 1990 there were 6.001 million households with an Hispanic householder, so the total impact of discrimination on the housing wealth of Hispanics comes to $23,327 multiplied by 6.001 million, or $200 billion.[7]

These figures give gross, not net, housing wealth: they do not account for the fact that most homeowners still owe money to a lender. Accounting for outstanding mortgages lowers the housing wealth gap between white and minority households, but not by as much as one might think. If homeowners in all three groups still owed the bank, say, 45 percent of their house value, on average, then the net wealth gaps would equal only 55 percent of the above gross wealth gaps. In fact, however, blacks and Hispanics are less likely than whites to have paid off their mortgage (or never to have borrowed), and the outstanding mortgage balance is a larger fraction of house value, on average, for blacks and Hispanics than for whites.[8] Thus, average net wealth in 1990 equaled $47,925 for black homeowners and $70,510 for Hispanic homeowners, compared to $82,436 for white homeowners. Combining these figures with the homeownership shares for each group reveals that expected net housing wealth is $20,799 for black households, $29,896 for Hispanic households, and $56,963 for whites. Hence the aggregate impact of discrimination on net wealth is $361 billion for blacks and $163 billion for Hispanics.

These calculations apply to 1990. The consumer price index increased at a 3.5 percent annual rate between 1990 and 1993. With continued growth at this rate, the 1994 aggregate gap in net housing wealth would be $414 billion for blacks and $186 billion for Hispanics, for a grand total of $600 billion.[9]

These findings add perspective to the earlier result that current discrimination alone imposes an annual cost of about $2.6 billion on black households and $1.5 billion on Hispanic households. The current discrimination results represent annual flows, whereas the household wealth calculations presented here represent asset values. Using well-known formulas for the determination of an asset price, these asset values can be translated into equivalent annual flows.[10] In particular, the above impacts of past and current discrimination on housing wealth correspond to a long-term annual loss of about $12.4 billion per year for black households and about $5.6 billion per year for Hispanic households. Roughly speaking, therefore, current discrimination as observed by HDS and the recent mortgage discrimination studies accounts for one-fifth to one-fourth of the gap in housing wealth between whites and minorities, and past discrimination, including discrimination in markets other than housing, accounts for the rest.

A key component of these housing wealth differences is the difference in homeownership rates between white and minority households. A recent study based on national data from the 1989 American Housing Survey (AHS) provides a careful, sophisticated estimate of the extent to which the homeownership deficit for minority households is due to the fact that they have lower endowments, particularly lower permanent incomes, than whites. The study finds that "81 percent of the differences between the predicted probability of ownership between black and white households are due to differences in group endowments."[11] The comparable figure for Hispanics is 78 percent. In other words, 19 percent of the homeownership gap for blacks (and 22 percent for Hispanics) is due to "direct effects," which most scholars associate with current discrimination in housing and mortgage markets. Previous studies based on earlier data obtained similar results.[12]

In short, recent evidence indicates that roughly 20–25 percent of the minority–white gaps in both homeownership rates and overall housing wealth can be attributed to current discrimination. The rest of these gaps represents the legacy of past discrimination in housing and other markets. The cumulative impact of past and current discrimination is very large; the share of minority households that own their own homes is over 20 percentage points lower than the share for white households, and the net housing wealth of minority households is estimated to be $600 billion lower than it would be in a world without discrimination.[13]

Because homeownership is the principal method by which American households accumulate wealth, these differences in net housing wealth shed light on the likely magnitude of the overall wealth differences between white and minority households. In 1992 net housing wealth constituted 31 percent of total net household wealth in the United States.[14] If past and current discrimination have the same proportional impact on the ability of minority households to accumulate nonhousing wealth as they have on their ability to accumulate housing wealth, then discrimination lowers the total net wealth of black households by $1,335 billion and of Hispanic households by $600 billion. Adding these together gives $1,935 billion; by this rough estimate, the legacy of discrimination is a wealth gap of almost two trillion dollars.[15]

Housing Quality

Black and Hispanic households are far more likely than white households to live in overcrowded conditions, to live in housing with severe or moderate structural problems, or to devote an excessive share of their income toward housing.[16]

According to the 1989 AHS, fewer than 2 percent of white households, compared to 5 percent of black households and 15 percent of Hispanic households, had more than one person per room, which is the census definition of overcrowded conditions.[17] These intergroup disparities are even greater among poor households. Only 4 percent of poor white households were overcrowded, compared to 9 percent of poor black households and 26 percent of poor Hispanic households. In fact, the share of *nonpoor* Hispanic households living in overcrowded conditions, 11 percent, was over two and one-half times as great as the comparable share for *poor* whites. Moreover, the 1990 census, which is based on a larger sample than the AHS, finds even larger overall disparities in overcrowding, with a rate of 3 percent for whites, 10 percent for blacks, and 27 percent for Hispanics.[18]

The U.S. Bureau of the Census, in conjunction with the U.S. Department of Housing and Urban Development, has developed a detailed definition of deficient housing, which includes all housing with severe or moderate physical problems. A housing unit is placed in the "severe" category if it has one or more of the following problems: a lack of complete plumbing; frequent plumbing breakdowns; serious electrical problems or a lack of electricity; a lack of hallway lighting, hallway railings, adequate stairs, or adequate elevators; and at least five basic maintenance problems, such as water leaks.[19] A housing unit's deficiencies are said to be "moderate" if they include one or more of the following: occasional plumbing breakdown; unvented heaters as a primary heat source; lack of sink, refrigerator, stove, or oven; three of the four above hall or stairway problems; and three of the five basic maintenance problems.

According to this definition, 9 percent of white households lived in deficient housing in 1989, compared to 20 percent of black households and 17 percent of Hispanic households.[20] As in the case of overcrowding, these disparities are larger among the poor. Housing was classified as deficient for 13 percent of poor white households but for 29 percent of poor black households and 23 percent of poor Hispanic households. Moreover, the likelihood of deficient housing was the same, 12 or 13 percent, for nonpoor black and Hispanic households as for poor whites.

Despite the fact that they live in poorer quality housing and more overcrowded conditions than whites, black and Hispanic households are also more likely than whites to pay more than 30 percent of their income in housing expenses, which include rent and utilities or mortgage payments, utilities, property taxes, housing insurance, and housing maintenance. In 1989, 25 percent of white households, 39 percent of black households, and 42 percent of Hispanic households devoted more than 30 percent of their income toward housing.[21] In addition, the housing cost burden exceeded 50 percent of income for 9 percent of white households, compared to 18 percent of black and Hispanic households. These disparities do not exist among poor households, for whom the share paying more than 30 percent of income is slightly higher for whites (76.8 percent) than for blacks (72.8 percent) and for Hispanics (76.4 percent).

These disparities reflect both current discrimination and endowment and other differences associated with past discrimination. No recent study provides evidence on the extent to which these disparities still exist after accounting for racial and ethnic differences in endowments.[22] On the basis of evidence concerning homeownership disparities, however, it seems safe to conclude that both past and current discrimination contribute to the relatively high incidence of overcrowding, housing deficiencies, and excess housing cost burdens among minority households.

■ RESIDENTIAL SEGREGATION

Racial and ethnic residential segregation is one of the most dramatic features of urban areas in the United States. Blacks and whites, and to a lesser extent Hispanics and whites, tend not to live in the same neighborhoods.

The Extent of Segregation

The most popular measure of residential segregation is the so-called dissimilarity index, which indicates the extent to which two groups live in different neighborhoods.[23] A value of 100 for this index indicates complete segregation of the two groups from each other, and a value of zero indicates that the two groups are evenly spread throughout all neighborhoods. Intermediate values can be interpreted as the share of the population of either group that would have to move to achieve an even distribution.

Black–white segregation indexes have been quite high, above 70, for many decades. Between 1950 and 1970, black–white segregation increased somewhat in the average metropolitan area. One study of 137 metropolitan areas found that the average black–white segregation index went from 74.3 in 1960 to 74.7 in 1970.[24] The trend then shifted and black–white segregation indexes exhibited a slow but widespread decline between 1970 and 1980. Among the thirty metropolitan areas with the largest black populations in 1980, which contain over one-half of the black population in the United States, the index dropped almost 6 percentage points on average over this period, from 81.3 to 75.4.[25]

This downward trend in segregation continued during the 1980s. As shown in Table 7.1, a recent study reveals that among the twenty-three urban areas with the largest black populations in 1990, which together contain about 46 percent of the nation's black citizens, the average segregation index dropped from 78.8 in 1980 to 74.5 in 1990.[26] Similar results appear in other samples. Among the 232 metropolitan areas with at least 20,000 blacks in 1990, the average index fell from 68.8 in 1980 to 64.3 in 1990.[27] Moreover, segregation decreased in all the forty-six central counties with 50,000 or more black residents, except for no change in Essex County (Newark) and increases of one point in Fulton County (Altanta) and two points in Wayne County (Detroit).[28] Segregation also decreased in six of the seven suburban counties with more than 50,000 blacks and remained unchanged in the seventh.[29]

Despite these widespread declines, however, black–white segregation remains high in metropolitan areas with large black populations, with an average 1990 index of 74.5.[30] On average, three-quarters of the blacks (or of the whites) would have to move in these areas to achieve an even racial distribution. Only one of these twenty-three metropolitan areas, Norfolk, has a 1990 index below 60, and only six others, five in the South plus Oakland, have a 1990 index below 70. Moreover, six northern areas have 1990 indexes above 80.[31] Among the forty-six central counties with at least 50,000 black residents in 1990, the average index is 72.0, only two counties have an index below 60, and only eighteen more have indexes below 70.[32] Seven of these central counties, including Fulton and Baltimore counties in the South, have indexes of 80 or more.[33]

Hispanics are considerably less segregated from non-Hispanic

TABLE 7.1 1980 AND 1990 INDEXES OF BLACK–WHITE SEGREGATION
FOR THE 23 METROPOLITAN AREAS
WITH THE LARGEST BLACK POPULATIONS IN 1990

	1980	1990
Northeast		
Boston	76	70
Newark	84	83
New York	78	78
Philadelphia	83	82
Midwest		
Chicago	91	87
Cleveland	89	86
Detroit	89	89
Kansas City	81	76
St. Louis	85	81
South		
Atlanta	79	73
Baltimore	78	75
Birmingham	80	79
Charlotte	68	65
Dallas	81	66
Houston	78	69
Memphis	76	76
Miami	81	75
New Orleans	76	74
Norfolk	65	57
Richmond	68	64
Washington, D.C.	71	68
West		
Los Angeles	80	71
Oakland	75	69
Average	78.8	74.5

SOURCE: Farley and Frey (1993, Table 9) and appendix table supplied by Farley. These
dissimilarity indexes are calculated using a census block group as the neighborhood
scale.

whites than are blacks, but Hispanic–white segregation is moderately
high and is growing in many urban areas. Table 7.2 presents the Hispanic–white dissimilarity index for the twenty urban areas with
more than 200,000 Hispanic residents. These areas contain 59 percent
of the nation's Hispanics. The background of the Hispanic population is largely Puerto Rican in New York, Cuban in Miami, mixed
in Washington, D.C., and Mexican in the other areas. The average

TABLE 7.2 1980 AND 1990 INDEXES OF HISPANIC–WHITE
SEGREGATION FOR THE 20 METROPOLITAN AREAS
WITH THE LARGEST HISPANIC POPULATIONS IN 1990

	1980	*1990*
Northeast		
New York	55.0	54.0
Midwest		
Chicago	66.0	66.0
South		
Brownsville	46.0	50.0
Dallas	49.0	50.0
El Paso	56.0	52.0
Houston	50.0	49.0
McAllen	52.0	53.0
Miami	57.0	56.0
San Antonio	57.0	53.0
Washington, D.C.	33.0	41.0
West		
Anaheim	43.7	52.7
Denver	48.7	46.7
Fresno	47.3	46.3
Los Angeles	53.1	53.1
Oakland	33.7	34.7
Phoenix	50.5	48.5
Riverside	39.0	38.0
San Diego	39.1	43.1
San Jose	43.0	45.0
San Francisco	41.4	45.4
Average	48.0	48.9

SOURCE: Farley and Frey (1993, Table 2). These dissimilarity indexes are calculated using a census block group as the neighborhood scale.

segregation index for these areas increased slightly during the 1980s, from 48.0 to 48.9. Nine areas experienced an increase in segregation over this period, and two areas experienced no change. Although two areas, Washington, D.C., and Anaheim, experienced increases of 8 points or more, and three others, Brownsville, San Diego, and San Francisco, experienced an increase of 4 points, only two areas, San Antonio and El Paso, experienced declines of as much as 4 points.

The highest Hispanic–white segregation can be found in Chicago, where the index is 66. Nine other areas, only two in the west, have indexes of 50 or above, and two areas in California, Riverside and

Oakland, have indexes below 40. These levels are not high by the standards of Table 7.1, but they do represent significant segregation. Similar results are found in a larger sample; in the 153 metropolitan areas with more than 20,000 Hispanics, the average 1990 index was 42.7, up one half a point from 1980.[34]

The racial dimension of the Hispanic designation reveals itself in the extent of residential segregation between Hispanics who place themselves in different racial groups. A study of Caribbean Hispanics in the United States in 1980 found that black and white Hispanics were highly segregated from each other, with a segregation index averaging 60.9 in ten major metropolitan areas.[35] Black Hispanics also were far more segregated from non-Hispanic whites, with an average index of 80.0, than were white Hispanics, with an average index of 51.9.

Moreover, Hispanics identifying themselves as something other than white or black, which presumably means they have a mixed racial ancestry, were almost as segregated from non-Hispanic whites as were black Hispanics, with an average 1980 index of 71.9. This result suggests that even though mixed-race Hispanics do not identify themselves as "black," the social and economic forces they encounter in the housing market are similar to those encountered by black Hispanics.[36] Finally, the average index for the segregation of mixed-race and black Hispanics, 56.7, was much closer to the average index for white and black Hispanics, 60.9, than to the average index for mixed-race Hispanics and white Hispanics, 40.0. This result suggests that "it is race and not class that is crucial to understanding patterns of residential segregation among Caribbean Hispanics in U.S. cities."[37]

Residential segregation is a complex phenomenon, and the dissimilarity index measures only one of its dimensions. Scholars have discovered that exclusive focus on this index can lead to a misleading impression of racial and ethnic residential patterns. The dissimilarity index focuses on the extent to which the members of a minority group are evenly distributed across neighborhoods. Other dimensions of residential segregation include the extent to which a group is isolated from other groups, the extent to which a group is clustered in a contiguous area, the extent to which a group is concentrated in a small area, and the extent to which a group is centralized within an urban area.[38]

A recent study provides one simple measure of the isolation of blacks from whites in 1990. As shown in Table 7.3, the share of the black population that lives in a neighborhood that is 90 percent or more black declined slightly between 1980 and 1990 in most urban areas.[39] Declines of more than 10 percentage points were experienced

Table **7.3** ISOLATION OF BLACKS IN SELECTED LARGE
METROPOLITAN AREAS: 1990 AND 1980–1990 CHANGE

	Percentage of Blacks in Isolation, 1990	*Percentage Point Change in Black Isolation, 1980–1990*
Chicago	71	−9.1
Cleveland	67	0.4
Detroit	61	4.0
Memphis	58	−0.6
St. Louis	54	−3.3
Baltimore	53	−5.4
Philadelphia	53	0.1
Buffalo	48	2.6
New Orleans	47	−3.2
Kansas City	44	−6.0
Atlanta	43	−6.1
Milwaukee	42	−7.0
Newark	41	−2.6
Indianapolis	39	−6.0
Washington, D.C.	37	−9.3
Cincinnati	34	0.5
Fort Lauderdale/Hollywood	34	−29.6
Miami/Hialeah	33	−8.3
Orlando	32	−22.4
Charlotte/Gastonia	32	−0.9
Pittsburgh	32	−2.4
New York	31	3.0
Nashville	31	−4.6
Houston	30	−19.5
Tampa/St. Petersburg	30	−11.0
Average for 50 Areas	37	−6.7

Source: Gillmore and Doig (1992, p. 50). "'Isolation' is defined as living in a block group that is at least 90 percent of the same race." The average is for the 50 largest metropolitan areas. Isolation typically is higher within central cities; for example, the index is 69 within Washington, D.C.

by three urban areas in Florida, Fort Lauderdale, Orlando, and Tampa, and by Houston, Texas. In contrast, however, several urban areas in the Midwest and Northeast, namely, Buffalo, Cincinnati, Cleveland, Detroit, New York, and Philadelphia, experienced small increases in black isolation during the 1980s. The largest increase occurred in Detroit, which lost 200,000 white residents over this decade. Despite a slow trend toward lower black–white segregation by some measures, other dimensions of black–white segregation in many cities appear to be remarkably resistant to change.

In some urban areas, black–white segregation is high on many dimensions, not just the dimensions in Tables 7.1 or 7.2. One study defines a hypersegregated area as one that is highly segregated on at least four of the five dimensions defined above.[40] In 1980, sixteen urban areas were hypersegregated: Altanta, Baltimore, Buffalo, Chicago, Cleveland, Dallas, Detroit, Gary, Indianapolis, Kansas City, Los Angeles, Milwaukee, New York, Newark, Philadelphia, and St. Louis. These areas contained 35 percent of the nation's black population in 1980.

All sixteen of these areas were still hypersegregated, or close to it, in 1990.[41] Moreover, five new urban areas appeared on the hypersegregation list: Birmingham, Cincinnati, Miami, New Orleans, and Washington, D.C.[42] In general, the measures of segregation in these urban areas did not change very much between 1980 and 1990, but a few areas experienced increases in several dimensions of segregation. In Newark and Buffalo, for example, segregation increased on all five dimensions, and in Detroit it increased on four dimensions, two of them substantially. Overall, the share of the nation's black population living in hypersegregated areas reached 44 percent.

Hypersegregation is not experienced by Hispanics, however. In most metropolitan areas with significant Hispanic populations, Hispanics faced extensive segregation on only one of the above five dimensions (usually centralization), and they did not face extensive segregation on more than three dimensions in any metropolitan area. In some areas, including Miami, Hispanics do not face extensive segregation on any of these dimensions. Overall, therefore, "Despite their immigrant origins, Spanish language, and high poverty rates, Hispanics are considerably more integrated in United States society than are blacks."[43]

A final irony in the story of segregation is that some of the most segregated neighborhoods in the country can be found in housing projects that are publicly owned and operated. In 1990, for example, nine of the twelve family housing projects run by the Houston Housing Authority were between 87 and 99 percent black. The other three projects all had a black majority, and two of them were 20 percent or more Hispanic.[44] At the national level, blacks and Hispanics made up half the tenants in all federally assisted housing in 1989. This concentration is even more striking in federal public housing, for which the minority share in FY1993 was 69 percent in all units and 90 percent for the units operated by the largest public housing authorities.[45] Housing projects with so few white tenants make a powerful symbolic and substantive contribution to the perpetuation of residential segregation.

Racial and Ethnic Transition

The relative stability of segregation over time masks considerable racial and ethnic change at the neighborhood level. In fact, many neighborhoods undergo transition from largely white to largely black, but only a few make a transition from largely black to largely white or remain integrated for a long period of time.[46]

In urban areas where segregation declined between 1970 and 1980, two-thirds of the largely white census tracts with a significant increase in black population also experienced a decline in white population during that period.[47] Moreover, in the nation's twenty-five largest cities, only about one census tract in twenty began the 1970s with a mixture of black and white residents and did not experience racial transition during the decade.[48] Finally, for a sample of sixty major metropolitan areas, the probability that a census tract would experience a decline in its white population between 1970 and 1980 increased both with the share of the tract's population that was black and with the proximity of the tract to a largely black neighborhood. In a largely white suburban tract located 25 miles or more from the nearest black neighborhood, for example, the probability of a loss in white population during the decade was only 16 percent, whereas in a city neighborhood that was 30–40 percent black and within 5 miles of a largely black neighborhood, the probability was 92 percent; that is, white population loss was almost certain.[49]

A broad consensus has emerged among scholars on the link between racial attitudes and neighborhood racial or ethnic transition.[50] In particular, stable integration cannot be maintained unless the preferences of whites and blacks (or whites and Hispanics) meet certain conditions. Consider an existing all-white neighborhood. No racial integration will take place there unless at least one black family is willing to be a pioneer. Moreover, once blacks move in, integration cannot be maintained at any given percentage white unless enough whites are willing to live there to maintain that percentage. For example, a neighborhood cannot remain at 90 percent white unless enough whites are willing to live there to make up 90 percent of the population. If this condition is not met, if an insufficient number of whites is willing to live there, the neighborhood has passed what is called a "tipping point," and it will "tip" from all-white to all-black.

What are the actual neighborhood preferences of whites and blacks? A 1992 Detroit survey provides the necessary information.[51]

This survey found that the vast majority of blacks prefer to live in an integrated neighborhood where blacks make up at least 50 percent of the population, and that almost all blacks would be willing to move into an integrated neighborhood where the black population share fell between one-third and three-quarters. Only 20 percent of blacks state a preference for an all-black neighborhood, and only 4 percent prefer to be in an otherwise all-white neighborhood. However, 79 percent of blacks would be willing to move into an all-black neighborhood, whereas only 28 percent are willing to be pioneers, that is, to be the first black to move in. Blacks' reluctance to live in a largely white neighborhood has increased over time. In a 1976 Detroit survey, only 66 percent of blacks were willing to move into an all-black neighborhood, and 38 percent of blacks were willing to be pioneers.[52]

A survey of black attitudes in 1990 by the National Opinion Research Center paints a similar picture for the nation as a whole. Sixty percent of blacks said they were in favor of, and only 6 percent said they were opposed to, living in a neighborhood that was half black and half white.[53] The limited available evidence indicates that Hispanics' attitudes toward integration with non-Hispanic whites are similar to those of blacks.[54]

These survey results indicate that, at least on average, black attitudes do not constitute a major barrier to stable integration. Enough blacks are willing to be pioneers for integration to be started, and most blacks state a willingness to live in a neighborhood with a significant white population. The same conclusions probably hold for Hispanics. Nevertheless, there are some signs that blacks are now somewhat more hesitant about integration than they were in 1980.

In the case of white attitudes, the 1992 Detroit survey reveals that 4 percent of whites would move out of a neighborhood that was 7 percent black, 15 percent would move out of a neighborhood that was 20 percent black, and 41 percent would move out at 33 percent black.[55] With an average set of whites (at least an average for Detroit), integration therefore could be maintained in the short run at 7 or 20 percent black, but not at 33 percent black.[56] White prejudice may be stronger in Detroit than in other metropolitan areas. In Cleveland in 1991, for example, only 14 percent of whites said they would move out of a neighborhood that was one-quarter black, and only 35 percent of whites would move out when a neighborhood had an equal share of blacks and whites.[57] The limited available evidence suggests that whites' aversion to living with Hispanics is similar to, but somewhat weaker than, their aversion to living with blacks.[58]

These are only short-run results, however, because many people move for nonracial reasons. Stable integration in the long run requires whites to be willing to move into an integrated neighborhood.[59]

On this point the Detroit survey results are less encouraging for stable integration. In particular, 27 percent of whites said they would not be willing to move into a neighborhood that was 7 percent black, and this percentage increased to 50 percent at 20 percent black and to 73 percent at one-third black.[60] With an average set of whites from Detroit, therefore, integration cannot be sustained in the long run at any racial composition.[61]

The Causes of Segregation

This type of analysis has led some observers to conclude that white prejudice, which appears here as a white unwillingness to move into neighborhoods with a significant black or Hispanic population, is the key cause of residential segregation.[62] After all, the argument goes, segregation cannot be expected to decline unless integrated neighborhoods can be sustained. Indeed, this view has been expressed by the U.S. Supreme Court. In a 1992 school desegregation decision, *Freeman* v. *Pitts,* the majority opinion said, in part:

> The District Court has heard evidence that racially stable neighborhoods are not likely to emerge because whites prefer a racial mix of 80 percent white and 20 percent black, while blacks prefer a 50 percent–50 percent mix. Where resegregation is a product not of state action but of private choices, it does not have constitutional implications. It is beyond the authority and beyond the practical ability of the federal courts to try to counteract these kinds of continuous and massive demographic shifts.[63]

Despite the imprimatur of the Supreme Court, however, this conclusion is simply not correct. For six important reasons, one cannot say that white prejudice is the key cause of segregation.

First, not all neighborhoods contain whites with average preferences.[64] The Detroit area, for example, contains over one million white households. According the Detroit survey, 30 percent, or over 300,000 households, are willing to move into a neighborhood that is 53 percent black; and 44 percent, or over 440,000 households, are willing to move into a neighborhood that is one-third black. Even in Detroit, which appears to have unusually strong white prejudice, there are enough willing white households to fill many integrated neighborhoods.

A recent study of racial transition in Cleveland during the 1970s explores this issue in detail.[65] This study finds that the extent to which whites leave a neighborhood in response to a given concentration of black residents depends heavily on the degree of white prejudice in the neighborhood.[66] For the most prejudiced neighborhoods, tipping

will occur as soon as the first black moves in, but in the least prejudiced neighborhoods integration might be sustained at a composition
of 50 percent black or more.

Indirect evidence from other cities also supports the view that
white attitudes sometimes are conducive to integration. One study
found, for example, that "About one-tenth of the metropolitan Chicago white population in 1980 lived in areas where there had been a
significant black or Hispanic population for more than a decade and
no major racial change was taking place."[67] Most of these areas were
in the suburbs and away from the path of the ghetto expansions to
the west and south of the city. And in the twenty-five largest cities,
about one census tract in twenty remained stably integrated throughout the 1970s.[68] Thus, racial transition is by no means inevitable, at
least not within a fairly long time span.

Second, whites' neighborhood preferences reflect both their racial
and ethnic prejudices and their opportunities in other neighborhoods. If all neighborhoods were integrated, not even the most prejudiced white would have an incentive to move out of a neighborhood
because a black family moved in.[69] Hence, whites' neighborhood preferences as expressed in the Detroit and other surveys are influenced
by racial discrimination in housing and by any other factor that preserves all-white neighborhoods to which whites can flee.

The third reason is that white prejudice itself is a product of past
and current discrimination in housing and other markets.[70] The distinction between blacks and whites (or between Hispanics and
whites) has no intrinsic power but has gained power in this society
because of a long history of discrimination against blacks and Hispanics and the resulting disparities in social and economic outcomes.
Whites prefer white neighborhoods because they are taught that
blacks or Hispanics are inferior,[71] find support for this view in the
relatively poor average outcomes for these minority groups, and, because of extensive segregation, rarely experience the kind of interracial contact that breaks prejudice down.[72] The fiction of black or Hispanic inferiority that is at the heart of white prejudice is thus
supported by a powerful vicious circle: Prejudice builds on observed
disparities in social outcomes, is protected by the lack of contact that
goes with segregation, and then supports the continuing discrimination by which these disparities and this segregation are preserved.[73]

Stating that white prejudice is a cause of segregation is equivalent,
therefore, to the statement that past discrimination continues to promote segregation through its legacy of white prejudice. The common
conclusion by scholars that segregation is caused by both prejudice
and discrimination provides a way to separate the role of past and
current discrimination, but the scholarly literature gives no support

to the claim that segregation is inevitable because whites "simply" do not want to live with blacks or Hispanics.[74] Thus, it is profoundly disturbing that the Supreme Court would justify a passive acceptance of racial segregation on the basis of white prejudice that would not persist if racial segregation were to disappear.

Fourth, a household's neighborhood preferences are influenced by many factors other than current or expected racial composition. Households care, for example, about crime rates, school quality, and housing deterioration. Racial or ethnic transition by itself has no significant impact on these amenities. However, because neighborhood amenities tend to decline as income declines and because racial or ethnic transition often is accompanied by income transition,[75] many people associate racial or ethnic transition with a decline in housing quality or an increase in crime. Moreover, governments may provide poorer services in poorer neighborhoods or even discriminate against minority neighborhoods, so many people also may associate racial or ethnic transition with a decline in public services, such as education and police protection. Some surveys of prejudicial attitudes attempt to account for neighborhood amenities in the wording of their questions, but no survey can determine the extent to which expressed prejudice reflects perceptions about events that accompany transition as opposed to attitudes about racial or ethnic composition as such.

One study in Chicago in the early 1980s, for example, found that white households' intentions to move were strongly associated with their expectations about neighborhood tipping and with their racial prejudices.[76] However, when their perceptions about neighborhood crime and housing deterioration were introduced into the analysis, the impact of racial factors disappeared. Moreover, a 1991 survey in Cleveland asked whites "what it would take for them to move into a mostly minority neighborhood."[77] Sixty percent of whites said a better education for their children, 58 percent said a guarantee of their personal safety, and 52 percent said an improvement in city services.[78] Racial and ethnic attitudes are not so strong for most people that they cannot be overcome by other neighborhood factors.

Fifth, current racial and ethnic discrimination plays a major role in promoting segregation quite apart from its link to whites' racial attitudes. Audit studies demonstrate that discrimination sometimes serves to exclude minorities from certain neighborhoods.[79] Even when the discriminatory barriers are not absolute, however, steering and other forms of discrimination channel black and Hispanic demand for housing into certain integrated neighborhoods and thereby hasten racial transition there.[80]

Discrimination also can lower the likelihood that blacks and Hispanics will move at all.[81] Moreover, minority households' willingness to be pioneers in an all-white neighborhood, which appears to be declining, undoubtedly reflects the possibility that they will encounter blatant discrimination or even violence after making such a move.[82] Thus, discrimination pushes minority households toward minority neighborhoods. This effect now appears in suburbs as well as in central cities. In 1990, 32 percent of urban blacks lived in the suburbs, compared to 26 percent in 1980; and the appearance of stable, middle-class communities in some urban areas, including Miami, St. Louis, Atlanta, and Washington, D.C., pulls some middle-class blacks away from the largely white areas to which they might otherwise turn.[83]

A recent study provides clear, direct evidence of the link between current discrimination and residential segregation.[84] Using 1980 data for a large sample of metropolitan areas, this study finds that two dimensions of segregation for blacks—centralization and exposure to whites—are influenced by current discrimination. All else equal, the higher the incidence of sales market discrimination in the area, as measured by fair housing audits, the more centralized blacks are relative to whites and the lower the index of residential exposure.[85]

The final reason is that an exclusive focus on white prejudice does not consider the important role of neighborhood, market, and government institutions. In some cases, the actions of real estate brokers, lenders, and government officials magnify the forces that cause racial or ethnic transition. In other cases, community groups, real estate brokers, and public agencies have acted together to break the vicious cycle and maintain integration. The underlying process that promotes racial or ethnic transition is strong, but as the case studies in the following sections reveal, institutional factors can boost the speed with which this transition takes place or, under some circumstances, prevent it from happening at all.

Overall, therefore, residential segregation is one outcome of a complex system in which prejudice, segregation, discrimination, and racial or ethnic economic disparities are simultaneously determined.[86] Each of these phenomena influences the others. Because of their complexity, these relationships are difficult to study, but most scholars now recognize that racial and ethnic prejudice and discrimination are both causes and consequences of residential segregation.

Blockbusting and Neighborhood Decline

The recent history of Boston's Mattapan neighborhood, which was stable, white, and largely Jewish in 1970, shows how powerful institutional factors can be in promoting racial transition.[87] After Martin

Luther King, Jr., was assassinated in 1968, Boston, like many other cities, experienced riots in its low-income black neighborhoods. In response, Mayor Kevin White and most of the banks in Boston set up the Boston Banks Urban Renewal Group (BBURG) to expand home-ownership opportunities for blacks. When the program started in 1968, blacks in Boston were largely confined to a poor neighborhood called Roxbury, and BBURG made available $20 million in FHA-insured mortgages to help blacks in Roxbury buy houses in better neighborhoods.

Whatever the intentions of the mayor, however, the BBURG program was a disaster. Perhaps the most striking feature of the BBURG program was that, for both political and economic reasons, the participating banks drew, literally, a line around Roxbury, Mattapan, and parts of nearby neighborhoods and issued BBURG loans only inside this line.[88] The BBURG line had the effect of focusing all the increased black demand for homeownership in a small area and magnifying all the pressures for racial transition.

In addition, many banks skimped on the inspections that were required for the FHA loans. In fact, one survey discovered that almost two-thirds of the houses purchased with BBURG loans required major repairs within two years.[89] Because the loans required little or no down payment and were given to people with little or no savings, the new homeowners were left in the impossible position of living in houses with major structural defects or defaulting on their loans. Many of them chose default; and abandoned properties, which often fell victim to vandalism or structural deterioration, soon started to appear within the BBURG line. This decline lowered the value of neighboring houses. The lenders were not upset by all this because the FHA loans were fully insured by the federal government.

Finally, many unscrupulous real estate agents took advantage of the situation by engaging in aggressive blockbusting and speculation activities. These agents called white households in Mattapan and told them that they should sell immediately before blacks moved in. Indeed, "Telephone calls by the realtors became a daily routine."[90] Panic selling ensued. These agents not only made commissions when houses turned over but also profited from speculation. Before the BBURG banks stopped the practice in 1969, agents often purchased a property from a frightened white family and resold it within one or two weeks to a black family at twice the price. The city did not step in until 1971, when it passed an anti-blockbusting ordinance.

The rate of racial transition in Mattapan was phenomenal. One white resident said ". . . it became a nightmare. . . . Out of 141 white families on my street, only 7 were left within 2 years." The Wellington and Blue-Hill/Norfolk neighborhoods in Mattapan, which had been 99.9 percent white in 1960, were 48 percent black by 1970 and 85 percent black by 1976.[91]

Although the story of Mattapan is a particularly tragic example of racial transition, similar stories can be told about neighborhoods in several other cities, including Chicago and Detroit, during the 1960s and 1970s. Blockbusting is explicitly outlawed by the 1968 Fair Housing Act, and many communities have passed anti-blockbusting ordinances, such as bans on for-sale signs. Perhaps as a result, the incidence of such dramatic episodes of racial transition appears to have abated. Nevertheless, the potential for exploitation of racial fears remains.

■ INTEGRATION MAINTENANCE AND AFFIRMATIVE HOUSING

With the help of community groups and, in most cases, local governments, several communities have sustained racial or ethnic integration for a long period of time or otherwise eased racial or ethnic tensions in their housing markets. These communities include Oak Park and Park Forest, suburbs of Chicago; Shaker Heights and Cleveland Heights, suburbs of Cleveland; Park Hill in Denver; West Mt. Airy in Philadelphia; Butler Tarkington in Indianapolis; and the 19th Ward in Rochester.[92]

Integration Maintenance and Affirmative Housing Programs

A wide range of programs has been employed to maintain integration and ease racial and ethnic housing conflicts. These programs fall into four broad categories.[93]

The first category consists of programs that improve the flow of information in the housing market:

> *Race-conscious housing counseling by a private or government housing center.* This type of counseling encourages homeseekers to consider moving into neighborhoods where their own racial or ethnic group is not concentrated.

> *Affirmative marketing by real estate brokers.* Marketing of this type, which might be required or encouraged, involves making an effort to inform customers about housing possibilities in neighborhoods

where their own racial or ethnic group is not concentrated and thereby to expand their choices.[94]

Collection and dissemination of racial or ethnic information about neighborhoods by a private or government housing center.[95] The information collected usually includes the racial or ethnic composition of the residents and current homeseekers in various neighborhoods. This information can help to prevent the rumors and misperceptions that often arise in unregulated episodes of racial transition.

Requiring or encouraging notification, to a private or government housing center, of the desire to sell one's house. This policy is designed to ensure that all housing can be included in a program of race-conscious counseling or affirmative marketing before it is sold.

A second category of program is designed to improve neighborhood quality and thereby to offset the common perception that neighborhood quality declines when racial or ethnic transition occurs. This perception may lead whites either to keep minorities out or to leave once minorities start to move in — actions that do not support integration. Programs to break this cycle include:

Programs to maintain housing quality in changing neighborhoods. These programs, which involve strict code enforcement or financial assistance for housing maintenance, are designed to directly counter the perception that racial or ethnic transition inevitably leads to a decline in neighborhood housing quality.

Programs to maintain or even boost public service quality in changing neighborhoods. These programs are intended to reassure residents that the local government is committed to maintaining public service quality in all neighborhoods. Programs to boost school quality may be particularly important because many parents are more concerned about school integration than about neighborhood integration.[96] Programs to boost police protection also can offset the perception that neighborhood transition leads to more crime.[97]

Programs to promote intergroup understanding. Negative perceptions about neighborhood transition and about entering groups also can be addressed directly through educational, recreation, and other programs.

The third category involves programs aimed at preventing behavior that fosters neighborhood transition:

Programs to combat housing discrimination, especially racial and eth-nic steering. Steering and other forms of discrimination by real es-tate agents have the opposite impact of affirmative marketing; that is, they promote segregation. Programs to combat housing discrim-ination therefore can play an important role in promoting integration.

Anti-blockbusting ordinances, such as solicitation bans or the prohibi-tion of for-sale signs. Blockbusting tactics by real estate agents can undercut efforts to maintain integration. Bans on unwanted solici-tation of homeowners by agents and bans on the posting of for-sale signs in front of houses help prevent some of the worst kinds of blockbusting behavior.

The final category of programs provides financial or other incen-tives for individuals to take pro-integrative actions. These programs are designed to offset the reluctance of many households, particularly white households, to move into integrated neighborhoods:

Low-interest loans for households who move into neighborhoods where their group is underrepresented. This approach provides a fi-nancial incentive for households to help maintain an integrated neighborhood. Similar financial incentives can be provided through lower downpayment requirements, tax credits, or rent relief.

Home equity insurance. Many whites believe that house values de-cline when racial transition occurs.[98] Home equity insurance, or assurance as it often is called, is designed to reassure people that they will not lose money even if this belief is correct.

Oak Park

The Chicago suburb of Oak Park has employed most of these tools in its efforts to maintain integration.[99] These efforts began in 1963 when the Oak Park village government established the Community Rela-tions Commission to oversee the real estate industry and the housing market. In 1968, the village passed a Fair Housing Ordinance, which prohibited discrimination and forbade panic selling and unrequested solicitation of homeowners by real estate brokers, as well as requiring licensing of all real estate businesses in the village. Fines and injunc-tive powers gave the ordinance some teeth, and it was later comple-mented by a ban on for-sale signs and a testing program to uncover discrimination. The Commission, which enforced the ordinance, began, with the cooperation of the local real estate community, a race-conscious counseling program in the fall of 1971 and was reorganized into the Community Relations Department of the village government in 1972. The counseling program was complemented by the activities of a private Housing Center, which began operations in 1972, and various other community organizations.

The village's objective was officially expressed in an April 1973 resolution called "Maintaining Diversity in Oak Park." This resolution said, in part, "Efforts to achieve diversity are nullified by the resegregation of neighborhoods from all white to all black. . . . A free and open community — equal and diverse — can only be achieved through dispersal: a mixture of racial and ethnic groups throughout the Village."[100] Throughout the 1970s additional policies were enacted to promote this objective. The village required licensing of apartments along with annual inspections, required reports on the race of occupants, and strengthened code enforcement. It also set up a program to inspect the exterior of owner-occupied housing and suggest repairs to the owners. It made certain that the quality of garbage collection, police protection, and other public services was maintained in integrated neighborhoods. Finally, in 1978 Oak Park set up an "equity assurance plan," "that reimburses residents for up to 80 percent of any losses incurred in the sale of their homes after 5 years."[101] This program was designed to offset white homeowners' fears that they would lose money on their houses if their neighborhood underwent racial change.

These efforts had success for many years, but their long-term impact is not yet clear. Oak Park was 11 percent black in 1980 and increased to 18 percent black by 1990.[102] These figures suggest stable integration, but the white population of Oak Park has declined rapidly, by 24 percent between 1970 and 1980 and by 33 percent between 1980 and 1990. Moreover, despite the city's affirmative marketing program, the tracts on the city's eastern border, which are next to black tracts in Chicago, are all 25–40 percent black. It is not clear, therefore, whether white flight from Oak Park can be slowed in the 1990s.

Shaker Heights and Cleveland Heights

Similar plans were implemented in two Cleveland suburbs, Shaker Heights, a upper-middle-income community, and Cleveland Heights, its middle-income neighbor. In Shaker Heights, community groups devoted to integration arose in response to the bombing of a black resident's home in 1954.[103] These groups gained foundation support and eventually turned to the task of attracting white families into integrated neighborhoods. This same objective was embraced by the city of Shaker Heights, when it established the Shaker Heights Housing Office in 1967.[104]

Meanwhile, community efforts in Cleveland Heights were also triggered by the bombing of a black person's home.[105] The city of Cleveland Heights focused on preventing racial steering by brokers and filed a highly publicized lawsuit against a large real estate company in 1979. The suit contended that this agency steered whites away from Cleveland Heights and blacks to Cleveland and thereby "contributed to the erosion, interference and obstruction of integrated housing opportunities."[106]

From these beginnings, the efforts in these two suburbs expanded to include:

> (1) information dissemination designed to convince blacks that the communities welcomed integration and to convince whites that integration would not lead to racial transition; (2) aggressive enforcement of tough fair-housing laws; (3) stringent housing codes coupled with home maintenance subsidies; (4) enhancement of public service quality (especially education); and (5) housing brokerage services that explicitly attempted to allocate vacancies in ways which created and maintained racial balances in all neighborhoods.[107]

These city and community activities were complemented by a loan program of the Ohio Housing Finance Agency. This program set aside a pool of mortgage money for whites or blacks who moved into neighborhoods where their racial group was underrepresented. By 1991, 115 pro-integrative mortgages were provided, most of them to whites.[108] This program has been followed by similar programs, financed by area foundations, to provide small second mortgages for people who make pro-integrative moves.[109]

Although the racial balance is not the same in every neighborhood, these two communities appear to have achieved relatively stable integration. Shaker Heights went from 13 percent black in 1968 to 29 percent black in 1986 and Cleveland Heights went from 3 to 30 percent black over the same period. The late 1980s brought little additional change; by 1990, the black population share was 31 percent in Shaker Heights and 37 percent in Cleveland Heights.[110]

Conclusion:
When Can Integration Maintenance Succeed?

Although formal evaluations of the effectiveness of these programs, either individually or in combination, have not yet been conducted, several scholars have identified circumstances under which integration maintenance programs do or do not succeed. One recent study identified two "important, but not critical" conditions for the success of an integration maintenance program, and two other conditions that are absolutely necessary.[111] The first two conditions are that the community or neighborhood must have housing quality and neighborhood amenities of sufficient quality to be successfully marketed and that the program must be supported, if not conducted, by local government. These two conditions clearly were met in the cases discussed above.

The second two conditions are the absence of a concentration of public housing in the community and the absence of racially identifiable schools. The presence of public housing seems to promote whites' perception that a community is going to undergo both racial and income transition, thereby making it difficult to prevent white flight. Moreover, the presence of racially identifiable schools appears to encourage white flight by magnifying whites' fears about the extent and nature of impending racial transition.[112] Some cities or neighborhoods have no control over the racial or ethnic character of their schools because they are part of a larger school district. Places that do have control, however, can minimize white fears by making integration as even as possible and by aggressively maintaining school quality.

The Sherman Park area of Milwaukee, which was described at the beginning of this chapter, appears to have faltered on several of these conditions. It was hit by "a school redistricting plan that has resulted in racially identifiable schools, the development of large amounts of publicly assisted housing within the area, the withdrawal of state funding for a prointegrative program, and internal instability of the community organization" that was promoting integration.[113]

Starrett City

The problems and possibilities for integration maintenance are particularly well demonstrated by the story of Starrett City, a large, subsidized, middle-income rental housing project in Brooklyn, New York.[114] This project, which opened in 1974, was built with extensive loans from the New York State Housing Finance Agency. It contains about 15,000 residents in 5,881 apartments and 46 buildings. The developer was Starrett City Associates, an affiliate of the Starrett Housing Corporation, which has built many other housing projects in the New York metropolitan area as well as the Empire State Building.[115]

Starrett City's site has many disadvantages for attracting middle-income households, particularly middle-income whites. Moving clockwise from the southeast, Starrett City is surrounded by landfill mounds, 50 or 60 feet high, which block the view of Jamaica Bay, at least for the lower stories; the wide, polluted Fresh Creek basin, with high, litter-strewn banks; a large junk yard; large housing projects; and a sewage treatment plant. The only pleasant view is to the east, where residents can see the remains of the marsh that once covered the entire site. The housing projects on the northern corner of the site were integrated in 1974 when Starrett City opened, but they are now almost entirely black. The closest projects are for middle-income families, but numerous lower-income projects appear as one moves northward away from Starrett City. Moreover, East New York, one of the poorest black neighborhoods in the city, is located just a few blocks to the north. Canarsie, an all-white, working-class neighborhood, lies to the southwest of Starrett City, but it is separated from the site by the above-mentioned creek. Overall, it is ironic that such an important experiment with integration took place on a site where integration would prove to be so expensive to maintain.

When Starrett City opened in 1974, no whites applied. So the Starrett City management began a three-part strategy to attract whites and maintain integration. The first part was to provide amenities that would make the site more attractive to whites, and in particular to counter whites' perceptions that crime, school decline, and neighborhood deterioration inevitably accompanied racial integration.[116] Starrett City built a large fence around the project, hired a large security force with guard dogs, and placed a large sign at the northern entrance to the project proclaiming its commitment to safety. It convinced the city to build two schools inside the project; constructed parks and playgrounds; hired a large maintenance crew to keep the grounds attractive; built tennis courts, a swimming pool, and a community center; put up a shopping center; and provided an express bus to Manhattan.

The second part of the strategy was an extensive advertising campaign designed to attract whites. Starrett City advertised extensively in white ethnic newspapers, emphasizing its commitment to safety and to neighborhood stability.[117] No comparable advertising campaign was conducted in black neighborhoods. When no whites applied at first, Starrett City altered its construction plans to start at the southern edge, near the Belt Parkway, instead of at the northern edge, nearest East New York.[118] Moreover, it placed a large, welcoming sign at the southern entrance to the project, right by a parkway exit, where it would be seen by thousands of commuters, most of whom were white.[119]

The third, and most controversial, part of the Starrett strategy was to impose a ceiling quota on the number of minority residents, not only within the project as a whole, but also within each building and even on each floor.[120] This quota originally was set at 30 percent minority. Because of the quota, black and Hispanic families made up 9,000 of the 14,000 people on the Starrett waiting list in the early 1980s.[121] A black family on the list could expect to wait 20 months for a two-bedroom apartment, whereas the wait for a white family was only 2 months, on average.

These policies ultimately produced a stably integrated community. As one observer put it: "Starrett City thrives on the paradox of achieving integration by discriminating against blacks."[122] Because the number of white applicants was so low at the beginning, the project filled up slowly, and was not fully occupied for several years. The original ceiling quota was loosened somewhat over time, and by the early 1980s, the project was 65 percent white and 35 percent minority.[123] About three-quarters of the minority residents were black; almost all the rest were Hispanic.

In 1979 five black applicants, with the support of the NAACP, sued Starrett City for discriminating through its quota.[124] Because of its financial involvement with the project, the State of New York also was named as a defendant. After 5 years of litigation, this suit was settled out of court. Starrett agreed to add 175 black families to the project over the next 5 years but did not agree to eliminate its ceiling quota. New York State agreed to ask for voluntary affirmative action programs from the eighty-six projects (involving 69,755 units) funded under the same program as Starrett City. By one estimate, between one-quarter and one-half of these projects were 85 percent or more white.[125] Moreover, Starrett agreed to distribute waiting list announcements from state projects to minorities on the Starrett waiting list. Starrett did not agree to affirmative action programs at any of its own other projects, however, or even to inform minorities on the Starrett waiting list about its vacancies elsewhere.

In June 1984 this settlement was challenged in court by the U.S. Justice Department, on the grounds that it continued to rely on an illegal quota.[126] Lower courts agreed, and the suit eventually went before the U.S. Supreme Court, which ruled in favor of the Justice Department in November 1988.[127] Thus, Starrett City no longer employs a quota of any kind, although it remains committed to maintaining integration.[128] Between 1988 and 1990, the share of whites in Starrett City dropped sharply from 62 to 50 percent. However, the project remained very diverse, as the population share increased from 23 to 26 percent for blacks, from 8 to 16 percent for Hispanics, and from 5 to 8 percent for Asians.[129] It remains to be seen whether Starrett City can find tools to replace its quotas to maintain this degree of racial and ethnic integration.

This case illustrates four key lessons about integration maintenance programs. The first lesson is that racial and ethnic integration can work. Residents of Starrett City consistently give strong support to the integrated nature of their community.[130] Blacks, Hispanics, and whites can learn to live together.

Second, this case shows that the dynamics of neighborhood change and particularly the so-called tipping point are subject to some control and manipulation. Because of its site, Starrett City could not attract any whites when it first opened, but by aggressively altering its amenities and influencing whites' perceptions about the project, Starrett was able to attract many whites, indeed almost two-thirds of its population, into an integrated environment. These steps were facilitated by Starrett City's scale; that is, by the ability of the developer to directly influence such amenities as safety and recreation. More typical neighborhoods with fragmented ownership require community or government organizations to carry out the same steps.

The third lesson from Starrett City is that policies to eliminate discrimination and policies to promote integration sometimes are in conflict with each other. The managers of Starrett City believed that their quota was necessary to maintain integration, but this quota clearly discriminated against blacks on the waiting list. Any policy to maintain integration must address this conflict or find a way to avoid it.

Finally, the Starrett story shows how difficult it is to promote integration in a single neighborhood, even a large one, especially near a low-income minority neighborhood.[131] In the first place, the net impact of Starrett City on integration may have been quite modest because of the white flight it apparently caused from the housing projects immediately to the north. Moreover, all three aspects of the Starrett strategy—the amenities, the advertising, and the quota— were dramatic and expensive. The cost of the quota did not fall on Starrett or its residents, but instead fell on minority applicants; this cost, like the cost of housing discrimination in its other forms, may have been quite high. The original settlement with the state explicitly recognized this issue by making a connection between Starrett City and other comparable housing projects. In other words, the requirement that waiting list applications for these projects be made available to minorities on the Starrett City waiting list was a step, although a limited one, toward removing the cost of the ceiling quota from minority households.[132]

Thus, the great limitation of the original settlement and the tragedy of the subsequent Justice Department suit are that more direct connections were never made, either by the Starrett Corporation or by New York State, between the minority applicants on the Starrett City waiting list and opportunities at other housing projects. Starrett City clearly had (and indeed still has) the power to promote integration without imposing costs on minority applicants by offering such applicants information about available housing at its other projects as well as at state-financed projects. If offering information proved insufficient to induce racial balance on the Starrett waiting list, the Starrett Corporation could demonstrate its commitment to integration by offering moving expenses or a free month's rent or some other inducement to people on any of its waiting lists who were willing to move to other Starrett projects where their racial or ethnic group was underrepresented. The state could take similar steps. In any case, efforts to maintain integration in a single neighborhood face enormous obstacles when blacks and Hispanics do not have information and access to all other neighborhoods and when whites have many all-white neighborhoods to which they can flee.

■ CONCLUSIONS

Discrimination has had, and indeed continues to have, a dramatic impact on urban housing markets.

Blacks and Hispanics are far less likely than whites to own their own homes. The homeownership rate is only 43.4 percent for blacks and 42.4 for Hispanics, compared to 69.1 percent for whites. Moreover, the homes that minorities do own are worth far less than the homes owned by whites, and minorities are much more likely than whites to live in crowded conditions or in deteriorated housing or to face a high rent burden. Overall, discrimination has produced a deficit in net housing wealth of about $414 billion for blacks and $186 billion for Hispanics.

Racial residential segregation continues to be extremely high, especially in metropolitan areas with large black populations. In the average such area, three-quarters of the black population (or of the white population) would have to move to achieve an even population distribution. Hispanics live in less segregated conditions, but in the areas with the largest Hispanic populations, about half of Hispanics (or whites) would have to move for an even population distribution to be achieved.

Using this measure of the evenness of segregation, black–white segregation declined somewhat and Hispanic–white segregation increased slightly during the 1980s. However, black–white segregation increased on other dimensions, such as racial isolation, in many cities, and the number of hypersegregated cities, which are cities highly segregated on at least four of the five dimensions identified by scholars, increased significantly during this period.

Segregation remains high despite frequent neighborhood change because of the predominance of complete racial and ethnic transition: most neighborhoods into which minorities enter eventually become dominated by minorities. This transition is influenced by existing patterns of segregation, continuing discrimination, and racial and ethnic prejudice, all of which influence each other. It is not correct to say that racial and ethnic transition, and hence segregation, is simply the product of white prejudice against living with minorities. After all, white prejudice itself is heavily influenced by group separation and by the intergroup disparities in economic and social outcomes that are the legacy of past discrimination. Moreover, complete neighborhood transition, although common, is not inevitable.

Community organizations, local governments, and the real estate business can either encourage rapid neighborhood transition or promote stable integration. Cities around the country provide examples of both types of response. Communities that have successfully sustained integration over long periods have used a wide range of programs, including "public relations and advertising; education; promotion of sales and rental housing, including the use of financial incentives; liaison with the real estate industry and affirmative marketing; maintenance of the housing stock through zoning, point-of-sale inspections, and code enforcement; fair housing monitoring; commercial redevelopment and revitalization; and school desegregation."[133]

The Impact of Housing Discrimination on Education, Employment, and Poverty

■ THE SYSTEM OF DISCRIMINATION

Proviso West High School was built in Hillside, a western suburb of Chicago, in 1958.[1] Along with Proviso East High School, it draws students from Hillside and nine nearby suburbs, which range from working-class to well-to-do. When Proviso West was built, and indeed up until 1970, these suburbs were, with one exception, 99 percent white. The one exception, Maywood, was 42 percent black in 1970 and represented the beginnings of black movement into the western suburbs. Magnified by widespread housing discrimination in the Chicago area, this movement increased dramatically after 1970.[2] Between 1970 and 1980, the white population in the ten Proviso suburbs dropped by 40 percent and the black population tripled.

At first, this neighborhood racial change had little impact on Proviso West because most minority students in the district were assigned to Proviso East. In 1976, however, at the urging of the federal government, the district voluntarily altered the boundaries for assigning students to high schools. In 1973–1974, 4,500 students attended Proviso West, of whom 98 percent were white. By 1993–1994, the number of students had dropped to 2,300 and only 18 percent of them were white, whereas 56 percent were black and 22 percent were Hispanic.

This change has had a dramatic impact on Proviso West. As in many other cases, the racial and ethnic change has been accompanied by income change. As recently as 1990–1991, only 11 percent of the students came from low-income families; by 1993–1994, this figure had jumped to 19 percent. Moreover, many of the new students at Proviso West had attended distressed elementary schools in the city. Thus, Proviso West has been confronted with more and more students who have poor preparation or serious learning problems. The extremely high unemployment rates for minority youth in Chicago also severely undermine motivation. "Many students see little point in succeeding in school because success in school has no relevance."[3] In one recent semester, 40 percent of students at both high schools had at least one failing grade.

To make matters worse, public support for the schools has fallen off dramatically. Even though whites are now a minority in the schools, they still make up a majority of the population in the district, and all recent referenda to increase the school property tax rate have been defeated. Support also has dropped off at the state level: the state's contribution has declined from 12 percent of the district's budget in 1984 to 7 percent in 1993–1994.

Under these circumstances, integrated schools can do little to promote racial understanding.[4] Racial and ethnic hostility is high and segregation within the school is common, not only in social situations but also in the classroom. A recent honors class in American studies, for example, had fifty-two students, of which seven were black and four Hispanic. As one white student put it, "We don't start out as racist. We are all racist now."[5]

This story illustrates a crucial feature of discrimination in housing: it influences and is influenced by many other spheres of urban life. This chapter explores these lines of influence and, in particular, investigates the connections among housing discrimination, education, employment, and poverty. Together, these phenomena form a system of discrimination.

The framework for this chapter is presented in Figure 8.1, which shows that events in the housing market, including housing discrimination and residential segregation, are linked to outcomes for public schools, to outcomes in the labor market, and to racial and ethnic prejudice.[6] This chapter explores the available evidence on all these lines of influence, which are designated by the arrows in this figure, with an emphasis on the role of housing discrimination. It examines, for example, the connection between housing discrimination and school segregation, the consequences of school segregation for the educational achievement of minority children, and the feedback from these school outcomes to the housing market.

Although Figure 8.1 includes the most important elements of the system of discrimination, neither it nor this chapter as a whole is

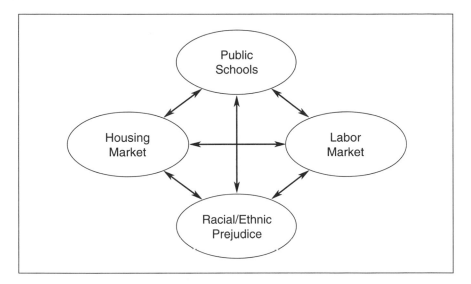

FIGURE 8.1.   Elements of the Discrimination System

intended to be comprehensive.[7] The chapter does not include, for example, any discussion of the links between housing discrimination and housing segregation on the one hand and health care, criminal victimization, or criminal activity on the other.[8] These linkages further reinforce the discriminatory system.

■ HOUSING DISCRIMINATION AND EDUCATION

Racial and Ethnic Disparities in Educational Outcomes

School outcomes traditionally are defined in terms of both attainment and achievement, with attainment measured by years of schooling and achievement by scores on standardized tests. The gap in educational attainment between blacks and whites has closed steadily over time and is now small by historical standards. Nevertheless, a significant gap remains. One survey finds that in 1990 the share of young adults between the ages of 16 and 24 who had not completed high school and were not currently enrolled was 13.2 percent for blacks and 32.4 percent for Hispanics, compared to 9.0 percent for whites.[9] Another survey of people aged 18–21 found 1991 dropout rates of 16.6 percent for blacks, an astonishing 35.1 percent for Hispanics, and 13.9 percent for whites.[10] These results, which are based on national surveys, may understate existing racial disparities, however, because they appear to undercount high school dropouts.[11]

Racial and ethnic disparities in educational achievement have also declined over time, but large gaps remain for tests in many subjects. On tests administered to 17-year-olds in 1990, blacks scored 10.1 percent lower than whites in reading, 6.8 percent lower in mathematics, and 15.9 percent lower in science.[12] The comparable disparities between Hispanics and whites were 7.4 in reading, 8.4 in math, and 13.0 in science.[13] In all of these cases except the science test for blacks, the disparities are smaller than in 1977.[14]

The minority–white test score disparities are even larger for younger children. The 1990 reading disparity for nine-year-olds, for example, was 16.1 percent for blacks and 12.9 percent for Hispanics. To some degree, minority youth may catch up with whites as they move through school, but in 1977 the black–white reading disparity actually was larger for 17-year-olds, 17.1 percent, than for nine-year-olds, 14.4 percent. The reversal of this relationship in 1990 suggests that the black–white test score disparities may rise when the 1990 cohort of 9-year-olds reaches high school.[15] Moreover, these racial and ethnic disparities appear to be much larger in some large cities. Tests administered in the spring of 1994 in New York City public schools found that 70.4 percent of white students, but only 42.7 percent of black students and 36.7 percent of Hispanic students could read at or above their grade level, and that math ability was at or above grade level for 74.0 percent of whites but only 40.6 percent of blacks and 42.5 percent of Hispanics.[16]

School Segregation

Racial and ethnic disparities in educational outcomes are closely linked to the fact that public schools for minorities still are, in many cases, separate and unequal, even though it has been 40 years since the *Brown* v. *Board of Education* decision by the U.S. Supreme Court.

A recent comprehensive report examines the extent of racial and ethnic segregation in the nation's schools.[17] This report measures the share of black and Hispanic students who attend schools with student bodies that are more than 50 percent minority or more than 90 percent minority.[18] By either measure, the level of segregation in 1991–1992 is strikingly high. As shown in Table 8.1, two-thirds of all black and Hispanic students attend schools that are mostly minority, and one-third attend schools in which less than 10 percent of the students are white.

TABLE 8.1 THE PERCENTAGE OF BLACK AND HISPANIC STUDENTS
IN PREDOMINANTLY MINORITY AND 90–100 PERCENT
MINORITY SCHOOLS: 1968–1992

School Year	Predominantly Minority		90–100 Percent Minority	
	Black	Hispanic	Black	Hispanic
1968–69	76.6	54.8	64.3	23.1
1972–73	63.6	56.6	38.7	23.3
1980–81	62.9	68.1	33.2	28.8
1986–87	63.3	75.1	32.5	32.2
1991–92	66.0	73.4	33.9	34.0

SOURCE: Orfield et al. (1993, Table 1).

NOTE: Minority students include blacks, Hispanics, Native Americans, and Asian Americans.

Table 8.1 also reveals that segregation has been increasing during recent years. In fact, earlier declines in segregation for black students have been offset by recent events, and segregation for blacks is back to the level of 1971, the year of the Supreme Court's first busing decision. Segregation for Hispanic students has increased steadily since 1968. The recent increases in segregation reflect demographic changes, a lack of federal school desegregation efforts during the 1980s, and "case law permitting both the abandonment of desegregation plans and return to segregated neighborhood schools under some circumstances. . . . The 1991 Oklahoma decision gave Supreme Court approval to a process of ending desegregation plans that began earlier."[19]

Although school segregation is high throughout the nation, it is highest in the Northeast and lowest in the South and the Border states, "the only regions to face a serious federal enforcement effort."[20] In Illinois, Michigan, New York, and New Jersey, over 50 percent of black students attend schools that are more than 90 percent minority, and over 40 percent of Hispanic students attend such schools in New York, New Jersey, and Texas. Extensive school integration appears to require either metropolitan school districts, as in North Carolina and Virginia, or interdistrict desegregation plans, as in Delaware, Kentucky, and Nevada.

School segregation also differs by type of community, with the highest levels of segregation in large central cities. In fact, in large cities the share of minority students in schools where most of the students are minorities reaches an astonishing 92.4 percent for blacks and 93.8 percent for Hispanics. Levels of segregation are smaller, but still disturbingly high, in smaller central cities, in suburbs, in small towns, and in rural areas. In the suburbs of large central cities, for example, 57.9 percent of blacks and 63.9 percent of Hispanics attend schools in which minorities make up more than half of the student body. The comparable figures for the suburbs of small metropolitan areas are somewhat smaller: 43.0 percent for blacks and 51.4 percent for Hispanics.[21] Thus, for blacks and even more so for Hispanics, moving to the suburbs does not imply moving to integrated schools. Even though blacks and Hispanics are now moving to the suburbs in record numbers, there is little reason to anticipate a movement away from school segregation.[22]

Schools for minority children are not only separate from schools for white children, they often are unequal as well; that is, they provide lower-quality educations.[23] Racial and ethnic disparities in school quality persist because the schools that minority children attend are concentrated in large central cities and often have large concentrations of poor students.

Over half of black and Hispanic school-aged children live in a central city, compared to about one-quarter of whites. This disparity is even greater in the Northeast and Midwest regions, where central cities are the home of about three-quarters of black children, and only in the West do more than one-quarter of black children live in the suburbs.[24] Central cities tend to have lower wealth per pupil and greater service responsibilities than suburbs. At any given property tax rate, therefore, central cities cannot provide as much support for their schools.[25]

Moreover, the relationship between minority composition and poverty concentration in schools is striking. As shown in Table 8.2, 60 percent of largely white schools, which are defined as schools with a student body less than 10 percent minority, draw very few students, below 10 percent, from poor families. In sharp contrast, a majority of the students come from poor families in almost 60 percent of largely minority schools, that is, schools with more than 90 percent minority students. In addition, a "student in an intensely segregated African American and Latino school was 14 times as likely to be in a high poverty school as [was] a student in a school with less than a tenth black and Latino students."[26]

Concentrated poverty clearly has a dramatic impact on a school's ability to deliver a high-quality education. Poor families do not have as many resources as other families to support their children's education, and the family stresses often associated with poverty make it difficult for a child to succeed at school.[27] Schools with many students

TABLE 8.2 THE PERCENTAGE OF SCHOOLS WITH VARIOUS
COMBINATIONS OF MINORITY CONCENTRATION
AND CONCENTRATION OF STUDENTS
FROM POOR FAMILIES: 1992

Percentage of Students from Poor Families	*Percent Minority*					
	0–10	*10–20*	*20–30*	*30–40*	*40–50*	*90–100*
0–10	60.2	46.0	35.8	30.2	28.2	36.2
10–25	22.2	24.8	26.8	18.8	12.4	1.7
25–50	13.6	21.1	29.8	36.7	31.6	5.6
50–100	4.0	4.4	7.6	14.2	22.0	56.5
Addendum: Percentage of all Schools	56.5	9.2	7.0	5.6	4.4	6.0

SOURCE: Orfield et al. (1993, Table 15). This source includes columns for schools between 50 and 90 percent minority, also in 10-percentage-point ranges. None of the
columns omitted here contains more than 3.6 percent of all schools.

NOTE: Minority students include blacks and Hispanics. The percentage of students
from poor families is measured by the percentage of students who receive free lunches.

from poor families must spend more time and resources dealing with
these issues than do other schools and therefore cannot, without additional resources and exceptional leadership, provide comparable educational services.[28] In the Atlanta area, for example, test scores are
directly related to poverty concentration, as measured by the share
of students receiving free lunches. Among the ten high schools with
the highest percentage of students receiving free lunches, the highest
average test score was far below the lowest average test score among
the ten schools with the lowest percentage of students receiving free
lunches.[29] The high concentration of minority students in high-
poverty schools therefore helps to explain the continuing racial and
ethnic disparities in educational outcomes.[30]

Finally, racial and ethnic segregation by itself appears to undermine academic success for minority students. Most researchers agree
that integrating schools leads to modest gains in academic achievement for black children, with no appreciable loss for whites.[31] The
consensus among scholars is that:

Experience in a desegregated class may motivate minority students, giving them hope that they will have an opportunity as adults to escape segregated job markets, that successfully competing in an interracial school
can lead to later life success. Educators and community leaders may hold
higher expectations for achievement for students in integrated schools,

compared to low expectations of minority schools with many low income students.[32]

A recent study in Chicago supports this conclusion; children in black families that moved to the largely white suburbs had lower dropout rates, higher rates of participation in a college preparatory track, and higher college attendance rates than black children in comparable families that moved within the central city.[33]

The Role of Housing Discrimination

Segregation in housing obviously leads to segregation in schools.[34] In most cases, a child must live in a school district in order to attend school there. When minorities and whites live in different places, their children go to school in different places. Thus, the factors that cause segregation in housing, including current and past discrimination in housing, are among the principal culprits in school segregation.

Housing segregation is not the whole story, of course. Segregated public schools can persist even when a school district is integrated if white residents decide to send their children to private schools. Studies of the initial desegregation plans in the South discovered some white flight to private schools, especially when public schools became more than half minority.[35] This response by whites also appears to explain some of the school segregation in the Proviso School District described earlier.

However, there is no evidence that recent increases in school segregation are associated with renewed white flight from public schools. In fact, the share of whites in private schools has actually declined in recent years. There was a 14 percent drop in white enrollment in public schools between 1972 and 1992, but an even larger drop, 18 percent, in white enrollment in private schools.[36] Moreover, private schools still play a relatively small role, even for whites. In 1992, 89 percent of white children, compared to 95 percent of black children and 92 percent of Hispanic children, went to public elementary schools. Even among high-income whites, only one-sixth of the children attended private elementary school, and private school enrollment is even smaller, among all groups, for high school students.

In addition, housing segregation at the neighborhood level does not imply school segregation if students are able to attend schools outside their neighborhood. This possibility arises in two cases. The most common case is when a school district is large enough to include both minority and white neighborhoods. In this case a pupil assignment plan, which might include busing or an intradistrict school choice plan, would give minority children access to largely white schools. North Carolina and Virginia, for example, tend to have large countywide school districts, and both states have several examples of districts that are successfully integrated, such as Charlotte. A countywide school district also has facilitated integration in Las Vegas. A few metropolitan areas, including Louisville and Wilmington, even have consolidated school districts to facilitate this sort of desegregation.[37] School choice plans specifically designed to help foster integration have been implemented in Boston, Cambridge, Kansas City, and Seattle, and a plan enabling a few poor families to send their children to private schools has been operating for 4 years in Milwaukee.[38]

The second case is a desegregation or choice plan that encompasses both minority (typically central city) and white (typically suburban) school districts. City–suburban desegregation plans have been implemented successfully in some cities in North Carolina, and also in Louisville, Wilmington, Indianapolis, and St. Louis.[39] Interdistrict choice plans are rare. A statewide choice plan exists in Minnesota, which has few minority residents, but few parents take advantage of it.[40]

The use of metropolitanwide desegregation plans has been quite limited, however, in large part because the Supreme Court ruled, in the 1974 *Bradley* v. *Milliken* case, that desegregation orders should be limited to a single school district unless it could be shown that specific actions by state or suburban officials were the cause of segregation in the city. Despite the important role that discrimination plays in restricting minority access to suburbs, this standard is difficult to meet, that is, specific actions by government officials are difficult to identify.[41] Because most large central cities have their own school districts, this unfortunate ruling has made it impossible for federal officials to impose metropolitanwide school desegregation orders, which are the only ones likely to be effective in most metropolitan areas. This is particularly true in the states with the most fragmented school systems, including Illinois, Michigan, New York, and New Jersey, which have the highest levels of school segregation.

Feedback from School Outcomes

As illustrated in Figure 8.1, school segregation and racial and ethnic disparities in educational outcomes are causes as well as consequences. Many households select the location of their housing in part on the basis of the perceived school environment there, and many white households avoid locations with integrated or minority schools.[42] Moreover, the appearance of a school identified as "minority" appears to ensure that racial or ethnic neighborhood transition will take place, that is, that whites will leave.[43] In either case, events in the schools act to preserve housing segregation. This effect can be seen even across urban areas; one study found that higher school segregation leads to higher residential segregation.[44]

School integration also can help to promote housing integration. Not only do thoughtful school integration policies ease the fears of white parents, but school integration throughout a city or metropolitan area eliminates the ability of prejudiced white parents to escape integrated schools by moving.[45] Hence, an areawide integration plan can greatly weaken the forces that promote racial or ethnic transition.

An example of the positive influence of school integration policies can be found in Oak Park, Illinois, a Chicago suburb.[46] The Oak Park Board of Education joined the village's desegregation efforts early on with a 1971 "'human dignity' statement, a policy paper affirming the value of cultural diversity and accepting promotion of cultural awareness as a task for the schools."[47] Moreover, the board devoted special programs and curricula for the schools on the east side of the village that were closest to Chicago and had the highest minority representation. In 1976, the board went further and transformed these two schools into junior high schools for the entire village, a plan that "required busing of 1,555 children the first year."[48] Although somewhat controversial, this "plan did aid the community's efforts to achieve residential integration by at least forestalling racial tipping in east Oak Park schools."[49] The board was also determined to maintain educational quality in the high school that served Oak Park and River Forest, a neighboring suburb. This high school, which is now 28 percent black and 4 percent Hispanic, maintains average test scores that exceed the averages at the state, national, and Chicago-area levels.[50]

The case of Yonkers, New York, started out on a very different note. As of the mid-1980s, 27 subsidized housing projects had been built in the city, but with the explicit intention of "creating and maintaining racial segregation in the public schools." All but one of these projects was located in southwestern Yonkers, a largely minority neighborhood.[51] Furthermore, "school district boundaries were gerrymandered to concentrate minorities in schools located in the southwestern district of the city. When blacks attended schools with predominantly white student bodies they were assigned almost exclusively to segregated remedial classes."[52]

In 1985, a U.S. District Court found that school and housing segregation in Yonkers were deliberately promoted by city officials. The Court required the desegregation of the city's schools and ordered the construction of subsidized housing in other parts of the city.[53] Using magnet schools and busing, Yonkers succeeded in desegregating at the school level in only 1 year. As late as 1993, however, the Court still found "vestiges of segregation" in the city's schools, caused in part by school board practices, such as "racial and ethnic segregation within some schools" and "teaching methods that favor upper-middle-class white students."[54]

Racial and ethnic educational disparities also feed directly into the labor market.[55] As demonstrated by dozens of studies, educational attainment is a key determinant of employment status and earnings, and the relative disadvantage of having low skills appears to be growing.[56] Persisting educational disparities help to explain persisting disparities in employment and earnings, which are considered below. Moreover, school segregation itself may undermine job success for minority youth, as it limits both job contacts and skills for succeeding in a white-dominated labor market.[57] One study, for example, found that "black students who were randomly assigned to integrated suburban schools rather than segregated city schools were less likely to have dropped out of high school, gotten into trouble with the police, [or] borne a child before age 18."[58]

Finally, school segregation and racial and ethnic educational disparities help maintain the racial and ethnic prejudice that supports the discriminatory system.[59] The relatively low average educational attainment and achievement of blacks and Hispanics supports the stereotype that blacks and Hispanics are less capable than whites.[60] Moreover, contact between minority and white people, especially when they are young, may be necessary to break down prejudice.[61] Stereotypes and misinformation thrive without personal contact. School integration may not be sufficient to eliminate prejudice, of course, because it sometimes is associated with racial or ethnic tension. The story of Proviso West High School at the beginning of this chapter provides one sad example.[62] Nevertheless, it is difficult to imagine how prejudice will decline without regular, nonhostile contact between children of different racial and ethnic groups. This view is backed up by research: between 1958 and 1972, when most of the desegregation orders were implemented, the share of southern whites who said they would not "have any objection to sending your children to school where half of the children are black" rose from 20 to 66 percent. The 1972 figure was almost as high as the comparable figure, 70 percent, for northern whites.[63]

▌ HOUSING DISCRIMINATION AND EMPLOYMENT

Labor Market Outcomes for Minorities

Throughout the postwar period, the unemployment rate for blacks has been at least twice as high as the rate for whites. Disparities between Hispanics and whites are almost as large.[64] In 1994 the black male unemployment rate, 12.0 percent, was more than twice as high as the white male rate, 5.4 percent; and the Hispanic male unemployment rate, 9.4 percent, was almost twice as high. Unemployment gaps are nearly as large for female workers, with 1994 rates of 11.0 percent for blacks, 10.7 percent for Hispanics, and 5.2 percent for whites.[65] Moreover, these official unemployment rates underestimate the employment gap between blacks and whites because they do not account either for so-called discouraged workers, who have given up actively looking for a job, or for part-time workers.[66]

The employment situation is even bleaker for minority youth. The 1993 unemployment rate was 40.1 percent for black males aged 16–19 and 37.5 percent for black females of the same age.[67] These rates are about 2½ times the rates for comparable white youth. Moreover, after adjusting for black–white differences in labor force participation, the unemployment rate for black youth was at least 3¼ times as large as the rate for white youth in every age category and at every level of education. For high school graduates, for example, the adjusted 1990 unemployment rate was 56.7 percent for black youths without a high school diploma and 31.3 percent for black youths who had graduated from high school. The comparable rates for whites were 16.7 and 7.2 percent.[68]

Per capita income also is substantially lower for minorities than for whites. In 1991 per capita income was $18,807 for blacks and $22,629 for Hispanics, compared to $31,566 for whites. The ratios of black to white per capita income, 0.60, and of Hispanic to white per capita income, 0.72, have not declined at all since 1975.[69] Similar disparities appear in median household income, which was $19,532 for blacks, $22,886 for Hispanics, and $32,960 for whites in 1993.[70]

One of the key questions in interpreting these disparities is whether equally qualified minorities and whites are paid different wages for the same jobs. Until recently, most research answered this question in the affirmative; after accounting for all observable characteristics of workers and jobs, both blacks and Hispanics were paid less than whites. The most recent evidence indicates that this may no longer be true. In fact, one recent study of black men aged 22–29 in 1987 found that black–white differences in years of schooling, achievement test scores, and work experience explained virtually all of the gap between black and white earnings.[71] To put it another way, this study found that blacks and whites with the same education, test scores, and experience would be paid the same wages. This conclusion has been confirmed by three subsequent studies,[72] so the available evidence indicates that current wage discrimination may not be a major cause of continuing minority–white income disparities.[73]

In contrast, recent audit evidence indicates that some employers do discriminate in hiring: they are more likely to hire a white than an equally qualified black or Hispanic.[74] Employment audits are more complicated than housing audits because it is difficult to match audit teammates on all characteristics that employers might consider in making a hiring decision. Because of this complexity, two recent studies carefully selected and extensively trained the auditors and restricted the audits to relatively low-skilled, entry-level jobs, which have relatively simple requirements.[75] These studies discovered that both blacks and Hispanics were significantly less likely than whites to be allowed to complete applications, to be given interviews, or to be offered jobs. Black–white audits were conducted in Chicago and Washington, D.C., where the net incidence of discrimination was 9 and 15 percent, respectively. The Hispanic–white audits found a net incidence of discrimination equal to 27 percent in Chicago and 16 percent in San Diego.

These audit results provide clear evidence of continuing hiring discrimination against minorities, at least in entry-level jobs. This type of discrimination undoubtedly plays an important role in preserving minority–white employment disparities. However, other factors also appear to be at work. As we will see, there is considerable evidence that one of these factors is discrimination in housing.

The Spatial Mismatch Hypothesis

Jobs in metropolitan areas, particularly low-skilled jobs, have been steadily suburbanizing in the United States.[76] The spatial mismatch hypothesis is that housing discrimination restricts the ability of minorities to obtain suburban jobs and therefore is one cause of poor labor market outcomes for minorities.[77] The link between housing

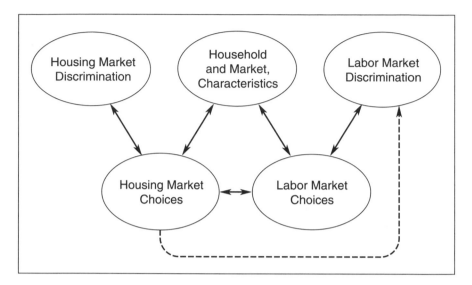

FIGURE 8.2. Elements of the Spatial Mismatch Hypothesis

discrimination and labor market outcomes can operate through several channels. People cannot find jobs without information about them. To the extent that housing discrimination keeps minorities in central cities while jobs are in suburbs, it may be difficult for minorities to find out about job opportunities. Moreover, housing discrimination may make a new job less desirable for a minority than for a white worker because it limits the minority worker's housing options and may force her to select an inadequate house or neighborhood or to deal with a long commute. Another channel involves the demand for labor: housing discrimination helps to maintain all-white areas in the suburbs, where employers may discriminate against minorities to please their predominantly white employees or customers.

The spatial mismatch hypothesis has received a lot of attention because it says that two easy-to-observe features of metropolitan areas, namely residential segregation and job suburbanization, help explain an outcome of great social concern — high minority unemployment rates. It also has proven to be difficult to pin down, however, because, as illustrated in Figure 8.2, it involves complex connections between the housing and labor markets.[78] A household's housing choices, such as whether or not to move and what type of house to buy, are influenced by its characteristics, by the characteristics of the housing market in which it searches for housing, and by housing discrimination.[79] Similarly, a household's labor market choices, such as whether to take a new job, are influenced by its characteristics, by labor market characteristics, and by labor market discrimination. The central idea of the spatial mismatch hypothesis is that housing discrimination spills over from housing choices into labor market choices: because of housing discrimination, minorities make different labor market choices than they otherwise would. This influence begins with the long arrow on the left of Figure 8.2 and then shows up in the short arrow that runs between choices in the housing and labor markets. It also may show up, according to the demand-side version of the spatial mismatch hypothesis, in the dotted line that runs from housing market choices to labor market discrimination: housing choices that lead to residential segregation give employers in white areas an incentive to reject black applicants.

It is therefore not surprising that the empirical findings in the spatial mismatch literature have proven to be difficult to interpret. Some of the evidence is consistent with the spatial mismatch hypothesis but also has other plausible interpretations. For example, several studies have now documented a trend toward higher wages and employment rates for blacks who live in the suburbs than for comparable blacks who live in central cities.[80] This trend might indicate that there are employment opportunities for blacks in suburbs but that their ability to take advantage of them is restricted by housing discrimination. However, it also might indicate that many more blacks, particularly those with high skills and high motivations, are now moving from central cities to suburbs.

Several other studies provide stronger evidence for a spatial mismatch of some sort but do not reveal the channel or channels by which housing discrimination affects labor market outcomes. In general, these studies also do not reveal whether current or past housing discrimination is involved. The following sections explore this evidence concerning spatial mismatches both for minority youth and for minority adults.[81]

Housing discrimination and youth unemployment.   For the most part, teenagers live with their parents and do not make their own housing decisions. As a result, teenagers' housing market choices can be taken as given, and analysis of the spatial mismatch hypothesis is somewhat simpler for youth than for adults. The housing choices of minority teenagers' parents may be constrained, of course, by discrimination. If discriminatory constraints keep some minority households in the central city while jobs are moving to the suburbs, minority teenagers may have poorer access to jobs than do white teenagers. This lack of access could involve both poor information about job availability and extra commuting costs if a job is found.

Two scholars have provided extensive evidence about the spatial mismatch for minority youth in 1980.[82] These scholars find that access to jobs, measured by the average commuting time of low-wage workers who use automobiles, is a key determinant of employment for both minority and white youth. However, the average access to jobs is much higher for whites than for blacks or Hispanics. In fact, differences in job accessibility explain a large portion of the unemployment gap between white and minority youth. In their most comprehensive study, these scholars find that for youth aged 16–19 who were in school, differences in job accessibility explained 27 percent of the black–white unemployment gap and 35 percent of the Hispanic–white unemployment gap. For youths aged 16–19 who were not in school, job accessibility differences explained 21 percent of the black–white unemployment gap and 13 percent of the Hispanic–white gap. The comparable figures for youths aged 20–24 who lived at home were 22 percent for blacks and 26 percent for Hispanics.[83]

Some evidence suggests that job accessibility plays a larger role in the largest cities. In Philadelphia, where unusually good data were available, the poor accessibility of black youth to jobs explained about one-third of the black–white unemployment gap for youth aged 16–19, whether or not they were in school, and for youth aged 20–24 who lived at home.[84] Moreover, the problem of accessibility appears to be particularly large for black men, especially those not in school or not living at home; not only do these young men live in places with poor job accessibility, but a given lack of accessibility has a larger impact on their likelihood of employment than it does on comparable white youth. This additional factor explained another half of the black–white unemployment gap for these young men. Finally, job accessibility not only influences employment prospects, it also undermines the incentives of young black men to stay in school. In fact, if blacks had the same access to jobs as whites, the black–white difference in school enrollment rates might be cut in half.[85]

Overall, these results provide strong confirmation of the view that a lack of access to jobs is one of the key explanations for high unemployment among minority youth.[86] Although these studies do not directly show that housing discrimination is a cause of minority youths' poor job accessibility, the circumstantial evidence in support of this point is very strong. Dozens of studies find that job accessibility is a desirable feature of a residential location, and housing discrimination clearly results in poorer housing outcomes for minority than for white families.[87] Blacks are more centralized than comparable whites, for example, an outcome that places blacks relatively far from rapidly suburbanizing jobs.[88] These studies do not establish, however, the extent to which current, as opposed to past, housing discrimination is at work.

The spatial mismatch for adults.   Studies of the spatial mismatch for adult workers require complex data sets and clever methodology. As shown in Figure 8.2, a spatial mismatch cannot be isolated without accounting for all the factors that influence housing choices and labor market choices. Moreover, household choices across locations cannot be compared without accounting for differences in wage rates, housing prices, and commuting distances. Workers may accept lower wages at one work site than another, for example, if selecting that work site allows them to buy equivalent housing at a lower price or makes it possible for them to live closer to work.

One study takes advantage of a unique data set that indicates the racial composition of the workforce and the geographical location for samples of firms in Chicago and Los Angeles in 1974 and 1980.[89] In both cities, the black employment share fell steadily with distance from largely black neighborhoods. In Chicago in 1980, for example, moving 20 miles from the black ghetto was associated with a 19.4 percentage point drop in the black employment share, after accounting for other firm characteristics. Moreover, distance from the black ghetto also helped explain the change in a firm's black employment; firms located farther from the ghetto experienced greater declines in their black employment share between 1974 and 1980.

These results clearly reveal some kind of spatial mismatch, but they do not indicate the specific role played by housing discrimination. They are consistent both with the demand-side view that employers in white areas discriminate against black applicants and with the supply-side view that due to poor information or housing discrimination black workers do not apply for jobs in white areas. In addition, they are consistent with an even more complicated spatial mismatch in which residential segregation leads to educational disparities between blacks and whites and hence to a skill disparity between the residents of largely white and largely black areas. In this case employers requiring the highest skilled workers locate farthest from the black ghetto.[90] Residential segregation is implicated in all of these cases, but the study cannot isolate the role of current housing discrimination.[91]

Another study estimates households' decisions to move and to change jobs using a national sample for 1983–1984 and the framework in Figure 8.2 (without the dotted line).[92] This study is able to directly observe the interaction between housing and labor market choices, which is at the heart of the mismatch idea, by determining how joint decisions to move and change jobs differ from decisions to move and change jobs taken separately.[93] Not only are blacks less likely to move and less likely to change jobs than are comparable whites in comparable locations, but blacks are also significantly less likely than whites to make a joint move and job change even after accounting for their propensity to take these two steps separately. This is clear, direct evidence that the racial dimension of housing market outcomes spills over into the labor market.[94]

This study also finds that the racial dimension of joint moves can be almost entirely explained by the fact that the black population is more centralized than the white population, an outcome that is due in large part to housing discrimination.[95] Like previous research, however, this study cannot determine whether the observed mismatch is due to past or current discrimination.

The Gautreaux and Special Mobility Programs.   No discussion of the spatial mismatch hypothesis would be complete without a discussion of several programs that directly address its consequences. The first program, called the Gautreaux Program, grew out of a lawsuit filed in 1966 against the Chicago Housing Authority (CHA) and HUD.[96] The plaintiffs were public housing tenants who argued that CHA discriminated both in the selection of sites, with a strong tendency to place projects in largely minority neighborhoods, and in the placement of tenants, with a strong tendency to place minorities only in minority projects. Courts agreed with the plaintiffs, and on various appeals, HUD and CHA were ordered to cooperate and to find a metropolitanwide solution to the segregation in the public housing system. In April 1976 the Supreme Court ruled for the plaintiffs and ratified the call for a metropolitanwide solution.

Two months later, the parties in the case announced an agreement, called the Gautreaux Assisted Housing Program, which was to be administered by a local fair housing group. Under this program, Section 8 rental certificates were offered to CHA tenants (or those on the CHA waiting list) to help them gain access to housing throughout the metropolitan area, and in particular to largely white neighborhoods. The program also involved landlord outreach and participant counseling.[97] This program was originally conducted as a HUD demonstration project; in 1981 it was renewed as a consent decree and has been operating ever since.

Since its inception in 1976, the Gautreaux Program has assisted about 5,600 families, virtually all of them African Americans, in finding housing at a cost of about $1,000 per family. About half of the participating families end up moving to the suburbs. Judging by the 10,000 to 15,000 calls received by applicants for the program's annual 2,000 slots (which are whittled down to 325 participants), the program is very popular.[98] A recent analysis of the outcomes of this program reveals that participants who moved to the suburbs were more likely to have a job than participants who stayed in the central city.[99] Another study that tracked children in Gautreaux families found a higher likelihood of attending college, higher employment rates for those not attending college, higher wages, and higher job benefits for children in families that moved to the suburbs than in families that moved within the city.[100] This evidence is consistent with the view that a lack of access to suburban jobs, due in part to current and past housing discrimination, helps explain minority–white employment disparities.

Similar programs now exist in Cincinnati, Dallas, Hartford, Memphis, Omaha, Parma (Ohio), and Yonkers.[101] All of them were created by consent decrees or (in the case of Hartford) negotiated agreements under threat of litigation. The program in Cincinnati, called the Special Mobility Program (SMP), was created by an out-of-court settlement between HUD and the Cincinnati Housing Authority in 1984. This decree expired in 1990, but the program continues to operate on a voluntary basis. The program, which is operated by a local fair housing group, relies on Section 8 housing certificates and helps about 40 families a year.[102] The families must move into integrated census tracts. By 1994, 723 households had participated and about one-quarter of these households had moved out of Cincinnati. Virtually all of the participating families are African American.

A recent evaluation of SMP finds a high level of satisfaction among participants and a cost similar to that of the Gautreaux Program, namely, $1,080 per family.[103] Moreover, participants have significantly higher levels of employment and earnings than people who remain in public housing. For example, participants' average wage rate after moving was $5.86 per hour, compared with their average of $4.93 before joining the program and a $4.89 average for a random sample of public housing residents.

Feedback from Labor Market Outcomes

As illustrated in Figure 8.1, labor market outcomes have important feedback effects on housing markets, schools, and attitudes. Racial and ethnic income disparities play a role in maintaining residential segregation because people with different incomes tend to live in different places.[104] Moreover, there is mounting evidence that many minority youth are discouraged from working hard or even continuing in school because they do not think they can find a job, even with a high school degree. This discouragement factor was seen in the Proviso West story and has been documented by several studies.[105] Finally, labor market disparities support the stereotype that blacks and Hispanics are less capable or less motivated.[106] This stereotype is part of the foundation for racial and ethnic prejudice.

◼ HOUSING DISCRIMINATION AND POVERTY

Racial and Ethnic Disparities in Poverty Rates

The continuing power of the system of discrimination is clearly revealed in poverty rates. In 1993 the poverty rate was 33.1 percent for blacks and 30.6 percent for Hispanics, compared to only 12.2 percent for whites.[107] These disparities are particularly striking for children; the 1992 poverty rate was an astonishing 46.3 percent for black children, 38.8 percent for Hispanic children, and 16.0 percent for white children.[108] Thus, a black child is almost three times as likely to be in poverty as a white child.

The Neighborhood Dimension of Poverty

The first link between housing discrimination and poverty arises because an individual's success in life may be influenced by the characteristics of her neighborhood. In particular, people who live in distressed neighborhoods may have a difficult time breaking out of poverty. This concept, which was popularized by a 1987 book called *The Truly Disadvantaged,* is the subject of a great deal of recent research.[109] But most of this research ignores the role of housing markets and of residential segregation despite the fact that concentrated poverty and distressed neighborhoods are housing market outcomes.[110] Poor people do not live together by chance: they are concentrated by the operation of the housing market, including the forces that lead to residential segregation, such as housing discrimination.[111] It follows that a link between living in a distressed neighborhood and being poor implies a link between housing discrimination and poverty.

Although the evidence about the link between neighborhood characteristics and individual outcomes is somewhat mixed and the precise role of neighborhoods has proven to be difficult to identify, a consensus that neighborhood effects are significant is beginning to emerge.[112] Several studies have found, for example, that after accounting for her own and her family's characteristics, an individual's educational achievement is greater if she lives in a less distressed neighborhood. The measures of distress in these studies include the male unemployment rate, the share of female-headed or welfare-dependent families, and the share of managerial or professional workers. Other studies find that various employment outcomes are worse for people who live in neighborhoods with a high concentration of poor families, unemployed males, or welfare recipients, again after accounting for personal and family traits.[113]

One careful recent study observes men aged 25–32 in a representative sample of families in 1983.[114] This study examines the impact on economic outcomes, namely earnings, wage rate, and hours worked, of disadvantage in a person's zip code, as measured primarily by the percentage of the population on welfare.[115] The authors are able to control for a wide range of background characteristics, both of the young man and of his family. In a family with no welfare income, moving from a zip code with no welfare recipients to one in which one-fifth of the population receives welfare is associated with a 30 percent drop in the son's hourly wage and a 19 percent drop in his earnings. The neighborhood effects are considerably smaller for families with substantial welfare income. "[E]ven after controlling for other observable family and community characteristics, the presence of *either* family welfare receipt or a high community participation rate is associated with negative outcomes (although the combination of the two does not make matters much worse than they are with either one alone)."[116]

Several scholars have also explored the role of racial and ethnic residential segregation in the concentration of poverty.[117] Because minorities have higher poverty rates than average and because different income classes are not perfectly segregated from each other, either for minorities or whites, racial and ethnic segregation implies that minorities will be sorted into neighborhoods that inevitably are poorer, on average, than neighborhoods for whites. One careful simulation reveals, for example, that if the overall minority poverty rate is 20 percent, moving from no residential segregation to a level of segregation typical of most large cities would raise the poverty rate of the neighborhood in which the typical poor minority household lives from 25 to 35 percent.[118] With an overall minority poverty rate of 30 percent, moving from no to high segregation would boost the poverty rate experienced by the typical poor family even more, from 30 to 45 percent.

Not surprisingly, therefore, the actual concentration of poverty tends to be much higher in the neighborhoods where poor black families live than in those where poor whites live, with intermediate outcomes for Hispanics. In sixty large urban areas in 1980, for example, the typical poor black family lived in a neighborhood with a poverty rate of 29.7 percent, and the typical Hispanic poor family's neighborhood povery rate was 23.5 percent, compared to a neighborhood poverty rate of 13.7 percent for the typical poor white family. The difference was even more striking in hypersegregated cities, where the neighborhood poverty rate was 33.2 percent for the typical poor black family and only 12.8 percent for the typical poor white family.[119] Moreover, the poverty concentration among blacks in some cities has been exacerbated by federal housing policies that have placed large public housing projects in largely minority neighborhoods and filled these projects with poor minority households.[120]

Overall, therefore, existing research supports the view that housing discrimination has a significant impact on poverty among black and Hispanic families. Current and past housing discrimination are among the key causes of racial and ethnic residential segregation. This residential segregation, in turn, plays an important role in boosting the rate of poverty in the neighborhood where the typical poor minority family lives. With this concentration of poverty comes concentrated distress, in the form of high unemployment and extensive welfare dependency. Finally, regardless of an individual's own or family characteristics, living in a distressed neighborhood raises the likelihood that he or she will experience poor academic achievement, unemployment, and other outcomes associated with poverty.

The Direct and Indirect Impact of Housing Discrimination on Poverty

The linkage between housing discrimination and poverty has also been addressed at a more abstract level. In an ambitious series of studies conducted over the last few years, one scholar has made the best use of available data to estimate all the connections, direct and indirect, illustrated in Figure 8.1.[121] The most recent version of this work, which applies to a sample of fifty-nine metropolitan areas in 1980, simultaneously explores the determinants of black residential centralization, interracial residential exposure, class segregation among blacks, school segregation, black school dropout rates, and black poverty. Explanatory variables in the analysis include measures of racial prejudice (indirectly based on surveys) and of housing discrimination (indirectly based on audit results). The analysis finds, for example, a strong simultaneous linkage between black poverty rates and black school dropout rates, examples of the two-way arrow on the upper right of Figure 8.1. In addition, it finds evidence to support the view that housing segregation has a direct impact on poverty. Other results support several of the other arrows in Figure 8.1.

This analysis provides strong evidence that once all the channels in Figure 8.1 are accounted for, both current and past housing discrimination lead to higher poverty rates for blacks. In particular, considering all the indirect connections, a 1 percent increase in the current incidence of housing discrimination in either the sales or rental market is found to boost the black poverty rate by 0.07 percent.[122] This impact on black poverty is about two-thirds as large as the impact of a 1 percent increase in the school failure rate. This analysis also implies that if all current housing discrimination were eliminated, the black poverty rate would fall by 14 percent.[123] The legacy of past discrimination, as measured by low black–white exposure rates, high black centralization, school segregation, and high black failure rates, also contributes significantly to black poverty.

In many ways, this research provides a fitting summary for this chapter because it draws together the many elements of the system of discrimination. It provides strong evidence concerning some of the key linkages in this system and establishes that many of the outcomes in this system influence each other. Moreover, it is broadly consistent with the less aggregated research reviewed earlier, and it explicitly shows the link between housing discrimination and poverty. This study raises complex methodological and data issues, and the magnitudes it estimates should be taken as very rough guides until confirmed by further research.[124] Nevertheless, it provides the most direct evidence now available that current housing discrimination is one of the key causes of relatively high poverty rates among minority families.

■ CONCLUSIONS

The discriminatory system is a central feature of urban areas in the United States. No one can hope to understand the relatively poor outcomes for minorities in school and in work without examining this system. A vast body of research documents the mutually reinforcing connections among the elements of this system.

Because a household's access to public schools is directly tied to its residential location, any factor that influences residential choices, including discrimination, has a direct impact on access to schools. Central city schools and schools in poorer jurisdictions tend to be of poorer quality than suburban schools, particularly those in high-income suburbs. The fact that discrimination in housing contributes to residential segregation, and to segregation with a centralized pattern, therefore implies that discrimination restricts minority households' access to high-quality schools. The causation runs in both directions, of course: whites' concerns about integration in schools is a principal support for continuing discrimination in housing.

Discrimination in housing also has an important influence on labor market outcomes, both directly and indirectly through its impact on education. For teenagers, the direct impact operates through the residential choices made by their parents. If discrimination restricts their parents' housing choices in suburban areas, minority teenagers have limited access to suburban jobs. For adults, the connection between housing and labor markets is more complex but has been carefully explored by recent research on the spatial mismatch hypothesis. This research finds that current and past housing discrimination restrict the access of minority workers to suburban jobs.

To the extent that housing discrimination leads to lower educational attainment for minorities, it also affects labor markets indirectly. Moreover, labor market discrimination, which leads to lower incomes for minorities than for whites, influences housing market outcomes, and in particular limits minority households' access to more desirable neighborhoods. Labor market outcomes also feed back to schools: high unemployment rates for young black and Hispanic men discourage many students and help keep minority dropout rates so high.

Finally, racial and ethnic disparities in housing, schooling, and employment all feed the stereotypes on which racial and ethnic prejudice is built. Prejudice against minorities thrives when minorities and whites tend not to live together and when minorities achieve less success than whites, on average, in school and in work. Moreover, prejudice feeds back into the system; as we will see, prejudice is a key cause of discrimination by landlords, real estate agents, lenders, and others.

CURES:
PUBLIC POLICY
TO COMBAT
DISCRIMINATION

The Causes
of Discrimination
in Housing

In a survey of ninety real estate brokers on the south side of Chicago in 1955–1956, two-thirds of the respondents were "firmly convinced that they would suffer harmful consequences" if they sold a house to a black household in a white neighborhood. "One group stressed business consequences only, and a larger group spoke only of social consequences, but most mentioned both."[1] One-third of the brokers in another survey in San Francisco in the late 1950s felt that "there is a sizeable threat to the business of the broker who is thought to have arranged" a sale to a black in a white neighborhood.[2] Moreover, a 1972 survey of real estate brokers in the New York metropolitan area concluded that "The white community is the source of almost all their business and brokers fear that many whites would not give listings to agencies that show homes to blacks."[3]

Discrimination has now been illegal for over 25 years, and brokers are no longer so willing to discuss their discriminatory behavior. Moreover, since these surveys were taken, white prejudice has declined; the real estate business has changed considerably, with expansion in the use of multiple listing services and franchises; and discrimination by brokers has become less widespread and more subtle. Nevertheless, evidence from the Housing Discrimination Study (HDS) and other audit studies demonstrates that discrimination by real estate brokers is still influenced by economic factors. Although the evidence is more limited, a similar conclusion appears to apply to landlords and loan underwriters. Discrimination in housing and mortgage markets is not caused simply by the bias of housing agents and lenders.[4]

Audits provide a unique opportunity not only to measure discrimination in housing but also to determine the circumstances under which it occurs. Although characterizing these circumstances is difficult because of the many factors involved, audit data can shed light both on the causes of discrimination and on antidiscrimination policy. Since the most basic type of discrimination with the most obvious consequences for minority households is the denial of access to available housing units, this chapter will concentrate on discrimination in the number of housing units actually shown to a customer.[5]

▇ CONSTRAINTS AND INCENTIVES

Discriminatory behavior by a housing agent is constrained by his opportunity to discriminate and influenced by the locational and other attributes of the transaction.

The Opportunity to Discriminate

Perhaps the most crucial factor influencing discrimination in housing availability is the agent's opportunity to discriminate. Agents cannot discriminate unless they have the opportunity to do so; that is, unless they have access to some housing units available for sale or rental. Moreover, the extent to which they can discriminate depends on the number of available units. The analysis presented here focuses on the concept of marginal discrimination, which is the extent to which the difference between the number of units shown to white and minority customers increases when another unit becomes available.[6]

The concept of marginal discrimination may seem a bit abstract, but it has a simple, straightforward interpretation. When another housing unit becomes available, it is either shown to both audit teammates, shown only to the white, or shown only to the minority.[7] If it is shown to both teammates, it has no impact on discrimination in the number of units shown; but if it is shown only to the white teammate, measured discrimination increases by one unit; and if it is shown only to the minority teammate, measured discrimination decreases by one unit. Hence, marginal discrimination is simply the probability that an additional unit is shown only to the white auditor minus the probability that it is shown only to the black auditor.

A value for marginal discrimination equal to one indicates that agents always take advantage of the opportunity to discriminate against minorities, whereas a value of minus one indicates that additional units are all reserved for minority customers. A value of 0.5 implies that the probability of an additional unit being shown to whites is 50 percentage points higher than the probability it will be shown to minorities; the probability could be 60 percent for whites compared to 10 percent for minorities, for example. Moreover, when marginal discrimination equals 0.5, adding one available unit increases the difference in units shown to whites and minority customers by 0.5 units, and adding 4 available units increases this difference by $(0.5)(4) = 2.0$ units.

The concept of marginal discrimination applies to advertised units as well as to units similar to the advertised unit. Most of the time, only one advertised unit was inspected, but multiple advertised units were inspected in 143 of the black–white sales audits and 132 of the Hispanic–white sales audits. These cases correspond to developments, to condominiums, or to agents who advertise housing types instead of individual houses. In the rental market, an advertisement often applies to more than one apartment in a building or development, but for reasons outlined below, the number of advertised apartments cannot be determined with precision.

Estimating marginal discrimination requires a count of the number of units available in each audit. HDS data make it possible to observe the number of both advertised and similar units inspected by either auditor. In the sales audits, address information on each unit inspected can be used to count the total number of units available, accounting for units shown to both auditors.[8] Because of seriously incomplete address information, however, this matching process is not feasible for the rental audits. As a result, the total number of units available is approximated by the maximum of the units shown to either the white or minority auditor.

Locational Incentives in the Sales Market

Many locational factors influence a real estate agent's decision to take advantage of an opportunity to discriminate. The first such factor is the location of his office. An agent whose office is located in a white neighborhood is likely to derive most of his business from white clients, and he has an economic incentive to protect his reputation with whites.[9] Because many whites are prejudiced, this agent's reputation among whites—and hence his business prospects—may be damaged if he sells to a black or Hispanic household.[10] This type of action may also damage his reputation among other brokers who work in that community and thereby lead to a lack of cooperation from them.[11]

The incentives of real estate agents with offices in integrated neighborhoods are not so clear. If integration is stable at a low minority composition or if the neighborhood has stable, largely white areas near integrated areas, a housing agent may still expect most of his business to come from white clients. In this case, agents in integrated neighborhoods have the same incentives as do agents in white neighborhoods; namely, incentives to discriminate. But if racial or ethnic transition is taking place or integration is perceived to be unstable, causing agents to expect that most of their future customers will be minorities, then the agents' incentives to discriminate disappear. Indeed, because real estate agents' incomes come from commissions, they have an incentive to encourage turnover by selling to minority households in neighborhoods where racial or ethnic transition has begun or is anticipated.

Agents located in largely minority neighborhoods may not have incentives to discriminate, particularly in the rental market. However, few real estate brokers, even those located in minority neighborhoods, specialize in minority neighborhood sales, so brokers in minority neighborhoods may also look to please white customers who do not live near their offices.[12]

This analysis must also consider the role of a multiple listing service (MLS). An MLS gives a real estate agent access to units far from his office and far from the customers his personal contacts are likely to attract. To some degree, this breaks the link between office location and incentives to discriminate. The incentive to protect personal contacts might also be weaker in a larger, more established real estate firm than in a smaller one. However, an MLS may increase an agent's opportunity to discriminate because it may provide the agent with access to units in largely white neighborhoods, which can be reserved for white customers. This effect is most likely to be observed when the units available to the agent through his own contacts are concentrated in integrated or minority neighborhoods.

An agent's incentives may also be affected by the location of the available housing units. In their attempts to please customers, agents may attribute different neighborhood preferences to customers from different racial or ethnic groups.[13] Following widely available survey evidence about preferences, for example, agents may assume that white customers prefer not to live in integrated or minority neighborhoods and that black or Hispanic customers prefer not to be pioneers in largely white areas. If so, agents may perceive that they will save time if they do not show houses in integrated or minority neighborhoods to whites or houses in white neighborhoods to blacks or Hispanics.

An alternative explanation for discrimination in largely white areas is that white homeowners refuse to sell to blacks or Hispanics.[14] In this case, a real estate agent may believe that he is saving himself and his minority customers both time and trouble by not showing them houses owned by whites. Although some white sellers may indeed behave this way, most houses are now sold through an MLS or some other cooperative listing arrangement, and the broker who brings the buyer to the transaction often has not even met the seller. Unless the brokers participating in an MLS have a tacit agreement to follow the wishes of white sellers and some subtle mechanism for communicating these wishes, seller preferences cannot be the driving force behind agent discrimination.[15]

Finally, an agent's incentives may be different for the advertised housing units about which auditors inquire than for similar units that are available. The inquiry signals that the unit appears acceptable to the customer and thereby overrides, to some degree, the agent's perceptions about customer preferences.[16] Moreover, agents may be less likely to advertise housing units they do not want to sell to minorities; after all, advertisements can be read by anyone. An agent may be able to stall or mislead a customer about an advertised unit, but it is clearly more difficult to withhold information about a unit that has been advertised than about a unit whose availability is known only to the agent.

An agent's incentives concerning advertised units may depend on whether similar units are available outside minority neighborhoods; an agent may be less likely to withhold an advertised unit from minority customers, for example, when he can reserve similar units in white neighborhoods for white customers. Similarly, an agent's incentive to withhold units similar to the advertised unit may depend on whether the advertised unit or units are still available and are located outside minority neighborhoods.

The distinction between advertised and similar units complicates the notion of marginal discrimination. To begin, this distinction suggests that adding another advertised unit may have a different impact on discrimination than adding a similar unit. Moreover, agents may change their behavior toward advertised units when another unit similar to the advertised unit becomes available (or vice versa).[17]

The HDS audits make it possible to explore all of these possibilities. In particular, the HDS data make it possible to estimate the magnitude of marginal discrimination both for the advertised unit and for units similar to the advertised unit and to determine how marginal discrimination varies with the racial or ethnic composition of both the agent's neighborhood and the neighborhoods in which available housing is located.

Locational Incentives in the Rental Market

Rental agents face a somewhat different set of locational incentives to discriminate; they do not depend so heavily on developing contacts in a community, but they must deal with their customers for longer periods of time.

The principal incentives facing a rental agent operate at the level of an apartment building. In particular, an agent with an all-white building may induce his prejudiced white tenants to leave if he rents to minorities. The resulting turnover will boost his costs for credit checks, apartment cleaning, and apartment repair. If the exodus of whites is rapid, it also may result in longer vacancies and an associated loss of rent. These extra costs give rental agents with prejudiced white tenants a strong incentive to discriminate.[18] A rental agent may also assume that white auditors prefer white buildings in white neighborhoods and minority auditors prefer integrated or minority buildings in integrated or minority neighborhoods. Moreover, the location of a rental agent's office may reveal something about his own preferences, with the most prejudiced agents avoiding minority or even integrated areas.

Many of the rental agents encountered in HDS are themselves owners of the advertised apartments. When the roles of owner and agent are separated, however, rental agents, like real estate brokers, may sometimes discriminate to accommodate a prejudiced owner. In fact, rental agents have a stronger incentive to behave in this way than do real estate brokers. The rental market has no analog to a multiple listing service, and a rental agent is likely to know the racial preferences of the owners he serves and may discriminate to retain his prejudiced white owners. Although no formal study of this possibility has been conducted, anecdotal evidence suggests that many rental agencies explicitly record and act on the racial and ethnic preferences of their owner clients.[19] In short, intermediaries are less common in the rental market than in the sales market but, when they exist, are more likely to meet the discriminatory wishes of white owners.

The HDS data provide information about minority composition at the neighborhood scale but not at the scale of an apartment building. Moreover, rental offices are often located in the same apartment building as the advertised unit. As a result, locational incentives to discriminate are more difficult to untangle in the rental market than in the sales market. Nevertheless, the racial or ethnic composition of an apartment building is positively correlated with the racial or ethnic composition of the surrounding neighborhood, so some of these incentives may show up at the neighborhood scale. When a rental agent's office is located in a different neighborhood than his available apartments, it also may be possible to separate the incentives associated with office location from those associated with apartment location.

As in the case of the sales audits, some insight into locational incentives can be gained by determining the extent to which marginal discrimination varies with both the location of the agent's office and the location of the available unit. The analysis presented here predicts that marginal discrimination will be higher when the agent's office or the available units or both are located in largely white neighborhoods, although high marginal discrimination also may be observed in integrated areas in some cases. Marginal discrimination may also depend on whether some of the available apartments are the ones about which the auditor has inquired.

Other Incentives to Discriminate

Not all of an agent's incentives are associated with neighborhood composition. Three other types of incentive have been explored in the literature. First, an agent may have a stronger incentive to discriminate against minority households with characteristics most likely to upset their potential white neighbors (and hence the agent's potential white customers).[20] Because prejudiced whites often are more upset about school integration than about residential integration, one such characteristic is the presence of children in the household. In addition, minority neighbors appear to be less threatening to whites in high-income or high-wealth neighborhoods, where minority demand for housing is limited. Thus, marginal discrimination may be lower when the value or rent of the advertised unit or the associated assigned income is higher.

Second, in order to conserve his own effort, an agent may not provide as much assistance to households he believes will not be able to obtain financing.[21] Minority households who are highly overqualified for a mortgage, whose income is far higher than needed to buy the house in question, may encounter less discrimination than those with lower incomes. This effect may be difficult to distinguish, however, from the link between house value or income and the preferences of potential white neighbors.

Third, agents may discriminate because of their own prejudice.[22]

Although no direct measure of agent prejudice is available, several observable factors can be associated with agent prejudice. The most obvious factor is the agent's own race or ethnicity. Compared to white agents, black agents are less likely to be prejudiced against black customers and Hispanic agents are less likely to be prejudiced against Hispanic customers. A finding that marginal discrimination is lower when the agent is black or Hispanic, therefore indicates that, to some degree, agent prejudice is at work.[23] In addition, prejudiced agents may prefer to deal with minority females than with seemingly more threatening minority males. In the case of auditors playing the role of a spouse, this preference can be isolated from the preferences of potential white neighbors; a housing agent may prefer to deal with females, but potential white neighbors cannot possibly know or care whether the husband or wife of a minority couple does the house hunting. Thus, a finding that marginal discrimination is higher when the "wife" does the shopping also would indicate the impact of agent prejudice.[24]

∎ THE GEOGRAPHY OF DISCRIMINATION IN THE SALES MARKET

An exploration of these possibilities in the HDS sales audits reveals several key patterns in the geography of discrimination.

First, when no units similar to the advertised unit are available outside of minority neighborhoods, marginal discrimination for advertised units is not affected by neighborhood factors. In other words, one cannot reject the view that marginal discrimination is the same regardless of the racial or ethnic composition of the neighborhood in which either the agent's office or the advertised unit is located. This result, which applies to both the black and Hispanic audits, indicates that agents tend to advertise only those units that they are willing to show to anyone.

Second, when units similar to the advertised unit are available outside of minority neighborhoods, the contribution of neighborhood factors to marginal discrimination for advertised units sometimes is negative; that is, in some neighborhood settings additional advertised units are more likely to be reserved for minorities than for whites. This result is presented in Table 9.1. For both blacks and Hispanics, marginal discrimination is negative when both the agent's office and the advertised unit are located in an integrated neighborhood. In other words, agents with offices in integrated areas who have a variety of houses to sell tend to advertise the units they prefer to sell to minor-

TABLE **9.1** MARGINAL DISCRIMINATION FOR ADVERTISED UNITS
WHEN SIMILAR UNITS ARE AVAILABLE
IN WHITE NEIGHBORHOODS: SALES AUDITS

Type of Neighborhood in which Average Advertised Unit Is Located	Type of Neighborhood in which the Agent's Office Is Located		
	White	Integrated	Minority
Black–White Audits			
White	0.317**	−0.119	[a]
Integrated	−0.087	−0.537**	[b]
Black	[b]	[a]	[a]
Hispanic–White Audits			
White	−0.287**	−0.794**	[a]
Integrated	−0.331	−0.644**	[b]
Hispanic	[b]	−1.011	[a]

NOTES: Based on Appendix Tables A.4 and A.5. Two asterisks indicate significance at the 5 percent level (two-tailed), and one asterisk indicates significance at the 10 percent level. A white neighborhood is defined as less than 10 percent minority, an integrated neighborhood as 10 to 75 percent minority, and a minority as more than 75 percent minority. The significance indicators refer solely to the coefficients of the neighborhood variables, but the values in the table correct for the estimated impact of other variables on marginal discrimination, evaluated at the mean value of each variable.

[a]No audits observed in this cell.
[b]Only one audit in this cell; marginal discrimination cannot be estimated.

ities. In the case of Hispanics, this tendency appears even when the advertised unit or units are in white neighborhoods, and, although the results are less significant statistically, it sometimes appears when the agent's office is in a white neighborhood.[25]

These negative values for marginal discrimination support the view that agents indeed do tend to advertise units they do not mind showing to minorities. But the results are stronger than this; negative marginal discrimination implies that additional advertised units are *more* likely to be shown to minorities than to whites. When the advertised unit is in an integrated neighborhood, this result is consistent with the view that many agents believe that minorities, but not whites, prefer to live in integrated areas. When the agent's office is in an integrated neighborhood, it is consistent with the view that many agents whose principal business is in integrated areas believe that most of their future customers will be minority households.

Multiple advertised units are most likely when an advertised unit is part of a development or is a condominium. In these cases, the relevant neighborhood scale is the development or the building, not the census tract. A largely minority development or building can exist within an integrated or even a white tract. Negative marginal discrimination for advertised units could also arise if minorities are more likely to live in developments and condominiums, causing agents to steer white customers away from these types of projects. This possibility might help to explain why marginal discrimination is negative for Hispanics even when both the advertised unit and the agent's office are in white neighborhoods.[26]

There is one clear exception to this pattern of negative marginal discrimination for advertised units: When the agent's office and the advertised unit(s) are in a white neighborhood, agents are more likely to withhold advertised units from blacks than from whites. In this case, an agent's incentives to discriminate, based on both the prejudice of potential white customers and the agent's perceptions of customer preferences, are strong enough to produce systematic discrimination in advertised units, even though similar units unknown to the customer are available.

The third set of results, presented in Table 9.2, concerns marginal discrimination for units similar to the advertised unit when advertised units outside minority neighborhoods are not available for inspection.[27] For both blacks and Hispanics, marginal discrimination in this case tends to be positive; that is, when units are unknown to a customer, agents are more likely to withhold them from minorities than from whites. For blacks, the strongest evidence for positive marginal discrimination can be found when the agent's office is in a white neighborhood and the advertised units are in either a white or integrated neighborhood.[28] This finding supports the view that agents discriminate when most of their business comes from the white community. For Hispanics, the strongest evidence for positive marginal discrimination can be found when both the agent's office and the advertised unit are in integrated neighborhoods.[29] This result suggests that agents with business in integrated areas are particularly concerned about bringing in new Hispanic neighbors. Somewhat surprisingly, this behavior is not associated with ethnic steering; these agents often withhold additional units from Hispanics, but they do not tend to show Hispanics only those units in highly Hispanic areas.[30]

The final case to consider is marginal discrimination in units similar to the advertised unit when advertised units outside minority neighborhoods are available (see Table 9.3). In this table, marginal discrimination tends to be positive; that is, housing units about which customers have no initial knowledge are far more likely to be withheld from minority than from white customers. For both blacks and

TABLE **9.2** MARGINAL DISCRIMINATION FOR UNITS
SIMILAR TO THE ADVERTISED UNIT
WHEN ADVERTISED UNITS ARE NOT AVAILABLE
IN WHITE NEIGHBORHOODS: SALES AUDITS

Type of Neighborhood in which Units Similar to the Advertised Unit Are Concentrated	Type of Neighborhood in which the Agent's Office Is Located		
	White	Integrated	Minority
Black–White Audits			
White	0.285**	0.063	[a]
Integrated	0.330**	0.290	[a]
Black	[a]	[a]	0.058
Mix	0.218	[a]	[a]
Hispanic–White Audits			
White	−0.016	0.051	[a]
Integrated	0.248	0.316**	[a]
Hispanic	[a]	[a]	[a]
Mix	−0.546	0.319	0.635

NOTES: Based on Appendix Tables A.4 and A.5. Two asterisks indicate significance at the 5 percent level (two-tailed), and one asterisk indicates significance at the 10 percent level. A white neighborhood is defined as less than 10 percent minority (20 percent for the Hispanic columns), a minority neighborhood as more than 75 percent minority, and an integrated neighborhood as anything in between. Units are said to be in mixed neighborhoods when neither white, integrated, nor minority neighborhoods hold a majority of the available units. The significance indicators refer solely to the coefficients of the neighborhood variables, but the values in the table correct for the estimated impact of other variables on marginal discrimination, evaluated at the mean value of each variable.
[a]No audits observed in this cell.

Hispanics, marginal discrimination is positive and significant when the agent's office is in an integrated neighborhood (or in a white neighborhood in the Hispanic-white audits) and the available units are mostly in integrated neighborhoods. These results suggest that, in order to maintain their existing community contacts, agents try to manipulate events in integrated areas. They accomplish this by selectively withholding units from minority customers, not by steering.[31]

Table 9.3 also reveals that blacks face positive marginal discrimination when the advertised unit is in an integrated or black neighborhood and the houses available through an MLS are in mostly white neighborhoods. Indeed, when the agent's office is in an integrated neighborhood, the estimate of marginal discrimination is above 0.8; that is, the probability that a black customer will be shown an addi-

TABLE 9.3 MARGINAL DISCRIMINATION FOR UNITS
SIMILAR TO THE ADVERTISED UNIT
WHEN ADVERTISED UNITS ARE AVAILABLE
IN WHITE NEIGHBORHOODS: SALES AUDITS

Type of Neighborhood in which Units Similar to the Advertised Units Are Concentrated	Type of Neighborhood in which the Agent's Office Is Located		
	White	Integrated	Minority
Black–White Audits			
White	−0.075	0.192	b
	(0.553)**	(0.820)**	
Integrated	0.018	0.479**	a
Black	−0.126	a	a
Mixed	−0.274	0.544*	a
Hispanic–White Audits			
White	0.008	−0.061	b
Integrated	0.231**	0.345**	a
Hispanic	1.380	a	a
Mixed	0.053	b	a

NOTES: Based on Appendix Tables A.4 and A.5. Entries in parentheses apply when the advertised unit is in an integrated or black neighborhood and the agent uses an MLS directory. Two asterisks indicate significance at the 5 percent level (two-tailed), and one asterisk indicates significance at the 10 percent level. Neighborhood definitions are the same as for Table 9.2. The significance indicators refer solely to the coefficients of the neighborhood variables, but the values in the table correct for the estimated impact of other variables on marginal discrimination, evaluated at the mean value of each variable.

[a]No audits observed in this cell.
[b]Only one audit in this cell; marginal discrimination cannot be estimated.

tional unit is 80 percentage points lower than the probability for a white customer. With available units in white neighborhoods but without an MLS, however, marginal discrimination against blacks is close to zero. In this case, agents still withhold additional advertised units from blacks (Table 9.2) but do not systematically withhold additional similar units.

These results indicate that an MLS facilitates discrimination against blacks. When an agent can use an MLS to find units in white areas and has advertised a unit in a black or integrated area, he has a strong tendency to show the advertised unit to black customers but to reserve the units in white areas for whites. The role of the MLS apparently is crucial; when units in white areas are available in their own files, agents do not tend to withhold those units from blacks.

The MLS plays a fundamentally different role in the treatment of Hispanics. In fact, marginal discrimination is systematically lower against Hispanics when the agent draws listings from an MLS directory.[32] This result suggests that, to some degree, an MLS insulates agents from the harmful business consequences of selling to Hispanics; units located through an MLS presumably are located relatively far from the agent's potential white clients, so selling these units to Hispanics has little impact on the agent's reputation among whites.

These results also reveal that real estate brokers' actions often contribute to the current high levels of residential segregation. In the black–white audits, the highest levels of discrimination are registered by brokers who have advertised a house in an integrated or black neighborhood and have access to houses in white neighborhoods through an MLS. Brokers clearly do not make use of an MLS's potential for opening up white neighborhoods to blacks.

When both the agent's office and the available units are in an integrated neighborhood, additional advertised units are more likely to be reserved for minority customers than for whites, whereas additional units similar to the advertised unit are more likely to be reserved for white customers than for minorities.[33] This type of action is not associated with steering as it is traditionally defined; it does not arise because agents are directing minorities to minority neighborhoods. Nevertheless, it represents a kind of behavior in which minority customers are steered to the advertised units and white customers are steered to others.

Thus, when additional advertised units become available, a relatively rare event, agents' showing of these units tends either to promote integration if the units are in neighborhoods with a small minority percentage, or to encourage racial transition if the units are in neighborhoods where the minority percentage is at or above a tipping point. Similarly, agents' showing of units similar to the advertised unit tends either to preserve white areas when the units are located in neighborhoods where the minority percentage is small, or to promote integration when the units are located in neighborhoods near the tipping point. Because the minority percentage varies widely among both advertised and similar units even within integrated areas, both pro- and anti-integrative actions by agents can be observed in the IIDS data. Some agents act to protect their existing client base in integrated areas while others appear to maximize their commissions by promoting racial or ethnic transition. A more complete statement about the net impact of agents' actions on segregation in these cases requires more detailed information than HDS provides. In the case of units similar to the advertised unit, however, any pro-integrative steps by agents are achieved only through discrimination against minorities.[34]

Overall, the picture painted here is that agents do not systematically take advantage of the opportunity to discriminate when customers have good information about available units — that is, when only the advertised unit or units are available. It is difficult to mislead customers about units that have been advertised and, for the most part, agents appear to advertise only those units that they are willing to sell to minorities. For units similar to the advertised unit, however, marginal discrimination is positive under most combinations of office and unit neighborhood composition; with these units, agents control the information a customer receives and usually take advantage of the opportunity to discriminate when it arises.[35] When both advertised and other units are available, negative marginal discrimination for advertised units is often combined with positive marginal discrimination for other units; that is, agents have a tendency to show advertised units to minorities and to reserve other units for whites. However, when the incentives facing agents are particularly strong, as in the black audits when both the agent's office and the advertised unit are in a white neighborhood, marginal discrimination is positive for any available unit.[36]

■ THE GEOGRAPHY OF DISCRIMINATION IN THE RENTAL MARKET

The minority composition of a neighborhood also influences marginal discrimination in the rental market. Because advertised units cannot be identified with precision, however, marginal discrimination for advertised units alone cannot be estimated.[37]

The first case to consider is marginal discrimination when no advertised units are available for inspection.[38] The results for this case are presented in Table 9.4. Marginal discrimination is positive and significant in most cells of this table. Moreover, the value of marginal discrimination is close to one in several cases, including, for both blacks and Hispanics, the case in which the agent's office is in an integrated neighborhood and the available units are all in white neighborhoods. Despite the location of their offices, the agents in these audits almost always show additional available units to whites and withhold them from minorities.

The only negative entries appear when the available units are all in minority neighborhoods or the agent's office is in a minority neighborhood, that is, where an agent has strong incentives not to discriminate. In fact, the value of marginal discrimination in the Hispanic audits equals negative one when the agent's office and the avail-

TABLE 9.4 MARGINAL DISCRIMINATION FOR UNITS
SIMILAR TO THE ADVERTISED UNIT
WHEN ADVERTISED UNITS ARE NOT AVAILABLE
IN WHITE NEIGHBORHOODS: RENTAL AUDITS

Type of Neighborhood in which Units Similar to the Advertised Unit Are Located	Type of Neighborhood in which the Agent's Office Is Located		
	White	Integrated	Minority
Black–White Audits			
White	0.487**	1.029**	−0.806
Integrated	0.744**	0.594**	0.590
Black	a	0.193	−0.151
Mix	0.945**	a	b
Hispanic–White Audits			
White	0.304**	0.840*	b
Integrated	0.500	0.064	−0.288
Hispanic	b	−1.278	−0.996**
Mixed	0.161**	0.154	a

NOTES: Based on Appendix Tables A.6 and A.7. Two asterisks indicate significance at the 5 percent level (two-tailed), and one asterisk indicates significance at the 10 percent level. A white neighborhood is defined as less than 10 percent minority, an integrated neighborhood as 10 to 75 percent minority, and a minority neighborhood as more than 75 percent minority. Units are said to be in mixed neighborhoods when available units are not entirely concentrated in white or integrated or black neighborhoods. The significance indicators refer solely to the coefficients of the neighborhood variables, but the values in the table correct for the estimated impact of other variables on marginal discrimination, evaluated at the mean value of each variable.

aNo audits observed in this cell.

bOnly one audit in this cell; marginal discrimination cannot be estimated.

able units are in Hispanic neighborhoods. In this case, agents always reserve additional units for Hispanics.

Table 9.5 presents the analogous results for marginal discrimination when at least one advertised unit is available for inspection. The results in this table are not exactly comparable to those in the corresponding table for the sales audits, Table 9.3, because incomplete address information makes it impossible to determine the exact number of advertised units available. Hence, the results in this table describe marginal discrimination for any unit, advertised or other.

The results in Table 9.5 reveal a pattern similar to those in Table 9.4, except when the agent's office is in a white neighborhood. In this case, in the first row of the table, marginal discrimination against blacks is essentially zero, instead of large and positive as in Table 9.4. This result may reflect a tendency of agents to advertise only those

Table 9.5 **MARGINAL DISCRIMINATION FOR UNITS**
SIMILAR TO THE ADVERTISED UNIT
WHEN ADVERTISED UNITS ARE AVAILABLE
IN WHITE NEIGHBORHOODS: RENTAL AUDITS

Type of Neighborhood in which Units Similar to the Advertised Unit Are Located	Type of Neighborhood in which the Agent's Office Is Located		
	White	Integrated	Minority
Black–White Audits			
White	-0.132^{++}	0.937^{**}	a
Integrated	-0.046^{++}	0.855^{**}	0.474
Black	b	-1.011	a
Mix	-0.509^{+}	0.280^{**}	a
Hispanic–White Audits			
White	0.285^{**}	0.397^{**}	a
Integrated	0.051	0.166^{*}	a
Hispanic	a	c	-0.062
Mixed	0.459^{**}	0.577^{**}	b

Notes: Based on Appendix Tables A.6 and A.7. Two asterisks indicate statistical significance at the 5 percent level (two-tailed), and one asterisk indicates significance at the 10 percent level. Neighborhood definitions are the same as for Table 9.4. The significance indicators refer solely to the coefficients of the neighborhood variables, but the values in the table correct for the estimated impact of other variables on marginal discrimination, evaluated at the mean value of each variable. Two plusses indicate that the contribution of neighborhood factors to marginal discrimination is positive and significant at the two-tailed 5 percent level (one plus for the 10 percent level) but is not sufficiently positive to offset the negative contribution of other factors.
[a]No audits observed in this cell.
[b]Only one audit in this cell; marginal discrimination cannot be estimated.
[c]Only two audits in this cell; estimate of marginal discrimination is not meaningful.

units they are willing to rent to any customer, but this possibility cannot be firmly established since advertised units cannot be accurately identified. In any case, this result reveals once more the complexity of discriminatory behavior: a tendency to discriminate does not emerge whenever the incentives to discriminate appear strong. For Hispanics, however, marginal discrimination is positive when the agent's office and the available units are in white neighborhoods, regardless of whether an advertised unit is available.

With the agent's office in an integrated neighborhood, the availability of advertised units does not alter the pattern of positive marginal discrimination when the available units are in white, integrated, or a mixed set of neighborhoods, combined with negative marginal discrimination when the available units are all in minority neighborhoods. Moreover, as before, marginal discrimination against blacks approaches a value of one when the agent's office is in an integrated neighborhood and the available units are all in white neighborhoods; in this case, additional available units always are reserved for whites.

In sum, marginal discrimination against blacks and Hispanics in the rental market is consistently large and positive unless either (1) the agent's office or the available units are in minority neighborhoods or, in the case of blacks, (2) the agent's office is in a white neighborhood and at least one advertised unit is available for inspection. Although the specific incentives cannot be identified with precision, these results demonstrate that rental agents, like real estate brokers, tend to discriminate when their incentive to do so is highest.

Moreover, rental agents' actions tend to perpetuate segregation in largely white areas and to have mixed effects in integrated and minority neighborhoods, sometimes promoting integration by denying units to minorities, and sometimes promoting racial change. Because HDS does not provide any information about the racial or ethnic composition of apartment buildings, the impact of rental agents' actions on integration within buildings cannot be determined.

▉ OTHER EVIDENCE ABOUT INCENTIVES TO DISCRIMINATE

Not all incentives to discriminate are associated with neighborhood minority composition, and this analysis of the HDS data provides several other insights into these incentives.[39]

To begin, there is some evidence that agents are more likely to discriminate against those minorities most likely to upset their potential white clients. In particular, marginal discrimination in the sales audits is higher against both black and Hispanic auditors whose family assignment includes children.[40] The magnitude of this effect is about the same in both cases: marginal discrimination is 10 percentage points higher for black households with children and 12 percentage points higher for Hispanic households with children. A similar result appears for the Hispanic rental audits: both single men and single women encounter less discrimination than couples.

Marginal discrimination in the sales audits is higher against single black men and significantly lower against single black women than against black couples. These results are consistent with the views that agents do not want to deal with black men and that future white neighbors prefer black females to black males. But these results are partially reversed in the rental market, where single black women encounter more discrimination than do single black men or black couples. This effect is quite large; perhaps because agents associate them with welfare dependency or out-of-wedlock births, single black women renters face marginal discrimination that is 24 percentage points higher than that faced by other blacks.[41] This result also could be driven by the prejudices of housing agents or of their prejudiced white customers.

Two other results clearly support the view that the prejudice of housing agents themselves is sometimes at work. Marginal discrimination in the sales audits is significantly lower if the agent is from the same group as the minority auditor.[42] This effect is quite large. The impact of a minority agent on marginal discrimination is about −0.25 for both the black and Hispanic audits; this is equivalent to lowering the probability that a unit will be reserved for whites by 25 percentage points. In addition, marginal discrimination is lower in the black sales audits and the Hispanic rental audits when the "wife" does the shopping.[43] As explained earlier, this result indicates an agent aversion to dealing with black men.[44] In the black rental audits, however, black agents are more likely than other agents to take advantage of the opportunity to discriminate when the advertised unit is in a black or integrated neighborhood. Personal feelings do not always overcome incentives to discriminate.

The relationship between income and house value also appears to matter, at least in the black audits.[45] Remember that every audit team is assigned an income that qualifies them, generously, for the advertised unit. This assignment did not follow an exact formula, however, and some auditors are more overqualified than others. Marginal discrimination against blacks increases with the stated value of advertised houses, controlling for assigned family income.[46] This result suggests that agents are more likely to withhold units from blacks who are just qualified for a mortgage than from those who are overqualified; they do not "waste their time" on blacks who are believed to be unlikely to obtain a mortgage. In the black rental audits, marginal discrimination decreases with income, controlling for rent.[47] This result indicates that rental agents are more likely to serve overqualified blacks, perhaps because they believe such blacks are more likely than other blacks to pass their credit checks. In a similar vein, older black auditors encounter less discrimination in the rental market than younger ones. These results should be interpreted with care, however, because they also are all consistent with the view that higher-income minorities are less threatening than lower-income minorities to a housing agent's prejudiced white customers. Because relatively few minority households have high incomes, whites in high-income neighborhoods may be less concerned than other whites about racial or ethnic change.

In both the black and Hispanic sales audits, marginal discrimination declines with the age of the housing agent. Each year of agent age lowers marginal discrimination by 0.007 for blacks and by 0.005 for Hispanics. So, switching to an agent who is 20 years older lowers marginal discrimination by (0.007)(20) = 14 percentage points for blacks and by (0.005)(20) = 10 points for Hispanics. Because older people tend to be more prejudiced, this result does not support the view that agents are prejudiced, but instead suggests that older agents may work in types of firms that are less likely to discriminate or may, because of their experience, be more careful to avoid discriminatory behavior.

Marginal discrimination against blacks also decreases with agency size, as measured by the number of agents an audit team encounters. This result supports the view that larger agencies are not as dependent as are smaller agencies on connections in a single community and therefore are not as affected by selling to black customers.

Finally, marginal discrimination against an Hispanic auditor appears to be related to her skin color and Spanish accent—but in a puzzling manner. Recall that, at each site, Hispanic auditors were selected so that some of them had light skin, some had dark skin, some had no accents, and some had heavy accents. In the sales audits, marginal discrimination is equally high against Hispanics with both dark skin and a heavy accent and Hispanics with neither dark skin nor a heavy accent. However, it is lower against those with dark skin and no accent and even lower against those with a heavy accent but no dark skin. In the rental audits, marginal discrimination is also lower against Hispanic auditors with dark skin.[48] When the agent is Hispanic, however, Hispanic auditors with dark skin encounter slightly more discrimination than others, and Hispanic auditors with heavy accents encounter the least discrimination. In other words, Hispanic agents are more averse to dark-skinned clients and less averse to clients with heavy accents than are white agents.[49] Although somewhat surprising, all these results are highly significant statistically.[50]

◼ EVIDENCE FROM PREVIOUS STUDIES

Several previous studies have used audit data to explore the circumstances under which discrimination occurs. With one exception, previous studies do not consider the constraints imposed by the opportunity to discriminate; that is, they do not estimate marginal discrimination.[51] Moreover, most of these studies have limited information about an audit's neighborhood setting.

Two studies, one looking at the sales market and the other at the rental market, are based on the nationwide audits conducted in 1977.[52] Two of the results from examination of sales audits are consistent with the results presented here: discrimination in inspections is lower against women and at higher house values, controlling for assigned income. This study also finds that there is less discrimination in inspections when assigned families include children, a result that contradicts the view that agents exclude minorities most likely to upset their white neighbors.[53] The rental market study finds only one variable with a significant impact on discrimination in inspections; black males encounter more discrimination than black females.[54]

Another study is based on 1981 sales and rental audit data from selected Boston neighborhoods. In the sales market, discrimination in inspections was higher against lower-income blacks, against blacks with children, and against black males.[55] The first two results support the view that agents are more likely to discriminate against those blacks most likely to upset their potential white neighbors, and because almost all the auditors were assigned the role of a spouse, the last result supports the view that agents prefer to deal with (and therefore discriminate less against) black females than black males. In the rental market, no agent, auditor, or non-neighborhood audit characteristic had a significant impact on discrimination.

When these Boston audits were conducted, most real estate agents in the broad neighborhoods studied did not make use of an MLS and often knew about listings only within their neighborhoods. This feature of the market made it possible to explore how discrimination varied across neighborhoods and to determine the types of neighborhood in which discrimination was particularly high. Three neighborhoods had an inflow of blacks during the previous decade of less than 2 percent; two of these neighborhoods were less than 5 percent black and the third was 19 percent black. The level of discrimination in these neighborhoods was uniformly high. Discrimination was also high for some types of agent behavior in two other neighborhoods. One neighborhood was highly integrated, at 41 percent black, but it was also experiencing extensive gentrification and inflow of whites in certain blocks. The other was a large neighborhood that was about one-quarter black overall but still highly segregated and experiencing a rapid inflow of blacks and outflow of whites. The only neighborhood without any significant discrimination had a modest level of integration, 8 percent black, combined with a modest inflow of blacks, 7 percent during the last decade, and a significant outflow of whites, 25 percent.

These results support the view that agents discriminate to protect their established business with prejudiced whites but contradict the view that agents discriminate to satisfy the perceived neighborhood preferences of their clients. To be specific, blacks could be expected to want to move into the integrated neighborhood that was experiencing gentrification, but agents discriminated extensively there, presumably to protect their business with potential white entrants. Moreover, the neighborhood that was 19 percent black had many integrated sub-areas that would be acceptable to most blacks, but discrimination was also high there, presumably to protect agents' business with white residents. Finally, the neighborhood with 8 percent black had few sub-areas with significant black representation, so agents there who were relying on black preferences could be expected to turn blacks away. In contrast, the outflow of whites and inflow of blacks indicate that most new business in the neighborhood would come from blacks, so agents working to protect their business with likely future clients would not discriminate, as in fact was the case.

A study of sales audits in Memphis and Cincinnati concludes that agents discriminate in order to maximize racial turnover.[56] This conclusion is based primarily on the finding that when an audit began with a request for a house in an integrated neighborhood, the white auditor, but not the black, was shown other houses in white areas. This finding is comparable to the HDS finding that agents with a house to sell in an integrated or black neighborhood use an MLS to find housing in white neighborhoods for whites. This type of behavior does indeed encourage turnover in the neighborhoods where the advertised unit is located, just as it encourages stability in the white neighborhoods from which blacks are excluded.

In my judgment, this study goes too far in two ways. First, it concludes that this behavior is motivated by a desire to cause transition in integrated areas. Although this motivation undoubtedly applies in some cases, it also may be true that agents believe that whites do not want to live in integrated areas or that blacks do not want to live in white areas. Under some circumstances, audit evidence may not support the view that agents are motivated by their perceptions of customer preferences, but audits also cannot definitively rule out this view without direct measures of what agents perceive.[57] Second, whatever agents' motivations when they take actions that encourage racial transition, they also take some actions that support integration, at least at the census tract level. Discrimination in integrated neighborhoods usually does not consist of steering minorities to those places where the minority concentration is greatest; agents sometimes with-hold houses in integrated neighborhoods from minority but not white customers, thereby promoting integration—by discriminating.

Overall, real estate agents clearly play a role in encouraging racial transition under some circumstances, but the evidence supports neither the conclusion that a desire to maximize turnover is their principal motivation nor the conclusion that all their actions in integrated areas promote neighborhood change.

Finally, a study of 569 black–white rental audits conducted in Detroit during the 1980s supports several of the HDS results.[58] In particular, this study finds that discrimination in inspections is lower when the agent is black than when the agent is white, that discrimination is higher against blacks with school-aged children, and that discrimination declines with income. This study also finds that older agents discriminate more than younger agents and that discrimination declines when the auditor's assigned role includes a college education.

On the neighborhood dimension, the Detroit study finds less discrimination when the advertised unit is in a black or integrated area than when it is in a white area, where integrated areas are defined as those with between 2.5 and 60 percent black. Moreover, marginal discrimination, which is positive in all locations, is relatively low when the advertised unit is in one particular integrated area and relatively high when it is in one predominantly white area.[59]

Even though Detroit is one of the HDS sites, these results cannot be directly compared to the HDS rental results, which do not calculate marginal discrimination based on the racial composition of the neighborhood in which the advertised unit alone is located. Nevertheless, the Detroit and HDS results have qualitatively similar implications for the impact of rental agents' actions on segregation. In particular, the Detroit results indicate that it is highly likely that additional units will be withheld from blacks who inquire about houses in white areas, thereby preserving segregation there. In integrated areas, however, additional units sometimes are withheld from blacks, which preserves integration through discrimination, and sometimes offered to blacks, which promotes racial transition.

■ THE CAUSES OF DISCRIMINATION BY LENDERS

A few scholars have explored the circumstances under which lenders might discriminate, but no empirical study of the causes of lending discrimination has yet been published.[60]

Circumstantial evidence suggests that the key cause of lending discrimination may be that lenders believe the unobserved credit characteristics of minority applicants are less favorable, on average, than those of white applicants. This belief may lead lenders to be more likely to turn down minority applicants than white applicants with the same observable characteristics. This type of discrimination is called *statistical discrimination*.[61] Although no study formally shows that this type of statistical discrimination exists, several studies find that minority borrowers are more likely to default, controlling for their characteristics that can be observed at the time the loan was granted.[62] This result indicates that lenders have an incentive to practice statistical discrimination, at least some of the time, but it does not prove that they actually do. Furthermore, lenders themselves recognize that "perceptions of the expected behavior of a group of people may subtly affect the way in which information is evaluated or a particular loan is processed."[63]

Although statistical discrimination may be rational in the sense that it maximizes profits with imperfect information, it still is discrimination. When lenders decide whether to grant a loan, they are expected to consider the observable characteristics of a loan applicant that are related to his or her ability to pay back a loan. According to widely held values and the law, however, they may not use the average unobservable characteristics of a group to make inferences about the unobservable characteristics of an individual.[64]

Statistical discrimination may not be practiced by lenders who plan to sell their mortgages in the secondary market, who are now a majority of lenders.[65] All these lenders care about, one might argue, is whether a borrower meets the underwriting criteria established by the secondary market institutions.[66] Once an individual loan is sold, after all, the originator may no longer care about default. However, statistical discrimination may still occur if these lenders believe that the documentation needed for underwriting standards tends to be less definitive for minority applicants or that sales to minorities will lead to so many defaults that secondary market institutions will have to investigate. These beliefs are important because each secondary market institution

> subjects a certain portion of its purchases to a post-purchase quality control audit. In the event that this audit uncovers significant deviations from established underwriting guidelines which cannot be resolved, the lender will be required to repurchase the loan. This can be a major issue for lenders who do not otherwise hold loans in portfolio and for smaller

institutions for whom repurchase of even a single loan can cause problems.[67]

In short, lenders may discriminate against minorities to avoid anticipated problems with secondary market institutions. Moreover, loans with loan-to-value ratios above 95 percent also are audited more often, so lenders are more likely to retain them, which implies that the above stronger incentives for statistical discrimination remain in place, or to avoid them altogether, which implies that households who can afford only a small down payment, including many minority households, have fewer lenders to choose from.

Discrimination by lenders undoubtedly has other causes as well.[68] Some lenders may deny loans to creditworthy minority applicants, for example, because of their own personal prejudice against minorities.[69] Other lenders may discriminate against minority customers, at least in certain neighborhoods, to protect their reputation with potential white customers or with the real estate brokers from whom white customers get lender referrals.[70] Unfortunately, however, no research yet provides any direct evidence on the importance of these various possible causes of lending discrimination.

■ CONCLUSIONS

This chapter provides several insights into the nature of discrimination in housing and the appropriate design of antidiscrimination policy.

First, discriminatory behavior is complex and does not have one simple cause. The evidence from the HDS and other studies supports the view that some agents discriminate because of their own personal prejudice against minorities, but agents also face a variety of incentives to discriminate under some circumstances and to favor minorities under others. Of course, many housing agents understand and obey the law and therefore do not discriminate even when they have a strong economic incentive to do so. However, the evidence strongly supports the view that many other agents tend to protect their current and potential business with prejudiced whites. The evidence also suggests that some agents avoid investing time in minority customers who are unlikely to complete a transaction or act on perceptions that whites do not want to live in integrated areas and that minorities do not want to be pioneers in all-white areas.

Discrimination in housing also has a complex set of connections with other aspects of the discriminatory system. The analysis of housing availability in this chapter along with the evidence in Chapter 4 concerning steering and discrimination in marketing demonstrate that housing agents play a key role in perpetuating residential segregation. By denying minorities access to housing in white neighborhoods or by showing multiple advertised units in integrated neighborhoods only to minorities, housing agents preserve the all-white character of some locations and hasten racial or ethnic transition in others. However, discrimination by housing agents also serves to promote integration in some cases, at least at the census tract scale. To be specific, withholding available housing in integrated areas from minorities slows the pace of racial or ethnic transition. It is not possible with the HDS data to determine how often agents' actions foster integration at a scale smaller than a census tract or to determine what circumstances lead an agent to encourage transition instead of promoting integration.

The analysis of the HDS audits presented here does provide some evidence about the power and complexity of the linkages between outcomes in the housing and other markets. Because many prejudiced white parents do not want to send their children to integrated schools, housing agents clearly discriminate more against black and Hispanic households with children. The only case in which this is not true, the black–white rental audits, reveals discrimination against single black women, whom an agent may expect to have children based on their high rate of out-of-wedlock births. Racial and ethnic prejudice, a key product of the overall system, also clearly influences housing discrimination. Not only do black and Hispanic agents discriminate less under many, but not all, circumstances, but white agents are more willing to deal with minority females than minority males, except in the case of black renters. Finally, the influence of neighborhood minority composition on agent behavior is evidence of another key linkage in this system, as existing patterns of segregation are determined not only by past discrimination in the housing market but also by racial and ethnic prejudice and economic disparities.[71]

The analysis in this chapter yields several important lessons for antidiscrimination policy.

The first lesson is that an exclusive focus on advertised units will miss a great deal of discrimination. Under many circumstances, marginal discrimination for advertised units is zero if not negative: advertised units sometimes tend not to be withheld from minority customers. But agents often deny minority customers access to available units about which they have not explicitly inquired. Because actual housing search typically involves the inspection of units introduced to the customer by the agent, this type of denial constitutes an important limitation on minority access to housing. Enforcement strategies based on audits to determine the availability of a given unit may therefore miss a large portion of the discrimination that minorities actually encounter.[72] Indeed, any complaint-based strategy, which almost by definition involves units about which the minority customer is aware, inevitably ignores a large portion of existing discrimination.

A second lesson is that discrimination against minorities is not confined to white neighborhoods. In fact, some of the highest levels of marginal discrimination against minorities are found when either the agent's office, the available housing, or both are located in integrated areas. Because minority households tend to search for housing primarily in integrated areas, it is crucial that such areas be included in any enforcement campaigns.

A related lesson is that current policy leaves events in integrated neighborhoods largely in the hands of the real estate community, which usually does not have an incentive to maintain integration. Although real estate brokers sometimes have participated in a community program to promote integration, the evidence from HDS and other audit studies clearly indicates that brokers sometimes encourage racial or ethnic transition by reserving units in integrated neighborhoods for minority customers and sometimes support integration by actively discriminating against minorities in integrated neighborhoods. These two types of behavior may be supported by economic incentives, but neither one is in the public interest. Policy makers, particularly at the local level, and community groups that want to support integration need to be given tools to help them offset these actions by brokers, or better still, to enlist brokers into their cause.

Finally, MLSs appear to play a crucial role in discrimination, particularly against blacks. In the case of Hispanics, access to an MLS weakens an agent's ties to a given community and therefore weakens his incentive to discriminate. In contrast, the HDS results provide strong evidence that agents use an MLS to draw white customers away from integrated and minority areas—without bringing black customers along. Further investigation of this type of behavior clearly is warranted.

The History of Fair Housing and Fair Lending Policy

◼ FAIR HOUSING LAW BEFORE 1968

Racial and ethnic discrimination in housing used to be the law of the land. Between 1910 and 1917, fifteen state courts upheld the right of local governments to enact racial zoning ordinances that explicitly forbade the entry of blacks or members of other minority groups into white-zoned neighborhoods.[1] These ordinances were struck down by the U.S. Supreme Court in the 1917 *Buchanan* v. *Warley* decision.[2]

When racial zoning was outlawed, the real estate community turned to race-restrictive covenants, which were restrictions on deeds or agreements among the property owners in a given area to prevent sales to minority households at any time in the future. These covenants became widespread, and between 1917 and 1948, nineteen state courts upheld their legality.[3] Another step away from discrimination was taken in 1948 when the U.S. Supreme Court ruled in *Shelly* v. *Kraemer* that it was unconstitutional for any government to enforce a racial restrictive covenant. Such covenants could be included in deeds, the Court said, but they could not be enforced in a court of law.[4]

The first tentative federal initiative appeared in 1962, when President Kennedy issued Executive Order 11063, which required federal agencies to "take all necessary and appropriate action to prevent discrimination" in all housing programs that received federal support.[5] Housing suppliers who violated the order could, in principle, have lost their federal contracts or been made ineligible for other forms

187

of federal assistance. Even though the order was complemented by the Civil Rights Act of 1964, which outlaws discrimination by any organization that receives federal funds, this order was largely ignored, and even the regulations needed to implement it were not completed until 1980.

■ THE 1968 FAIR HOUSING ACT

In 1968 two crucial events fundamentally altered the legal status of discrimination in housing. The first event, in April, was the passage of the Civil Rights Act of 1968.[6] Title VIII of this act, which is known as the Fair Housing Act, explicitly outlaws discrimination in the sale or rental of housing on the basis of race, color, religion, or country of origin.[7] Two months later, the Supreme Court ruled, in *Jones* v. *Mayer,* that the 1866 Civil Rights Act, which bans racial and ethnic discrimination in all forms of contracts and which had been largely ignored for a century, applies to housing market transactions.[8]

The Fair Housing Act (FaHA) explicitly bans racial and ethnic discrimination in a wide range of housing agent actions, including the provision of information about available housing units, decisions to sell or rent, and statements about the terms and conditions of sale or rental. According to the Supreme Court, its provisions also prohibit racial steering.[9] FaHA bans both blockbusting, which is defined as the use of comments about racial or ethnic change to encourage panic selling, and discrimination in real estate advertising.[10] Moreover, FaHA outlaws racial and ethnic discrimination in the acceptance of mortgage loan applications or in mortgage terms and conditions. Finally, several federal courts have concluded that FaHA bans redlining, defined here as the refusal to grant loans or insurance based solely on the racial or ethnic composition of the neighborhood in which a property is located.[11]

A key issue in civil rights law is the distinction between discriminatory intent and discriminatory effect. The so-called effects test, or effects theory, places a lower standard of proof on a plaintiff, who must show that a defendant's actions had discriminatory effect but need not show that the defendant intended to discriminate.[12] The FaHA is based on the effects test and therefore does not require proof of discriminatory intent. This issue has been considered by many courts. The outcome, according to one of the leading experts on fair housing law, has been as follows:

By 1988, therefore, a strong consensus had developed among the circuits that the proper meaning of Title VIII included a discriminatory effect standard. Only the First, Tenth, and D.C. Circuits have not been heard from on this issue. Not a single court of appeals currently espouses the view that the effect theory is inappropriate for Title VIII.[13]

In order to ensure its passage, the Fair Housing Act contained several key compromises.[14] In particular, single-family houses sold by the owner and apartments in owner-occupied housing with four or fewer units were exempt from coverage; punitive damages in suits brought by individual plaintiffs were limited to $1,000; attorney's fees could be awarded only to plaintiffs who were unable to afford these fees themselves; the statutes of limitations was set at only 180 days (from the time of the alleged act of discrimination) both for civil suits and complaints to HUD; the enforcement role of the federal government was limited to the prosecution of pattern and practice suits, in which a landlord, real estate broker, or lender engaged in a widespread or systematic discrimination;[15] and pattern and practice suits could result in injunctive relief but not in compensatory or punitive damages. In fact, the only role for the federal government outside of pattern and practice suits was for HUD to act as a conciliator in discrimination cases — if both parties so requested. This ludicrously limited role placed virtually all enforcement power in the hands of state and local civil rights agencies, many of which had no legal basis for or interest in enforcing antidiscrimination laws. In many states, therefore, the only legal remedy available to someone who encountered discrimination was the costly one of a civil suit.

Because of the limitations in FaHA, the resurrection of the 1866 Civil Rights Act (CiRA) was an important event. Although it did not give the federal government any enforcement powers, and indeed cannot even be used by the Justice Department in a pattern and practice suit, this act also did not place any limits on damages or on the awarding of attorneys' fees in civil suits.[16] It did, however, limit standing to parties actually injured by discrimination and it required proof of discriminatory intent, not just discriminatory effect — limits not included in FaHA. Thus, the 1866 CiRA greatly strengthened the hand of an individual who encountered racial or ethnic discrimination and brought a civil suit against the discriminator, but only if the evidence was sufficient to establish discriminatory intent. Over time, more and more civil suits that could meet this test were brought, and the magnitude of the awards to victims of discrimination gradually grew; in fact, "single-victim settlements and awards during the past few years have generally exceeded $20,000 and commonly approach $100,000."[17]

The limitations of the enforcement system in FaHA were obvious, and many attempts to reform the act were made over the years.[18] In support of amendments proposed in 1980, for example, a report by the House of Representatives concluded that[19]

> The primary weakness in the existing law derives from the almost total dependence upon private efforts to enforce its provisions. For financially capable victims of housing discrimination, the Act has provided litigation remedies. For the vast majority of victims, however, this course of action is not feasible. Alternative enforcement under Title VIII is limited to "pattern and practice" cases brought by the Attorney General. While these cases have dealt with virtually every important type of discrimination, and have had a significant impact on the state of the law, relief for individual victims of housing discrimination has not been readily available through this avenue.[20]

■ THE 1988 FAIR HOUSING AMENDMENTS ACT

The long-time dissatisfaction with the enforcement provisions of FaHA, combined with strong evidence of continuing discrimination from the Housing Market Practices Survey and other sources plus a backlash against the Reagan administration's reluctance to initiate pattern and practice cases and its rejection of the effects test, resulted in the Fair Housing Amendments Act of 1988 (FaHAA).[21] This act removed the limit on punitive damages in civil suits; lengthened the statute of limitations to 2 years for private suits and to 1 year for complaints to HUD[22]; set up a system of administrative law judges, with the authority to impose penalties, for hearing complaints brought to HUD; authorized both damage awards and civil penalties, which are paid to the U.S. Treasury, in pattern and practice cases[23]; and allowed the Secretary of HUD to initiate cases.[24]

The system of administrative law judges (ALJs) is the heart of FaHAA. This system fundamentally alters the way HUD handles an individual discrimination complaint. As with the original FaHA, state and local civil rights agencies with laws that are substantially equivalent to the federal law have prior jurisdiction, so a complainant who lives in a location with a substantially equivalent law must exhaust all state and local remedies before his complaint will be investigated by HUD. Complainants in jurisdictions without such a law can go directly to their HUD regional office. In either case, a complaint brought to a HUD regional office begins with an interview and, if warranted, an investigation. To facilitate this type of investigation, the FaHAA gives HUD subpoena power, backed by penalties for people who do not cooperate.[25]

If the investigation finds "probable cause" to believe that discrimination occurred, the case is sent to the HUD central office, which may accept the regional office's finding or request that further investigation be conducted.[26] The final determination on the case is made by HUD; this responsibility falls on the Office of the General Counsel (OGC) unless it is delegated by the HUD secretary to another office, such as the Office of Fair Housing and Equal Opportunity (FHEO).[27] If a "cause" determination is made, the case is sent to an ALJ, who hears the case under the Federal Rules of Evidence. ALJs, who are appointed by the Office of Personnel Management and are independent of HUD,[28] have the authority to award compensatory damages and attorneys' fees to the complainant and to impose civil penalties on the defendant of up to $10,000 for a first offense, $25,000 for a second offense, and $50,000 for a third offense.[29] In the early months of this new enforcement procedure, the administrative law judges revealed a willingness to impose large penalties in clear cases of discrimination.[30]

If either the complainant or the respondent "elects," a case is sent to the Justice Department for prosecution in federal court.[31] This route is more time-consuming than the ALJ route, largely because it depends on the backlog in the federal district court, and the potential penalties are somewhat different.[32] Federal courts cannot impose civil penalties in a case involving an individual complaint, but unlike ALJs, they can award punitive damages to the complainant. HUD also must send a case to the Justice Department if there is the possibility of interim relief, such as obtaining a disputed apartment, or any sign of danger to the complainant.[33]

This new system enhances HUD's role as a conciliator. At any point between the time a case is brought to HUD and is filed with an ALJ, HUD may attempt to negotiate a settlement between the two parties. The possibility of a hearing before an ALJ, along with the associated penalties, greatly increases HUD's leverage in this type of negotiation. Under the original FaHA, HUD could not even serve as a conciliator without the consent of both parties; now HUD can offer a mutually agreeable settlement as an alternative to an ALJ hearing or a case in federal court. Moreover, HUD-brokered conciliation agreements can be enforced in federal court by the Justice Department.

FaHAA also allows the secretary of HUD to initiate discrimination cases and, backed by HUD's full investigatory power, to bring them before an ALJ. A secretary-initiated case need not be based on a complaint brought to HUD; it could, for example, be based on a HUD auditing program or on the analysis of a data set, such as the HMDA data on loan applications and outcomes.

Moreover, FaHAA expands the HUD secretary's participation in the implementation of fair housing law. The HUD secretary was given the responsibility to write the regulations implementing the 1968 FaHA, a responsibility that was retained in FaHAA. In addition, FaHAA gives the HUD secretary, through OGC, a major role in developing case law for the new act. To be specific, OGC can review, and overrule, any decision by an ALJ. Of course any decision by the OGC, or by an ALJ for that matter, can be appealed to federal court and ultimately to the Supreme Court. Nevertheless, the FaHAA greatly expands the HUD secretary's role as both an interpreter and an enforcer of fair housing law.[34]

Overall, therefore, the 1988 FaHAA directly addresses most of the key weaknesses of the original FaHA. First, it greatly reduces the enforcement burden on the victims of discrimination. This reduction has three components. The first component is that FaHAA reduces the financial burden on victims by removing the $1,000 limit on punitive damages in civil suits based on the FaHA[35]; by allowing ALJs to impose (or Justice to argue for) compensatory damages, including damages for humiliation and embarrassment; by allowing punitive damages in "election" cases and in pattern and practice cases; by authorizing the awarding of attorneys' fees; and by lengthening the statute of limitations.

The second component is that FaHAA makes HUD a full partner in the resolution of complaints, complete with investigatory and prosecutorial powers. For victims in jurisdictions without a state or local law that is substantially equivalent to the amended FaHA, turning to HUD for help is now a viable alternative to a civil suit.

The third and perhaps the most significant component is that FaHAA helps to break the connection between complaints and enforcement activities. Ever since the original FaHA, Justice has been able to investigate and file pattern and practice cases that are not associated with complaints. FaHAA broadens this power to HUD and to non-pattern and practice cases; specifically, HUD can initiate discrimination cases based on evidence from audits or other types of investigation even if no complaint is involved. For the first time, therefore, HUD has an enforcement tool that can uncover discrimination, such as racial steering, that is too subtle for the victim to recognize or discrimination so seemingly intractable that the victim decides not to complain.

A second key weakness of the original FaHA was the limits it placed on penalties for discriminating. Thanks to FaHAA, the possibility of severe financial penalties, a necessary condition for an effective enforcement system, is now at the heart of fair housing law, not limited to civil suits based on the 1866 CiRA. The $1,000 limit on punitive damages in FHA-based civil suits is completely removed; civil penalties of up to $50,000 for repeat offenders are possible in ALJ proceedings; civil penalties of up to $100,000 are possible in pattern and practice suits.[36] In addition, compensatory damages are now authorized for ALJ proceedings and pattern and practice suits, compensatory and punitive damages are authorized for "election" cases, and attorneys' fees may be awarded to the complainant in all types of cases, without consideration of the complainant's financial position. The FaHAA does not, however, extend coverage to apartments in owner-occupied buildings with four or fewer units or to the sale or rental of single-family houses, with some exceptions, such as when a broker is used.[37] Discrimination cases for these units still must meet the stronger burden of proof in the 1866 CiRA.

Third, FaHAA greatly loosens the previous absurd limits on the enforcement powers of the federal government. Gone are the days when the federal role was limited to the prosecution of pattern and practice cases (with no possibility of damages or civil penalties) and the conciliation of cases in which both parties already wanted to negotiate. HUD can investigate and prosecute individual cases through the ALJ system, and HUD can initiate cases itself.

Although not directly connected to the perceived weaknesses in the original FaHA, one further aspect of FaHAA is relevant here; namely, its extension of coverage to cases based on familial status or handicap. The impact of this extension on racial and ethnic discrimination is not clear. On the one hand, some landlords may have used rules prohibiting families with children as a way to screen out minority families without seeming to discriminate. To the extent that this was true, the extension will help in the fight against racial and ethnic discrimination. On the other hand, many cases involving familial status and, I suspect, most cases involving handicap, have nothing to do with race or ethnicity. The extension of FaHA to these cases, while beneficial in its own right, will spread more thinly the resources of HUD, Justice, and other agencies involved in enforcing this law. Unless resources devoted to enforcement increase substantially, therefore, this extension is likely to weaken the ability of enforcement agencies to attack racial and ethnic discrimination.[38]

◼ ECOA, CRA, AND INTEGRATION MAINTENANCE

Although FaHA is the centerpiece of antidiscrimination law, several other laws and legal developments are germane to a discussion of fair housing policy reform. This section discusses the Equal Credit Opportunity Act of 1974 (ECOA), the Community Reinvestment Act of 1977 (CRA), and court decisions concerning integration maintenance programs.

The Equal Credit Opportunity Act

FaHA outlaws racial and ethnic discrimination in all aspects of a housing market transaction, including the issuing of mortgages. The mortgage discrimination prohibitions are complemented by those in ECOA. These laws clearly ban racial and ethnic discrimination in loan approval, in loan terms and conditions, and in loan applications procedures; they also ban racial redlining.[39] The definition of discrimination in this legislation is consistent with the definition in Chapter 5. ECOA, for example, outlaws racial or ethnic discrimination in "any aspect of a credit transaction . . . provided the applicant has the capacity to contract."[40]

Because courts have rendered almost no decisions concerning lending discrimination, it is not clear exactly what type of evidence courts would require to prove that lending discrimination exists. The U.S. Supreme Court has ruled that statistics in general and regression analysis in particular are legitimate evidence in labor market discrimination cases.[41] Moreover, a "Joint Policy Statement on Lending Discrimination" issued by HUD, Justice, and the financial regulatory agencies in March 1994 explicitly states: "A pattern or practice of disparate treatment on a prohibited basis may also be established through a valid statistical analysis of detailed loan file information, provided that the analysis controls for possible legitimate explanations for differences in treatment."[42] It seems likely, therefore, that a court would accept the type of evidence provided by the Boston Fed Study or the Decatur investigation. This statement goes on to say that "evidence of disparate impact in lending could also constitute discrimination under those laws (ECOA and FaHA) when a lender cannot show that a 'business necessity' exists."[43]

The lack of court decisions also implies that the range of lender actions covered by these laws is not yet clear. In its consent decree with Decatur Federal S&L and some later ones, the Justice Department argued that these laws also extend into some types of lender behavior covered by the CRA, including lenders' definitions of their lending territory, branching decisions, and advertising practices, as well as into lenders' uses of various types of loan products and hiring policies.[44] However, no court has yet ruled on these arguments.

Although ECOA is complementary to FaHA as a fair lending law, the primary responsibility for enforcing ECOA falls on the agencies that regulate lenders, not on HUD.[45] The regulatory agencies involved are the Office of the Comptroller of the Currency (OCC); the Federal Reserve Board (the Fed); the Federal Deposit Insurance Corporation (FDIC); the Office of Thrift Supervision; and the National Credit Union Administration. Each of these agencies is responsible for monitoring the compliance with the ECOA of lenders within their purview, as well as of these lenders' mortgage company subsidiaries. OCC, for example, monitors about 3,700 national banks, which include many of the largest lenders in the country; the Fed monitors the 1,000 or so state-chartered banks that are members of the Federal Reserve System; and the FDIC monitors about 7,500 state-chartered, federally insured savings banks.[46] These financial regulatory agencies all belong to the Federal Financial Institutions Council, which is an interagency organization for coordinating regulatory activities. The Federal Trade Commission (FTC) is responsible for monitoring the activities of independent mortgage companies. This monitoring activity is tangential, however, to the principal mandate of the FTC, which is to promote fair trade practices in all consumer markets. Until recently, therefore, independent mortgage companies have received relatively little monitoring for ECOA compliance.[47]

The regulatory agencies have a variety of tools to enforce compliance with FaHA and ECOA.[48] OCC, for example, has developed detailed procedures for examining the banks it supervises and for ensuring compliance with the law.[49] Moreover, the Fed regularly conducts consumer compliance examinations at every bank it supervises. Banks with poor records may be visited as often as every 6 months.[50] The regulatory agencies can require lenders who violate one of these acts to change their practices, to provide relief to victims, or to pay civil penalties.[51] The Fed recently demonstrated its power in this regard by blocking a merger between Shawmut National Corporation and the New Dartmouth Bank on the grounds that Shawmut had not complied with fair lending laws.[52]

Although the principal responsibilities for enforcing FaHA and ECOA fall on different agencies, the financial regulatory agencies, HUD, and Justice are all involved in enforcing both laws, and cooperation among these parties is continually evolving. Because FaHA is more explicit about enforcement than ECOA, and because these two laws have equivalent prohibitions concerning mortgage lending behavior, FaHA is the principal law for addressing mortgage discrimination. Nevertheless, ECOA strengthens both the legal prohibition against this type of discrimination and the role of the financial regulatory agencies. The regulatory agencies are required to refer to the Justice Department any cases involving a pattern and practice of violating ECOA or FaHA, and they are required to refer violations of FaHA to HUD.[53] Because the definition of pattern and practice is not always clear, and because the coverage of ECOA and FaHA is so similar, this process of enforcing two laws with many enforcement agencies inevitably leaves a great deal of discretion in the hands of the agency that first handles a case.[54]

Although the details of this enforcement system are still evolving, the recent rediscovery of discrimination in mortgage lending has resulted in a dramatic burst of fair lending enforcement activity by all the parties with enforcement responsibility.[55] HUD Secretary Henry Cisneros set as one of his top priorities the implementation of "new initiatives to combat discrimination and redlining in mortgage lending and property insurance."[56] Attorney General Janet Reno "is deeply committed to eliminating consideration of race or national origin from home mortgage lending" and has called for "bold and vigorous enforcement of fair housing laws."[57] In recent testimony, Eugene A. Ludwig, the Comptroller of Currency, began a description of the topics on which he would focus by saying, "First, I will devote a great deal of time and energy to eliminating discrimination in our financial services system."[58] Moreover, the Comptroller recently initiated a large testing program to look for discrimination in the pre-application procedures of the lenders it oversees.[59] Recent testimony by Chairman of the Federal Reserve Board Alan Greenspan added another clear voice to this debate.

> We simply cannot as a nation tolerate unfair and illegal activity that puts some of our citizens at a disadvantage as they try to participate in the credit markets. . . . We have a problem whose magnitude may be unknown but whose presence is undeniable. . . . Free market capitalistic systems rooted in individual freedom cannot and should not abide such unjust behavior.[60]

This new enforcement resolve is also reflected in the March 1994 policy statement by the Interagency Task Force on Fair Lending (1994, p. 1), which states: "Discrimination in lending on the basis of race or other prohibited factors is destructive, morally repugnant, and against the law. It prevents those who are discriminated against from enjoying the benefits of access to credit. The Agencies [on the Task Force] will not tolerate lending discrimination in any form."[61]

The Community Reinvestment Act

The Community Reinvestment Act, which is Title VIII of the Housing and Community Development Act of 1977, is another important piece of legislation for combating discrimination in mortgage lending by banks and thrifts. It does not apply to nondepository lenders, such as mortgage bankers. CRA was passed to address redlining and disinvestment in low-income and minority neighborhoods, which were then believed to be widespread.[62] It reinforced and strengthened the requirements in many lenders' charters, and it obligates each financial regulatory agency in evaluating each lender under its jurisdiction to

> (1) assess the institution's record of meeting the credit needs of its entire community, including low- and moderate-income neighborhoods, consistent with the safe and sound operation of [the] institution; and (2) take such record into account in evaluating an application for a charter, deposit insurance, branch or other deposit facility, office relocation, merger, or holding company acquisition of a depository institution.[63]

This language reveals that CRA focuses on the outcome-based definition of redlining given in Chapter 5; that is, on redlining defined as a relatively low flow of credit to the minority neighborhoods served by a lender.[64] Although discrimination in mortgage lending can be a cause of redlining by this definition, a lending institution may be guilty of redlining even if it treats comparable minority and white applicants exactly the same way. In principle, therefore, CRA imposes requirements that go beyond equal treatment of all applicants and neighborhoods.

The supporters of the original CRA legislation argued that lenders were obligated under the terms of their charters to meet the credit needs of their communities.[65] In addition, lenders can, and apparently sometimes do, discriminate in many ways that are difficult to observe, such as in advising applicants. By focusing on an outcome-based definition of redlining, CRA bypasses the need to identify individual acts of discrimination and gives lenders responsibility for the outcome. When the flow of funds to minority neighborhoods in a lender's service area lags behind the flow to comparable white neighborhoods, CRA establishes the presumption that the lender bears some responsibility for this outcome and therefore bears some responsibility for improving the situation.[66]

Because the CRA requirements are somewhat vague, however, this presumption is not so clear in practice. Over time, the regulatory agencies worked together to develop a set of twelve assessment factors for determining CRA compliance. These factors fell into five categories: ascertainment of community credit needs, marketing and types of credit offered and extended, geographic distribution of applications and loans and opening and closing of offices, discrimination and other illegal activities, and community development.[67] By March 1989 regulator coordination had progressed to the point at which the Fed, Federal Home Loan Bank Board (now the Office of Thrift Supervision), OCC, and FDIC issued a Joint Statement on the Community Reinvestment Act to clarify lenders' responsibilities under CRA.[68] This Statement called on lenders to implement detailed processes for evaluating community credit needs and to prepare an expanded CRA report that described the steps they had taken.

Despite this coordination, the regulatory agencies did not use CRA requirements to force significant changes in lender behavior. The twelve assessment factors were combined into a rating or grade for each bank, but the implicit standards in this rating system were lenient, and fewer than 3 percent of lenders were given failing grades.[69] Widespread dissatisfaction with the rating system led to provisions amending CRA in the 1989 Financial Institutions, Reform, Recovery and Enforcement Act (FIRREA). In particular, FIRREA established a more precise and demanding rating system and required public closure of each lender's CRA rating and evaluation. The new rating system uses the same twelve assessment factors, but tightens the standards and requires each lender's record in meeting community credit needs to be placed into one of four categories: outstanding, satisfactory, needs improvement, and substantial noncompliance.[70] Moreover, each lender must make its CRA rating and evaluation available at all of its offices and to anyone who requests it.[71]

Although many lenders have responded to CRA requirements by developing programs to assess the credit needs of neighborhoods in their lending area, and by taking advantage of opportunities for loans in low-income and minority communities, regulators have not used CRA to force a significant reallocation of credit toward minority neighborhoods.[72] In fact, no lender action was denied on CRA grounds until 1989, when the Fed turned down a merger request by Continental Bank Corporation of Illinois.[73] Even with the new rating system and reporting requirements in FIRREA, most of the CRA requirements have to do with bureaucratic procedures, not actual outcomes.

Moreover, regulators have long revealed an unwillingness to require loans that do not meet widely accepted underwriting standards; nothing in these amendments is likely to alter this tendency.

Discriminatory practices by lenders, such as advertising programs that ignore minority neighborhoods, decisions to limit branch offices to all-white neighborhoods, more favorable applications procedures for white than for minority customers, or stricter underwriting standards for minority than for white customers, will not be accepted by regulators.[74] However, these practices are already covered by FaHA and ECOA, and, as the strong evidence of continuing discrimination indicates, neither CRA nor these other laws have been effective in eliminating them. As implemented by regulators, therefore, CRA represents a tool for encouraging communication between banks and thrifts and the communities in which they operate and as a potential source of additional enforcement powers; namely, the threat CRA-based denials of requested lender actions, for lenders' ECOA mandate to eliminate discriminatory practices. Because the range of behavior covered under ECOA and FaHA is not yet firmly established by the courts, CRA may be a better tool for addressing some types of discrimination by banks and thrifts, such as advertising campaigns that neglect minority neighborhoods. If the courts follow the line of argument made by the Justice Department in the Decatur case, however, the types of discrimination covered by the three laws may converge.

Although regulators appear unlikely to push CRA enforcement very far beyond ECOA, CRA still represents a significant extension of the fair lending enforcement system because of the role of community groups. This role is not spelled out in the law, but CRA gives community groups "implicit standing" to challenge lender requests to regulators.[75] Thus, any lender request for a branch office or other deposit facility, for an office relocation, for a merger, or for holding company acquisition of a depository institution is subject to a CRA challenge by a community group. The lender action cannot take place until the appropriate regulatory institution has ruled that the lender meets its CRA obligations or the lender reaches an agreement with the community group or groups making the challenge. As a result, community groups are in a position both to delay and to raise the cost of lender actions. To avoid these costs, lenders have a strong incentive to improve their CRA rating and often to negotiate a settlement when a challenge is made.

Since 1985 about 200 CRA-based settlements have been reached between community groups and lenders, primarily large regional banks. These settlements cover mortgage lending programs, small business lending, and, in some cases, programs to help provide affordable housing.[76] Some observers claim that these settlements have brought billions of dollars in loans into low- and moderate-income communities, and one estimate places this flow as high as $20 billion.[77] These estimates do not, however, net out the loans that would have been made in these communities even without the settlements.[78]

The overall impact of CRA on lender behavior is difficult to evaluate. No credible evidence supports a claim that the regulatory agencies' enforcement of CRA requirements has had a significant impact either on discriminatory practices by lenders or on credit flows to minority neighborhoods. Moreover, the extent to which settlements between lenders and community groups go beyond what lenders would have done anyway has not been clearly established; many of the settlements undoubtedly opened up credit opportunities for minority households and businesses, perhaps with ancillary benefits such as affordable housing, but the extent of these benefits has not been accurately measured.

Court Cases Concerning Integration Maintenance

Hiding in the background of the debate over fair housing and fair lending policy is the issue of integration maintenance. This issue has been periodically addressed by policymakers throughout the last 25 years, but it has proven to be so controversial that federal policymakers have tended to shy away from it, and most of the important developments have taken place in court.

The question of whether promoting integration should be an objective of federal policy appeared in the original congressional debate over the Fair Housing Act. Senator Walter Mondale of Minnesota, one of the sponsors of the legislation, stated that FaHA was intended "to replace the ghettos by truly integrated and balanced living patterns."[79] Another sponsor, Senator Brooke of Massachusetts, stated that "America's future must lie in the successful integration of all our many minorities, or there will be no future worthy of America."[80]

The interpretation of congressional intent remains controversial, however, because the debate also suggested that eliminating discrimination was all that was necessary for the creation of integrated communities. Senator Mondale said that "the basic purpose of this legislation is to permit people who have the ability to do so to buy any house offered to the public if they can afford to buy it"; and Senator Brooke said America's "future does not require imposed residential and social integration; it does require the elimination of compulsory segregation in housing, education, and employment."[81] Thus, some people have argued that the federal government's affirmative mandate to promote "fair housing" and "freedom of choice" cannot be achieved unless people have the freedom to select from all types of neighborhoods, including integrated ones.[82] Others believe that racial and ethnic integration is simply a hoped-for outcome in a housing market without discrimination — not a legitimate objective of federal policy.[83]

The courts generally have sided with those who claim that integration is a legitimate federal objective under the Fair Housing Act.[84] In the 1977 *Linwood* case, which concerned a municipal ordinance banning for-sale signs, the U.S. Supreme Court acknowledged "the vital goal this ordinance serves: namely promoting stable, racially integrated housing." The Court went on to say, "There can be no question about the importance of achieving this goal. This Court has expressly recognized that substantial benefits flow to both blacks and whites from interracial association and that Congress has made a strong national commitment to promote integrated housing."[85] In the 1979 *Bellwood* case, in which the village of Bellwood, Illinois, claimed racial steering by real estate brokers, the Court cited its *Linmark* decision and went on to say that "if, as alleged, petitioner's sales practices actually have begun to rob Bellwood of its racial balance and stability, the village has standing to challenge the legality of that conduct."[86]

Despite this endorsement of integration as a legitimate federal objective, the legal standing of actual integration policies remains unclear because the Supreme Court also has set tough constitutional standards, called the "strict scrutiny" test, that must be met by any race-conscious policy, including one to promote integration.[87] In particular, any race-conscious policy must meet three tests. First, it must "further a compelling government interest." Second, it must be "necessary and effective for dealing with the issue and designed" specifically to address it. Third, it "must not stigmatize the minority group as inferior."[88]

Each of these tests places severe constraints on any policy designed to promote or maintain integration. Although courts have ruled that integration is a legitimate objective of government policy, they also have ruled that race-conscious policies are allowable only to offset the effects of past discrimination. There is, of course, ample evidence that past and current discrimination are important causes of the lack of stable, racially integrated neighborhoods.[89] In any particular case, however, it may be difficult to identify past discrimination and therefore to convince a court that it played a major role in preventing integration.[90]

The second test indicates that a race-conscious policy cannot be used if it is possible to use alternative policies that are not race-conscious. Because antidiscrimination enforcement efforts have been lax in many places, it may be difficult to prove that the possibilities for promoting integration by eliminating discrimination have been exhausted. Even active enforcement of antidiscrimination laws has not yet eliminated discrimination, however, and current discrimination is by no means the only reason that stable, racially integrated neighborhoods are so rare. "These arguments suggest that the case for the necessity of employing race-conscious [policies] is complex, but that it *can* be made."[91]

The third test requires policy makers to consider the burdens any race-conscious policy imposes on minorities. Policies that integrate by discriminating, for example, will not survive this test.

Even if these constitutional standards are met, an integration maintenance policy also must meet statutory standards, that is, it must not violate FaHA. According to one commentator,

> while the courts have generally agreed to the interpretation of Title VIII as promoting integration, difficulties exist in resolving issues when integration policies come into conflict with policies of antidiscrimination. Here antidiscrimination prohibitions are likely to prevail. Thus, in *U.S. v. Charlottesville* (1989) the Court argued that the antidiscrimination provisions of Title VIII are constraints within which the integration policies are pursued, and that these prohibitions against discrimination are usually primary unless race conscious actions to pursue integration can survive the strict scrutiny test.[92]

These legal principles have been applied to several types of integration maintenance policies, namely "quotas, controls on real estate solicitations, bans on for-sale signs, and affirmative marketing programs involving housing information and counselling services."[93]

Courts have not ruled that quotas always are invalid, but they have made it clear that quotas are acceptable only under very limited circumstances. As one scholar puts it:

> First, they should be imposed . . . in response to a prior finding of illegal discrimination and should be designed, under the "narrowly tailored" doctrine, to correct the segregation caused by this past discrimination. Second, the court appears more favorable toward access quotas or goals than limiting quotas. . . . Third, the quotas should be time limited.[94]

One example of a quota that the court did not accept is the ceiling quota used by Starrett City.[95] This quota attempted to prevent racial tipping by placing a ceiling on the share of minorities in any building (and indeed on any floor). As a result, minorities spent much longer on the waiting list than did whites—a form of discrimination. The Supreme Court ruled in 1987 that this quota was not permissible.

Some other integration maintenance policies have been accepted by the Supreme Court. In one case, *Barrick* v. *Gary* (1973), the Court accepted a municipal ban on for-sale signs on the grounds that the signs "had caused panic selling and white flight."[96] The Court also accepted a municipal ban on solicitations by real estate agents (*South Suburban Housing Center,* 1988) and ruled in favor of a private, non-profit housing assistance center that gave free advice only to people who wanted to make pro-integrative moves (*Steptoe* v. *Beverly,* 1987).[97] Moreover, a recent appeals court decision concerning race-conscious counseling by the South-Suburban Housing Center in Chicago "affirmed the legality of affirmative marketing techniques and stated that any activity that serves to increase competition among all racial groups for housing is precisely the type of robust multiracial market activity that the Fair Housing Act intends to stimulate."[98] To put it another way, "the court did not see a conflict between the goal of furthering integration and providing equal opportunities to homebuyers of all races."[99] The Supreme Court refused to hear this case, thereby ratifying the use of race-conscious counseling, without identifying circumstances under which such a policy would be inappropriate.

Finally, the Court has addressed the issue of integration in several cases involving public housing. The most important case, *Gautreaux,* was originally filed in 1966 against the Chicago Housing Authority (CHA) and HUD.[100] The plaintiffs were public housing tenants who argued that CHA discriminated both in the selection of sites, with a strong tendency to place projects in largely minority neighborhoods, and in the placement of tenants, with a strong tendency to place minorities only in minority projects. Courts agreed with the plaintiffs, and on various appeals, HUD and CHA were ordered to cooperate and find a metropolitanwide solution to the segregation in the public housing system. In April 1976 the Supreme Court ruled for the plaintiffs and ratified the call for a metropolitanwide solution. The resulting Gautreaux Program has been back in the news recently because evaluations of its results have been published, because comparable programs have been tried and evaluated in other metropolitan areas, and because HUD has implemented a new version of the program as a demonstration in a few sites.[101]

◼ CONCLUSIONS

The year 1968 was a watershed for fair housing policy; it outlawed discrimination in housing and mortgage lending through the passage of the Fair Housing Act and the resurrection by the Supreme Court of the 1866 Civil Rights Act. These events did not provide the federal government with strong enforcement powers, however, and for the next 20 years, the burden of enforcing these laws fell largely on state and local civil rights agencies, private fair housing groups, and the victims of discrimination.

The Fair Housing Amendments Act of 1988 dramatically increased the federal government's enforcement powers. This act increased the penalties on convicted discriminators, authorized HUD to bring discrimination complaints before an administrative law judge, expanded the role of the Justice Department, and allowed the Secretary of HUD to initiate discrimination cases on the basis of HUD's own investigations. These provisions provide a wide range of effective enforcement tools for any administration that chooses to use them.

In combating discrimination by lenders, the Fair Housing Act is complemented by the 1974 Equal Credit Opportunity Act and the 1977 Community Reinvestment Act. ECOA gives enforcement powers to the agencies, such as the Federal Reserve Board and the Office of the Comptroller of the Currency, that regulate lenders. Thanks to the recent rediscovery of discrimination in mortgage lending, these financial regulatory agencies have revamped their procedures for finding and addressing discriminatory practices. Independent mortgage lenders, who now handle a large share of home mortgages, are regulated by the Federal Trade Commission, which has more limited powers and experience than the financial regulatory agencies. It remains to be seen whether the FTC can provide adequate monitoring of discrimination by these lenders.

The Community Reinvestment Act requires thrifts and commercial banks to meet the credit needs of all the neighborhoods in their market area, including minority neighborhoods. Lenders who do not live up to this requirement face challenges by community groups to their branching, merging, and other business decisions, as well as sanctions from the appropriate financial regulatory agency. CRA clearly adds to the set of laws that outlaw blatantly discriminatory practices, such as discrimination in loan approval, but it also establishes the presumption that lenders must take responsibility for credit outcomes in minority neighborhoods. Hence lenders may be required to expand credit in minority neighborhoods even without clear evidence that they engage in discriminatory practices. Although CRA has led to numerous settlements between lenders and community groups, the net impact of this legislation on credit opportunities for minority households has not yet been accurately measured.

Finally, developments in fair housing and fair lending policy over the last quarter-century have been accompanied by a debate, concentrated in the nation's courts, about programs to promote integration. In several cases, the Supreme Court has concluded, on the basis of the Fair Housing Act, that integration is a legitimate objective of federal policy. However, the Supreme Court has also established strong constitutional standards, called the "strict scrutiny" test, that must be met by any race-conscious policy, including one designed to promote integration. In particular, any such policy must be "necessary and effective" and it must not "stigmatize" the minority group.

Several local government programs to promote integration, including bans on for-sale signs and real estate solicitation, have passed the strict scrutiny test. Moreover, a recent Supreme Court decision ratified a program that involved race-conscious housing counseling. Other types of programs, including ceiling quotas, have been rejected by the Supreme Court. In addition, the Supreme Court has approved programs, such as the Gautreaux Program, that provide suburban housing opportunities to public housing residents when public housing authorities have a history of discrimination in site selection and other decisions.

Public Policy to Combat Discrimination in Housing: A Comprehensive Approach

■ THE LEGACY OF THE KERNER COMMISSION

On March 1, 1968, the National Advisory Commission on Civil Disorders, which had been appointed by President Lyndon Johnson almost a year earlier to investigate the causes of urban riots, issued its final report. This report, commonly referred to as the *Kerner Commission Report,* contained the famous conclusion:

> Our nation is moving toward two societies, one black, one white — separate and unequal.

> Reaction to last summer's disorders has quickened the movement and deepened the division. Discrimination and segregation have long permeated much of American life; they now threaten the future of every American.

> This deepening racial division is not inevitable. The movement apart can be reversed. Choice is still possible. Our principal task is to define that choice and to press for a national resolution.

> To pursue our present course will involve the continuing polarization of the American community and, ultimately, the destruction of basic democratic values.[1]

This conclusion is still remarkably accurate today.[2] Progress has been made over this quarter century: levels of overt discrimination in housing, lending, and employment are lower than they were; some of the most dramatic racial disparities, including those in educational achievement and wage rates, have narrowed significantly; and many black families have moved into the middle class.

Nevertheless, blacks continue to face widespread discrimination in housing and mortgage markets; American neighborhoods remain highly segregated along racial lines; racial prejudice continues to be high; black–white disparities in homeownership, education, and income remain large; and some racial disparities appear to be more serious and more intractable than they were in 1968. The growing concentration of poverty in central cities, for example, affects all racial and ethnic groups, but the system of discrimination is particularly hard on blacks. Moreover, unemployment rates for black youth in cities, along with the associated rates for dropping out of school, teenage pregnancy, drug abuse, and criminal activity, are staggeringly high.

The Hispanic population in the United States has grown dramatically since 1968. Although the designation of "Hispanic" does not carry the legacy of slavery and masks enormous diversity, it is connected with conflicts concerning immigration, oppression of Native Americans, and, in some cases, the powerful symbolism of skin color. Thus, many disparities between Hispanics and whites have exhibited trends similar to those of black–white disparities.[3] Hispanics are neither as segregated from whites nor, by most measures, as disadvantaged relative to whites as are blacks, but they face high levels of discrimination in housing and mortgage markets, Hispanic–white residential segregation is growing, and the disparities faced by some Hispanic groups, particularly Puerto Ricans and Mexican Americans, often approach and occasionally reach the levels faced by blacks.

In short, most black and Hispanic citizens continue to be caught in the system of discrimination. This system has many components, but one of the most central is discrimination in housing. The evidence presented in this book shows that continuing, widespread discrimination in housing and mortgage markets makes an important contribution to the perpetuation, and in some cases the worsening, of racial and ethnic disparities in economic and social outcomes.

The *Kerner Commission Report* also presented a framework for public policy. To be specific, it offered three "choices" for the nation: the "present policies choice," the "enrichment choice," and the "integration choice." As the earlier quotation makes clear, the Commission rejected the present policies choice as inadequate. The enrichment choice "would aim at creating dramatic improvements in the quality of life in disadvantaged central-city neighborhoods—both white and Negro. It would require marked increases in federal spending for education, housing, employment, job training, and social services."[4] The integration choice, on the other hand, was to directly attack the separation between blacks and whites by "creating strong incentives for Negro movement out of central-city ghettos and enlarging freedom of choice concerning housing, employment and schools."[5]

This conceptualization of the policy issues has dominated the debate over urban policy in the years since 1968.[6] Dozens of books and articles have been written defending either the proposition that the federal government should develop the ghetto or the proposition that the federal government should actively promote racial integration. Although there have been many thoughtful contributions to this debate, many of which are reviewed below, the Kerner Commission framework has outlived its usefulness.

First, the two "choices" now often appear simply as caricatures. The enrichment choice, labeled by some as "gilding the ghetto," is said to perpetuate existing patterns of separation and to ensure outcomes that are separate and unequal.[7] The integration choice, labeled by some as "dispersal," has been called both an attempt to diffuse black political power and an attempt to legislate preferences; that is, to force antagonistic blacks and whites to live together against their wills.[8] As we will see, these caricatures badly distort the truth and mask important substantive issues, but they are now so firmly fixed in some people's minds that these two choices no longer appear useful as guides to policy.

Second, and more important, the Kerner Commission choices make it seem as if we must select one route or another, that we must either develop the ghetto or promote integration. Perhaps hoping that the problems themselves will prove to be simple, people often embrace simple solutions, but the truth is that complicated problems, such as those brought on by racial and ethnic divisions, require complicated, balanced solutions—not simple extremes. One cannot hope to untangle the system of discrimination by focusing on only one of its elements. Effective policy must attack many elements of this system and account for the many interconnections it contains.

The question, of course, is how to find the right balance. Somewhat ironically given the subsequent debate, the Kerner Commission itself searched for a balance. In fact, the integration choice it favored explicitly called for "large-scale improvement in the quality of ghetto life"[9] and included many specific actions, such as job creation or training programs, that were designed to develop the ghetto. After all, it argued, policies to promote integration would not have an immediate impact on many existing disparities. Nevertheless, neither the Kerner Commission nor the subsequent policy debate provide much guidance in finding the right balance.

This chapter attempts to recast the debate by presenting five principles to help find a balanced policy for fair housing and fair lending.[10] The principles presented here are my own, but they build on widely held values, many of which are expressed in current legislation or in Supreme Court decisions, and on evidence about the discriminatory system presented throughout this book.

■ PRINCIPLES FOR FAIR HOUSING POLICY

Principle 1: Eliminate Market Discrimination

The first principle is the obvious one—racial and ethnic discrimination in housing, in lending, and in related markets must be eradicated. This discrimination violates principles of fair treatment that are fundamental to American democracy, poisons the relationships among groups in our society, helps perpetuate the system of discrimination, and is clearly illegal according to many longstanding laws. To the extent that existing laws and policies do not succeed in eliminating discrimination, stronger, more effective laws and policies must be developed.

This principle is about freedom of choice. We must strive for a system in which current racial and ethnic discrimination no longer constrains the housing choices of black and Hispanic families.

An important corollary is that discrimination also must be attacked on a broad front because different types of discrimination reinforce each other. Some of this reinforcement is direct. For example, real estate brokers appear to discriminate in part because they anticipate trouble finding mortgages for minority customers, at least under some circumstances. Indirect reinforcement can be equally powerful, however, as discrimination by landlords, real estate brokers, lenders, insurers, and employers all support the racial and ethnic economic disparities on which stereotypes feed. These stereotypes are key supports of racial and ethnic prejudice—and ultimately of discrimination. Attacking only one type of discrimination leaves most of the discriminatory system still in place; such a limited strategy is like mopping up a spill while the water is still running.

Principle 2: Avoid Government Discrimination

The second principle, closely related to the first, is that, except under extreme circumstances, government programs themselves should avoid discrimination, either against or in favor of minorities. Government policies that discriminate against minorities, whatever their intended objectives, directly offset the gains from eliminating discrimination in private markets. Policies that discriminate against white individuals undercut white support for an antidiscrimination program[11] and implicitly promote the view that minority households are somehow incapable of competing in a free marketplace.[12] Moreover, any government-sanctioned discrimination contradicts the principle of equal treatment and thereby undermines the argument for stronger antidiscrimination enforcement efforts.[13]

Quotas or tenant selection policies that explicitly favor minority individuals over white individuals (or vice versa) are examples of policies that violate this principle.[14] Quotas are a "know-nothing" approach in the sense that they do not address the underlying causes of discrimination and racial transition but simply attempt to overrule them.[15] In fact, however, these underlying causes are powerful and will not disappear when quotas are applied. By attempting to force the issue, quotas almost inevitably involve discrimination of one type or another. The Starrett City ceiling quota, for example, did not address black households' lack of access to housing in other locations and clearly discriminated against black households on the waiting list.[16] Moreover, rigid floor quotas almost inevitably involve reverse discrimination, that is, discrimination against whites.

According to a longstanding legal principle, policies that favor minorities are an acceptable remedy in the case of individuals or firms with a history of discrimination against minorities. In general, application of this principle requires proof of discriminatory effect, not the stronger standard of discriminatory intent.[17] Whatever the standard for proving past discrimination, however, this legal principle provides an important exception to the rule of equal treatment and should, in my judgment, continue to be used in individual cases.

The question is whether this exception applies to government actions as well as to actions by private actors. Before we can address this question, we must consider the other side of the coin; namely, why government action that goes beyond eliminating discrimination is needed in the first place.

Principle 3: Offset the Effects of Past Discrimination

The third principle is that government programs must find ways to offset the effects of past discrimination against blacks and Hispanics. This principle is supported by two main arguments. First, existing racial and ethnic disparities in economic and social outcomes are major components of the discriminatory system, which poisons intergroup relations in this country, with great costs for all of us, and which places minority citizens at a severe and unfair disadvantage.[18] Thus, the legacy of our discriminatory past plays a significant role in preserving an unequal present: addressing these disparities is a key step in promoting justice and equal opportunity.

The second argument is that government should recognize that it bears a large share of the responsibility for existing racial and ethnic disparities. To be specific, the federal government has engaged in discriminatory acts both of commission, such as enforced segregation in public housing, and of omission, such as poor enforcement of antidiscrimination laws. Although the federal government has already taken some steps to offset the consequences of its past actions, racial and ethnic disparities continue to be severe and the federal government is obligated to continue its search for policies to ameliorate them.

The crucial role of existing disparities in the system of discrimination is worth reviewing. Centuries of discrimination by private actors and governments ensure that the average black or Hispanic household falls behind the average white household on virtually every measure of socioeconomic achievement, including income, education, and housing quality. This situation is a key source of the racial and ethnic stereotypes on which current prejudice and discrimination feed. Many whites see the concentration of disadvantage in some minority neighborhoods and conclude that letting minority households into their neighborhood would lead to neighborhood deterioration — a conclusion that gives landlords and real estate brokers a strong incentive to discriminate. Of course, racial or ethnic transition, as distinct from income or class transition, does not imply neighborhood deterioration, but the strong correlation between minority status and economic deprivation overpowers this fact both in whites' perceptions and in neighborhood transition as it often is experienced. Hence, this nation will find it impossible, I fear, to eliminate current discrimination without facing up to its discriminatory past.

Now we can return to the question: Can the federal government offset existing disparities without practicing reverse discrimination itself? As explained earlier, reverse discrimination by the federal government, in the form, say, of a floor quota that explicitly selects minority applicants over more qualified whites, undermines both the principle of equal treatment and public support for antidiscrimination programs. Because these costs are so high, policies that explicitly favor minorities should be used only as a last resort. Can such policies be avoided? Can we find policies that expand opportunities and resources for minorities without explicitly selecting minorities over whites?

I believe that the answer to these questions, at least for fair housing policy, is clearly affirmative.[19] Policies that offset existing disparities without discrimination are available. Some policies, such as floor quotas, clearly involve a conflict between principles two and three, but other policies are available in which no such conflict is present. We must not let the specter of quotas prevent us from addressing the grim legacy of our past.[20] To do so would be to leave intact one of the principal supports for current discrimination.

The key to finding policies that offset disparities without reverse discrimination is to identify social and economic outcomes for which racial and ethnic disparities are particularly large and then provide assistance to all people disadvantaged in that outcome, regardless of their race and ethnicity.[21] This could be called a "disparate benefits" approach because it focuses on policies that treat all racial and ethnic groups the same but have disparate benefits for disadvantaged minorities.[22] Perhaps the clearest example appears in education. Remember that almost 60 percent of schools that are 90 percent or more minority have family poverty rates above 50 percent, whereas only 4 percent of largely white schools have poverty rates this high.[23] Programs to provide aid to all schools with high poverty rates, which will be discussed in more detail below, therefore directly address a key consequence of past discrimination, while avoiding any hint of reverse discrimination. This approach requires that some of the funds go to helping poor white students, but this is a desirable outcome in its own right and, if programs focus on outcomes that exhibit large racial and ethnic disparities, the benefits will be relatively concentrated on poor black and Hispanic students; that is, they will help offset the consequences of past discrimination.

Programs to address social problems that fall particularly heavily on minorities obviously must operate in markets other than the housing market, even when housing discrimination is a principal cause of the racial and ethnic disparities. A comprehensive program to address discrimination in housing therefore must include programs to address social problems in education and labor markets, as well as others.

Principle 4: Make Integration a Real Choice

One cannot eliminate discrimination without making racial and ethnic integration a real choice.[24] To put it another way, effective antidiscrimination policy must recognize the important role that racial and ethnic residential segregation plays in supporting the discriminatory system in housing, schools, and employment. Segregation is not simply an incidental outcome of the discriminatory system but is, in fact, a key reason why discrimination is so hard to eliminate—an outcome that becomes a cause.

The role of segregation begins with the fact that racial and ethnic prejudice can thrive only in a world in which different racial and ethnic groups rarely live in the same places. This nation cannot break down the stereotypes and ignorance that feed prejudice without providing extensive, stable opportunities for different racial and ethnic groups to live and work together. Moreover, prejudiced white households flee racially or ethnically changing neighborhoods in part because they have almost no examples of stable integration to observe and in part because they have so many stable all-white areas to which they can flee.

This white prejudice and these white actions in turn give landlords, real estate brokers, and perhaps lenders an incentive to discriminate in relatively stable white areas and to encourage racial or ethnic transition once it has begun.[25] Thus, segregation plays a key role in giving housing agents an incentive to manipulate the racial and ethnic composition of neighborhoods by discriminating in some cases and encouraging transition in others.[26]

Policies that identify and prosecute discriminators are important, but they are seriously incomplete because they do little to eliminate the segregated system that gives landlords, real estate brokers, and lenders an incentive to discriminate in the first place.[27] Even with an effective enforcement system, many housing agents will find a way to discriminate if they have a strong economic incentive to do so. Thus, a strategy that focuses on enforcement alone leaves one key component of the discriminatory system, the extent of racial segregation, in the hands of the discriminators themselves. An effective strategy to combat discrimination therefore must include government support for stable integration.[28]

Some scholars have argued that principles two and four are contradictory, that one cannot promote integration without discriminating—that is, without using some policy to limit the flow of minorities into integrated areas.[29] Other scholars have responded, far more persuasively in my view, that these two principles are fundamentally complementary: one cannot eliminate discrimination without promoting integration and vice versa.[30] Whether or not one believes in integration for its own sake, one must recognize that segregation—the inverse of integration—supports mistrust and misperception across groups and thereby supports prejudice and discrimination.

Proponents of the Starrett City ceiling quota, for example, claimed that it was the only way to preserve integration there.[31] Although it is true that one can design policies, such as the Starrett City quota, in which the objectives of eliminating discrimination and of promoting integration are contradictory, it is equally true that alternative policies without this contradiction are available.[32] The Starrett Corporation itself weakened the conflict between these objectives by adding amenities that made Starrett City more attractive to whites.[33] More importantly, Starrett Corporation had (and indeed still has) access to policies that probably could eliminate the contradiction altogether. These policies include informing families on its waiting list about housing that is available in one of its other developments and paying moving expenses for any family on a waiting list at any Starrett project who is willing to live in a project in which its racial or ethnic group is underrepresented.[34]

Principles three and four return us to the debate inspired by the Kerner Commission: One must choose, some scholars say, between "dispersal" of the minority population and "gilding the ghetto."[35] In my judgment, these two objectives are complementary, not competing. It makes no more sense to strive for a situation in which everyone lives in an integrated environment than to strive for a world that is "separate but equal." The problems of prejudice and discrimination arise from the nation's failure to provide opportunities for stable integration as well as its failure to redress the costs imposed on minorities by past discrimination. The only way to eliminate discrimination is to attack both these problems.[36] We must expand the opportunities for people who would consider living in an integrated environment while revitalizing minority communities, with their unique political, economic, and cultural contributions. Indeed, both of these routes are necessary to eradicate discrimination.

This principle does not say that all minorities or all whites should move to integrated neighborhoods. Indeed, it is not intended to force anyone to live anywhere.[37] Instead, this principle builds on the well-established conclusion that without government intervention, stable racial integration rarely occurs, and stable ethnic integration, at least between Hispanics and whites, is uncommon. Despite moderating white prejudice, opportunities for interracial or interethnic living in this country are very scarce; even if minority and white families prefer a multiracial or multicultural environment, they usually cannot find stable integrated neighborhoods into which they can move. To promote true freedom of choice, governments must intervene to make integration a possibility for anyone, minority or white, who wants it. Moreover, the only legitimate way for governments to intervene is to support people who want to build integrated communities—not to force them to do so.

The debate between development and dispersal has a long history within the minority community as well as among academics and government policymakers.[38] The principle that integration should be a choice is offered here purely as guidance for public policy, not as advice for either the minority or the white community. Blacks or Hispanics in a particular urban area have the right to remain in minority neighborhoods and not take advantage of incentives to integrate, just as they have the right to live in integrated neighborhoods if they so prefer. Whites have a right to remain in white neighborhoods—as long as they do so without discriminating—and a right to choose integration. It is not appropriate for me or for the federal government to tell people where to live. But it is, I believe, the responsibility of the federal government to address the fact that past and current discrimination—not neutral market forces—virtually eliminate integration as an option even for families who prefer it.

An important corollary is that an antidiscrimination program should recognize the power of the market forces that cause racial and ethnic transition in neighborhoods. They are so powerful that stable integration with significant minority representation rarely arises without active intervention from private fair housing groups and local governments and cooperation from the real estate industry. Moreover, as illustrated by the Starrett City case, even concerted efforts to promote integration may fail if they are concentrated in a single location, particularly a location near an impoverished minority neighborhood. Casual or half-hearted or spatially limited attempts to promote integration face serious obstacles.[39]

Recognizing the power of the forces causing transition does not imply, however, that the government should accept those forces as given. Continuing high levels of white prejudice and apparently increasing preferences for all-black neighborhoods among blacks are products of the discriminatory system. Recognizing the existence of white prejudice is not the same thing as believing that is inevitable. In fact, white prejudice has been declining over time, and programs to make integration a choice, along with other programs discussed in this chapter, would almost certainly lower prejudice still further among both whites and minorities.[40]

Principle 5: Support Personal Responsibility

The fifth principle is that government antidiscrimination programs and rhetoric should be careful to support the personal responsibility of all individuals, including those who have encountered discrimination as well as those who have practiced it. Enforcement programs are one way to emphasize personal responsibility; so are programs that support community involvement.

Most black and Hispanic people in this country lead normal, respectable lives, and some lead inspirational lives, in spite of discrimination. However, one of the most tragic features of a discriminatory system is that some people respond to discrimination and associated economic disparities by engaging in self-destructive or socially destructive behavior. Others simply don't put forth their best effort because they anticipate that discrimination will hold them back. These behavioral responses, in turn, feed the stereotypes that support continuing discrimination. The problem is that statements about the continuing existence of discrimination or the need for new policies are sometimes interpreted as excuses for anti-social behavior or lack of success. But they are explanations, not excuses—a crucial distinction that our leaders can help to make.

Individuals must be given hope and opportunity, not excuses. While recognizing and combating discrimination, public officials must be careful to emphasize that government action is not a substitute for individual initiative. There are, thank goodness, limits to the ability of governments to influence the efforts of individuals, and most efforts to promote responsibility must come from community leaders.[41] Nevertheless, governments can help to build a context in which the efforts of individuals and community organizations can pay off. Public officials can emphasize, for example, that individual initiative will be accompanied by aggressive attempts to eliminate discrimination and equalize opportunities for all, and governments can provide funds to support community initiative, particularly when it also serves other goals, including offsetting existing racial and ethnic disparities and supporting stable integration.

■ POLICY RECOMMENDATIONS

An antidiscrimination program that is consistent with these principles must focus not only on enforcement activities but also on more comprehensive policies that attack the foundations of discrimination. These more comprehensive policies must strive for a balance that supports stable integration, helps to revitalize disadvantaged communities, and promotes individual and community responsibility.[42]

Public Rhetoric

It is important to acknowledge the role played by public rhetoric about race relations and discrimination. During the Reagan/Bush years, the public rhetoric on these matters was decidedly mixed: statements deploring discrimination were accompanied by statements supporting tax exemptions for a university that practiced discrimination and statements weakening longstanding government support for effect, not intent, as a standard of proof in discrimination cases.[43] Policy actions sent out the same mixed signals: support for the 1988 amendments to the Fair Housing Act and assistance to state and local enforcement agencies were combined with a dramatic cutback in the prosecution of fair housing cases at the Justice Department.[44]

It is not possible to determine the extent to which these mixed signals influenced the perceptions or actions of the nations' citizens, but I am convinced that they gave comfort to people who wanted to discriminate and heightened the prejudicial attitudes that lead many blacks and whites to prefer not to live with each other.

Public rhetoric, combined with effective action, can have a powerful impact on actual outcomes. One telling example from recent history is the strong, consistent message against violence sent out by both Nelson Mandela and F.W. de Klerk in the period leading up to the first free elections in South Africa. The level of violence during and after these elections was far lower than anyone had predicted, partly, I believe, because of this strong public rhetoric.

The president and other national leaders could have a significant positive impact on race relations in this country with a regular series of strong public statements against racial and ethnic prejudice and discrimination.[45] President Clinton already has made some steps in this direction, with a statement in support of "fair housing and fair lending" in his 1994 State of the Union Address. Moreover, at a celebration of the 30th anniversary of the *Brown* v. *Board of Education* decision, President Clinton called the decision a "miracle" and spoke of the "unfinished business of helping us to live together as one people."[46] Secretary of Housing and Urban Development Henry Cisneros and Attorney General Janet Reno have also made several clear statements, along with policy steps reviewed below, against discrimination. For example, Cisneros has said that racism is a "malignancy" and "the great Achilles' heel of our nation's future."[47] Nevertheless, the public rhetoric on these problems is still limited: more forceful and more regular statements are needed from the president and other leaders.[48]

The key problem is that prejudice and discrimination are complex issues about which many people are ill-informed. Racial and ethnic stereotypes breed, and discriminators thrive, in an atmosphere of ignorance and silence. The president is in a unique position to address the widespread misunderstanding on these issues not only through effective policies but also through consistent public rhetoric. Racial and ethnic divisions pose serious threats to the long-run health of this nation, and I hope that President Clinton and all the presidents who follow him will use their "bully pulpit" to educate the nation about the continuing power of discrimination and to foster understanding and compassion across racial and ethnic lines. Other national leaders can contribute to this effort as well. After all, everyone, regardless of race or ethnicity, region, or political party, loses if our racial and ethnic divisions are not healed.

The message I hope the president and other national leaders convey is that in a democratic society we must all avoid stereotypes and learn to look for the strengths and weaknesses of each person we meet. To paraphrase Martin Luther King, Jr., we must learn to judge people not by the color of their skin but by the content of their character. All people, regardless of perceived race or ethnicity, are drawn from essentially the same genetic pool, with wide differences in traits across the individuals *within* any socially defined group but no meaningful differences in average traits *between* socially defined groups. People from all racial and ethnic backgrounds have valuable and unique contributions to make to the nation based on their culture and experience. Despite some progress, both current discrimination and a legacy of past discrimination still exist and place an enormous burden on the nation as a whole. The nation desperately needs a fair, nondiscriminatory program that attacks current discrimination, closes the disparities that hold back so many of our black and Hispanic citizens, and promotes individual and community responsibility.

Improved Fair Housing Enforcement

The centerpiece of fair housing policy should continue to be enforcement of the Fair Housing Act (FaHA). Thanks to the 1988 Fair Housing Amendments Act (FaHAA), the federal government now has extensive enforcement powers. By all accounts, it also is making great strides in learning how to put these powers to work. In this section I discuss recent developments in fair housing enforcement and propose several new policy initiatives.[49]

Complaint processing.   The first task of the fair housing enforcement system is to ensure that complaints are effectively handled. Because

HUD now has an expanded enforcement role, the number of complaints received by HUD has increased significantly in recent years, from 3,952 in FY1989 to 6,131 in FY1993.[50] To some degree, this increase undoubtedly is temporary. HUD initially processes a complaint only if the relevant state or local agency does not have a fair housing law that is "substantially equivalent" to FaHA, as amended. Because the 1988 amendments were so extensive, it has taken a while for state and local agencies to amend their own fair housing laws so that they are equivalent.[51] In the meantime, complaints originating in jurisdictions without upgraded laws will come directly to HUD.

As of October 1994, thirty-eight states and thirty localities had laws considered to be substantially equivalent to the amended FaHA.[52] Ultimately HUD will review complaints that (1) arise in a jurisdiction that refuses to pass a substantially equivalent fair housing law; (2) are not acted upon by the state or local agency within the required 30 days; (3) are referred to HUD by a state or local agency; or (4) are part of HUD's oversight of a state or local agency. Despite HUD's enhanced enforcement powers, it is difficult at this point to predict how many complaints HUD will process in the long run.

HUD has taken many steps in recent years to improve complaint processing.[53] It has, for example, improved intake procedures so that cases requiring a rapid response can be better identified and sent to the Justice Department for prompt legal action.[54] It has devised better incentives for managers so that rewarding for the number of cases closed does not give a manager an incentive to push for a rapid conciliation that is not in the interest of the complainant. These clearly are steps in the right direction.

When processing a complaint, HUD's responsibility is first to attempt a conciliation and then, if conciliation fails, to determine whether there is "cause" to believe that discrimination took place. If a "cause determination" is made, the case is then brought before an administrative law judge (ALJ). In FY1993, HUD received 6,131 FaHA-based complaints, concluded successful conciliations on 2,054 complaints, and issued "no cause" determinations in 1,035 cases and "cause" determinations in 211 others.[55] In about 60 percent of the cases with a "cause" determination, one party or the other elects to have the case heard in U.S. District Court, instead of in front of an ALJ.[56] These "election" cases are then prosecuted by the Justice Department. Over the last few years, HUD has improved its process for making its "cause" rulings, and both HUD and Justice have been developing expertise in prosecuting cases for which "cause" is found.

These enforcement mechanisms appear to be effective in resolving complaints and in sending strong signals to would-be discriminators.

The cases conciliated by HUD in FY1993 resulted in an average compensation to the victims of discrimination equal to $1,103, and 28 percent of the victims received some form of housing relief. The "cause" cases sent to ALJs sometimes result in out-of-court settlements and sometimes in judgments by the ALJ.[57] In FY1993, 47 settlements resulted in compensatory damages and civil penalties totaling over $215,000, and 14 decisions by ALJs resulted in damages and civil penalties of almost $300,000. In the 4 cases involving racial discrimination, the average award to the victim was $44,370.[58] In FY1994, the Justice Department handled 125 election cases, of which 34 were based on race and one on national origin. Damage awards in the race and ethnicity cases have been as high as $61,000.[59]

It is imperative that the federal government continue to support this element of the fair housing enforcement system. Because so many of the complaints handled by HUD and Justice are based on familial status, it is also imperative that the resources be sufficient to maintain support for cases based on race and ethnicity.[60]

Supporting state and local agencies.   As more and more state and local agencies operate under laws and procedures that are substantially equivalent to the amended FaHA, the burden of complaint processing will continue to shift from HUD to the state and local agencies.[61] In addition to providing oversight and training, the federal government supports these agencies through the Fair Housing Assistance Program (FHAP), which was originally implemented in 1984.[62] FHAP support comes in two forms. First, state and local agencies receive funds for "capacity building" during their first 2 years of participation in the program; that is, in the first 2 years after HUD has ruled that their law is "substantially equivalent" to FaHA. Second, agencies then receive funding based on the number of complaints they process.

The available evidence indicates that this program leads to more effective complaint processing by the so-called FHAP agencies.[63] Because these agencies will eventually process most fair housing complaints, this federal funding plays an important role in supporting the overall enforcement system and should be continued.

Taking the enforcement burden off the victims.   The principal strength of FaHAA is that it greatly expands the ability of the federal government to take the responsibility for enforcing fair housing law off the victims of discrimination. Under the original FaHA, most of the enforcement occurred through suits or complaints brought by victims. The only exception was pattern and practice suits brought by the Justice Department, which could lead to injunctive relief but not to damages or penalties on the discriminator. Now HUD and Justice, along with state and local agencies with substantially equivalent laws, have many tools for relieving victims of the enforcement burden.

The first set of new enforcement tools makes the complaint route more appealing to someone who believes that he or she is a victim of discrimination.[64] HUD can prosecute cases in front of ALJs, with the possibility of compensatory damages for the complainant and of civil penalties imposed on the defendant. The complainant (as well as the defendant) can also elect to have the case prosecuted by the Justice Department in Federal Court, without the possibility of civil penalties, but with the possibility of compensatory and punitive damages. These possibilities greatly enhance the enforcement system. Thus, it is imperative that HUD and Justice be given adequate funds to make full use of them.[65]

Second, the Secretary of HUD can now initiate fair housing cases that are not connected with a complaint. Because of HUD's new complaint-based enforcement tools and the recent increase in complaints processed by HUD, the agency's attention has so far been focused largely on improving complaint processing, not on developing a broad program for secretary-initiated cases. Several secretary-initiated investigations were conducted during the Bush administration, and a few cases were filed as a result.[66] The use of this tool has expanded somewhat in the Clinton administration, with investigations focusing on discrimination in housing advertising and (as discussed below) the activities of mortgage bankers.[67]

As more state and local agencies enter the "substantially equivalent" category, and the burden of complaint processing shifts away from HUD, this tool should become a central part of the fair housing enforcement system. Audits conducted on a random sample of housing units in areas where the HUD has reason to believe that discrimination may be high could have an enormous impact on discriminatory behavior. For example, the Housing Discrimination Study indicates that discrimination is particularly high in integrated areas and that multiple listing services often are used to facilitate racial steering.[68] Auditing programs that focus on integrated areas and on the role of MLSs therefore could have a powerful enforcement payoff.

FaHAA also added effectiveness to the federal government's original enforcement tool, the pattern and practice suit. In particular, these amendments not only made it possible for Justice to ask for compensatory and punitive damages in pattern and practice suits, they also authorized civil penalties in these suits of up to $100,000 for repeat offenders.

By all accounts, the Justice Department has been making full use of these enhancements during the Clinton administration.[69] It has set up an auditing program for rental housing, using federal employees and employees of private fair housing organizations as auditors. Through August 1994 this program has resulted in the filing of 18 pattern and practice suits, including 6 in Detroit that have generated over $1 million in settlements. Another case in Akron, Ohio, resulted in monetary relief of $175,000. Pattern and practice cases can also be based on complaints originally filed with HUD or on Justice Department investigations, which have recently covered discrimination in property insurance and zoning, as well as in housing. Overall, 15 pattern and practice suits based on race or national origin were filed in 1994, up from 5 in 1991.[70] These actions by the Justice Department are very valuable and should be continued.

Finally, state and local fair housing organizations, both public and private, play an important role in taking the enforcement burden off victims. In addition to supporting public agencies through FHAP, HUD supports private fair housing groups and a few public fair housing agencies through the Fair Housing Initiatives Program (FHIP), which was created in 1986 and made permanent in 1992. This program provides funds for testing and other enforcement activities, as well as for education and outreach.[71] In FY1993, 62 public and private agencies received FHIP support.[72] The testing programs supported by this act often are effective. A fair housing organization in the New York area, for example, initiated cases based on FHIP-supported testing that resulted in settlements of $90,000 and apartments set aside for minorities.[73] Moreover, a recent study finds evidence that a well-publicized testing program can result in lower levels of housing discrimination.[74]

By promoting community involvement, FHIP enhances the effectiveness of the fair housing enforcement system and also enhances community responsibility. It deserves continued federal funding.

New initiatives. The current fair housing enforcement system is vastly improved over the pre-1988 version. Recent experience in fair lending enforcement suggests, however, that two additional steps would strengthen the system still more. The first step, which reflects experience with HMDA, would be to gather regular, broad-based information about the racial and ethnic dimension of housing market outcomes. The second step, which reflects recent experience with CRA, would be to give real estate intermediaries formal responsibility for providing all neighborhoods with equal access to available housing.

One of the great lessons of HMDA is that broad-based information can be an effective tool both for focusing attention on an issue and for identifying potential discriminators. The problem is that broad-based information is more difficult to collect in the housing market, particularly the rental market, than in the mortgage market.

The rental market contains many small sellers who are largely unregulated. In some regions, many of the rental transactions involve an intermediary—a rental agency—but focusing on such agencies would yield an incomplete picture of the rental market as a whole. In the rental market, therefore, there does not appear to be a better mechanism for gathering broad-based information than an audit study based on a random sample of advertised apartments. Such a study would acknowledge the responsibility of landlords and rental agencies for housing market outcomes without imposing a large cost on them.[75] Hence, a national audit study of the rental housing market should be conducted by HUD at least every 5 years.

In the case of the sales market, however, the vast majority of transactions involve real estate brokers. Although real estate brokers are not regulated at the federal level, they are licensed at the state level and are widely regarded as performing services with important public implications. Moreover, many brokers, especially those who participate in an MLS, already use information collection and storage techniques that would facilitate the provision of information about their listings and sales activities, and perhaps even about the treatment of people who inquire about available housing. Thus, it appears far more feasible to collect broad-based information in the sales market than in the rental market.

The most feasible type of information to collect is the location and date of each listing and each sale. This information, which every broker must have, would be relatively easy to assemble. Because so many listings are placed on a multiple listing service, much of it could be collected from MLSs instead of from individual brokers, thereby minimizing the paperwork burden. This information would provide great insight into the locational dimension of brokers' activities. It would indicate the extent to which brokers attract listings in minority neighborhoods as well as their relative success in selling such listings. Hence, I propose a Home Sales Disclosure Act, which would require brokers to submit annually to HUD, either directly or through an MLS to which they belong, the address, listing date, and sale date of every listing they receive.

Another set of broad-based information about broker activities; namely, the race or ethnicity of each person who inquires about housing along with the number of units he or she inspects, could shed light on the search behavior of households and the marketing behavior of brokers. However, this type of information would be far more costly to collect because it involves so many people and is not now systematically collected by brokers. Although a pilot project to collect this type of information from a few large MLSs might prove valuable, it seems to me far more reasonable to gain insight into the treatment of potential buyers through an audit study. Hence, regular national audit studies of the sales market, say every 10 years, also would be valuable.

The second weakness in the current fair housing enforcement system is that it does not formalize real estate brokers' responsibility for housing market outcomes.[76] The fundamental premise of CRA; namely, that lenders are responsible not only for treating each customer equally but also for providing equal service to all neighborhoods in their service area, can reasonably be applied to real estate brokers, who handle virtually all housing sales and are widely acknowledged to be important gatekeepers into the housing market. Moreover, the evidence from HMPS, HDS, and many smaller audit studies shows definitively that, despite the clearly expressed support for fair housing by the National Association of Realtors, many real estate brokers continue to discriminate against blacks and Hispanics who inquire about available housing.[77] Less extensive evidence reveals broker discrimination in marketing houses for sale in minority neighborhoods.[78] Although other aspects of broker behavior are not so widely studied, some brokers undoubtedly discriminate in advertising their services and in placing their offices, actions that hit minority neighborhoods particularly hard. There is a strong case, therefore, for policies that require brokers to serve a broad range of neighborhoods. The question is whether there exist any practical policies of this type.

Because real estate firms often are small and often specialize in a particular area, it would not be reasonable to require every firm to serve all types of neighborhoods. However, MLSs, which are now widely used, virtually always cover a large area and are the natural focus of a CRA-type policy for real estate brokers. Moreover, the Housing Discrimination Study clearly demonstrates that MLSs play a key role in racial steering. Thus, I propose a Community Brokerage Act (CBA), which would require all MLSs, either by themselves or in coalition with other MLSs, to provide equal service to all types of neighborhoods in their metropolitan area. An MLS that now covers middle-income suburbs could meet its CBA requirements either by expanding into (and adequately serving) inner-city areas or by forming a coalition with another MLS that operates in the inner city.[79]

The CBA service tests would be based on the share of houses for sale that are attracted as listings and on the share of listings that are sold. An MLS coalition that listed a smaller share of the houses that sold in the minority neighborhoods in their service area than of the houses that listed in the largely white neighborhoods would be in violation of the CBA requirements unless it could show that this smaller share was not due to a lack of advertising or service in minority neighborhoods. In addition, an MLS coalition that sold a smaller fraction of the houses it listed in minority neighborhoods than of the houses it listed in all-white neighborhoods would be in violation of the CBA requirements unless it could show that this smaller share was not due to a lack of a marketing effort for the minority-area listings.

Enforcement of CRA is facilitated by the fact that federal financial regulatory agencies have the power to block mergers and branch closings by the lenders they regulate and by the implicit standing that community groups have to provide input on these decisions. No comparable federal regulatory apparatus exists for MLSs, and regulation of real estate brokers and their organizations is confined to the state level. Thus, state governments may be better positioned to implement a CBA.

However, only a federal CBA can provide the necessary broad coverage, so an alternative enforcement mechanism is needed. I propose a CBA in which HUD is given the authority to fine, and affected community groups are given standing to sue, MLS coalitions that do not meet the CBA requirements.[80]

Improved Fair Lending Enforcement

Thanks to the rediscovery of discrimination in mortgage lending, as well as FaHAA, the fair lending enforcement system has also improved considerably in recent years.

Complaint processing. Complaints form a relatively small portion of the enforcement system for fair lending. In FY1993, for example, HUD received only 512 complaints involving financing, about 8 percent of its total complaints, and the federal regulatory institutions received 289 complaints, of which about 188 involved residential discrimination and were referred to HUD.[81]

Taking the burden off victims. The most fundamental tool for enforcing fair lending is an examination by a federal regulatory agency. In FY1993, the financial regulatory agencies were responsible for the oversight of over 20,000 lending institutions.[82] These agencies conducted over 5,000 fair lending examinations and found over 10,000 violations. Most of these were technical violations involving record keeping and were easily resolved. In most other cases, the lender voluntarily corrected its discriminatory policies, and regulatory enforcement measures were not necessary.[83] In one case, however, the Federal Reserve Bank took more dramatic action by blocking a merger between Shawmut National Corporation and the New Dartmouth Bank on the grounds that Shawmut had not complied with fair lending laws.[84] This valuable regulatory activity should be continued.

Over 40 percent of the home-purchase loans in the United States are now issued by mortgage companies that are regulated by the Federal Trade Commission.[85] Although it has begun to investigate mortgage lenders, the FTC has neither the broad regulatory powers nor the experience of the financial regulatory agencies.[86] This is a troubling gap in the fair lending enforcement system because mortgage companies are overrepresented among the lenders with the poorest records in reaching out to minority neighborhoods. One recent investigation found that in 1992 mortgage bankers made up 79 percent of the large lenders who had relatively poor penetration in largely black areas.[87] If the FTC cannot close this gap by improving its oversight procedures, the Justice Department and perhaps HUD will have to step in.

The Justice Department helps to combat mortgage discrimination using pattern and practice suits. Its recent interest in lending discrimination began with the case filed against Decatur Federal Savings and Loan in 1989, a case that was revived by the release of the 1990 HMDA data and finally settled in 1992 for $1 million. This program was expanded by the Clinton administration, and the Attorney General has made it "one of the Department's highest priorities."[88] The current program investigates discrimination not only in loan approval but also in marketing and other aspects of the lending process.

During the first 10 months of 1994, the Justice Department filed four major mortgage discrimination cases, all of which have been settled.[89] Two of these cases are particularly relevant here.[90] In December 1993 Justice brought a case against the Shawmut Mortgage Company in Boston based on discrimination in mortgage loan approval. The settlement resolving this case involved compensation of almost $1 million for minority applicants who had been turned down for loans, as well as extensive revisions in the banks' underwriting procedures.[91] In August 1994 Justice filed a suit charging that the Chevy Chase Federal Savings Bank (CCFSB) in Washington, D.C., refused to market its loan products in black neighborhoods, and "placed black areas of Washington off-limits for mortgage lending," which is, of course, redlining.[92] The settlement calls for CCFSB to provide special low-interest loans, combined with grants toward down payments, for the residents of the redlined neighborhoods, to open mortgage offices and branches in largely black areas, and to make efforts to hire black employees. This settlement will cost CCFSB up to $11 million.

The Justice Department's strategy in these cases has been to work for a settlement; that is, to try to find a solution involving voluntary compliance by the lender.[93] The resulting settlements do not have the precedential value of a court ruling, but they give Justice leverage in future negotiations with other lenders. Moreover, the Decatur and Chevy Chase settlements have helped to bring discriminatory actions other than loan denial to the attention of lenders and policymakers. The Chevy Chase settlement in particular requires the lender to open branch offices in minority areas, a type of action that has not been required in any previous settlement under FaHA, ECOA, or CRA.[94] These are important steps toward recognizing the complexity of discrimination by lenders. Overall, this enforcement activity by Justice is vital and should continue.

Although not a central player in fair lending enforcement, HUD participates through two routes in addition to processing the few financing-related complaints it receives.[95] First, it supports community enforcement efforts through FHIP. Starting in FY1992, for example, HUD has used some FHIP money to support testing of lenders by local fair housing groups.[96] Second, the HUD secretary has initiated several investigations into lending discrimination, particularly by mortgage bankers who are not covered by the financial regulatory agencies. These are valuable steps that should be expanded.

Because so many agencies are involved in fair lending enforcement, coordination issues inevitably arise. Two of these issues are particularly important. First, the FTC, HUD, and Justice must make certain that adequate enforcement mechanisms are in place for mortgage bankers and department store lending departments. Because the foundations of fair lending enforcement by FTC, namely, the FTC's general regulatory mandate and ECOA, do not appear to be as powerful as the new enforcement tools available through FaHAA, HUD and Justice will have to play a major role, at least in the short run. HUD already has some secretary-initiated investigations of independent mortgage companies; the Shawmut case settled by Justice involved a mortgage company; and these two agencies have agreed to conduct joint investigations with a focus on independent mortgage companies.[97] Further investigations of mortgage bankers and department store mortgage programs by HUD and Justice clearly are warranted.

The second coordination issue concerns the assignment of lending cases to an enforcement agency.[98] Some people argue that virtually all cases of lending discrimination are pattern and practice cases because it would be unusual for a lender to discriminate against a single minority customer. For two reasons, however, neither HUD nor the regulatory agencies are likely to turn all lending cases over to the Justice Department.[99] First, lending plays a central role in the missions of both HUD and the regulatory agencies, and these parties are unlikely to relinquish all their power to enforce antidiscrimination legislation in this activity. Second, both HUD and the regulatory agencies have some unique investigatory and enforcement powers that complement those of Justice. Unlike Justice, for example, HUD can issue subpoenas during its preliminary investigations, and it can initiate cases and bring them before an ALJ. Moreover, the financial regulatory agencies have considerable influence over the lenders under their jurisdiction and often can induce them to alter their lending practices, or even to make settlements with applicants, without resorting to court proceedings. HUD, Justice, and the regulatory agencies all belong to the Task Force on Fair Lending and need to continue coordinating their actions to make sure that each case is handled by the agency with the most appropriate enforcement tools.[100]

Community Reinvestment Act regulations.   In December 1993 the Clinton administration proposed a strengthening of the CRA requirements.[101] This proposal received extensive comments from lenders, community groups, regulators, and policymakers, and a revised proposal was made in October 1994.[102] The final version, a joint product of the U.S. Department of the Treasury and the four federal banking agencies, was adopted in April 1995. Both the original and the revised proposals call for replacing the twelve CRA assessment factors with three tests, covering lending, service, and investment.[103] The three tests are designed both to lessen paperwork and to shift from process-oriented to performance-oriented standards.[104] They emphasize the geographic pattern of the loans made by each lender, both across different types of neighborhoods and compared to other lenders. The initial plan also called for the new rules to be enforced with new sanctions, including binding orders and fines, but in December 1994 the Justice Department ruled that the regulatory agencies do not have the authority to use such measures.[105]

These new tests, which reflect over a decade of experience with CRA, are also designed to push regulators away from the implausible current outcome that virtually all lenders are given a satisfactory CRA rating. As a result, the new tests probably will give both regulators and community groups somewhat more leverage in negotiating with lenders. Even without new sanctions, therefore, the new rules provide a valuable, albeit modest, boost to the effectiveness of the CRA requirements.[106]

These rules do not apply to mortgage bankers and department store mortgage offices, which are exempt from CRA. This is an unfortunate omission. The central premise of CRA; namely, that lenders have a responsibility to ensure that all neighborhoods have equal access to mortgage credit, is seriously undermined by the exemption for nondepository lenders, who now provide such a large share of mortgage loans. Hence, CRA should be amended to apply to all lenders.[107] This extension would not only reaffirm the central premise of CRA, it also would boost the weak enforcement powers of FTC and give an expanded enforcement role to community groups, which have played a crucial role in expanding the geographic range of lending by depository lenders.

This extension would be complicated by the fact that many mortgage bankers specialize in loan products most suitable for borrowers in middle-income areas and rely on intermediaries (mortgage brokers and real estate brokers) to bring them business.[108] The best way to account for these features of the market is to allow mortgage bankers and department store mortgage departments to form coalitions for CRA purposes. The CRA rules would then be applied to the coalition, not to its individual members.[109] Hence, a mortgage bank could meet its CRA obligations either by expanding into minority neighborhoods itself, perhaps with the help of intermediaries, or by joining a coalition with another mortgage bank or department store that specialized in loans to the minority community.

Information about discrimination.   Thanks to HMDA, there is, at one level, far more information about the treatment of minorities in mortgage markets than about their treatment in housing markets. Discrimination is a more complicated concept in mortgage lending, however, and much less is known about it.

In the case of loan approval, discrimination is now defined as a higher denial rate for minority than for white applications, after accounting statistically for everything the lender can think of that might affect creditworthiness. But this is inherently a very conservative approach. Skillful lenders or analysts can find variables that are plausibly (but not actually) related to credit risk and that are highly correlated with minority status and, by using them as control variables, can "show" that no discrimination exists when in fact it does.[110] Moreover, standard underwriting criteria used by lenders or by secondary mortgage market institutions may still include such variables.

The problem is that the true return on a loan is difficult to determine because it requires observations spread out over a long period of time. Neither scholars nor lenders have evaluated the data necessary to fully understand the impact on loan returns of borrower, property, and loan characteristics. If this information were available, it would be possible to determine whether minorities applicants were more likely to be denied, controlling only for those characteristics actually related to loan returns. Thus, I urge both HUD and the secondary mortgage market institutions to make research on this topic one of their top priorities.[111]

In addition, relatively little is known about the extent of discrimination in the marketing of mortgage products, in pre-application treatment, and in application counseling. Although recent Justice Department settlements have covered some of these types of discrimination, HUD and the secondary mortgage market institutions could also make a valuable contribution by supporting research on this topic.

Support for Stable Integration

The federal government should support stable integration through a three-part program that funds state and local efforts to promote integration, provides aid to integrated school districts, and expands programs to help disadvantaged city residents find housing in the suburbs. These programs are a vital part of an overall antidiscrimination strategy. According to Principle 4, some stable integrated neighborhoods are needed to help undermine the incentives that support the discriminatory system. Moreover, fair housing enforcement in integrated neighborhoods, where discrimination often is relatively high, may be self-defeating if it encourages racial and ethnic transition and thereby heightens racial and ethnic tensions, which are a key support for discriminatory behavior.

Stable neighborhood initiatives program. The first part of this program is a new FHIP-like program to provide funding for efforts by state and local governments and community groups to promote integration without discriminating. A program of this type is motivated primarily by Principle 4 but, to be consistent with Principle 2, it also should avoid discriminating itself; and to be consistent with Principle 5, it should encourage community participation.[112]

The program proposed here, which I call the Stable Neighborhood Initiatives Program (SNIP), would provide grants to state and local programs according to the following rules, which are designed to make the program consistent with Principles 2 and 5 and with the tests developed by the Supreme Court.[113]

> No money would be given to organizations that maintain integration through quotas, either ceiling quotas or floor quotas, even if those quotas are not part of the program for which funding is requested.
>
> Programs that provide race-conscious counseling, which has now been ratified by the Supreme Court, would be eligible for funding, but only if they were accompanied by a commitment to prevent discrimination—that is, only if they expand choice instead of restricting it.[114]
>
> The maximum grant size would be greater in neighborhoods (i.e., census tracts) with more balanced integration. In particular, the largest grants would be available in neighborhoods in which at least 40 percent of the population is white and at least 40 percent is minority. Lower levels of funding would be available in neighborhoods in which both whites and minorities make up at least 20 percent of the neighborhood. The symmetry in these rules is important to send the signal that both white and minority neighbors are equally valued.[115]
>
> Community groups, local governments, and coalitions between them could compete for the grants, but only one award would be made in each jurisdiction. The maximum grant within one jurisdiction would depend on the share of neighborhoods in the jurisdiction that fell into each category defined above.
>
> SNIP funds would be focused on programs that often appear to be effective in other communities, including (a) housing centers that collect and disseminate information about neighborhood change, provide housing counseling, and prevent rumors from spreading; (b) programs to provide extra housing maintenance in changing neighborhoods; (c) programs to boost public services, such as education or police and fire protection, in changing neighborhoods; and (d) police, recreation, or other programs that promote intergroup understanding. Other programs would also be considered for funding, however.
>
> No money would be provided for integration-enhancing payments to individuals, such as the Shaker Heights loan programs or the Oak Park equity assurance plan, although agencies running such programs would not be prohibited from applying for funds for other purposes. These types of programs have two important weaknesses. First, the payments tend to go to whites, which makes them a curious method for attacking the system of discrimination.[116] Second, they appear to reward people for their prejudice. Although these programs may be acceptable in some communities, these flaws make them inappropriate for federal support.[117]
>
> Maximum possible funding should be higher for programs that cover more people or that coordinate with programs in other nearby communities.[118]

Bonuses should be provided for metropolitan-level organizations that work with several integrated communities. Although SNIP funds could not be used for fair housing enforcement activities, such as testing, coordination with local or FHIP-funded enforcement programs would enhance an organization's chance for SNIP funding.

This program would not force anyone to live in an integrated community but would provide, for the first time, systematic federal support for the integration option.[119] The success of this program should be judged on whether it expands choice, for both minority and white families, not on whether it leads to neighborhoods that remain integrated indefinitely.[120] Some communities may be able to sustain integration for an extended period through SNIP-supported activities, others may be able to prevent rapid racial or ethnic transition and intergroup conflict, and still others may be able to open up neighborhoods for minorities. All such outcomes would be desirable.

If the facts about racial and ethnic transition were better known, this type of program would attract widespread support from people of all political persuasions. At the present time, neighborhood transition is heavily influenced by housing agents who can profit by encouraging transition, which imposes large costs on displaced white residents. These housing agents may promote neighborhood stability under some circumstances, but their primary tool for doing so is discrimination against minorities, a tool that violates basic social norms and which is under attack from increasingly effective antidiscrimination laws. Every household can gain if choice is expanded and change is orderly.

To prevent the dramatic losses, both for the affected families and for general race relations, that come from rapid neighborhood transition, while simultaneously promoting increased choice for minority households, this nation must turn to a strategy that cultivates both freedom of choice and neighborhood stability. SNIP would be a clear step in this direction.[121]

Revive the Emergency School Aid Act (ESAA).[122]   Added support for integrated schools plays an important role in offsetting the forces that cause racial and ethnic transition and intergroup conflict.[123] ESAA, which was passed in 1972 and bolstered in 1978, was designed to help school districts support the process of integration. It "helped hundreds of districts in teacher training, human relations, and curriculum development to make the transition from segregated to desegregated schools more effective. It avoided the busing controversy by specifying that none of the federal money could be used for local transportation costs."[124] Moreover, "evaluations of the program were extensive and positive, both in terms of better human relations and in terms of improved academic achievement."[125] Nevertheless, in 1981 ESAA and seven other acts were merged into two block grants with far less funding and no focus on desegregation.

School segregation supports the discriminatory system by contributing to educational disparities, by preventing intergroup communication, and by magnifying the pressures that lead to neighborhood transition. Moreover, school desegregation is a complex process that requires special programs to facilitate communication and to help prevent domination, either in or out of class, by one group. As shown by the Proviso West story, school desegregation without skilled leadership and adequate resources may not promote understanding along racial and ethnic lines.[126] The federal government therefore can take an important step in fighting discrimination by reviving this program. The revived version should include support for inter-district desegregation efforts and for districts that undertake integration-enhancing consolidations.[127]

Expand Gautreaux-type programs. The concentration of minority households in poor neighborhoods has become one of the most dramatic features of residential segregation. This concentration is a key component of the system of discrimination, as it both reflects and perpetuates racial and ethnic disparities in economic and social outcomes. Moreover, federal policy has contributed directly to this concentration by placing many public housing projects in largely minority neighborhoods.[128]

The system of discrimination makes it difficult for minority households to break out of neighborhoods in which poverty is concentrated. Housing search for all households tends to focus on nearby neighborhoods, and the housing search patterns of minority households are further constrained by actual and anticipated discrimination.[129] Indeed, the restrictions on housing search imposed by past and current discrimination are so severe that housing assistance programs, such as the Section 8 certificate program, that help low-income households pay for the housing of their choice have little impact on the neighborhoods that recipients select.[130] As one observer put it in describing families eligible for Section 8, "These families are typically inexperienced housing consumers who typically seek housing in the context of a discriminatory dual housing market."[131]

Although standard housing assistance programs do not promote mobility, we now have enough evidence to say with confidence that Gautreaux-type programs, which combine Section 8 housing certificates with housing search assistance for public housing or other inner-city residents, are a cost-effective way to help loosen the barriers that past and present housing discrimination impose on many minority families.[132] These programs appear to improve the employment outcomes of participants and the educational outcomes of their children without negative consequences for suburban neighborhoods.[133] Moreover, by focusing on public housing tenants or families eligible for Section 8, these programs primarily have served minority households without using race or ethnicity as a selection criterion.

An extension of Gautreaux-type programs, called Moving to Opportunity (MTO), was proposed during the Bush administration, passed by Congress in 1992, and initiated in five cities in 1994.[134] The five cities are Baltimore, Boston, Chicago, Los Angeles, and New York. The program was designed to provide over 6,000 Section 8 certificates or vouchers as well as housing counseling to households moving from a high-poverty area, defined as a census tract with a poverty rate of at least 40 percent, to a neighborhood where the poverty rate is 10 percent or below. Participating families will be followed for 10 years to facilitate evaluation of the program.

MTO is a sensible, cost-effective application of the lessons learned from earlier Gautreaux-type programs. By helping many minority families to break out of poverty neighborhoods, this program clearly helps offset the disparities caused by past discrimination (Principle 3) — and it does so with race- and ethnicity-neutral rules (Principle 2). MTO also provides support for residential integration (Principle 4) and promotes individual responsibility for housing choice (Principle 5). Overall, MTO is an excellent addition to the nation's set of antidiscrimination policy tools.

Unfortunately, however, MTO ran into severe opposition in the suburbs of Baltimore, the second year of funding was cut off, and the Clinton administration's proposal to extend the program beyond the original five sites was killed in Congress.[135] Moreover, opponents of the program have made extreme, and often incorrect, claims about it, saying, for example, that it gives poor families access to middle-class housing and brings crime and drugs into the suburbs.[136] These claims simply are not true. In fact, MTO provides modest housing assistance and counseling to a few low-income families, and it is inconceivable that a program the scale of MTO could have a significant negative impact on any suburb. Suburban residents have far more to gain from moderating the social costs of concentrated poverty through programs like MTO than they do from discouraging the movement of a few public housing residents into their communities.[137]

Although MTO has been put aside by Congress (at least for now), the Clinton administration has proposed the Choice in Residency program, which provides housing counseling for recipients of Section 8 certificates or vouchers with no requirements imposed on the neighborhoods that recipients choose.[138] The funding for this program would be focused on residents of neighborhoods with relatively high concentrations of poverty. The future of this program is not clear, but it probably could be implemented, at least in part, through changes in the Section 8 regulations, without congressional action.[139] In any case, programs of this type deserve continued support from both the executive and legislative branches of the federal government.

A recent HUD "Reinvention Blueprint" expands the mobility concept into all project-based federal housing assistance, including public housing, by calling for the conversion of all current housing subsidies into portable housing certificates.[140] Residents of private projects supported by project-based subsidies, such as the Section 8, New Construction program, "would be allowed to move to apartments of their own choice," taking their housing subsidy with them. Moreover, the Blueprint calls for the conversion of current "operating subsidies for public housing agencies into rental assistance for residents, who would be given the choice to stay where they are or move to apartments in the private rental market." As part of this proposal, HUD would give more flexibility to public housing authorities that are doing a good job, help other housing authorities learn how to compete for low-income tenants, and help demolish the most troubled projects (and relocate their residents).

The striking change in strategy would expand residential choice for residents in public and assisted housing projects, who are disproportionately minorities, while protecting their ability to stay in their current housing, at least in all but the most troubled projects.[141] Given the seemingly intractable segregation and concentrated disadvantage in many public and assisted housing projects, this approach would make a significant contribution to the expansion of housing choice and the elimination of segregation.[142]

Attacking Racial and Ethnic Disparities

Finally, a comprehensive antidiscrimination program should include policies to support communities that bear the scars of past discrimination. To the extent possible, these programs should not contain any racial or ethnic preference. Instead, policymakers should identify the social and economic outcomes for which the minority–white disparities are greatest and then design programs that assist all people, regardless of race or ethnicity, who fall short of acceptable standards on those outcomes. A full treatment of these policies is beyond the scope of this book, but this section provides a few thoughts on policies of this type that are closely connected to the system of discrimination as presented here.[143]

Support low-income homeownership. Minority–white disparities in homeownership are dramatic and at the heart of the system of discrimination. The federal government provides extensive assistance to homeowners in the form of income tax deductions. In fact, one recent study places the value of these income tax breaks at $109 billion.[144] Unfortunately, however, low-income homeowners often use the standard deduction and therefore gain no advantage from homeowner deductions. Moreover, even when low-income homeowners itemize deductions, they receive a smaller subsidy than do high-income homeowners, both because they have smaller mortgage interest and property tax payments and because their marginal tax rate, which determines the value of each dollar of deduction, is smaller. These income-tax provisions therefore do not go very far in promoting homeownership among low-income households.

The most effective way to promote homeownership among low-income homeowners would be to increase the subsidy they receive from existing income tax breaks. One way to do this would be to turn the itemized deductions for mortgage interest and property taxes into "adjustments," which are available to all taxpayers, regardless of whether they itemize. An even more effective reform would be to change the itemized deductions into a tax credit, which would ensure that all taxpayers receive the same benefit per dollar of mortgage interest or property tax payment. A tax credit of 15 percent would help low-income homeowners while raising federal revenue by about $10 billion.[145]

The federal government also gives direct assistance to low-income homeowners through the Home Investment Partnership Program, which was started in 1992. This program provides $1.5 billion (about 1.4 percent of the amount spent on homeowner tax breaks!) to localities, both directly and through their states, for subsidizing low-income homebuyers. Participants must have incomes below 80 percent of the area median and their housing must remain "affordable" for 15 years after their initial purchase. Preliminary indications are that this program is an effective way to promote homeownership and community responsibility.[146]

Another possible way to promote homeownership among public housing tenants is to sell them their units. Several pilot programs of this type have been conducted and have met with some success for relatively high-income tenants in relatively high-quality projects. This route does not appear reasonable, however, for the vast majority of public housing tenants, whose incomes are too low to support the costs of homeownership. Moreover, many public housing projects are so deteriorated and in such undesirable neighborhoods that massive investment would be required before anyone — including low-income tenants — would want to own them.[147] The transformation of public housing subsidies into housing certificates strikes me as a much more promising approach.

Retain and revise Title 1.   Title 1 is a large federal program that provides about $7 billion in assistance to schools with a concentration of poor students. This program was first passed as part of the Elementary and Secondary Education Act of 1965 and was recently renewed and amended by the Improving America's Schools Act of 1994.[148] In spirit, this program exactly fits the principles outlined earlier: It provides aid to all disadvantaged students, not just to minorities, but it helps offset the legacy of past discrimination because it is focused on a key outcome, educational achievement, for which racial and ethnic disparities continue to be large.[149] A program of this type therefore has an important role to play in an antidiscrimination program.

The amount of money allocated to a county through Title 1 depends on the poverty rate among poor school-aged children in the county and on education spending by the state. This formula spreads the available money quite broadly. About 95 percent of the school districts and half of the schools in the nation receive some Title 1 funding.[150] The Clinton administration proposed a greater concentration of Title 1 funds on schools with the highest poverty rates among their students, but the 1994 legislation allocates only a share of future funds above the FY1995 appropriations for additional allocations to high-poverty schools. Because concentrated poverty magnifies the problems that a school faces, a tighter focus on high-poverty school districts would make the program more cost-effective.[151]

Future revisions of the allocation formula must be careful, however, not to replace a measure over which a district has little control, namely, poverty in the surrounding county, with a measure over which a district has considerable control, namely, the concentration of poverty within a single school.[152] With a school-based measure, a school district might be able to increase its Title 1 funding by putting all of its poor students in one school — clearly not a desirable outcome. This problem does not arise, however, if a county-level poverty measure is replaced with a poverty measure for each school district.

Within a county, Title 1 funds programs for children who are both poor, as indicated by participation in a free school lunch program, and performing below grade level. In the original legislation, this structure penalized success because school districts or individual schools that succeeded in bringing up the test scores of their disadvantaged students received less aid.[153] The 1994 legislation moderated this problem by ensuring that "schools with high concentrations of poverty will continue to receive Title 1 aid."[154]

Another feature of the Title 1 formula is also troubling, namely, its use of state educational spending.[155] One could argue that the federal government should encourage states to spend more on education themselves, but this approach not only encourages spending it also rewards states with higher incomes, and it ignores the fact that some states have higher educational costs than others. Some steps to correct this problem were taken in the 1994 legislation, which added supplemental Title I grants to states that have a high ratio of spending per pupil to income per capita or that demonstrate "equity" in their school finance program. These steps do not, however, account for educational cost differences across states.[156]

Support employment and training programs.   Some of the seemingly most intractable racial and ethnic disparities appear in employment, particularly for young men. Many different employment and training programs have been implemented and evaluated in recent years. Some training and job-search programs have met with success for adult men and women in the sense that the participants had higher earnings than a comparable group of nonparticipants.[157] The earnings gains tend to be larger for women than for men, and a few programs focusing on welfare recipients have resulted in particularly large earnings gains. However, no large-scale training or job-search program has yet been shown to have a significant impact on employment for young men.

The federal government should continue to fund large-scale programs for adults and pilot programs for youth, with an evaluation component, until we can identify programs that work for young men. To maximize the effectiveness of these programs in offsetting racial and ethnic disparities in employment, they should be concentrated in areas where poverty and unemployment are relatively high.

■ CONCLUSIONS

The federal policies in this chapter are designed to be balanced and comprehensive. Balance is achieved by making the policies consistent with five principles of fair housing policy that are based on widely held values and recent Supreme Court decisions. These principles call for eliminating private discrimination, avoiding government discrimination either against or in favor of minorities, offsetting the legacy of past discrimination, supporting integrated neighborhoods, and emphasizing personal and individual responsibility. Although some specific policies that have been proposed or enacted in the past contradict one or more of these principles, the policies proposed here are consistent with all of them.

An antidiscrimination program must also be comprehensive to recognize the complexity of the forces that support discrimination. Simply enforcing antidiscrimination legislation is not sufficient to eliminate discrimination because it leaves intact many social and economic outcomes that lead to discriminatory behavior. Enforcement tools are not powerful enough to eliminate all discrimination, especially when many actors in the system, including landlords, real estate brokers, and lenders, have strong incentives to discriminate. Hence the program in this chapter calls for continuation and in some cases strengthening of current antidiscrimination enforcement efforts; policies to support community integration efforts; policies to enhance individual neighborhood choice; and race-neutral policies to address some of the economic and social outcomes, such as homeownership, school quality, and employment, for which the minority–white disparities are greatest.

The federal program in this chapter would not cost a great deal of money. The enforcement efforts could be funded by a modest increase in the current enforcement budgets of HUD and Justice. A 20 percent increase in funding for the Office of Fair Housing and Equal Opportunity at HUD, for example, would cost only about $10 million.[158] The Stable Neighborhoods Initiatives Program would likely have a cost similar to that of the current Fair Housing Initiatives Program, for which the FY1993 budget was $10.6 million. Although it was cancelled after one year, the national mobility program, Moving to Opportunity, originally was scheduled to cost $234 million over 2 years.[159] A revised version of the program with a budget of this size could make a valuable contribution.

The programs to alleviate key racial and ethnic disparities are more open-ended, but several effective steps could be taken without a great deal of expenditure. Greater focus of Title 1 educational aid on school districts with relatively high concentrations of poor students, for example, would not require any additional funding, and numerous educational and training experiments in high-poverty neighborhoods could be conducted with relatively little money.

Moreover, one of my specific proposals, namely to change the income tax deductions for homeowners into a 15 percent credit, actually would save about $10 billion, which is far more than needed to pay for every other policy. Given the importance of healing this nation's racial and ethnic divisions, the program proposed here is cost-effective even without this tax savings. Indeed, the annual cost of this program is less than the $4 billion cost that housing and mortgage discrimination impose on African American and Hispanic families each year.[160] Despite the current constraints on federal spending, therefore, prohibitive cost is not an excuse for refusing to attack housing discrimination.

Opening Doors, or How Liberals and Conservatives Can Join to Fight Discrimination

This nation is still divided along racial and ethnic lines. The divisions are fainter in some ways and sharper in others than they have been in the past, but there is no sign that they are going away. After decades of battle and some success, many people would no doubt like to declare victory in the war against discrimination. Such a declaration would be decidedly premature. The evidence in this book demonstrates conclusively that African American and Hispanic citizens continue to encounter extensive discrimination in housing and mortgage markets, with reverberations throughout the nation's economic and social life. This chapter provides a summary of this evidence—and of the federal policies to which it leads.

▉ THE EVIDENCE: I HEAR YOU KNOCKING, BUT YOU CAN'T COME IN

The 1989 Housing Discrimination Study used a state-of-the art research technique, called a fair housing audit, to compare the treatment of comparable minority and white homeseekers in urban areas throughout the country. Perhaps the most striking findings concern housing availability. Housing agents show about 25 percent fewer housing units to potential black and Hispanic homebuyers and black renters than to equally qualified whites, and between 5 and 10 percent of the time, black and Hispanic homeseekers are excluded from available housing altogether. Black and Hispanic homeseekers are also offered far less assistance in identifying housing that fits their needs and often are steered to neighborhoods with minority concentrations or low house values.

Additional recent research reveals that black and Hispanic applicants are about 60 percent more likely to be turned down for a loan than are whites with the same credit qualifications. Minority households also receive far less help in completing mortgage applications than do white households, and they sometimes receive mortgages on less favorable terms. Other recent evidence indicates that minority neighborhoods face a severe disadvantage relative to white neighborhoods in the marketing of houses that are for sale, in the flow of housing credit, and in the provision of homeowner's insurance.

All this housing discrimination imposes a high cost on minorities in the form of greater search expenses and less satisfactory housing outcomes. This discrimination "tax" is estimated to be roughly $3,000 every time a minority family wants to search for a new house, with a cumulative burden on blacks and Hispanics of over $4 billion per year. The effects of current and past discrimination are visible in the form of large racial and ethnic disparities in homeownership and housing quality. For the past two decades, for example, the homeownership rate has remained over 20 percentage points lower for blacks and Hispanics than for whites, and minority households are twice as likely as white households to live in deficient housing.

Housing discrimination also contributes directly to extensive residential segregation. In a typical large urban area, about three-quarters of black households (and half of Hispanic households) would have to move to achieve an even distribution of minorities and whites. Some analysts have argued that residential segregation is "simply" the result of people preferring to live with their "own kind." In fact, however, racial prejudice is not an inherent trait but is instead a product of the discriminatory system. Moreover, current discriminatory practices not only steer minorities away from some neighborhoods and whites away from others but also magnify the pressures that often cause rapid neighborhood transitions from mostly white to mostly minority residents. By concentrating contacts between whites and minorities in neighborhoods undergoing traumatic neighborhood changes, housing discrimination helps to sustain racial and ethnic prejudice. This prejudice, in turn, provides landlords and real estate brokers with economic incentives to continue practicing discrimination.

In addition, housing discrimination is a principal component of a self-reinforcing system of discrimination that leads to large racial and ethnic disparities in educational and labor market outcomes.

Residential segregation contributes heavily to a school system in which one-third of black and Hispanic children attend schools that are at least 90 percent minority and in which minority schools are far more likely than white schools to have students from disadvantaged backgrounds and to be located in fiscally stressed cities. Large racial and ethnic disparities in dropout rates and educational achievement are the result. A national reading test administered to 17-year-olds in 1990, for example, found that whites' scores exceed blacks' scores by 10.1 percent and Hispanics' scores by 7.4 percent. School segregation itself helps reinforce this system because it plays a major role in magnifying racial and ethnic transition in neighborhoods and in preventing the types of contacts that might help to break down stereotypes and intergroup hostility.

The impact of housing discrimination also appears in minority–white disparities in employment, income, and poverty. This contribution is both direct, because housing discrimination restricts minority access to suburban employment, and indirect, because housing discrimination contributes to educational disparities, which play such a crucial role in the labor market. The resulting disparities are striking. The 1994 unemployment rate for white men, 5.4 percent, was less than half the rate for black men, 12.0 percent, and less than three-fifths the rate for Hispanic men, 9.4 percent. Moreover, the poverty rate reaches the astonishing level of 50 percent for black and Puerto Rican children, compared to only 16 percent for white children.

These divisions and disparities impose a large cost on all Americans, not just on minority households whose choices are severely restricted by discrimination. We all lose when the exclusion of minorities from some neighborhoods leads to disruptive change in others and thereby limits the neighborhood choices of all households. We all lose when discrimination and its legacy undermine the productivity of some citizens and promote mistrust and intergroup conflict. We all have an interest in attacking the system of discrimination.

Although current and past policies have made progress against this system, it has proven to be a strong and resilient opponent. Without effective leadership and a comprehensive antidiscrimination program, some racial and ethnic disparities, particularly those associated with concentrated poverty, are likely to get worse. What the Kerner Commission said in 1968 is still true:

> It is time to make good the promises of American democracy to all citizens—urban and rural, white and black, Spanish-surname, American In-

dian, and every minority group. . . . There can be no higher priority for national action and no higher claim on the nation's conscience.[1]

■ A COMPREHENSIVE PROGRAM TO COMBAT DISCRIMINATION

Despite this strong substantive case for government action, the political obstacles facing new antidiscrimination policy are formidable. Not only do many politicians deny the importance of continuing discrimination, but a growing public rejection of policies perceived to give preferences based on race or ethnicity has also undermined the consensus that supported antidiscrimination efforts in the past. Some liberals have responded to this situation by defending the principle of affirmative action without searching for new policies that have broader appeal. Some conservatives have responded by moving to scrap all efforts that go beyond enforcing antidiscrimination laws on the grounds that they inevitably involve discriminatory quotas. Both responses are extreme; some existing policies attack discrimination without racial or ethnic preferences and other such policies could be designed.

Principles for Fair Housing Policy

The program for governmental action developed at length in Chapter 11 provides a new balance that avoids these extreme positions. This balance builds on five principles, which are derived from widely held values and recent Supreme Court decisions:

1. Government programs should strive to eliminate racial and ethnic discrimination in housing, lending, and related markets.

2. Government programs themselves should avoid discrimination, either against or in favor of minorities.

3. The government has a continuing obligation to help offset the effects of past discrimination against blacks and Hispanics.

4. The government should help to make neighborhood integration a real choice for households who want it.

5. Government antidiscrimination programs and rhetoric should support the personal responsibility of all individuals, including those who have encountered discrimination as well as those who have practiced it.

Careful application of these principles helps to resolve the confusion and disagreement in the current debate. Liberals tend to emphasize the first and third principle, while neglecting the second and fifth. Conservatives acknowledge the first principle but downplay or reject the third, while emphasizing Principles 2 and 5. Moreover, few politicians anywhere on the political spectrum provide clear support for the fourth principle, although it is stressed by some scholars and community leaders.[2] In my judgment, these emphases are outmoded. In fact, all five principles are important and widely accepted, and federal policies that simultaneously promote all five principles are available.

Liberals need to recognize that programs based on preferences for minorities undermine not only the principle of equal treatment but also political support for an antidiscrimination program. In 1994, for example, only 28 percent of whites agreed with the statement: "Do you believe that where there has been job discrimination in the past, preference in hiring or promotion should be given to blacks today?"[3] Furthermore, a clear role for personal and community responsibility is necessary to encourage everyone's participation in attacking the system of discrimination.

Conservatives need to recognize that the products of past discrimination, particularly racial and ethnic disparities in social and economic outcomes, contribute to the stereotypes that feed ongoing prejudice and thereby support current discrimination. Some of these disparities show no signs of fading away. In addition, conservatives need to acknowledge that even though some policies to combat the legacy of past discrimination, such as quotas, violate principle two; other policies, some of which are presented below, combat this legacy with no hint of racial or ethnic preference. Flaws in a particular policy do not validate the rejection of that policy's objectives.

Finally, all parties in this debate must recognize that residential segregation is not only an *outcome* but also a *cause* of continuing discrimination. Segregation helps to sustain stereotypes and prejudice and is a principal source of the incentives that lead real estate brokers and other participants in housing markets to discriminate.

Moreover, stable integration, the inverse of segregation, rarely occurs without government intervention. Federal support for integration would offset a key consequence of our discriminatory past and weaken the incentives that support current discrimination.[4]

A four-part federal program to meet all five principles was developed in Chapter 11. It includes public discussion, antidiscrimination enforcement, promoting integration and neighborhood choice, and offsetting the legacy of past discrimination.

Public discussion: An expanded national conversation on matters of race and ethnicity. Despite their importance to our nation's future, matters of race and ethnicity receive little public attention. The tone set by our public officials can make a difference, so I propose:

- An effort by national leaders, especially the president, to promote intergroup understanding through regular public statements.

Such statements would stimulate national discussion of these important but neglected topics, a discussion to which community leaders and public officials at all levels of government could contribute.

Antidiscrimination enforcement. The first two policies in this part of the program involve the use or expansion of existing tools that relieve the victims of discrimination of the enforcement burden.

- A continuation of current enforcement efforts by the U.S. Department of Housing and Urban Development (HUD), the Justice Department, and the financial regulatory agencies, including financial and technical support for state and local enforcement agencies, both public and private.

- An expansion of investigations by the secretary of HUD into discriminatory behavior, especially in neighborhoods where discrimination is expected to be high, and by mortgage bankers, who are not adequately covered by the current enforcement system.

Three other policies in this part are designed to track our progress in fighting discrimination and to expand our knowledge about key aspects of housing discrimination that are now poorly understood. The first builds on the success of previous audit studies in providing information about discrimination, the second builds on the success of the Home Mortgage Disclosure Act in making people aware of racial and ethnic disparities in mortgage acceptance, and the third expands our understanding of mortgage discrimination.

- A national audit study of rental housing every 5 years, and a national audit study of sales housing every 10 years.

- A Home Sales Disclosure Act to assemble the information that real estate brokers already have on the location of all their listings and sales, and thereby to shed light on brokers' marketing and sales practices, which still involve discrimination.

- Federal support for research that refines our understanding of discrimination in mortgage markets.

The two final policies in this part close the gaps in the current enforcement system. They apply the central principle of the Community Reinvestment Act (CRA), namely, that depository lenders have a responsibility to ensure that all types of customers and neighborhoods are served, to two multiple listing services and mortgage bankers.[5] Some lenders complain about the burdens imposed on them by CRA, but its main thrust has been to initiate and to sustain a constructive dialogue between lenders and the communities they serve.[6] Given the important and growing role that MLSs and mortgage bankers play in providing access to housing, plus irrefutable evidence that they contribute to the system of discrimination, it is time to include them in this exchange. The two policies are:

- A Community Brokerage Act to give multiple listing services a formal responsibility to provide service to all types of neighborhoods.

- An extension of the Community Reinvestment Act to cover nondepository lenders, such as mortgage bankers.

This set of enforcement policies would solidify and build upon the progress that has been made in fighting housing and mortgage discrimination since the passage of the 1988 Fair Housing Amendments Act.

Promoting integration and neighborhood choice.   The policies in this part promote integration but are designed to be consistent with the other principles as well. The first policy provides financial backing for community efforts to maintain integration, building on the model of the Fair Housing Initiatives Program, a highly successful federal program that supports community efforts to fight discrimination. This policy does not force anyone to live in an integrated neighborhood; instead, it assists in providing the integration option for people who want it. It does not allow communities to integrate by discriminating against minorities, it defines integration in such a way that minority and white residents are given equal weight, and it does not involve preferences for members of any particular racial or ethnic group.

- A Stable Neighborhood Initiatives Program to support community efforts to maintain stable racial and ethnic integration without discrimination.

The second policy in this type has been pursued by both the Bush and Clinton administrations. It builds on experience with several programs, starting with the Gautreaux Program in Chicago, that have helped low-income families move out of distressed and often segregated inner-city neighborhoods to more suitable environments for raising their children, without any evidence of problems for the neighborhoods to which they move.[7]

- An expansion of Gautreaux-type programs to provide public housing tenants and residents of poor inner-city neighborhoods with both rental assistance and information about housing opportunities outside the central city.

The third policy associated with Principle 4 builds on the important role that schools can play both in supporting neighborhood integration and in providing opportunities for children from different racial and ethnic groups to learn to get along with each other. It calls for a reenactment of a highly successful federal policy from the 1970s.

- A revival of the Emergency School Aid Act to help school districts manage the process of desegregation.

The principal objective of these three policies is to expand the range of neighborhood options that are available to both minority and white families. These policies do not force anyone to live in an integrated neighborhood. They do recognize, however, that without government intervention, housing markets rarely provide integration as an option, even for families who prefer it, and that additional integration and expanded choice can help to dismantle the system of discrimination.

Offsetting the legacy of past discrimination.   The final part of the program involves policies to lessen some of the most significant racial and ethnic disparities in housing, education, and labor market outcomes without any racial and ethnic preference. These policies work by identifying social and economic outcomes that involve large disparities across racial or ethnic groups and then by providing assistance to all individuals, minority and white, who are disadvantaged on those outcomes. Over the last few years, several scholars have offered versions of this approach as substitutes for affirmative action programs that give preference to members of specific racial or ethnic groups.[8]

- Replacement of the current income tax deductions for mortgage interest and property tax payments with an adjustment to income for the same items or, better still, with a 15 percent income tax credit, which would expand the tax advantages of homeownership for low- and moderate-income households.

- Continued support for, and possible expansion of, the Home Investment Partnership Program, which makes homeownership affordable for low- to moderate-income families.

- Continued support for Title 1 education aid, which goes to schools with a concentration of poor students, along with reforms to focus this aid more heavily on school districts with the most concentrated poverty.

- Federal support for local education and training programs in communities with the highest concentrations of poverty and the highest unemployment rates.

Although these policies are directed at all disadvantaged individuals, regardless of race or ethnicity, they address social and economic outcomes for which minority–white disparities are particularly high and therefore disproportionately benefit minority households. When applied to carefully selected outcomes, this approach appears to be both effective and politically viable.

Program Cost

Although it is comprehensive, this program would not require extensive new federal spending. As shown in Chapter 11, this program requires an annual budget far below the $4 billion burden imposed on minority families each year by housing and mortgage discrimination.

▊ CONCLUSION

Implementing all these policies will require bold leadership to explain why healing our racial and ethnic divisions is so important for the nation as a whole. It will require new recognition and debate about the importance of discrimination in housing and mortgage markets. It will require a shift in priorities and perhaps a modest amount of new federal funding. It will require vision and coordination. These are demanding requirements under the best of circumstances and are exacerbated by the extreme positions and misperceptions that often arise in matters of race and ethnicity. Thus, we risk failing to act and thereby following a path along which many of the most jarring racial and ethnic disparities will continue to grow—at great cost to us all.

The program proposed here provides a way out. It is built on widely held principles that appeal to people throughout the political spectrum; it combines continued enforcement of antidiscrimination legislation with policies that address the underlying causes of discriminatory behavior; it expands choices for millions of families, both minority and white, without resorting to racial or ethnic preferences; and it does not require a significant increase in federal spending.

Discrimination in housing and mortgage markets continues to oppress our African American and Hispanic citizens and impose costs on us all. A balanced, comprehensive attack on this discrimination would make a vital contribution to the goals of fair treatment and equal opportunity, which remain central to our potential as a free, democratic—and diverse—nation.

◼ Analysis of Discrimination in Number of Units Inspected

The analysis in this appendix is based on a multiple regression analysis of discrimination in the number of units inspected. It gives detailed definitions of the variables and presents the full regression results. Interpretation of the results is presented in Chapter 9.

An audit is the unit of observation. The regression is conducted for all audits in which at least one unit was inspected by one of the auditors; that is, for all audits in which discrimination in inspections was possible. (Only a few audits—34 for black–white sales audits, 27 for Hispanic–white sales audits, 53 for black–white rental audits, and 32 for Hispanic–white rental audits—involved no inspections. The results are virtually identical whether or not these audits are included in the regressions.) The dependent variable is the total number of units actually inspected by the white auditor minus the number of units inspected by the minority auditor.

The explanatory variables are defined in Tables A.1–A.3. Two key variables are ADINSP, the number of advertised units available for inspection, and SIMINSP, the number of units similar to the advertised unit available for inspection. These two variables do not appear by themselves but are used to define many interaction terms. With some exceptions (identified below), variables that begin with an A are interacted with (that is, multipled by) ADINSP, and variables that begin with an S are interacted with SIMINSP.

Table A.1 DEFINITIONS OF INTERMEDIATE EXPLANATORY
VARIABLES

Variable	Definition
ADINSP	Number of advertised units available for inspection (very approximate for rental audits)
SIMINSP	Number of units similar to the advertised unit available for inspection (includes advertised units in rental audits)
AO	Zero-one variable indicating no advertised units available for inspection outside minority neighborhoods
AP	Zero-one variable indicating a positive number of advertised units available for inspection outside minority neighborhoods
SO	Zero-one variable indicating no units similar to the advertised unit available for inspection outside minority neighborhoods
SP	Zero-one variable indicating a positive number of units similar to the advertised unit available for inspection outside minority neighborhoods
OFWHITE	Zero-one variable indicating that the agent's office is in a white neighborhood
OFINTEG	Zero-one variable indicating that the agent's office is in an integrated neighborhood
OFBLACK	Zero-one variable indicating that the agent's office is in a black neighborhood
OFHISPA	Zero-one variable indicating that the agent's office is in an Hispanic neighborhood
NEWHITE	Zero-one variable indicating that the advertised unit is in a white neighborhood
NEINTEG	Zero-one variable indicating that the advertised unit is in an integrated neighborhood
NEBLACK	Zero-one variable indicating that the advertised unit is in a black neighborhood
NEHISPA	Zero-one variable indicating that the advertised unit is in an Hispanic neighborhood
OW-ANW	Zero-one variable indicating the agent's office and the average advertised unit are in white neighborhoods
OW-ANI	Zero-one variable indicating the agent's office is in a white neighborhood and the average advertised unit is in an integrated neighborhood
OW-ANM	Zero-one variable indicating the agent's office is in a white neighborhood and the average advertised unit is in a minority neighborhood
OI-ANW	Zero-one variable indicating the agent's office is in an integrated neighborhood and the average advertised unit is in a white neighborhood
OI-ANI	Zero-one variable indicating the agent's office and the average advertised units are in integrated neighborhoods
OI-ANM	Zero-one variable indicating the agent's office is in an integrated neighborhood and the average advertised unit is in a minority neighborhood

TABLE A.1 (*continued*)

Variable	Definition
OM-ANW	Zero-one variable indicating the agent's office is in a minority neighborhood and the average advertised unit is in a white neighborhood
OM-ANI	Zero-one variable indicating the agent's office is in a minority neighborhood and the average advertised unit is in an integrated neighborhood
OM-ANM	Zero-one variable indicating the agent's office and the average advertised units are in minority neighborhoods
OW-SMW	Zero-one variable indicating the agent's office is in a minority neighborhood and a majority of units similar to the advertised units are in white neighborhoods
OW-SMI	Zero-one variable indicating the agent's office is in a white neighborhood and a majority of units similar to the advertised unit are in integrated neighborhoods
OW-SMM	Zero-one variable indicating the agent's office is in a white neighborhood and a majority of units similar to the advertised unit are in minority neighborhoods
OW-SMX	Zero-one variable indicating the agent's office is in a white neighborhood and units similar to the advertised unit are in neighborhoods with varying racial/ethnic composition
OI-SMW	Zero-one variable indicating the agent's office is in an integrated neighborhood and a majority of units similar to the advertised unit are in white neighborhoods
OI-SMI	Zero-one variable indicating the agent's office is in an integrated neighborhood and a majority of units similar to the advertised unit are in integrated neighborhoods
OI-SMM	Zero-one variable indicating the agent's office is in an integrated neighborhood and a majority of units similar to the advertised unit are in minority neighborhoods
OI-SMX	Zero-one variable indicating the agent's office is in an integrated neighborhood and units similar to the advertised unit are in neighborhoods with varying racial/ethnic composition
OM-SMW	Zero-one variable indicating the agent's office is in a minority neighborhood and a majority of units similar to the advertised unit are in white neighborhoods
OM-SMI	Zero-one variable indicating the agent's office is in a minority neighborhood and a majority of units similar to the advertised unit are in integrated neighborhoods
OM-SMM	Zero-one variable indicating the agent's office and a majority of units similar to the advertised unit are in minority neighborhoods
OM-SMX	Zero-one variable indicating the agent's office is in a minority neighborhood and units similar to the advertised unit are in neighborhoods with varying racial/ethnic composition

TABLE A.2 **DEFINITIONS OF NEIGHBORHOOD VARIABLES**

Variable	Definition	Variable	Definition
APSO	(AP)(S0)	S1WW	(A0)(SIMINSP)(OW-SWW)
APSP	(AP)(SP)	S1WI	(A0)(SIMINSP)(OW-SWI)
AOFWHITE	(ADINSP)(OFWHITE)	S1WM	(A0)(SIMINSP)(OW-SWM)
AOFINTEG	(ADINSP)(OFINTEG)	S1WX	(A0)(SIMINSP)(OW-SWX)
AOFBLACK	(ADINSP)(OFBLACK)	S1IW	(A0)(SIMINSP)(OI-SIW)
AOFHISPA	(ADINSP)(OFHISPA)	S1II	(A0)(SIMINSP)(OI-SII)
A1WW	(S0)(ADINSP)(OW-AWW)	S1IM	(A0)(SIMINSP)(OI-SIM)
A1WI	(S0)(ADINSP)(OW-AWI)	S1IX	(A0)(SIMINSP)(OI-SIX)
A1WM	(S0)(ADINSP)(OW-AWM)	S1MW	(A0)(SIMINSP)(OM-SMW)
A1IW	(S0)(ADINSP)(OI-AIW)	S1MI	(A0)(SIMINSP)(OM-SMI)
A1II	(S0)(ADINSP)(OI-AII)	S1MM	(A0)(SIMINSP)(OM-SMM)
A1IM	(S0)(ADINSP)(OI-AIM)	S1MX	(A0)(SIMINSP)(OM-SMX)
A1MW	(S0)(ADINSP)(OM-AMW)	S2WW	(AP)(SIMINSP)(OW-SWW)
A1MI	(S0)(ADINSP)(OM-AMI)	S2WI	(AP)(SIMINSP)(OW-SWI)
A1MM	(S0)(ADINSP)(OM-AMM)	S2WM	(AP)(SIMINSP)(OW-SWM)
A2WW	(SP)(ADINSP)(OW-AWW)	S2WX	(AP)(SIMINSP)(OW-SWX)
A2WI	(SP)(ADINSP)(OW-AWI)	S2IW	(AP)(SIMINSP)(OI-SIW)
A2WM	(SP)(ADINSP)(OW-AWM)	S2II	(AP)(SIMINSP)(OI-SII)
A2IW	(SP)(ADINSP)(OI-AIW)	S2IM	(AP)(SIMINSP)(OI-SIM)
A2II	(SP)(ADINSP)(OI-AII)	S2IX	(AP)(SIMINSP)(OI-SIX)
A2IM	(SP)(ADINSP)(OI-AIM)	S2MW	(AP)(SIMINSP)(OM-SMW)
A2MW	(SP)(ADINSP)(OM-AMW)	S2MI	(AP)(SIMINSP)(OM-SMI)
A2MI	(SP)(ADINSP)(OM-AMI)	S2MM	(AP)(SIMINSP)(OM-SMM)
A2MM	(SP)(ADINSP)(OM-AMM)	S2MX	(AP)(SIMINSP)(OM-SMX)

In the case of the sales audits, the addresses of the units shown to white and minority teammates were compared to determine which units were seen by both teammates. The above two variables were then defined as the number of unique housing units shown to either teammate. Address information was sometimes incomplete, especially for condominiums, which often did not have an apartment number. As a result, procedures were developed to rule out matches when units seen by teammates had similar but incomplete address information and differed on some observable characteristic, such as number of rooms or floor number.

In the case of rental audits, the address information was so poor that no such matching was attempted. Instead, approximations to the approach for the sales audits were used. To be specific, SIMINSP is defined as the maximum number of units inspected (advertised or similar) by either teammate. In addition, cases in which more than one advertised unit were available for inspection were identified by counting the maximum number of units inspected by either auditor in audits when at least one auditor inspected the advertised unit and

Table A.3 DEFINITIONS OF OTHER EXPLANATORY VARIABLES

Variable	Definition
Site Characteristics	
Site	Zero-one variable for every site defined in Table 2.1 with separate central city and suburb variables for the four in-depth sites (with New York central city as the left-out category)
Ssite	(SIMINSP)(Site)
Agent/Firm Characteristics	
AGNTAGE	Estimated age of housing agent who served white auditor
AGNTFEM	Zero-one variable indicating that a female housing agent served white auditor
SAGAGE	(SIMINSP)(AGNTAGE)
SAGFEM	(SIMINSP)(AGNTFEM)
SAGBLK	(SIMINSP)(Zero-one variable indicating a black housing agent served white auditor)
SAGBLKIN	(SAGNTBLK)(NEINTEG+NEBLACK)
SAGHIS	(SIMINSP)(Zero-one variable indicating an Hispanic housing agent served white auditor)
SAGHIDK	(SAGNTHIS)(DARK)
SAGHIAC	(SAGNTHIS)(HEAVY)
SSIZE	(SIMINSP)(Number of people encountered by white auditor)
SMLS	(SIMINSP)(Zero-one variable indicating that the housing agent made use of an MLS directory)
SMLSIW	(SMLS)(Zero-one variable indicating that the advertised housing unit was in an integrated or black neighborhood and that houses similar to the advertised unit were available in white neighborhoods)
Auditor Characteristics	
FAMINC	Family income assigned to audit team
SFINC	(SIMINSP)(FAMINC)
SFEMLK	(SIMINSP)(Zero-one variable indicating that the audit team's assigned role was a spouse and that the auditor was female)
SSFEM	(SIMINSP)(Zero-one variable indicating that the audit team's assigned role was a single person and that the auditor was female)
SSMAN	(SIMINSP)(Zero-one variable indicating that the audit team's assigned role was a single person and that the auditor was male)
SKID	(SIMINSP)(Zero-one variable indicating that the audit team's role was that of a family with school-aged children)
SCHILD	(SIMINSP)(Zero-one variable indicating that the audit team's role was that of a family with children)
SADAGE	(SIMINSP)(White auditor's age)

Table A.3 (*continued*)

Variable	Definition
DARK	Zero-one variable indicating that an Hispanic auditor had dark skin
ACCENT	Zero-one variable indicating that an Hispanic auditor had a heavy Spanish accent
SDARK	(SIMINSP)(DARK)
SACCENT	(SIMINSP)(ACCENT)
DA	Zero-one variable indicating that an Hispanic auditor had both a dark skin and a heavy Spanish accent
SDA	(SIMINSP)(DA)

Audit Characteristics

HOUSEVAL	Stated value of the advertised house that defines an audit
SHOUSEVAL	(SIMINSP)(HOUSEVAL)
SQUAL	(SIMINSP)(FAMINC)/(HOUSEVAL)
RENT	Stated monthly rent of the advertised apartment that defined the audit
AFTNOON	Zero-one variable indicating the audit began during the afternoon
AUDMAY	Zero-one variable indicating the audit took place in May (July is the left-out category)
AUDJUNE	Zero-one variable indicating the audit took place in June (July is the left-out category)
AUDAUG	Zero-one variable indicating the audit took place in August (July is the left-out category)
CONDO	Zero-one variable indicating the advertised unit was a condominium

Controls for Teammate Differences

ORDER	Zero-one variable for whether minority auditor went first
DAUDAGE	White auditor age minus minority auditor age
DAGNTAGE	Estimated age of agent seen by white auditor minus estimated age of agent seen by minority auditor
DAGNTFEM	Zero-one variable for whether white auditor saw female agent minus zero-one variable for whether minority auditor saw female agent
DAFTNOON	Zero-one variable for whether white auditor's visit was in the afternoon minus zero-one variable for whether minority auditor's visit was in the afternoon

Related Agent Behavior

RECOMM	Difference between white and minority auditor in number of units recommended but not inspected
SRECOMM	(SIMINSP)(RECOMM)
STEER	Index of steering from Turner, Mickelsons, and Edwards (1991)

both auditors were told that no units similar to the advertised unit was available. This approach understates the number of advertised units because it cannot identify additional advertised units that exist when units similar to the advertised unit are available.

Other key variables indicate the racial or ethnic composition of the neighborhoods in which the agent's office and the relevant units are located. In the sales audits, a white neighborhood is defined as a census tract with a population less than 10 percent black (for the black–white audits) or Hispanic (for the Hispanic–white audits); an integrated neighborhood is a tract that is 10–75 percent black or Hispanic; and a minority neighborhood is a tract that is over 75 percent black or Hispanic. The minority composition figures are estimates for 1988 (see Turner, Mickelsons, and Edwards, 1991). In the sales audits, a set of available units is said to be mostly from white (integrated) (minority) neighborhoods if more than 50 percent of the set is located in a white (integrated) (minority) neighborhood by the above definition. When no type of neighborhood contains more than 50 percent of the total, a set of available units is said to come from "mixed" neighborhoods. In the rental audits, a set of available units is said to be located in a white or integrated or minority neighborhood if all of the units in the set are in that type of neighborhood. If some of the units are in one type (e.g., white), and other units are in another type (e.g., integrated), then the units are said to be located in "mixed" neighborhoods.

The breakpoints of 10 and 75 were selected for two reasons. First, they are plausible breakdowns given what we know about preferences and neighborhood transition (see Chapter 7). Second, regressions based on these breakpoints have higher explanatory power than regressions with other breakpoints (at 5 point intervals). A well-known econometric result is that, under the assumption of normal error terms, selecting nonlinear parameters, such as these, according to the explanatory power (R-squared) of a regression is equivalent to a maximum likelihood estimating procedure. This approach roughly follows the logic of this theorem. For the Hispanic sales audits, breakpoints of 20 and 70 percent were used to define neighborhoods for units other than the advertised unit. This deviation from the breaks used elsewhere also was guided by the above theorem; raising the lower breakpoint from 10 to 20 increased the explanatory power of the regression.

In addition, four zero-one variables are used to define the type of units available: A0 indicates that no advertised units are available for inspection in white or integrated neighborhoods, whereas AP indicates that a positive number of advertised units are available in white or integrated neighborhoods. Similarly, S0 indicates that no units similar to the advertised unit are available for inspection in white or integrated neighborhoods, whereas SP indicates that such units are available in white or integrated neighborhoods. Because few units are located in largely black or Hispanic neighborhoods, one obtains very similar results using definitions for A0, AP, S0, and SP that omit the phrase "in white or integrated neighborhoods."

These racial/ethnic composition and opportunity variables, along with ADINSP and SIMINSP, are used to define four sets of interaction terms. The first two sets contain nine variables each, defined by a table in which the racial/ethnic composition of agent's neighborhood (that is, of the neighborhood in which his office is located) form the rows (white, integrated, minority) and the racial/ethnic composition of the average advertised unit form the columns (white, integrated, minority). The first set equals a set of nine zero-one variables identifying these nine categories multiplied by ADINSP and S0; the second set is identical except that S0 is replaced by SP. In short, the first set captures marginal discrimination for advertised units when no similar units are available and the second captures marginal discrimination for advertised units when similar units are available.

Because rental advertised units could not be identified with precision, these two sets were not included in the rental audits. Instead, the zero-one variables were included without the interactions with ADINSP, and the approximated ADINSP variable was interacted with a set of three dummy variables to indicate the racial or ethnic composition of the neighborhood in which the agent's office was located.

Sets three and four contain twelve variables each, defined by a table in which rows refer to the racial/ethnic composition of the agent's neighborhood (white, integrated, minority), and the columns refer to the racial/ethnic composition of the neighborhoods in which available units similar to the advertised unit are located (mostly white, mostly integrated, mostly minority, and mixed). In the rental audits, the columns are more restrictive; they define audits in which all of the units are in white, integrated, or black areas, and in which units are drawn from a mix of these three types of areas. Set three is made up of twelve zero-one variables identifying these twelve categories multiplied by SIMINSP and A0; the fourth set is identical except that A0 is replaced by AP. Thus, the third set captures marginal discrimination for units similar to the advertised one when no advertised units are available, and the fourth captures marginal discrimination for units similar to the advertised one when advertised units are available outside minority neighborhoods.

The regressions also contain two sets of site variables and controls for observable differences between teammates. The first set of site variables consists of a zero-one variable for each site, with the in-depth sites split into central city and suburb and with the New York central city as the left-out category. The second is the first with each variable multiplied by SIMINSP. This second set makes it possible to see how marginal discrimination varies by site. The controls for teammate differences add to the controls built into the matching process of the audit design. They include, for example, ORDER, which indicates whether the minority auditor went first, and DAUDAGE, which is the difference between the ages of audit teammates. The complete list of such controls is given in Table A.3.

In addition, the regressions include agent or agency, auditor, and audit characteristics. The final sets of these characteristics are listed in Table A.3. Variables in these categories, unlike all the variables discussed earlier, are not all included in the final regressions. Because the regressions include so many variables already, variables in these categories with t-statistics that were consistently below 1.0 were excluded. The reported results are all robust, however; that is, significant coefficients do not become insignificant when additional variables are added (and insignificant coefficients do not become significant), at least not in the alternative specifications that were examined.

Finally, the regressions include two other types of agent behavior. SRECOMM, which is SIMINSP multiplied by discrimination in the number of units recommended but not inspected, is included in both sales regressions. The coefficient of this variable indicates whether marginal discrimination in inspections declines when discriminatory possibilities exist in recommendations. RECOMM, which is the recommendations variable with no interaction, is in the Hispanic rental regression. In addition, the black sales regression includes a steering index, STEER, which determines whether the possibility of steering leads to more discrimination in inspections. The steering index is the one defined by Turner, Mickelsons, and Edwards (1991). This variable is not significant in the Hispanic regressions and was dropped. Results for other variables are not affected, for either the black or Hispanic audits, by excluding either or both of these variables.

Hausman (1978) tests were conducted to determine whether these variables are endogenous, that is, whether they are influenced by (as well as an influence upon) discrimination in inspections. The added instruments for these tests were the total number of units available to be recommended (but not inspected) for SRECOMM or RECOMM and whether recommendations outside integrated or minority areas were available for STEER. Neither test indicated endogeneity.

The final regression results are presented in Tables A.4–A.7.

TABLE A.4 REGRESSION RESULTS FOR BLACK-WHITE SALES AUDITS

Explanatory Variable	Estimated Coefficient	Standard Error	t-Statistic
Site Variables			
ONE	0.38681	0.43581	0.88757
ATLCC	$-5.39752e{-}02$	0.35285	-0.15297
ATLSUB	$-9.79281e{-}02$	0.34689	-0.28230
CHICC	-0.35220	0.32784	-1.07430
CHISUB	-0.51443	0.32390	-1.58822
LACC	$-1.40145e{-}02$	0.28355	$-4.94243e{-}02$
LASUB	0.24217	0.36747	0.65903
NYSUB	-0.23095	0.47007	-0.51258
AUSTIN	-0.27226	0.38235	-0.71207
BERGEN	0.66171	0.42069	1.57294
BERMHAM	$8.35139e{-}03$	0.40797	$2.04708e{-}02$
CINCINN	-0.23644	0.41106	-0.57520
DAYTON	-0.20470	0.34351	-0.59591
DENVER	-0.11821	0.35390	-0.33402
DETROIT	0.87363	0.43704	1.99895
HOUSTON	-0.14665	0.36733	-0.39924
LASIND	-0.17603	0.36370	-0.48400
MACON	0.19399	0.41052	0.47256
MIAMI	-0.21223	0.35118	-0.60434
NEWORLEA	-0.41185	0.40051	-1.02831
ORLANDO	-0.51384	0.35687	-1.43986
PHILLY	-0.43625	0.34472	-1.26553
PITTSBUR	-0.23785	0.37689	-0.63110
WASHDC	-0.58853	0.33383	-1.76296
SATLCC	0.20436	0.14605	1.39925
SATLSUB	0.16772	0.14329	1.17044
SCHICC	$6.75819e{-}02$	0.15506	0.43585
SCHISUB	0.23442	0.13603	1.72337
SLACC	-0.37676	0.11186	-3.36813
SLASUB	-0.70986	0.19572	-3.62689
SNYSUB	-0.16113	0.16026	-1.00540
SAUSTIN	0.39542	0.20869	1.89478
SBERGEN	-0.18072	0.13620	-1.32681
SBIRMHAM	0.26172	0.14994	1.74551
SCINCINN	1.32851	0.35843	3.70646
SDAYTON	0.39446	0.23474	1.68042
SDENVER	0.34472	0.14209	2.42604
SDETROIT	$3.95479e{-}02$	0.16669	0.23725
SHOUSTON	0.56282	0.27029	2.08230
SLANSING	-0.13923	0.17651	-0.78878
SMACON	0.42108	0.18651	2.25764
SMIAMI	0.36758	0.30210	1.21673
SNEWORLEA	0.23478	0.26814	0.87557
SORLANDO	0.26370	0.25035	1.05334
SPHILLY	0.10516	0.24362	0.43164
SPITTSBUR	0.23336	0.14460	1.61384
SWASHDC	0.50026	0.16794	2.97881

TABLE A.4 (*continued*)

Explanatory Variable	Estimated Coefficient	Standard Error	t-Statistic
Agent, Auditor, and Audit Characteristics			
AGNTAGE	5.83500e−03	5.01167e−03	1.16428
FAMINC	−3.63579e−06	2.45586e−06	−1.48045
HOUSEVAL	8.23997e−07	1.74471e−06	0.47228
AUDMAY	9.11515e−03	0.25513	3.57279e−02
AUDJUNE	−0.17772	9.10128e−02	−1.95265
AUDAUG	0.16655	0.18321	0.90906
CONDO	−0.10484	0.11199	−0.93614
STEER	0.18780	8.38801e−02	2.23895
SSIZE	−4.77808e−02	1.58412e−02	−3.01624
SHVAL	2.19744e−06	5.37622e−07	4.08733
SAGAGE	−6.96678e−03	2.43086e−03	−2.86598
SFEMLK	0.15085	4.27828e−02	−3.52601
SSFEM	−0.20511	0.12067	−1.69982
SSMAN	0.44936	0.14212	3.16176
SKID	8.59937e−02	4.09989e−02	2.09746
SRECOM	−4.88638e−02	9.86611e−03	−4.95270
SMLS	−4.56084e−02	4.57098e−02	−0.99778
SMLSIW	0.62753	0.23579	2.66139
SAGBLK	−0.25016	0.12181	−2.05377
Neighborhood Variables			
AOSP	−0.41694	0.24193	1.72339
SPSP	−0.21934	0.21556	−1.01753
OFINTEG	0.13921	0.33190	−0.41944
NEINTEG	0.54546	0.25557	2.13424
NEBLACK	1.07297	1.76589	0.60761
A1WW	−3.44944e−02	0.10750	−0.32088
A1WI	−0.32917	0.28033	−1.17420
A1WM	−1.07569	1.32892	−0.80944
A1IW	0.12167	0.26141	0.46545
A1II	−0.42273	0.26535	−1.59309
A1IM	−1.83105	2.12829	−0.86034
A1MW	3.03411e−02	1.15398	2.62924e−02
A1MI	0.18229	1.15525	0.15780
A1MM	−0.25354	2.09670	−0.12093
A2WW	0.31697	0.10202	3.10703
A2WI	−8.74726e−02	0.21039	−0.41576
A2WM	−1.26207	2.13979	−0.58981
A2IW	−0.11856	0.37058	−0.31993
A2II	−0.53687	0.25852	−2.07666
S1WW	0.40338	0.17947	2.24764
S1WI	0.48366	0.20621	2.34548
S1WX	0.33550	0.30022	1.11750
S1IW	0.18076	0.22149	0.81610
S1II	0.40776	0.31480	1.29531
S1MM	0.20344	0.59717	0.34067
S2WW	4.34078e−02	0.18351	0.23654

TABLE A.4 (*continued*)

Explanatory Variable	Estimated Coefficient	Standard Error	t-Statistic
Neighborhood Variables			
S2WI	0.13594	0.21951	0.61929
S2WM	−8.07313e−03	0.42617	−1.89434e−02
S2IX	−0.15617	0.21854	−0.71459
S2IW	0.31038	0.25291	1.22725
S2II	0.59734	0.20170	2.96147
S2IX	0.66243	0.34898	1.89818
S2MW	2.22975	1.22125	1.82580
Controls for Teammate Differences			
ORDER	−0.11523	7.37807e−02	−1.56181
DAGNTAGE	−3.21549e−03	4.96974e−03	−0.64701
DAGNTFEM	−8.46413e−02	9.52139e−02	−0.88896
DAUDAGE	1.71450e−03	6.82370e−03	0.25126
DAFTNOON	−0.15721	6.00243e−02	−2.61906
Number of Observations		1047	
R-squared		0.34158	
Corrected R-squared		0.26967	
Sum of Squared Residuals		1.19583e+03	
Standard Error of the Regression		1.12610	
Mean of Dependent Variable		0.29608	

TABLE A.5 REGRESSION RESULTS FOR HISPANIC–WHITE
                   SALES AUDITS

Explanatory Variable	Estimated Coefficient	Standard Error	t-Statistic
Site Variables			
ONE	1.15223	0.40514	2.84404
CHICC	−0.51580	0.30084	−1.71452
CHISUB	−0.54741	0.30891	−1.77208
LACC	−0.35234	0.28431	−1.23925
LASUB	−0.55688	0.32783	−1.69867
NYSUB	0.19700	0.46368	0.42487
SACC	−0.89910	0.29553	−3.04236
SASUB	−0.71654	1.51544	−0.47283
AUSTIN	−0.74713	0.31647	−2.36080
BERGEN	−0.45702	0.35491	−1.28771
DENVER	−0.74105	0.29278	−2.53111
HOUSTON	−0.75810	0.33426	−2.26799
MIAMI	−0.64740	0.30313	−2.13575
PHOENIX	−0.52779	0.34329	−1.53745
PUEBLO	−0.82711	0.33442	−2.47328

Table A.5 (*continued*)

Explanatory Variable	Estimated Coefficient	Standard Error	t-Statistic
Site Variables			
SANDIEGO	−0.42388	0.29796	−1.42258
TUCSON	−0.77016	0.31447	−2.44909
SCHICC	4.81336e−03	0.14091	3.41579e−02
SCHISUB	−0.16223	0.14181	−1.14401
SLACC	−8.38080e−02	0.13687	−0.61232
SLASUB	4.58727e−02	0.20437	0.22446
SNYSUB	−8.10667e−02	0.12494	−0.64885
SSACC	−0.18266	0.13893	−1.31480
SSASUB	0.51363	0.45099	1.13889
SAUSTIN	0.47228	0.15648	3.01822
SBERGEN	−0.18150	0.13257	−1.36906
SDENVER	−0.15207	0.12446	−1.22184
SHOUSTON	9.33132e−02	0.17410	0.53598
SMIAMI	0.31810	0.26768	1.18839
SPHOENIX	−0.14825	0.12079	−1.22741
SPUEBLO	8.27996e−02	0.28273	0.29286
SSANDIEGO	−0.10925	0.12676	−0.86189
STUCSON	0.19620	0.12889	1.52226
Agent, Auditor, and Audit Characteristics			
AGNTFEM	−0.13806	9.25898e−02	−1.49106
DARK	8.57894e−02	0.11743	0.73058
ACCENT	−7.52671e−02	0.12048	−0.62475
FAMINC	−2.97594e−06	1.64318e−06	−1.81108
AUDMAY	−0.13994	0.44677	−0.31322
AUDJUNE	7.89918e−02	8.98623e−02	0.87903
AUDAUG	0.18686	0.18756	0.99630
CONDO	5.14143e−02	0.12692	0.40510
SAGAGE	−5.17416e−03	1.82009e−03	−2.84281
SFINC	1.14618e−06	8.03742e−07	1.42606
SCHILD	0.11544	4.70290e−02	2.45465
SDARK	−0.13912	5.87896e−02	−2.36648
SACCENT	−0.31051	7.18427e−02	−4.32201
SDA	0.41335	7.73464e−02	5.34419
SQUAL	0.17784	9.24152e−02	1.92436
SMLS	−0.11481	3.85287e−02	−2.97993
SAGHIS	−0.24888	0.12218	−2.03702
SRECOM	−2.24075e−02	7.32551e−03	−3.05883
Neighborhood Variables			
AOSP	−0.17524	0.31247	−0.56083
APSP	0.25899	0.28900	0.89618
OFINTEG	−0.14882	0.26411	−0.56349
OFHISPA	−0.70940	1.00420	−0.70643
NEINTEG	2.40601e−02	0.17622	0.13654
NEHISPA	0.57281	0.99640	0.57487
A1XWW	−0.16303	0.20828	−0.78274

Table A.5 (*continued*)

Explanatory Variable	Estimated Coefficient	Standard Error	t-Statistic
Neighborhood Variables			
A1WI	−0.20631	0.23710	−0.87014
A2WM	−0.69070	1.22085	−0.56576
A1IW	7.06770e−02	0.28077	0.25173
A1II	2.06981e−02	0.18622	0.11115
A1IM	−0.25146	0.75048	−0.33506
A1MI	0.21881	0.85378	0.25629
A1MM	−1.98671e−02	1.51883	−1.30805e−02
A2WW	−0.28745	0.16534	−1.73851
A2WI	−0.33065	0.20151	−1.64084
A2WM	0.94629	0.88584	1.06823
A2IW	−0.79403	0.38481	−2.06343
A2II	−0.64389	0.23414	−2.75003
A2IM	−1.01166	0.80925	−1.25011
S1WW	0.20110	0.17595	1.14295
S1WI	0.46512	0.33021	1.40855
S1WX	−0.32850	0.29506	−1.11335
S1IW	0.26778	0.18426	1.45331
S1II	0.53304	0.20159	2.64423
S1IX	0.53614	0.50103	1.07008
S1MM	0.85245	0.55850	1.52633
S2WW	0.22468	0.16597	1.35370
S2WI	0.44782	0.19836	2.25765
S2WM	−1.59668	1.25405	−1.27322
S2WX	0.26977	0.22057	1.22303
S2IW	0.15591	0.17268	0.90284
S2II	0.56215	0.18050	3.11446
S2IX	0.46539	0.27916	1.66713
S2MW	−0.58379	0.81148	−0.71942
Controls for Teammate Differences			
ORDER	−5.98780e−02	7.76196e−02	−0.77143
DAGNTAGE	−3.02144e−03	4.90227e−03	−0.61633
DAGNTFEM	−0.11707	0.10567	−1.10792
DAUDAGE	−4.60423e−03	8.08275e−03	−0.56964
DAFTNOON	−0.15627	5.88000e−02	−2.65765

Number of Observations	1049
R-squared	0.24110
Corrected R-squared	0.16981
Sum of Squared Residuals	1.37972e+03
Standard Error of the Regression	1.20009
Mean of Dependent Variable	0.24881

Table A.6 REGRESSION RESULTS FOR BLACK–WHITE RENTAL AUDITS

Explanatory Variable	Estimated Coefficient	Standard Error	t-Statistic
Site Variables			
ONE	−0.31254	0.66171	−0.47232
ATLCC	−8.53164e−02	0.34825	−0.24499
ATHSUB	−0.43078	0.34776	−1.23872
CHICC	−8.45320e−02	0.29103	−0.29046
CHISUB	0.35514	0.49919	0.71129
LACC	−0.26206	0.28591	−0.91656
LASUB	−0.12098	0.33612	−0.35993
NYSUB	0.70150	0.67122	1.04511
AUSTIN	−6.53254e−02	0.34451	−0.18962
BERGEN	4.10365e−02	0.35120	0.11685
BIRMHAM	−0.11230	0.36268	−0.30964
CINCINN	−0.17970	0.34989	−0.51360
DAYTON	0.39589	0.33286	1.18934
DENVER	7.00097e−02	0.32622	0.21461
DETROIT	0.30890	0.39188	0.78826
HOUSTON	−8.88620e−02	0.31291	−0.28398
LANSING	−0.19657	0.32931	−0.59692
MACON	0.31925	0.35179	0.90752
MIAMI	0.35060	0.30515	1.14893
NEWORLEA	−8.29812e−02	0.36040	−0.23024
ORLANDO	−0.17494	0.38765	−0.45129
PHILLY	−0.13374	0.34901	−0.38321
PITTSBUR	0.13806	0.31418	0.43943
WASHDC	−0.25893	0.32266	−0.80249
SATLCC	−0.47601	0.26328	−1.80797
SATLSUB	−0.11109	0.26155	−0.42473
SCHICC	−8.89654e−02	0.17954	−0.49552
SCHISUB	−1.28341	0.42781	−2.99998
SLACC	−0.45904	0.24417	−1.88004
SLASUB	−0.38389	0.27963	−1.37285
SNYSUB	−1.59170	0.90509	−1.75860
SAUSTIN	−0.46897	0.26229	−1.78799
SBERGEN	−0.16615	0.21789	−0.76255
SBIRMHAM	−0.51614	0.28544	−1.80822
SCINCINN	0.18503	0.24095	0.76793
SDAYTON	−0.56075	0.31701	−1.76886
SDENVER	−0.18814	0.21859	−0.86070
SDETROIT	−0.46737	0.25479	−1.76505
SHOUSTON	−0.38984	0.28241	−1.38044
SLANSING	−0.69234	0.23133	−2.99287
SMACON	−0.60578	0.25773	−2.35043
SMIAMI	−0.64460	0.28843	−2.23486
SNEWORLEA	−0.18051	0.36158	−0.49924
SORLANDO	−0.45658	0.40811	−1.11876
SPHILLY	−0.24670	0.23090	−1.06844
SPITTSBUR	−0.74636	0.23987	−3.11158
SWASHDC	−0.14581	0.25278	−0.57681

Table A.6 (*continued*)

Explanatory Variable	Estimated Coefficient	Standard Error	t-Statistic
Agent, Auditor, and Audit Characteristics			
AGNTAGE	3.92999e−03	3.11095e−03	1.26328
RENT	7.65443e−06	9.24071e−06	0.82834
AUDMAY	0.30629	0.27305	1.12171
AUDJUNE	0.12672	8.63951e−02	1.46675
AUDAUG	−0.25973	0.26636	−0.97508
AFTNOON	1.01315e−03	0.10608	9.55091e−03
SAGBLKIN	0.24595	0.12563	1.95765
SADAGE	−1.93520e−02	4.71315e−03	−4.10596
SSFEM	0.24085	6.90924e−02	3.48588
SFINC	−6.45853e−06	2.08624e−06	−3.09578
Neighborhood Variables			
AOSP	−0.19693	0.59137	−0.33300
APSP	1.37919	1.44220	0.95631
AOFWHITE	0.16969	8.82464e−02	1.92296
AOFINTEG	−0.28809	0.17953	−1.60466
AOFBLACK	1.04036	0.49488	2.10226
A1WW	0.23694	0.59664	0.39713
A1WI	0.10642	0.62132	0.17129
A1WM	0.16812	0.87885	0.19129
A1IW	0.28611	0.67037	0.42680
A1II	0.34416	0.60056	0.57307
A1IM	0.89822	0.75399	1.19130
A1MW	6.65739e−02	1.08112	6.15786e−02
A1MI	0.66370	0.88209	0.75242
A1MM	0.29945	0.54892	0.54552
A2WW	−0.82927	1.55814	−0.53221
A2WI	−0.63361	1.56590	−0.40463
A2WM	−1.82029	0.91557	−1.98815
A2IW	−2.30348	1.58448	−1.45378
A2II	−1.69856	1.57037	−1.08163
A2MI	−1.77501	2.00554	−0.88506
S1WW	1.52811	0.26872	5.68662
S1WI	1.78526	0.35504	5.02829
S1WX	1.98600	0.41231	4.81674
S1IW	2.07041	0.60928	3.39810
S1II	1.63485	0.30828	5.30318
S1IM	0.84792	0.80618	1.05177
S1MW	0.23467	0.76973	0.30488
S1MI	1.63066	0.53976	3.02106
S1MM	0.89034	0.31756	2.80369
S1MX	2.42062	0.55943	4.32693
S2WW	0.90923	0.28574	3.18202
S2WI	0.99496	0.33724	2.95028
S2WM	−2.62259	1.73430	−1.51219
S2WX	0.53184	0.30894	1.72151
S2IW	1.97828	0.34365	5.75663

TABLE A.6 (*continued*)

Explanatory Variable	Estimated Coefficient	Standard Error	t-Statistic
Neighborhood Variables			
S2II	1.89581	0.30589	6.19764
S2IM	2.86067e−02	0.71709	3.98928e−02
S2IX	1.32054	0.34799	3.79473
S2MI	1.51545	0.92649	1.63569
Controls for Teammate Differences			
ORDER	3.68630e−02	6.99109e−02	0.52728
DAGNTAGE	8.32817e−04	5.53360e−03	0.15050
DAGNTFEM	0.24566	0.11490	2.13805
DAUDAGE	1.05315e−02	6.85943e−03	1.53534
DAFTNOON	−0.10800	8.39335e−02	−1.28676
Number of Observations		748	
R-squared		0.31423	
Corrected R-squared		0.20824	
Sum of Squared Residuals		5.00092e+02	
Standard Error of the Regression		0.87917	
Mean of Dependent Variable		0.24733	

TABLE A.7 REGRESSION RESULTS FOR HISPANIC–WHITE RENTAL AUDITS

Explanatory Variable	Estimated Coefficient	Standard Error	t-Statistic
Site Variables			
ONE	−1.03871	0.74074	−1.40227
CHICC	−0.35777	0.27794	−1.28722
CHISUB	−0.29670	0.41480	−0.71528
LACC	−0.57331	0.26067	−2.19933
LASUB	−0.77210	0.34365	−2.24679
NYSUB	0.73914	0.76840	0.96067
SACC	−0.64461	0.29788	−2.16397
SASUB	−0.51617	0.91157	−0.56624
AUSTIN	−0.67087	0.29148	−2.30160
BERGEN	−0.63164	0.29894	−2.11289
DENVER	−4.70014e−02	0.31481	−0.14930
HOUSTON	−0.68062	0.30357	−2.24208
MIAMI	−0.52947	0.29247	−1.81034
PHOENIX	−0.39918	0.30831	−1.29472
PUEBLO	−0.37153	0.31664	−1.17335
SANDIEGO	−0.48522	0.29835	−1.62636
TUCSON	−0.68774	0.30253	−2.27327
SCHICC	−0.16496	0.17780	−0.92780

Table A.7 (*continued*)

Explanatory Variable	Estimated Coefficient	Standard Error	t-Statistic
Site Variables			
SCHISUB	−8.80503e−03	0.37146	−2.37039e−02
SLACC	2.36570e−02	0.17963	0.13170
SLASUB	0.77025	0.24688	3.11997
SNYSUB	−0.57260	0.42229	−1.35594
SSACC	0.52036	0.24129	2.15655
SSASUB	−1.64709	1.52901	−1.07722
SAUSTIN	0.31610	0.17594	1.79666
SBERGEN	0.19950	0.17077	1.16822
SDENVER	−0.41089	0.17674	−2.32481
SHOUSTON	0.58575	0.23273	2.51683
SMIAMI	0.22732	0.20562	1.10551
SPHOENIX	−0.23969	0.18827	−1.27316
SPUEBLO	0.11588	0.23822	0.48645
SSANDIEGO	0.23103	0.20522	1.25770
STUCSON	0.26605	0.19428	1.36942
Agent, Auditor, and Audit Characteristics			
AGNTFEM	−0.26004	0.10126	−2.56794
DARK	0.28957	0.12377	2.25877
ACCENT	−0.24858	0.12636	−1.96716
DA	0.39208	0.15986	2.45270
FAMINC	6.22121e−06	3.86248e−06	1.61068
RENT	−1.06548e−05	1.60320e−05	−0.66459
AUDMAY	−0.54942	0.55294	−0.99362
AUDJUNE	−3.46080e−02	8.05357e−02	−0.42972
AUDAUG	−6.94874e−02	0.20523	−0.33858
AFTNOON	0.23261	0.10508	2.21367
SAGHIDK	0.69175	0.18557	3.72771
SAGHIAC	−0.45585	0.19264	−2.36627
SDARK	−0.63460	8.52544e−02	−7.44360
SAGFEM	0.41710	8.26821e−02	5.04461
SSFEM	−0.17208	8.72890e−02	−1.97138
SSMAN	−0.22239	8.91313e−02	−2.49510
SFEMLK	−0.27317	8.99717e−02	−3.03616
RECOMM	−0.11127	3.93286e−02	−2.82930
Neighborhood Variables			
AOSP	1.14131	0.67033	1.70260
APSP	−0.29141	1.53606	−0.18971
AOFWHITE	−0.24519	0.11346	−2.16098
AOFINTEG	0.34062	0.10142	3.35848
AOFHISPA	−0.80858	0.42071	−1.92197
A1WW	1.19322	0.68574	1.74005
A1WI	1.27785	0.69458	1.83975
A1IW	0.79931	0.72384	1.10426
A1II	1.33509	0.67440	1.97968
A1IM	1.24897	0.80463	1.55223

TABLE A.7 (*continued*)

Explanatory Variable	Estimated Coefficient	Standard Error	t-Statistic
Neighborhood Variables			
A1MI	1.58007	0.91385	1.72901
A1MM	1.30671	0.62296	2.09757
A2WW	1.08596	1.68965	0.64272
A2WI	1.55777	1.69161	0.92088
A2IW	0.98918	1.71627	0.57635
A2II	1.12695	1.68942	0.66706
A2MI	4.24824	1.38031	3.07773
S1WW	0.45532	0.20407	2.23115
S1WI	0.65115	0.43112	1.51035
S1WX	0.31235	0.15598	2.00255
S1IW	0.99060	0.58075	1.70574
S1II	0.21521	0.21070	1.02140
S1IM	−1.12727	1.00186	−1.12518
S1IX	0.30502	0.26948	1.13190
S1MW	$4.79351e{-}02$	1.02399	$4.68123e{-}02$
S1MI	−0.13675	0.35089	−0.38973
S1MM	−0.84498	0.34228	−2.46869
S2WW	0.43577	0.17728	2.45812
S2WI	0.20199	0.17784	1.13580
S2WX	0.60951	0.12717	4.79291
S2IW	0.54826	0.24468	2.24067
S2II	0.31705	0.17284	1.83430
S2IM	2.11447	1.80682	1.17027
S2IX	0.70759	0.19783	3.57667
S2MM	$8.88288e{-}02$	0.90295	$9.83766e{-}02$
S2MX	−0.94950	0.60172	−1.57798
Controls for Teammate Differences			
ORDER	0.10373	$6.67376e{-}02$	1.55426
DAGNTAGE	$-5.18679e{-}03$	$4.81405e{-}03$	−1.07743
DAGNTFEM	$-9.75903e{-}02$	0.11093	−0.87973
DAUDAGE	$-1.09082e{-}02$	$7.07812e{-}03$	−1.54111
DAFTNOON	−0.27681	$8.03535e{-}02$	−3.44485
Number of Observations		755	
R-squared		0.41380	
Corrected R-squared		0.33334	
Sum of Squared Residuals		$4.96101e{+}02$	
Standard Error of the Regression		0.86502	
Mean of Dependent Variable		0.12450	

CHAPTER 1: RACE AND ETHNICITY, PREJUDICE AND DISCRIMINATION

1. These examples are taken from the Housing Discrimination Study, which is described in detail in Chapters 2 through 5.

2. Schiller (1989). This book mentions residential segregation on pages 220 and 221. It says that the "Federal Housing Authority [sic] has been a major factor in the housing market," and "has chosen to encourage and extend rigid racial and class segregation," and that public housing "tends to intensify racial and economic isolation." Schiller also mentions the link between housing and school segregation, a topic that is addressed in Chapter 8.

3. Jaynes and Williams (1989, pp. 88–91 and 140–146). Not only is housing discrimination neglected in this generally excellent report, but some statements made about it are factually incorrect. The report summarizes a 1977 study by the U.S. Department of Housing and Urban Development as saying that blacks and whites are "steered into separate neighborhoods" (p. 142). As explained in detail in Chapters 3 and 4, this HUD study does not examine steering at all, and subsequent analyses find only modest levels of steering in this HUD data.

4. Among the scholars who have emphasized the importance of housing discrimination are Galster (1991, 1992b, 1993b), Massey and Denton (1993), and Orfield and Ashkinaze (1991). A more thorough review of the research linking housing discrimination to the broader system of racial and ethnic disparities, some of which was conducted before these studies, is provided in Chapter 8.

5. Herrnstein and Murray (1994). The authors never literally say that blacks

are inherently less intelligent than whites, but they do say: "It seems highly likely to us that both genes and the environment have something to do with racial differences" (p. 311). In an apparent effort to absolve themselves from blame for the implications of their work, they also state: "We cannot think of a legitimate argument why any encounter between individual whites and blacks need be affected by the knowledge that an aggregate ethnic difference in measured intelligence is genetic instead of environmental" (p. 313). Apparently they have never heard of stereotypes and prejudice! As Goldberger and Manski (forthcoming) put it, the Herrnstein/Murray "treatment of genetics and race is akin to standing up in a crowded theatre and shouting, 'Let's consider the possibility that there is a FIRE!'"

6. Some experts believe that racial differences in average intelligence test scores are due entirely to differences in environmental factors. Others believe that genetic factors also may be involved, but their role, if any, has not yet been determined. For example, using the term "bell curve" to indicate the distribution of IQs, a recent op-ed piece signed by fifty-two experts in intelligence and allied fields concludes: "Most experts believe that environment is important in pushing the bell curves [of different racial and ethnic groups] apart, but that genetics could be involved too" (Arvey et al., 1994). Moreover, the specific arguments used by Herrnstein and Murray (1994) to support the view that genetics matter have been widely criticized by the experts. See Allman (1994), Goldberger and Manski (1995), Gould (1994), Holt (1994), and Passell (1994). For a review and critique of previous claims that blacks are inherently less intelligent than whites, see Simpson and J. Milton Yinger (1985, Chap. 2) and Schiller (1989, Chap. 7).

7. Many different methods are used to observe and measure an individual's genes. See Cavalli-Sforza, Menozzi, and Piazza (1993), Levathes (1993), and Sokal, Oden, and Wilson (1991). Levathes, for example, reports that Cavalli-Sforza and his colleagues compare human genes by looking at the "DNA of mitochondria, cellular structures that supply energy and are inherited solely through the mother's line."

8. This discussion of these two processes is drawn from Cavalli-Sforza, Menozzi, and Piazza (1993).

9. Cavalli-Sforza, Menozzi, and Piazza (1993, p. 639). Genetic differentiation by location also may arise if the people who migrate are genetically different from the people who stay behind.

10. Cavalli-Sforza, Menozzi, and Piazza (1993, p. 641). Some experts believe that differences in skin color arise as people in different locations develop preferences for certain types of appearance—not as people adapt to different climates. See Diamond (1994b). In any case, skin color is determined by the interaction between light and five pigments in human skin. A detailed discussion of the racial dimension of skin color, as well

as of hair and eye color, hair texture, and facial features, can be found in Simpson and J. Milton Yinger (1985, Chap. 2). Moreover, all human beings have the enzyme needed to make black skin, but some also either produce this enzyme in inactive form or else produce "inhibiters" (see Wills, 1994). Both Simpson and Yinger and Wills also explain that these aspects of human appearance are influenced by multiple genes, and the exact mechanism by which they are inherited is not known. Hence it is difficult, if not impossible, "to define racial groups by specifying differences in the frequency distribution of certain genes" (Simpson and Yinger, 1985, p. 31).

11. Levathes (1993, p. C9).

12. This quotation is taken from Levathes (1993, p. C9). It is from a statement made before the Senate Committee on Government Affairs by Dr. Cavalli-Sforza and Dr. Mary-Claire King.

13. These six broad groups are black, Khoisan, Pygmy, white, Asian, and Australian aboriginals (see Diamond, 1994a).

14. Diamond (1994a) provides a detailed account of the competition between the three dark-skinned racial groups in Africa and explains how competition with blacks had kept down the populations of Pygmies and Khoisans even before the Europeans arrived and almost wiped them both out.

15. Cavalli-Sforza, Menozzi, and Piazza (1993). An earlier migration by a precursor to anatomically modern humans took place between 1 and 2 million years ago. Scholars disagree about the fate of these early migrants. Some believe they died out, whereas others believe that they experienced "parallel evolution," and that "humans who descended from their modern African ancestors expanded eastward and mixed to some extent with East Asians who were more direct descendants of archaic" humans, that is, of descendants of the earliest migrants. Again, see Cavalli-Sforza, Menozzi, and Piazza (1993).

16. Humans reached Australia between 55,000 and 60,000 years ago, after rafts and boats were common (Cavalli-Sforza, Menozzi, and Piazza, 1993). Australian aboriginals are genetically closer to Asians than to Africans, despite their dark skin. See Cavalli-Sforza, Menozzi, and Piazza (1993) and Levathes (1993). Native Americans, who migrated into the Americas from Asia, often are considered part of the broadly defined Asian race.

17. This genetic research, as well as the information on human migrations out of Africa, is described in Levathes (1993).

18. This discussion of human expansions into Europe is based on Cavalli-Sforza, Menozzi, and Piazza (1993), who find clear evidence of these expansions in examining the genes of people who come from various different parts of the world. This source also describes five expansions after 10,000 years ago which led to genetic mixing in other parts of the world. Genetic evidence concerning human expansions into Europe also is provided by Sokal, Oden, and Wilson (1991). Cavalli-Sforza, Menozzi,

and Piazza (1993) also explain that their genetic evidence of human expansions is supported by archeological evidence, which makes it possible to date the spread of tools and other human products, which accompanies human migrations. Moreover, human expansions show up to some degree in language. See Ross (1991) and Sokal, Oden, and Thomson (1992). Some experts in linguistics also believe that the relatively similar structures of all human language provide further evidence of the basic similarity of all humans. In describing the work of the linguists Pinker and Chomsky, Coe (1994, p. 8) writes: "Even though there are 4,000 to 6,000 languages today, they are all sufficiently alike to be considered one language by an extraterrestrial observer. In other words, most of the diversity of the world's cultures, so beloved to anthropologists, is superficial and minor compared to the similarities. Racial differences are literally only 'skin deep.' "

19. Because the dividing lines between racial groups are arbitrary and because new racial groups are continually emerging, scholars take many different approaches to the biological conception of race. Some define a different number of broad racial groups, others focus on a larger number of smaller racial groups, and still others reject the biological notion of race altogether. For a discussion of some other racial classification schemes, see Simpson and J. Milton Yinger (1985, Chap. 2). One well-known detailed scheme, which contains thirty-four racial groups, was developed by Dobzhansky (1962). For examples that reveal how arbitrary racial classification schemes can be, see Shreeve (1994) or Diamond (1994b). Diamond points out, for example, that a racial classification scheme based on fingerprint type would place most Africans, Asians, and Europeans in one race, Mongolians and Australian aboriginals in another, and the Khoisan people of southern Africa plus some central Europeans in a third.

20. Simpson and J. Milton Yinger (1985, p. 34). Simpson and Yinger also point out, on page 36, that the genetic makeup of African Americans' African ancestors is quite mixed, and can be one-eighth black or even less in some cases. Many African Americans also have Native American ancestors. Another way to express the extent of this genetic mixing is to say that "some 20 to 30 percent of the average African American's genetic material was contributed by ancestors who were either European or American Indian" (Shreeve, 1994, p. 58).

21. As one scholar put it: "In my family, like many families with African-American ancestry, there is a history of multiracial offspring associated with rape and concubinage." Quoted in Wright (1994).

22. The number of marriages between blacks and whites in the United States increased from 65,000 in 1970 to 246,000 in 1992. Over this same period the total number of interracial couples increased from 310,000 to 1,161,000. See U.S. Bureau of the Census, 1993d. Interracial marriages constituted 2.2 percent of all marriages in 1992, compared to 0.4 percent

in 1960 (Holmes, 1994a); moreover, about 10 percent of married black men have white wives and about 5 percent of married black women have white husbands (Wright, 1994, p. 49). Strictly speaking, intermarriage is neither necessary nor sufficient for genetic mixing. Interethnic couples may be childless and mixed-ethnic children can be born out of wedlock. Nevertheless, intermarriage and genetic mixing are highly correlated. For more on these topics, see J. Milton Yinger (1994, Chap. 4).

23. Simpson and J. Milton Yinger (1985, p. 34). In addition, many apparently white Americans have Native American ancestors.

24. A description of the racial groups in Africa when Europeans arrived, which included both whites and Asians, can be found in Diamond (1994).

25. J. Milton Yinger (1994, p. 20).

26. Shreeve (1994, p. 60). According to one calculation, 99.8 percent of genetic material is the same, on average, in every group of people. Eighty-five percent of the variation in the remaining 0.2 percent occurs within "any small group from any location in the world," 9 percent of this variation occurs "among ethnic and linguistic groups within a given race," and only 6 percent "represents genetic differences between races" Gutin (1994, p. 72).

27. A broader definition of an ethnic group is provided by J. Milton Yinger (1994, pp. 3–4): "(1) The group is perceived by others in the society to be different in some combination of the following traits: language, religion, race, and ancestral homeland with its related culture; (2) the members also perceive themselves to be different; and (3) they participate in shared activities built around their (real or mythical) common origin and culture." By this definition, African Americans could be considered an ethnic group.

28. In fact, the term ethnicity "was derived from the Greek work *ethos,* which . . . conveyed the notion of an ancestrally related group" (Connor, 1985, p. 4).

29. For a detailed discussion of the racial background of Mexican Americans, see J. Milton Yinger (1985). The Census Bureau explicitly notes that Hispanics can be of any race, or, it should be added, any racial mixture. See Garcia (1993).

30. In the 1980 census, 58 percent of Hispanics identified themselves as "white," 3 percent identified themselves as "black," and the rest gave other answers to the race question, all of which were coded as "Spanish race." See Denton and Massey (1989, Table 1).

31. To take the etymology of the word back another step, *Hispania* originally was "a Phoenician word for 'land of rabbits' that was used by the Romans during their conquest of the area that includes modern-day Spain." This quotation, which is found in Gonzales (1992), is by Ana Celia Zentella, a linguistics professor.

32. This count is from the introduction to Moore and Pinderhughes (1993, p. xi).

33. A similar point is made by J. Milton Yinger, who writes that "Race is important in social interaction primarily because of present and past correlation of racial differences with cultural and status differences" and "Socially visible 'racial' lines, based on beliefs about race and on administrative and political classifications, not on genetic differences per se, are the critical ones for social analysis" (1994, p. 20). This approach, like many if not most of the points in this book, can be traced back to Myrdal (1944) who writes that "The definition of the 'Negro race' is thus a social and conventional, not a biological concept. The social definition and not the biological facts actually determines the status of an individual and his place in interracial relations" (p. 115).

34. For comprehensive investigations into the role of ethnic conflict in human society, see Horowitz (1985b), Gurr (1993), and J. Milton Yinger (1994).

35. For a detailed discussion of the individual and cultural sources of prejudice and discrimination, see Simpson and J. Milton Yinger (1985, Chaps. 4 and 5).

36. For an examination of the personality responses to prejudice and discrimination, see Simpson and J. Milton Yinger (1985, Chaps. 6 and 7). Chapter 8 of this source discusses the negative personality consequences of prejudice and discrimination for people who are prejudiced or who practice discrimination.

37. According to NORC data for 1990, about 85 percent of blacks (compared to 75 percent of whites) believe that there is some or a lot of discrimination against blacks in housing and labor markets (Farley, 1993, pp. 174–175). Moreover, NORC data for 1985 to 1990 reveal that 71 percent of blacks endorse the view that "blacks have worse jobs, income, and housing than whites . . . mainly due to discrimination" (Farley, 1993, p. 176). These perceptions of differential treatment reach into a person's identity. Every year I ask my students to tell the class what group they identify with. The African American students always say "African American" or "black," the Hispanic American students usually say "Latino," and the white students usually say "just American," although one occasionally says "Jewish" or "Irish" or "Italian."

38. For a review of the evidence showing that violence is not connected to the genetic dimension of race, see Williams (1994).

39. Appearances can, of course, be deceiving. Wright (1994, p. 53) describes a study of infants who died from 1983 to 1985: "In an astounding number of cases, the infant has a different race on its death certificate from the one on its birth certificate."

40. Wright (1994, p. 48). The "one-drop rule" was, in effect, written into law in many southern states. As late as 1986, the U.S. Supreme Court refused

to review (and thereby upheld) "a lower court's ruling that a Louisiana woman whose great-great-great-great-grandmother had been the mistress of a French planter was black—even though that portion of her ancestry amounted to no more than three thirty-seconds of her genetic heritage" (Wright, 1994, p. 48). Many minority scholarship or affirmative action programs also are available to people with any identifiable minority ancestor.

41. Denton and Massey (1989, p. 791).

42. In an ironic and revealing twist, "coloureds" in South Africa, who once had their own, largely powerless Parliament, recently rioted because they believe the new, democratically elected government favors blacks and whites over coloureds. See Keller (1994).

43. Results presented in Chapters 7 and 9 demonstrate that the power of skin color as a symbol adds to the power of the Hispanic designation. The potential for conflict associated with immigration is illustrated by the passage in November 1994 of Proposition 187 in California. This proposition, which prohibits the provision of education, non-emergency health care, and other state and local government services to illegal immigrants and which has so far been blocked by the courts, both reflects and magnifies the conflicts between voters and illegal immigrants, almost all of whom are Hispanic. See, for example, Ayres (1994). Of course, not all interactions between immigrants and domestic workers involve conflict. The history of Mexican immigration to the United States and an analysis of its impact on both the immigrants and domestic workers can be found in Horowitz (1985a) and Rogers (1985).

44. Examples of the diversity in economic and social outcomes for different Hispanic groups can be found in Moore and Pinderhughes (1993). Other examples of this diversity, along with evidence for widespread discrimination against all Hispanics, are presented throughout this book.

45. In a controversial speech at the 1963 March on Washington, John Lewis, national chairman of the Student Nonviolent Coordinating Committee, gave a boost to this change in terminology when he said "black people" and "the black masses" instead of "Negro." See Branch (1988).

46. A recent newspaper article on the "name game" for minorities writes that "Black Haitians, Jamaicans and Cubans, for example, affirm that they are black, but not African American. . . . Cape Verdeans, from a country off the coast of Africa that was once part of Portugal, say they are neither Latino nor African American. But they are frequently referred to as both" (*The Boston Globe*, 1993).

47. See Wright (1994) and Holmes (1994a). The current racial and ethnic categories on government documents are set by the Office of Management and Budget's Statistical Directive 15, which was issued in 1977. This directive "acknowledges four general racial groups in the United States: American Indian or Alaska Native; Asian or Pacific Islander; Black; and

White" (Wright, 1994, pp. 46–47). Many decades ago, the Census Bureau attempted to count the number of blacks with various degrees of white ancestry. "After 1920, however, the Census Bureau gave up on such distinctions, estimating that three-quarters of all blacks in the United States were racially mixed already" (Wright, 1994, p. 48).

48. For a more detailed discussion of this debate, see Wright (1994).

49. Negative reactions to the term Hispanic are somewhat ironic given the fact that it was selected by the Census Bureau for the 1980 census after consulting the Census Advisory Committee on the Spanish-Origin Population, a nonprofessional group that included community activists, and after the formation of the Congressional Hispanic Caucus in 1977. Peterson (1986) describes in detail the history of this census decision. For a discussion of various recent reactions to the term *Hispanic,* see the article in *The New York Times* by Gonzales (1992) and the letters published in response (Krebs, 1992; Guadalupe, 1992; and Sundiata, 1992).

50. This quotation is from an author, Sandra Cisneros, and is taken from Gonzales (1992).

51. This quotation, also found in Gonzales (1992), is from Enrique Fernandez, the editor of "a Spanish language entertainment magazine." Antonio Molina, editor of a Spanish-language newspaper, says, "There never was a Latin race. It comes from a dead language and I am very much alive" (*The Boston Globe,* 1993).

52. This survey result is reported in Gonzales (1992). For additional survey evidence that supports the view that most "Hispanics" prefer to be identified by their place of origin, see J. Milton Yinger (1994, Chap. 4).

53. This definition is from Simpson and J. Milton Yinger (1985, p. 21), who provide a detailed discussion of the concept of prejudice. As noted earlier, this source also explores the individual and cultural sources of prejudice.

54. The perception that the members of a group are more likely to engage in some socially undesirable act, which may in fact be true, leads to a type of discrimination called *statistical discrimination,* which is defined as judging an individual based on the perceived average characteristics of the group to which that individual belongs. Examples include crossing the street to avoid a young black man based on the perception that young black men are more likely than others to commit crimes, or denying a loan to a black based on the perception that blacks are more likely to default than whites with the same observable credit characteristics. If the perceptions on which they are based are accurate, statistical discrimination may be rational, but the discrimination is always sad and troubling, and in many cases, including mortgage markets, illegal. We will return to this topic in Chapters 5 and 9.

55. For an in-depth analysis of the origins of prejudice, see Simpson and J. Milton Yinger (1985) or J. Milton Yinger (1994, Chap. 5). See also Goleman (1994). Some evidence on white perceptions of blacks is provided

by Farley (1993, p. 176). Surveys conducted by NORC between 1985 and 1990 reveal that 50 percent of whites believe that "most blacks just don't have the motivation or willpower to pull themselves out of poverty," and 19 percent of whites believe that "most blacks have less inborn ability to learn." A 1994 survey by L. H. Research found that 12 percent of whites "agreed with the stereotype that blacks have less native intelligence"; in a Harris survey in 1978, 25 percent of whites agreed with this stereotype. See Holmes (1994b).

56. Surveys of the racial attitudes of blacks also have been conducted but not over so long a time period. The racial attitudes of blacks are important in understanding neighborhood racial transition, and the results of these surveys are discussed in Chapter 7.

57. Other aspects of white prejudice also have been studied. For example, hate crimes are one indicator of the extent of extreme prejudice. Hate crime statistics have only recently been collected in a reasonably comparable manner nationwide, so changes in the number of hate crimes over time are difficult to document. Nevertheless, the number of hate crimes in the United States was disturbingly high in 1991, with 2,963 reported crimes motivated by racial hatred (including 1,689 against blacks) and 1,367 reported crimes motivated by ethnic or religious hatred (including 242 against Hispanics). Most of these crimes were classified as intimidation, vandalism, or assault. See U.S. Department of Justice (1992). By 1993, the number of race-based hate crimes was up to 4,764 (including 2,476 against blacks), although it is not clear whether this increase reflects improved reporting. See *The New York Times* (1994b).

58. A detailed recent review of this survey evidence can be found in Farley (1993), from which all the evidence in this section is taken. The trends in white attitudes toward fair housing policy are not so clear. In 1990, 54 percent of whites said they would vote for a law "that a homeowner cannot refuse to sell to individuals because of their race or color." This percentage is up from 1973 (36 percent) but down from 1989 (59 percent) (Farley 1993, Figure 6.2). Moreover, some researchers believe that new, more subtle forms of prejudice are on the rise among whites. Pettigrew (1985), for example, talks about how whites now express nonprejudicial views without internalizing them and how the success of a few blacks has made some whites more ready to blame other blacks who do not succeed.

59. These declines in racial prejudice have occurred both because prejudice has declined within specific age cohorts and because younger cohorts tend to be less prejudiced than older ones. See Schuman, Steeh, and Bobo (1985). However, some evidence suggests that the decline in prejudice between cohorts is slowing down, that is, that the "youngest generation is not as sharply differentiated from its immediate predecessor" as it was in the past (Schuman, Steeh, and Bobo, 1985, p. 134).

60. Farley (1993, pp. 167 and 169). Further analysis of the Detroit data revealed that "The shift toward more liberal attitudes was not restricted to

a particular group of whites" (Farley et al., 1994, p. 760); that is, it occurred at all ages, incomes, and educational levels.

61. See Farley (1993, p. 173). Farley also cites Clark (1991), who found for five major cities in the 1980s that 65 percent of whites preferred a neighborhood that was at most 10 percent black.

62. Keating (1994, p. 64).

63. This definition implies that an employer can discriminate in hiring decisions by using illegitimate criteria (e.g., criteria unrelated to productivity) or by neglecting to use available legitimate criteria. These issues also arise in mortgage lending discrimination; as discussed in Chapter 5, lenders sometimes discriminate by using underwriting standards that are not related to a person's creditworthiness.

64. A detailed analysis of the causes of discrimination in housing and mortgage markets is provided in Chapter 9.

65. These points are explored in detail in Simpson and J. Milton Yinger (1985, Chap. 1).

CHAPTER 2: THE HOUSING DISCRIMINATION STUDY

1. See, for example, Kain and Quigley (1975), Yinger (1979, 1987), and Yinger et al. (1979).

2. These studies not only provide an indirect test of the existence of discrimination but also measure the consequences of discrimination and are reviewed in more detail in Chapter 7.

3. Some people use the term *test* instead of audit when the purpose is enforcement. In this book an "audit" is a procedure that can be used for research or enforcement. Standards for enforcement audits or tests are discussed in Reed (1994).

4. For examples of these how-to manuals, see Murphy (1972), Kovar (1974), or Leadership Council for Metropolitan Open Communities (1975).

5. A few audit studies, such as Holshouser (1984), were explicitly designed for research and enforcement purposes. Some other studies, including HMPS and HDS, have provided information to enforcement officials. The audit technique also has uncovered discrimination by lenders and home insurers (see Chapter 5), by employers (see Chapter 8), and by automobile dealers (see Ayres and Siegelman 1995).

6. McEntire (1960) reports that
    In a Los Angeles study, 1955, a white couple representing themselves as possible house buyers, called on twelve real estate brokers doing business in a new residential area of 12,000 homes, chiefly FHA- and VA-financed. The couple was followed after a brief interval by a Negro, also purporting to be looking for a house to buy. To the white couple, all brokers offered listings and information that many houses were available with down payments as low as $1,000. None of the realtors

offered any listings to the Negro "prospect," some saying that no houses were available, others that down payments were prohibitively high—from $3,000 up (p. 239).

In the other study "in a large Southern California city," Johnson, Porter, and Mateljan (1975, first published in 1971) used two three-couple teams in which one couple was black, one was Mexican American, and one was white. The year in which the audits were conducted is not stated in this reference, but it clearly was between 1968 and 1971. Each couple inquired about apartment availability and recorded information on quoted rent and fees. Blacks encountered less favorable treatment than whites on at least 1 of these 3 variables in 15 of the 20 possible comparisons, Mexican Americans encountered less favorable treatment than whites in 12 of 22 cases, and whites received less favorable treatment than their minority teammates in 4 of 23 cases. The 1974–75 study by Pearce (1979), which focused on racial steering and was not available until 1979, is discussed in Chapter 4.

7. The results of the 1967 audits in Great Britain, as well as those of audits conducted in 1973–74, are presented in McIntosh and Smith (1974).

8. The HMPS results are presented in Wienk et al. (1979). The idea to use fair housing audits came from a series of papers HUD commissioned in the spring of 1975 to help it decide how to meet its responsibility to evaluate the enforcement of the Fair Housing Act of 1968. The contract for collecting the HMPS data was awarded, after a competition, to the National Committee Against Discrimination in Housing, a nonprofit fair housing organization. The audit procedures were designed by and the audit data were analyzed by researchers at HUD. See Wienk et al. (1979, pp. 4–11).

9. The HMPS results are discussed in detail in Chapter 3.

10. The Dallas results are presented in Hakken (1979).

11. The role of HMPS is explored more fully in Chapter 10.

12. All the audit studies except the most recent (Roychoudhury and Goodman, 1992) are reviewed in Galster (1990b and 1990d). The principal Boston study was conducted in 1981. See Feins, Bratt, and Hollister (1981), Feins and Bratt (1981), and Yinger (1986a). A follow-up study (Holshouser, 1984) was conducted in 1983. The Denver study is presented by James, McCummings, and Tynan (1984).

13. The results of these studies are presented in Chapters 3 and 4.

14. The main HDS reports are Struyk, Turner, and Yinger (1991), Yinger (1991b and 1991c), Turner, Mickelsons, and Edwards (1991), and Elmi and Mickelsons (1991).

15. This description of the objectives is from Struyk, Turner, and Yinger (1991). Similar statements of the objectives appear in all the HDS reports and in the request for proposals.

16. For clarity of presentation, this book refers to auditors as "she" and to housing agents as "he," even though auditors and agents are both male and female.

17. An audit need not be limited to a two-person team. In fact, three- or four-person teams might help solve some methodological problems that two-person teams encounter. See Heckman and Siegelman (1993) and Yinger (1993a). One early audit study of employer responses to resumes (McIntyre, Moberg, and Posner, 1980) used three-person teams, and some fair housing agencies use "sandwich" audits in which a visit by a minority homeseeker falls between visits by two comparable white homeseekers. However, all the audit studies discussed in this book (except the one in note 6) rely on two-person teams.

18. For a more detailed discussion of the need for comparability, see Yinger (1986a).

19. The following section describes these tools and their use in HDS.

20. For a fuller discussion of these ethical issues, see Fix and Struyk (1993) or Reed (1994).

21. These time figures are rough averages for the HDS audits.

22. For a detailed discussion of *Havens,* see Metcalf (1988, pp. 92–101).

23. For a more complete discussion of diversity in the Hispanic population, see J. Milton Yinger (1985) or Moore and Pinderhughes (1993).

24. This study is Hakken (1979).

25. For more details on assigned identities, see The Urban Institute (1991). Most aspects of the assigned identities were never communicated to the housing agent. In fact, housing agents rarely asked auditors about anything, including their income. Nevertheless, detailed identities were given to each auditor for each audit to make certain that any questions asked by the agent could be answered.

26. This instruction is quite different from the one used by HMPS. In HMPS, only one sample of advertisements was drawn in advance of the field work for each metropolitan area, and auditors did not explicitly ask for the advertised unit. By "anchoring" audits to specific advertised units, HDS ensured that the opening requests by both members of an audit team were identical. In addition, since both teammates initially requested a unit that was advertised as available within the last week, HDS measures of differential treatment with respect to housing availability are less likely to be affected by the possibility that the advertised unit was no longer available by the time an audit occurred. As discussed in Chapter 3, this methodological difference must be considered in comparing the HDS and HMPS results.

27. One procedural difference between HDS and HMPS is that HMPS, but not HDS, reimbursed an auditor for the number of units she inspected. The HMPS reimbursement scheme might encourage auditors whose actual

incomes were relatively low to try to inspect more units. Although HDS encouraged auditors to inspect as many units as possible, it gave each auditor the same reimbursement regardless of the number of units inspected. This issue was discovered by the HMPS researchers (Wienk et al., 1979, p. 119).

28. For arguments in favor of "blind" employment audits, see Heckman and Siegelman (1993b) and Yinger (1993b). "Blind" audits of lender behavior during the pre-application phase of a mortgage transaction have been successfully conducted. See Leeds (1993).

29. When the initial contact with the agent was through a telephone call, the second teammate made contact no sooner than 15 minutes and no later than 1 hour after the first. The timing procedures were more complicated when the initial contact was a visit to the agency. In the rental audits, the second teammate proceeded no sooner than 1 hour and no later than 4 hours after the first; in the sales audits the comparable times are no sooner than 4 hours and no later than 32 hours. These time frames differ from HMPS in two minor ways. The rental site-visit upper limit is 4 hours instead of the 1 hour used by HMPS to allow for the possibility that the agent may be showing the requested unit to the first auditor when the second one arrives. For the same reason, the sales site-visit lower limit is 4 hours instead of the 2 hours used by HMPS.

30. Evidence to support this claim, along with a detailed comparison of audits in which auditors did and did not see the same agent can be found in Ondrich, Ross, and Yinger (1994).

31. The first study to randomize order was Feins, Bratt, and Hollister (1981). HMPS did not randomize order but selected the order that the researchers believed would minimize estimated discrimination. This approach has two disadvantages. First, it depends on an assumption about the impact of order on treatment that cannot be tested and that may not be correct. Second, if the assumption is correct, this approach may significantly understate discrimination. However, the HDS approach does not appear to represent a significant departure from HMPS. The HDS audit data reveal that the auditors who go first are not treated significantly differently than the auditors who go second. See Yinger (1991c) and the Appendix.

32. National results presented in this report are weighted to account for the sampling scheme. Specifically, because the probability of selection varied with a metropolitan area's size, observations from metropolitan areas that are underrepresented in the sample are weighted more heavily than observations from metropolitan areas that are overrepresented in the sample. In the in-depth sites, the weights vary by week to reflect the number of advertisements in the paper each weekend. Details of this weighting procedure are presented in Yinger (1991b) and the derivation of the weights themselves is discussed in The Urban Institute (1991).

33. Because of their importance as places of residence for America's black

and Hispanic populations, 5 in-depth sites, listed below, were selected with certainty for inclusion in the HDS sample. The remaining 20 audit sites were selected at random, with a higher probability of selection for larger metropolitan areas. In other words, larger areas, where a larger share of the nation's black and Hispanic populations live, were more likely to be included in the sample. Separate samples were drawn for the black-white audits and the Hispanic-white audits. For more details, see The Urban Institute (1991).

34. This universe of 105 metropolitan areas consists of three categories: (1) 23 areas that are both more than 12 percent black and more than 7 percent Hispanic, from which 8 sample areas were selected for both black-white and Hispanic-white audits; (2) 62 areas that are more than 12 percent black but less than 7 percent Hispanic, from which 12 sample areas were selected for only black-white audits; and (3) 20 areas that are more than 7 percent Hispanic but less than 12 percent black, from which 5 sample areas were selected for only Hispanic-white audits.

35. In Chicago, Los Angeles, and Washington, D.C., the HDS researchers closely examined the role of newspapers other than the major metropolitan newspaper in providing information about available housing. They concluded that including these newspapers in the sampling frame would add little additional available housing—but a great deal of complexity. This conclusion is reinforced by two recent surveys that document the infrequent use of community or even secondary areawide newspapers for housing advertisements. See Newburger (1995) and Turner (1992).

36. Because condominiums are a significant part of the sales market in some metropolitan areas, HDS included condominiums among the units for sale that were eligible for inclusion in the sample. HMPS did not include condominiums.

37. A recent study of housing search behavior in the sales market in Boston (Newburger, 1995) found that blacks were far less likely than whites to use either of the major newspapers in the area but only slightly less likely to use a real estate broker. Two other recent studies show that houses for sale in largely black or integrated neighborhoods are less likely than houses for sale in white neighborhoods to be advertised in a newspaper or to have an open house. See Turner (1992) and Galster, Freiberg, and Houk (1987). These studies are discussed further in Chapter 4.

38. A dramatic example of this practice is described by Schemo (1994a, p. B1). The manager of an apartment referral agency on Long Island has been "accused of having programmed his company's computer to indicate the ethnic background of prospective tenants and landlords, along with the biases of the landlords" and has been taken to court by the State Attorney General. Apparently, many landlords (and perhaps other referral services) participate in attempts like this to screen out blacks and members of other minority groups. "About 100,000 of the 270,000 apart-

ments in Nassau and Suffolk Counties are illegal, untaxed units carved from basements and garages, the Long Island Regional Commission estimates. Such landlords are often reluctant to advertise, and use the referral services to attract and screen potential tenants." See also Winerip (1988). An apartment manager in Southern California was accused of identifying minority households by placing "happy face" stickers on their applications. See Feldman (1989).

39. For some estimates of the unfavorable treatment encountered by the average black and Hispanic homeseeker, see Yinger (1991c).

40. This study is Newburger (1995).

41. Some evidence on this point is presented in Chapter 9.

CHAPTER 3: DISCRIMINATION IN HOUSING

1 The net incidence and severity measures are related algebraically. As shown by Yinger (1993a), the severity measure depends not only on the relative incidence of unfavorable treatment of minority and white auditors but also on the relative severity of unfavorable treatment when it does occur.

2. These net incidence measures are all statistically significant using a fixed-effects logit model for paired data. This procedure was devised by Chamberlain (1980) and its application to audit data is described in Yinger (1993a).

3. The relevant HDS report (Yinger, 1991b) also presents an index of discrimination in housing availability, which is similar to the index devised for HMPS (Wienk et al., 1979). A simpler index along the same lines appears in Johnson, Porter, and Mateljan (1975). This index summarizes the probability of encountering discrimination in at least one aspect of housing availability and yields results that are similar to those for the total number of units available.

4. This statement holds generally. Few types of agent behavior involved significantly different treatment of Hispanics with different skin color or accent. See Yinger (1991c). However, Chapter 9 shows that different types of Hispanics face different types of discrimination in number of units shown. A 1979 audit study in Dallas, Hakken (1979), found a higher incidence of discrimination against dark-skinned Hispanics than against light-skinned Hispanics.

5. HDS uncovered a few cases in which minority auditors were unable even to make an appointment with a real estate broker. This problem virtually never arose for white auditors. The net incidence of discrimination for this "no appointment" variable was 3.6 percent in the black–white audits and 3.2 percent in the Hispanic–white audits, but was not statistically significant in either case.

6. In the sales market, minority auditors also are driven past fewer houses by the agent than are their white teammates. Moreover, because minority

auditors are recommended or shown fewer units, their interviews are significantly shorter than those of their white teammates. See Yinger (1991b).

7. These net severity measures are all statistically significant using a paired difference-of-means test, weighted to reflect the HDS sampling plan. More detailed calculations also reveal that, following the point in note 1, minority auditors not only are more likely to encounter unfavorable treatment than are white auditors, but the unfavorable treatment they encounter is more severe. For more on both these points, see Yinger (1993a).

8. This total is not the same as the number shown to the majority auditor plus the number shown to the minority auditor, because some units are shown to both auditors. Using the address information in the HDS data set, however, the units made available to both auditors can be identified, but only for the sales audits (see Chapter 9).

9. Figures 3.2 and 3.3 do not differentiate between the advertised and other units. This distinction may be important (see Chapter 9). The sales results in this figure and the following one are slightly revised versions of the results described in detail in Yinger (1993a). The rental results have not been presented elsewhere and are less reliable because the measure of the opportunity to discriminate is only approximate (see Chapter 9).

10. Yet another way to express this result is to focus on marginal discrimination, which is the increase in the severity of discrimination when another unit becomes available to be inspected. The HDS data reveal that when another house becomes available for inspection, the severity of discrimination increases by 0.135 houses for blacks and by 0.059 houses for Hispanics. The topic of marginal discrimination is discussed in more detail in Yinger (1993a) and in Chapter 9. Even higher levels of marginal discrimination are estimated by Roychoudhury and Goodman (1992) for rental housing in Detroit.

11. Chapter 9 explores the circumstances under which housing agents are most likely to take advantage of the opportunity to discriminate.

12. For some types of agent behavior, both an incidence and a severity measure of discrimination can be calculated. Note that queries about a customer's income have a somewhat ambiguous interpretation. They may be an extra annoyance or they may be an effort by an agent to move a transaction along. Therefore, not much weight should be placed on results for this variable.

13. This argument was first made by Wienk et al. (1979).

14. In Chapter 6 we explore the reasons why minority households are likely to search less than white households.

15. As first noted by Wienk et al. (1979), the probability of encountering at least one act of discrimination in n visits to housing agents, say P_n, is

related to the incidence discrimination in one visit, P_1, as follows: $P_n = 1 - (1 - P_1)^n$. This formula, which was used to construct the entries in Table 3.4, assumes that the n visits to housing agents are independent of each other.

16. See, for example, the work presented in Fix and Struyk (1993).

17. It should be noted that a gross measure does not literally correspond to the share of audits in which legal action is warranted. A court must consider many factors, such as the credibility of the witnesses and the importance of the discriminatory behavior, which are beyond the scope of a research study.

18. A standard weighted t-test (two-tailed) indicates that all these results are statistically significant at the 5 percent level or above. Strictly speaking, this test cannot be applied without restating the standard null hypothesis because even one audit in which the white auditor is favored is sufficient to reject the null hypothesis that the gross incidence is zero. The standard test can be applied, however, with a null hypothesis that the gross incidence is close to zero. See Yinger (1993a).

19. This assumption was explicitly made by Wienk et al. (1979).

20. One also could argue that it makes no sense to net them out in calculating the net incidence of discrimination; after all, steering does not represent favorable treatment of minorities. In other words, the net measure might not be correct even for the net concept. See Yinger (1993a).

21. These results are based on the steering index presented in Turner, Mickelsons, and Edwards (1991).

22. Ondrich, Ross, and Yinger (1994). This paper estimates a bivariate probit model in which the observations are visits to an agent by an auditor. There are two visits per audit, one for the minority auditor and one for the white. This model can account for the correlation between teammates' treatment and other elements of the error term in the model. In principle, this approach could be used to measure the net incidence of discrimination as well as the gross incidence, but a more precise modeling of the error term probably would not lead to a net measure that is significantly different from the simple net measure.

23. The upper and lower bounds are 5.7 and 11.3 for "advertised unit available," 7.0 and 12.9 for "advertised unit inspected," and 10.7 and 20.5 for "similar units inspected." See Ondrich, Ross, and Yinger (1994). Note that the last upper bound actually exceeds the simple gross measure. As pointed out by Yinger (1993a), the simple gross measure can understate the gross incidence of discrimination because random factors can make an agent who discriminates against minorities appear to be neutral or even favor minorities.

24. The lower bound, upper bound, and simple gross measures are 14.5, 24.5, and 25.9 for "auditor asked to call back"; 11.5, 18.9, and 20.6 for "follow-

up call"; 12.7, 21.5, and 21.1 for "ask about income"; and 10.5, 24.0, and 21.7 for "ask about housing needs." See Ondrich, Ross, and Yinger (1994).

25. The report is NCDH (1970); the quotation and the list of tactics are on page 17 of this report.

26. The NCDH report also lists racial steering as a common tactic (NCDH, 1970, p. 17). As discussed in Chapter 4, HDS also discovered that this type of discrimination continues to be practiced. Some of the tactics listed by this report cannot be observed by an audit study: these include refusing to allow an inspection or delaying until a white buyer is found or the seller removes the house from the market.

27. As a reminder, HMPS refers to the Housing Market Practices Survey, and is presented in Wienk et al. (1979).

28. For a detailed comparison of the two studies, see Elmi and Mickelsons (1991).

29. This number differs slightly from the comparable number in Table 3.1 because it is based on the HMPS variable definitions, not those used by HDS. See Elmi and Mickelsons (1991). Other numbers in this section may differ slightly from results presented earlier in this chapter for the same reason.

30. Seventy-one of these studies are reviewed in Galster (1990b); the other one is Roychoudhury and Goodman (1992). This list is quite comprehensive because Galster made an extensive effort to identify all audit studies, including those by fair housing groups. It includes only those studies based on a random sample of advertisements or housing agencies. These studies vary in quality, and the sample size (i.e., number of audits) ranges from 12 to 280. Three of the largest studies, plus HMPS and the follow-up to HMPS that measured discrimination against Hispanics in Dallas (Hakken, 1979), are reviewed in Yinger (1985). An audit study of the rental market in the city of Atlanta in 1988–89 is mentioned by Orfield and Ashkinazi (1991, p. 76), but few details of the study are given.

31. Galster (1990b) indicates that one study found discrimination against Asian-Americans and another found no discrimination against Native Americans.

32. The results in this paragraph are taken from Galster (1990b). The 1988–89 Atlanta rental audit study found discrimination against blacks 31 percent of the time, but Orfield and Ashkinazi (1991, p. 71) do not mention the types of agent behavior covered by this incidence measure. Summary indexes, similar to the availability indexes mentioned in note 3, also were calculated for HDS. See Yinger (1991b). For an alternative approach based on the number of acts of discrimination, see Yinger (1991a).

33. As Galster (1990b) makes clear, the studies differ enough in methodology and quality so that they cannot be combined to obtain a national estimate of discrimination. Galster also points out that repeat audit studies

in a few cities indicate a downward trend in discrimination, but only when the audits are part of a continuing local enforcement effort in that location. No evidence suggests a downward trend in discrimination without active local enforcement and no evidence reveals what would happen to discrimination if an existing local enforcement program were terminated. Roychoudhury and Goodman (1992) estimate a downward trend in discrimination involving the number of apartments recommended and number of apartments inspected but an upward trend in discriminatory rental terms. These results suggest that rental agents in Detroit may be changing their strategy for discriminating, perhaps in response to enforcement efforts.

34. This study is Feins, Bratt, and Hollister (1981). The data from this study are further analyzed in Feins and Bratt (1981) and Yinger (1986a).

35. The results from the Boston study are from Yinger (1986, Table 1).

36. The results of these studies are presented in Galster (1990b).

37. One of the studies that found no significant difference was a study of discrimination against blacks in the Denver area by James, McCummings, and Tynan (1984). Even in this study, however, audits in suburban (and largely white) areas revealed that blacks were told about two fewer houses than were their white teammates.

CHAPTER 4: RACIAL AND ETHNIC STEERING

1. I am grateful to Maris Mickelsons, who provided this example and the map in Figure 4.1 that shows the associated steering.

2. This type of constraint is illustrated in stage 3 of a housing market transaction in Figure 3.1.

3. For a thorough discussion of the link between steering and segregation, see Galster (1990c). We will return to this topic in Chapters 7 and 11.

4. The details of these data procedures, including information on the success rates for geocoding and mapping, are described in Turner, Mickelsons, and Edwards (1991).

5. Steering analysis was not conducted for the rental audits both because the rental address information, which involved an apartment and perhaps a building number in addition to a street address, was more difficult to work with and because the possibility for steering was limited by the relatively low number of apartments available in most audits.

6. Remember from Chapter 3 that net incidence is defined as the share of audits in which the majority auditor was "favored" minus the share in which the minority auditor was "favored." In this context, being "favored" means being showed houses in neighborhoods with a greater white concentration. This is not literally more favorable treatment, simply a way to identify steering. Remember also that net incidence mea-

sures are inherently conservative; that is, they tend to understate the incidence of discrimination to some degree.

7. These results are based on an index of the type discussed in Chapter 3. An auditor is "favored" in the index if she is "favored" on at least one of the three items in the index (in this case, the percentage white, per capita income, and median house value of the neighborhoods in which she was shown or recommended houses) and her teammate was not "favored" on any of them. See Turner, Mickelsons, and Edwards (1991) for a more detailed discussion of this index and for an alternative index.

8. Apparently, however, real estate brokers do not hesitate to steer whites away from an advertised unit in a largely Hispanic neighborhood (or Hispanics from an advertised unit in a largely white neighborhood), so excluding the advertised unit actually lowers the Hispanic steering result for minority composition.

9. The formula for these calculations is presented in Chapter 3, note 15.

10. This study is Turner and Mickelsons (1992).

11. The area in which units are concentrated is determined by a geographical technique called a standard deviation ellipse. See Turner and Mickelsons (1992).

12. In Atlanta, houses shown to blacks are concentrated in areas with a higher percentage black, lower income, and lower house value than the areas for whites, but the differences are not statistically significant. Moreover, the houses shown to blacks in Atlanta are closer to largely black areas than the houses shown to whites, but again the difference is not statistically significant. See Turner and Mickelsons (1992).

13. Remember from Table 3.3 that housing agents often make significantly more positive comments to white than to minority auditors.

14. These results, which do not appear in any HDS reports, are unchanged if one controls for the audit site and the racial composition of the tract in which the agent's office is located. They do not arise in the Hispanic–white audits, however.

15. One rough gauge of the potential impact of brokers remarks is to include negative comments about the neighborhood in the composite steering index. This increases the index by about two percentage points in the black–white audits and one percentage point in the Hispanic–white sales audits.

16. This effect is not quite as strong as in the sales market, but it is still statistically significant, even after controlling for site and for the racial composition of the agent's office. To be specific, a 100 percentage point increase in percent black for the tract in which the advertised unit is located leads to an increase of 0.4 in the difference between the negative comments about the apartment complex that whites hear relative to

blacks. This difference is offset somewhat by the location of the agent's office in a largely black neighborhood.

17. The first steering study is Pearce (1979). All thirty-six studies are reviewed in Galster (1990d), which is the source of the information presented in this section. The sample size of these studies ranges from 16 to 156. Twenty-three of the studies concern house sales and thirteen concern rentals.

18. The only study focusing on Hispanics and whites is James, McCummings, and Tynan (1984), which finds little evidence of steering.

19. A comparison of the HDS steering results with those of HMPS also suggests that blacks face less steering now than they did in 1977. As reported in Newburger (1989), for example, the HMPS net incidence of steering based on the average racial composition of the neighborhoods in which auditors were shown houses was 26.7 percent, which is considerably greater than the figures in Table 4.1. For two reasons, however, it is inappropriate to conclude on the basis of this comparison that racial steering has declined. First, as explained in Chapter 3, HMPS auditors did not ask about a specific advertised unit, so agents had more leeway to steer in the HMPS than in the HDS audits. Second, the 26.7 percent figure, unlike the figures in Table 4.1, includes audits in which the minority composition of the neighborhoods seen by audit teammates differed by less than 5 percentage points.

20. An analysis of the HMPS data by Pearce (1983) discovers that 38 white auditors but no black auditors were discouraged from considering listings in integrated neighborhoods. Only one study in South Bend (and a study focusing on Hispanics in Denver, namely, James, McCummings, and Tynan, 1984) looks for and fails to find this type of steering. See Galster (1990d).

21. This finding also explains why the severity of steering is fairly low. To be specific, the average difference in the racial composition of the neighborhoods in which black and white auditors are recommended or shown houses is only 1.4 percentage points, and the average difference in the ethnic composition of the neighborhoods in which white and Hispanic auditors are recommended or shown houses is only 0.9 percentage points. See Turner, Mickelsons, and Edwards (1991).

22. The units recommended or shown to the HMPS auditors also were heavily concentrated in largely white neighborhoods, although this fact was not mentioned in the main HMPS report (Wienk et al., 1979) and was not emphasized in the follow-up work on steering (Newburger, 1981). Moreover, the researchers who designed HDS, including myself, failed to recognize the significance of this finding.

23. These figures, along with those that appear later in this paragraph, are from Turner, Mickelsons, and Edwards (1991).

24. The average advertised unit was in a census tract with even fewer black residents, namely 7.9 percent.

25. A recent study by Newburger (1995) provides some evidence on household search methods in Boston. Among white house buyers, 75.3 percent used *The Boston Globe* and 91.8 used a real estate broker. The comparable figures for black house buyers are 49.1 percent and 86.8 percent. Black buyers are more likely than whites, 35.8 percent versus 14.3 percent, to use *The Boston Herald*.

26. The two studies that follow HDS are Newburger (1995), conducted in Boston, and Turner (1992), conducted in Washington, D.C. The third study, conducted in Milwaukee, is Galster, Freiberg, and Houk (1987).

27. With the exception of houses in one white tract in Washington, D.C., houses in largely white neighborhoods also were seldom advertised in community or alternative areawide newspapers.

28. The conclusion that firms in black neighborhoods are relatively unlikely to participate in an MLS was based on conversations with brokers and a few pieces of circumstantial evidence. For example, a significantly higher percentage of whites than of blacks (39.4 percent versus 17.8 percent) bought a house not listed with their agent's firm. See Newburger (1995). Although this topic was not addressed in the Washington study (Turner, 1992), Margery Turner has informed me that virtually all real estate firms, regardless of the neighborhoods in which they specialize, belong to the MLS in the Washington, D.C., area. In some other areas, different MLSs cover the central city and the suburbs, and a broker may belong to only one.

29. Auditors also recorded several other things that might be related to membership in an MLS, such as the use of a computer to identify listings. Bringing these other information sources into the analysis does not significantly alter the conclusions in the text.

30. This approach is not concerned with differences in the use of an MLS directory for minority and white auditors, only with whether there was any sign of such a directory in the agent's office during either auditor's visit.

31. To be specific, these results are based on logit regressions, which are not in any HDS report, of the probability that either auditor was shown houses from an MLS directory on a series of site dummies, whether the unit was a condominium, whether the advertised unit was in the central city, the percentage minority (black or Hispanic, depending on the class of audit) in the census tract of the agent's office, and the percentage minority in the census tract of the advertised unit. In both cases, the coefficient for percentage minority in the advertised unit's tract was negative and significant at the 5 percent level (one-tailed test). In the black–white regression, the coefficient of the central city variable also was negative and significant.

32. To put it another way, a household that buys a house in a largely minority or integrated neighborhood will receive far less assistance in selling its house when the time comes than will households who buy comparable houses in largely white neighborhoods.

33. The geographic dimension of household search behavior has not been widely studied, but existing evidence suggests that all households, but particularly black households, search for housing close to their current residence. See Peterson and Williams (1994), Leigh (1981), Rossi (1981), and Weisbrod and Vidal (1981). Indirect evidence on this point is abundant, however; minorities, particularly poor minorities, are far less likely than whites to move from poor to higher-income neighborhoods. See Nelson and Edwards (1993) and Gramlich, Laren, and Sealand (1992).

34. This issue is addressed more fully in Chapter 11.

CHAPTER 5: DISCRIMINATION AND REDLINING IN MORTGAGE LENDING

1. These studies are described in Smith and Cloud (1993).

2. A 1989 survey by the National Association of Realtors, which is described in Muist, Megbolugbe, and Trent (1994), found that 93 percent of home purchasers rely on a mortgage.

3. See Lawton (1993) and Smith and Cloud (1993).

4. The series is Dedman (1988). This series was followed closely by a similar article in *The Detroit News* (Blossom, Everett, and Gallagher, 1988), and somewhat later by one in *The Washington Post* (Brenner and Spayd, 1993). As explained in Chapter 10, community groups can challenge mergers and other actions by a lender who does not meet the credit needs of all neighborhoods in its service area. The "Color of Money" series followed an unsuccessful attempt by the Atlanta Community Reinvestment Alliance to challenge a merger by an Atlanta lender, apparently after someone working with this alliance gave the documents challenging the merger to *The Atlanta Journal and Constitution*. See Robinson (1992).

5. For more on the legislative history of HMDA, see Fishbein (1992).

6. Dreier (1991) reports that the 1989 amendments, which were included in the Financial Institutions Reform, Recovery, and Enforcement Act, were passed through the efforts of Rep. Joseph Kennedy (D-Mass.) and the Financial Democracy Campaign, "a coalition of community and consumer groups, unions, and public figures" (p. 17).

7. For a more detailed discussion of the data and reporting requirements in the HMDA amendments, see Canner and Gabriel (1992). Before 1989 HMDA reporting requirements applied to all depository urban lenders with assets over $10 million and their subsidiaries. The 1989 amendments extended coverage to unaffiliated nondepository lenders with at least $10 million in assets. Smaller lenders are now covered as well, thanks to legislation passed in 1991.

8. See Quint (1991) and Thomas (1991, 1992a, 1992b).

9. The investigation is described in Turner (1993). Despite the thoroughness of the investigation, the Decatur case has limited precedential value for future court proceedings because it ended in a consent decree, not a trial. Further developments on this topic are considered in Chapters 10 and 11.

10. The Boston Fed Study grew out of discussions held in Washington, D.C., with representatives from the Board of Governors of the Federal Reserve System, HUD, and the Boston Federal Reserve Bank, among others. These discussions resulted in an initial research design, which was then refined and implemented by the Boston Fed researchers. The authors of the Boston Fed study also received comments and suggestions from several leading academics and from researchers at the financial regulatory agencies. See the acknowledgments in Munnell et al. (1992).

11. More formally, the Boston Fed Study is Munnell et al. (1992).

12. Recent policy initiatives on mortgage discrimination are discussed in Chapter 10.

13. These process-based definitions of discrimination and redlining are consistent with the legal definitions in the 1968 Fair Housing Act and the 1974 Equal Credit Opportunity Act, whereas the outcome-based definition is close to the definition in the 1977 Community Redevelopment Act. See Chapter 10.

14. Statistical discrimination is discussed in more detail in Chapter 9.

15. Studies of redlining are considered in a later section of this chapter.

16. This point is clearly made by Bradbury, Case, and Dunham (1989).

17. The Associated Press (1994b).

18. For households with incomes equal to 120 percent or more of their area median income, for example, the denial rates were 18.2 percent for blacks, 17.1 percent for Hispanics, and 7.9 percent for whites. See The Associated Press (1994).

19. The information in the last two sentences comes from an analysis of the 1992 HMDA data by King (1994). An analysis of the 1990 HMDA data by Brown (1993) yields similar results.

20. See Spayd and Brenner (1993) and King (1994). Spayd and Brenner found, for example, that in Washington, D.C., "mortgage companies made two times as many loans in black neighborhoods as did local banks and thrifts" (p. A25).

21. The figures and explanations in this and the following paragraph come from Avery, Beeson, and Sniderman (1994a).

22. A partial correction for the lack of a credit history variable in the HMDA data has been devised in a set of related papers (Abariotes et al., 1994;

Myers, 1994; and Myers and Chan, forthcoming). These papers regress the HMDA variable that indicates when an application was rejected due to a poor credit history on applicant and census tract characteristics. The results of this regression are then used to obtain a predicted probability of poor credit for all applications, including those that were not rejected. This predicted probability is included in the loan approval equation. Abariotes, Myers et al. find that this correction for poor credit history leaves 57 percent of the black–white acceptance gap unexplained for mortgage loans in six midwestern states; Myers finds that it leaves between 7 and 40 percent of this gap unexplained for refinancing loans in the same states; and Myers and Chan find that it leaves 70 percent of this gap unexplained for mortgage loans in New Jersey. As the authors recognize, this procedure has limitations, but it may provide the best way to account for credit history with the HMDA data.

23. Avery, Beeson, and Sniderman (1994a) also point out that the minority–white denial rate differences after controls are similar across type of lender (commercial bank, thrift, or mortgage bank) and across type of loan (conventional or federally insured).

24. In addition to Munnell et al. (1992), studies of discrimination against minorities in loan approval include Black, Schweitzer, and Mandell (1978), King (1980), Schafer and Ladd (1981), and Maddala and Trost (1982). Schafer and Ladd, the best of the early studies, is reviewed at length in Yinger (1993c). Another recent study, Siskin and Cupingood (1993), examines discrimination in loan approval for a single lender, and another early study, Peterson (1981), looks at sex discrimination in consumer lending.

25. For example, Schafer and Ladd (1981) investigated the behavior of state-regulated lenders in New York and California in the late 1970s. Their data set included many applicant, property, and loan characteristics, including applicant wealth but not applicant credit history. They found strong evidence of discrimination against blacks in eighteen of thirty-two California study areas and six of ten New York study areas; in fact, black applicants were between 1.58 and 7.82 times more likely than comparable whites to be denied a loan.

26. Again, the reference for the Boston Fed Study is Munnell et al. (1992).

27. A few commentators claim to have found errors or problems of interpretation in the Boston Fed data and argued or implied that the study's conclusions are therefore invalid. See Liebowitz (1993) and Horne (1994). Neither of these commentators provides convincing evidence that data errors drive, or even influence, the Boston Fed Study's results. Some data errors may exist in the Boston Fed data, as they do in any complex data set, but most such errors are accounted for by standard statistical procedures. Moreover, the authors of the Boston Fed Study address, convincingly in my view, the criticisms raised by Liebowitz; they show that the "errors" identified by Liebowitz are in fact not errors at all but are in-

stead reflections of the complexity of actual loans, and they explain in detail their careful procedures for collecting and checking the data, which included extensive calls to lenders to verify items for individual loans. See Browne, McEneaney, and Tootell (1993) and Brown (1993). Finally, two careful reexaminations of the data used by the Boston Fed Study, which included detailed error-correcting procedures, found no reason to believe that data errors influenced the Study's conclusions. See Carr and Megbolugbe (1994) and Glennon and Stengel (1994). Additional research on mortgage discrimination would be desirable to determine whether the Boston Fed results hold in other urban areas, with other data collection procedures, and with controls for additional credit characteristics. Based on all the evidence now available, however, there is no basis for rejecting the Boston Fed Study's conclusions because of data errors or missing controls.

28. This result is highly significant statistically.

29. For a more detailed look at their alternative specifications, see Yinger (1993c), who points out that with one particularly compelling alternative, namely the one in which each neighborhood is identified, the minority denial rate is 90 percent higher than the white denial rate — instead of 56 percent in the version preferred by the Boston Fed researchers.

30. For criticisms of the Boston Fed Study, see Liebowitz (1993), Horne (1994), and Zandi (1994). For a response to Liebowitz, see Browne et al. (1993) and Browne (1993). For overviews of all this work, see Carr and Megbolugbe (1994) and Glennon and Stengel (1994). Carr and Megbolugbe point out, for example, that Zandi makes a critical error by using as a "control" variable the lender's subjective assessment of the applicant's credit history, a variable that clearly could reflect the lender's tendency to discriminate.

31. The two studies are Carr and Megbolugbe (1994), which is the one that found somewhat higher levels of discrimination, and Glennon and Stengel (1994). Glennon and Stengel also emphasize that some data and specification issues in the Boston Fed Study cannot be resolved without additional data and analysis.

32. A more detailed discussion of these four aspects can be found in Yinger (1993c). A fifth aspect, resampling rejected applicants, also might lead to a downward bias, but no study yet provides any information to support such a possibility. My judgment that the standard approach is likely to understate discrimination is not universally shared. Some scholars have argued that lending behavior is so complicated, with the simultaneous determination of at least four variables (application, terms, acceptance, and foreclosure), that it is not possible to determine the direction of the bias that arises when one of these variables is examined separately. See, for example, Rachlis and Yezer (1993) or Yezer, Phillips, and Trost (1994).

33. See Schafer and Ladd (1981) and Black and Schweitzer (1985).

34. This possible advantage appears to be offset, however, by higher interest rates and fees. See Schafer and Ladd (1981) and Black and Schweitzer (1985).

35. Yezer, Phillips, and Trost (1994) argue that estimates of discrimination may be biased upward because minority borrowers themselves select higher loan-to-value ratios (LTVs), all else equal. In my judgment, the limited available evidence is more consistent with the view that minority borrowers *are assigned* higher LTVs than with the view that they *select* higher LTVs—and hence that estimates of discrimination are biased downward.

36. This study is described in Kohn (1993).

37. A more complicated example was suggested to me by Geoffrey Tootell. The Boston Fed Study found that applications for mortgages on multi-unit buildings were more likely to be denied than those on single-family houses, all else equal, even though underwriting standards call for the higher risk on these buildings to be fully accounted for in the expected income stream from the building, which is accounted for in the denial regression. Because minority households are more likely than whites to apply for a loan on a multi-family building, this apparent divergence from standard underwriting practices has a disproportionate impact on minorities. In other words, lenders appear to be discriminating against minorities by raising the rejection rate on multi-unit loans.

38. This finding is reported in Munnell et al. (1992).

39. As discussed in Chapter 8, the same issue comes up in studying discrimination in employment.

40. In legal terms, a claim of discrimination can be based on "disparate impact" even if there is no "discriminatory intent." This issue is discussed at length in Chapter 10.

41. ICF (1991, p. 5).

42. See, for example, Board of Governors of the Federal Reserve System (1993), Calem (1993), and Fritz and Abdelal (1994).

43. Mills and Lubuele (1994, p. 258). Note that the term *community reinvestment* refers to the Community Reinvestment Act, which is discussed in detail in Chapter 10.

44. Quercia and Stegman (1992, p. 343).

45. In principle, the borrower can claim any remaining equity in the house by selling it before the bank forecloses. In some neighborhoods, however, an owner may not be able to sell his house quickly enough to make this claim.

46. The lender in question was Fleet Finance Inc. On June 14, 1993, the Georgia Supreme Court ruled, with obvious distaste, that Fleet's policy of pro-

viding high-interest loans and aggressively foreclosing when possible was legal. To be specific, the court said: "Although we do not condone Fleet's interest charging practices, which are widely viewed as exorbitant, unethical, and perhaps even immoral . . . , we are constrained to hold that the loans in question are legal." See The Associated Press (1993). Racial discrimination was not an issue in this case.

47. Although the lender role in defaults has been recognized in the literature, none of the studies reviewed in Quercia and Stegman (1993) examines defaults with a simultaneous equations model of borrower and lender behavior.

48. These findings are described in Turner (1993).

49. A related downward bias in estimated discrimination in loan approval arises when minorities are more likely to be discouraged from applying. See Bloom, Preiss, and Trussell (1983).

50. These columns are Becker (1993), Brimelow (1993), Brimelow and Spencer (1993), and Roberts (1993).

51. See Peterson (1981) and Berkovec et al. (1994).

52. The default approach only addresses discrimination in loan approval and cannot shed light on other types of discrimination. For example, Tootell (1993) shows how redlining does not affect default probabilities. For additional criticisms of the default approach, see Galster (1993a), Tootell (1993), and Ross (forthcoming).

53. The study is Berkovec et al. (1994). Two recent articles (Karr, 1995, and The Associated Press, 1995) have headlines proclaiming that the new study challenges the conclusion that there is discrimination in mortgage lending. A third article (Seiberg, 1995) claims that the Berkovec et al. article "is one of a handful of recent reappraisals of lending discrimination that challenges the conventional wisdom that banks discriminate against black Americans."

54. See Peterson (1981) or Tootell (1993) for a careful discussion of this issue.

55. See Berkovec et al. (1994).

56. See the excellent review of this literature by Quercia and Stegman (1992).

57. The same problem arises when a credit variable that is correlated with minority status is not observed by the researcher. See Tootell (1993).

58. In formal terms, even the most sophisticated versions of the default approach assume that credit characteristics not observed by lenders are uncorrelated with minority status. Berkovec et al. (1994, p. 287) acknowledge that "While we have sought to exploit the data set as fully as possible to account for relevant determinants of default likelihoods, we clearly have not accounted for all such determinants, and to the extent that they are correlated with race or ethnicity, biased estimates will result." As pointed out earlier, studies of loan approval also confront an omitted

variable problem, but that problem can be solved by observing all the credit variables the lender observes. This solution is not available with the default approach, which must control for not only these observed credit variables but also for credit variables that are unobserved by the lender. Moreover, the omitted variable bias in a default study works against finding discrimination. A cynic might say that this explains the current popularity of the approach; people who want to "prove" that discrimination does not exist may be drawn to a method that is rigged to support such a conclusion.

59. Recall that statistical discrimination, which is discussed in detail in Chapter 9, is just as illegal as discrimination based on any other motivation, such as lender bias.

60. Some scholars argue that the default approach isolates discrimination motivated by lender prejudice. For example, Berkovec et al. (1994, p. 288) say that their results "relate only to what has been called uneconomic discrimination. Estimation findings are not inconsistent with what has been called statistical or economic discrimination, even if the assumptions underlying the basic prediction hold." Distinguishing between statistical discrimination and discrimination based on prejudice (uneconomic discrimination) might make sense if one assumed that statistical discrimination eliminated the impact of unobserved characteristics on loan outcomes. (In fact, however, Ross, forthcoming, shows that even "perfect" statistical discrimination does not completely eliminate this impact.) But note how this assumption fundamentally changes the interpretation of a default study; *statistical discrimination must be assumed to exist before one can obtain evidence of discrimination based on prejudice.* Glenn Canner, one of the authors of the recent default study (Berkovec et al., 1994) is clear on this point; he told *The Wall Street Journal* that "it would be unfair to say the study proves lending bias doesn't exist. There are other forms of discrimination than the kind targeted by his study" (Karr, 1995).

61. This point is recognized by Berkovec et al. (1994, p. 288), who say that "if discrimination led lenders to foreclose more quickly on black borrowers than other borrowers, this could result in higher default rates for black borrowers."

62. See Quercia and Stegman (1992, p. 354). The Board of Governors of the Federal Reserve System (1993, Table 15) finds that a lender's profitability is not affected by the share of its loans that go to blacks. Berkovec et al. (1995) find that the loss given default is not higher for whites than for minorities, controlling for credit characteristics observed when the loan is granted. This procedure has the same weakness as the first one of the default approach itself; it depends on the unrealistic assumption that unobserved characteristics have the same distribution for whites and minorities. Otherwise, the impact of lender behavior (such as discrimination in foreclosure decisions) on relative minority loss rates might be swamped by the impact of unobserved credit characteristics.

63. The need to focus on returns is noted by Becker (1993), who says at one point that if banks discriminate, "the mortgage loans approved for minority applicants would be more profitable than loans to whites." Becker then returns to the default argument, however, when he says that "the rate of default on loans approved for blacks and Hispanics by discriminatory banks should be lower, not higher, than those on mortgage loans to whites."

64. These studies are described by Smith and Cloud (1993), Lawton (1993), and Galster (1993c).

65. See Turner (1993).

66. See Galster (1992c) and Munnell et al. (1992).

67. See Schafer and Ladd (1981) and Black and Schweitzer (1985).

68. The Justice Department has uncovered a few cases of this type of discrimination. In 1994 Justice settled a case with the First National Bank of Vicksburg, Mississippi, based on allegations "that the bank charged African Americans significantly higher interest rates (as much as 10 percent) than whites for unsecured home improvement loans." The settlement involved changes in bank policies and "monetary relief of $800,000." See Patrick (1994).

69. For evidence on this point and the point in the following sentence, see Spayd and Brenner (1993) and Wilke (1991). A similar problem arises with both home equity loans and with regular banking services. Evidence from the Richmond area in 1992 suggests that several large consumer finance companies specialize in providing high-interest home equity loans to low-income and minority neighborhoods. See Byers (1994). In addition, customers in many distressed neighborhoods must rely on expensive check-cashing services instead of on bank accounts. See Sexton (1994).

70. The evidence on this point is discussed in Chapter 7.

71. These figures are from Schnare (1993). The data cover 10 major metropolitan areas "chosen to reflect a range of conditions that might affect the treatment of minorities in the mortgage market and the relative reliance on FHA as a source of mortgage financing" (p. 1). Loans that are too large to qualify for FHA insurance are not included in these figures.

72. See Shear and Yezer (1985), Gabriel and Rosenthal (1991), Canner, Gabriel, and Woolley (1991), and Schnare (1993).

73. This result is from Canner, Gabriel, and Woolley (1991). A similar result is in Gabriel and Rosenthal (1991).

74. For evidence on this point see Schnare (1993).

75. A homebuyer's success in finding a mortgage also depends in part on her own behavior, and in particular in the way she searches for a loan. Of particular importance for our purpose is the possibility that minority

households may not even apply for mortgages because they expect to encounter discrimination. For some evidence in support of this argument from the 1983 Survey of Consumer Finances, see Wienk (1992, p. 230). This type of reaction is considered in detail in Chapter 6. Finally, for a thoughtful analysis of the system that links the housing and mortgage markets and of the connections among the actors in this system, see Galster (1992c).

76. This quotation comes from a discussion of in-depth interviews conducted with lenders in 1991. See ICF (1991, p. 5). Lenders also depend on mortgage brokers for referrals, but I know of no research on the behavior of these intermediaries.

77. This study is Feins, Bratt, and Hollister (1981). Several other audit studies have found discrimination by brokers in some aspect of housing finance. See Galster (1990b).

78. See Yinger (1991b).

79. In both cases the minority–white differences are statistically significant based on a logit model with fixed effects. This procedure is described in Yinger (1993a).

80. All of these differences except the FHA result for Hispanics are statistically significant.

81. For a detailed discussion of this history and this lawsuit, see Schwemm (1993).

82. Schafer and Ladd (1981). Using data from three metropolitan areas in the 1970s, King (1980) performs a test similar to the one in Schafer and Ladd and finds little evidence of discrimination in appraisals against Hispanics. As explained by Yinger (1993c), the methodology of these studies is very conservative, that is, it is rigged against finding discrimination. A series of interviews with lenders in 1991 found that "lenders also noted that appraisals are harder to conduct in minority areas" and that appraisers "may approach them with a culture of bias" (ICF, 1991, p. 5).

83. The examples and quotations in this paragraph are all from Feldstein (1994), which presents other examples as well.

84. These problems also are recognized in a recent report by the National Association of Insurance Commissioners, which "concluded that insurers don't offer homeowner policies in urban areas populated by minorities and people with low incomes. The study also showed the insurers charge higher premiums in these markets" (The Associated Press, 1994c, p. B4).

85. See Munnell et al. (1993). This study was unable to determine whether the disparities in mortgage insurance were associated with the minority status of the applicant or with minority concentration in the neighborhood where the applicant's property was located.

86. Squires and Velez (1988).

87. These audits were conducted by the National Fair Housing Alliance. See Tisdale, Smith, and Cloud (1994). The discrimination in this study included arbitrary limits on the age or value of houses the companies were willing to insure (which clearly have a discriminatory effect), as well as more stringent inspection or credit requirements and higher prices for houses in minority than in white areas. Insurers, like lenders, can discriminate by using underwriting criteria that are not related to risk but that are correlated with minority status. Moreover, minorities who find insurance may end up paying more even if no individual insurer discriminates in terms of price. As Feldstein (1994, p. 454) puts it, "blacks and other minorities are often able to get insurance only from state-sponsored 'pools,' which charge more money and offer less coverage."

88. This figure and all the other information in this paragraph come from Canner and Gabriel (1992).

89. This point is made by Galster (1992c) and Van Order (1993), both of whom provide a thoughtful discussion of the impact of secondary-market institutions on minority households' access to credit.

90. Some of these programs are described in Canner and Gabriel (1992). For example, both agencies recently implemented a "3-2" mortgage program in which a borrower can put down 3 percent, instead of the usual 5 percent, and borrow or receive a grant for the other 2 percent. HUD (1995) describes other programs, including Fannie Neighbors from Fannie Mae and Affordable Gold from Freddie Mac.

91. HUD (1995).

92. For a detailed discussion of the relationship between the two definitions of redlining, see Bradbury, Case, and Dunham (1989).

93. For a review of these studies and some recent evidence, see Schill and Wachter (1993).

94. Munnell et al. (1992). In a follow-up paper (Munnell et al., 1993), the same authors investigate redlining in more detail and come to the same conclusion. Avery, Beeson, and Sniderman (1994b) investigate the same issue using nationwide HMDA data for 1990 and 1991. They find that after accounting for the limited characteristics in the HMDA data, neighborhood racial composition has a small impact, about 5 percentage points, on the probability of loan denial for home purchase and refinancing loans. In the case of home improvement loans, however, the probability of denial is 15.6 percentage points higher in minority than in white neighborhoods, all else equal. They also find that home purchase and refinancing loan denial rates are higher in neighborhoods with median incomes below $20,000 than in those with higher incomes, all else equal (including the income of the applicant).

95. These studies, which include Bradbury, Case, and Dunham (1989) and Shlay (1988), are reviewed in Schill and Wachter (1993). One neighborhood-based study that does not find evidence of redlining is Hula (1991).

This study has been widely criticized for methodological flaws. See Galster (1992d), Galster and Hoopes (1993), and Shlay, Goldstein, and Bartlett (1992). One problem with the Hula study not mentioned in any of these critiques is that it uses the number of owners as an explanatory variable, even though this number clearly depends on the number of loans and therefore is endogenous. A recent study based on HMDA data and not covered in Schill and Wachter is Brown (1993).

96. This study is Bradbury, Case, and Dunham (1989). Dreier (1991) reports that a similar study, commissioned by the Boston Redevelopment Authority, an agency of the Boston city government, and conducted by Charles Finn, found even greater lending disparities between white and minority neighborhoods. This study covered a slightly different time period, 1981–1987, than the Bradbury et al. study, excluded federal- and state-insured loans, and defined minority neighborhoods in a somewhat different way.

97. One hint is provided by Avery, Beeson, and Sniderman (1994b), who find, using the 1990 and 1991 national HMDA data, that application rates for home purchase loans are only slightly lower for minority than for white neighborhoods, once other factors are accounted for. This finding suggests that discrimination in advertising and outreach may play a relatively small role.

CHAPTER 6: THE DIRECT COST OF CURRENT DISCRIMINATION

1. Measures of surplus from household search for housing were first provided by Courant (1978).

2. The framework presented in this section is based on Yinger (1994), which is in turn an extension of the search model developed by Courant (1978).

3. This example assumes that the homeseeker would not have any more success negotiating down the asking price with one house than with the other.

4. The cost of discrimination can also be calculated based on a search-rule strategy, which is to keep looking at individual houses as long as the expected gain from visiting another house exceeds the expected cost. This expected gain takes the form of the possibility that another search will turn up a house better suited to the household's preferences than anything seen previously. With this strategy, the household keeps searching until it finds a house or apartment with a surplus above a "stopping value." Once a housing unit with a surplus this high is found, the probability of finding even better housing is so low that further search is not warranted. This strategy, which is the one modeled by Courant (1978), is similar to searching by going to open houses, which is a common technique. Indeed, Newburger (1995) finds that 58.8 percent of white home buyers visited open houses. However, this strategy rules out the realistic possibility that a homeseeker makes contact with a broker at an open house and then visits the listings in that broker's files, which leads to the

unrealistic conclusion that no household will ever inspect more than one housing unit it is willing to buy or rent. Because this strategy is much less realistic than the one-stop strategy, it is discussed exclusively in footnotes. For more details, see Yinger (1994).

5. A household does not literally have to receive a mortgage to buy a house, but only the richest households are able to buy a house without a mortgage loan. A household that is turned down for a mortgage also might apply to another lender. This possibility is not considered here because little is known about the likelihood or outcome of another mortgage application and because, as explained later in the text, this approach probably understates the disadvantage minorities face in the mortgage market.

6. With a one-stop search strategy, this surplus also depends on the number of housing units a housing agent has to show. As explained below, evidence on the distribution of available housing units is provided by HDS. In addition, one must make an assumption about the distribution of surpluses among available houses. Yinger (1994) shows, however, that this assumption has a relatively small impact on the results.

7. This study is Munnell et al. (1992), which was discussed in detail in Chapter 5.

8. It is not literally linked to just the mortgage payment if the down payment is taken into account. Focusing on the mortgage payment is sufficient for now, however.

9. Housing search, credit application, and moving costs are one-time costs that are automatically in present value terms. To make the surplus figures comparable, they must be expressed as the present value of a stream of annual surpluses. The $10,000 figure is simply the present value of a 15-year stream of $960 per year with a real discount rate of 5 percent. The present value of a constant real annual flow equals the flow divided by $r^* = r/[1 - (1 + r)^{-T}]$, where r is real annual discount rate and T is the time horizon in years. For a more detailed discussion of these issues, see Yinger (1994).

10. The comparable figure for the search-rule strategy is similar, although the relationship in that case is linear.

11. As it turns out, the range of surpluses matters in this figure but the level of surpluses does not. Hence a constant could be added or subtracted to the origin of the horizontal and vertical axes in Figure 6.2 without altering the difference between the minority and white curves. See Yinger (1994).

12. With a search-rule strategy, the key issue for a minority household is the probability that it will be denied access to housing that actually is available. One way to measure this probability is by the severity of discrimination in available housing, as defined in Chapter 3. Strictly speaking, the severity of housing discrimination is not quite the right number because it measures the share of housing units minority households never learn

about, not the share of units they visit but are then prevented from buying or renting. In fact, however, these two shares may be closely related; real estate brokers or rental agents may not show minorities a housing unit if the owner refuses to sell or rent to minorities. The search-rule model presented here can therefore be interpreted as a highly simplified portrait of housing search in which real estate broker and landlords play no role, and buyers or renters must deal directly with the owner. To be specific, the severity of discrimination is the difference in the number of units shown or recommended to minority and white auditors, expressed as a percentage of the number of units made available to whites. From Table 3.2, we know that this percentage is 23.7 for the black–white sales audits and 25.6 for the Hispanic–white sales audits. With a 23.7 percent chance that a black household will be unable to buy or rent an available housing unit, the housing search costs for a black household equal the search costs for a white household multiplied by $1/(1 - 0.237) = 1.311$. This way of expressing the impact of limited housing access was first derived by Courant (1978). In other words, a black household must visit 1.311 houses to have the same chance of finding something available to them as a white household has in visiting a single house.

13. These effects were documented in Chapter 3.

14. The types of discrimination in this paragraph are documented in Chapter 5.

15. This type of discrimination is documented in Chapter 5.

16. See the evidence in Chapter 5.

17. See Chapter 5.

18. With a search-rule strategy, minority households respond to their higher search costs and to the probability they will be denied access to some units by visiting fewer houses. In a recent study of household search behavior, Newburger (1995) found evidence of this type of response: white families inspected 18.7 houses, on average, and black families inspected 9.4. Consequently, minority households' total search costs may not exceed those of white households even if their costs per search are much higher.

19. A survey in Detroit in 1992 (Farley et al., 1993, Figure 6) found that 29 (56) percent of blacks said that real estate agents "often" ("sometimes") will not sell to blacks, and 47 (43) percent of blacks said that lenders "often" ("sometimes") will not lend money to blacks to buy a home. A 1990 national survey found that 48 percent of blacks believed there was a lot of housing discrimination against blacks and an additional 38 percent believed blacks encountered some housing discrimination (Farley, 1993, Figure 6.6).

20. An underestimate of actual discrimination by a minority household also lowers its net surplus, because it prevents them from taking the appro-

priate evasive measures. Assuming that perceptions are accurate therefore gives a lower bound on the cost of discrimination.

21. The 17 percent figure from the Boston Fed Study (Munnell et al., 1992)
applies to both blacks and Hispanics, but there were few Hispanic applicants in Boston in 1990, and a separate estimate for Hispanics is not available. Evidence in Chapter 5 based on the HMDA data suggests that lending discrimination may be less common against Hispanics than against
blacks.

22. The comparable figures are lower with the search-rule strategy, namely
$1,272 and $372. Discrimination plays a much larger role with the one-
stop strategy because households often see more than one house with a
surplus above the minimum acceptable value. This never happens with
a search rule. With one-stop shopping, in other words, the potential gains
from search are much larger and so, therefore, are the costs of restricted
search. Because multiple listing services are an important feature of most
metropolitan housing markets, many households do inspect more than
one house that they are willing to buy. Thus the one-stop strategy is a
more realistic depiction of housing search than is the search-rule strategy. It follows that relying on the search-rule strategy, that is, ignoring
the possibility that households may inspect more than one house that
they would be willing to purchase, leads to an underestimate of the cost of
housing and mortgage discrimination. For more on this point, see Yinger
(1994).

23. The main tool is a demand curve. In particular, a constant-elasticity demand function is used for these calculations. Following Mayo (1981) and
Harmon (1988), the income and price elasticities of demand for housing
are assumed to equal 0.7 in absolute value, and the household with the
mean post-move income is assumed to spend 32.17 percent of its income
on housing, including its mortgage, property tax, and insurance payments and the opportunity cost on its investment. This 32.17 percent
figure is an average based on the house values in the data set described
later in the text. A demand curve is a useful tool in this context because
consumer surplus is defined to be the area under a demand curve less
actual spending. For all the technical details, see Yinger (1994).

24. Size and amenities are not specifically incorporated into the analysis but
are instead offered as examples of the features a household obtains when
it spends more on housing. See Yinger (1994).

25. The translation of an annual surplus into a total willingness to pay also
depends on the real interest rate, which is assumed to be 5 percent, and
on a household's time horizon, which is the time it expects to stay in its
new house. In some cases, the time until the next move (that is, the next
move after the 1984–1986 period) can be observed in the PSID data,
which runs until 1989. If so, the expected duration at the time of the move
in the sample is set equal to this actual duration; in other words, households who move again fairly soon are assumed to have accurate expecta-

tions about their next move. For households who do not move again before the PSID data ends, the expected duration at the time of a move is set equal to the maximum of the time from its last move until 1989 or 1.5 multiplied by the time since its previous move, whichever is greater. A household's past time between moves is multiplied by 1.5 to reflect the fact that households tend to move less often as they get older. Even with this assumption, however, the average time horizon for owner/movers in the PSID data is only 3.6 years, and few households are given a long time horizon through this procedure, even though many of them will stay in their houses for a decade or more. It follows that this procedure probably leads to a conservative translation of annual costs of discrimination into total costs. See Yinger (1994).

26. This study, Yinger (1994), uses a discrete choice analysis of moving behavior to estimate the impact of household composition and job changes on the utility gain associated with moving relative to the impact of an income change on this utility gain.

27. This data set is collected by the Survey Research Institute of the University of Michigan; for a detailed description, see Hill (1992). The beginning income is either the income at the household's previous move or the income at the household's formation if no previous move was observed. A "permanent" income measure is used. It is defined as average income during the year of the move (or of the household's formation) and the following two years. This measure assumes that households have foresight about their income. Income in prior years cannot be used because it is not defined when the starting point of a staying "spell" is the household's formation. Results are very similar when current income is used.

28. To be eligible for the data set, the household had to remain intact during the move; that is, households created by the move were not included.

29. There also is a technical reason for using white households: It is impossible to calculate the cost imposed on minorities who are discouraged from moving using a sample of minority movers.

30. As discussed below, the direct cost of current discrimination probably is lower for renters than for owners. Because of past discrimination, blacks and Hispanics are far more likely to be renters than are whites. Consequently, using the actual minority households who are homeowners instead of the white share would confuse past discrimination and current discrimination. Moreover, such a calculation implicitly makes the absurd claim that the impact of current discrimination is minimal because all the damage was already done in the past!

31. The 58 percent figure applies to the PSID sample. Some people who search for a house to buy may end up renting an apartment because they cannot find an appropriate house. There is no way to identify such household in the PSID data.

32. Even when income, household composition, and job changes are ac-

counted for, a few households have post-move surpluses that are estimated to be below their pre-move surpluses. This does not make sense;
a household would not move unless it gained from doing so. To account
for unobserved factors that affect the gain in surplus, starting surpluses
for these households are lowered until the revealed gain from search is
positive. See Yinger (1994).

33. The calculations require assumptions about the form of the demand function, the values of the demand elasticities, and the share of income spent
on housing. See note 23.

34. To be specific, the base case assumes that minorities pay 10 percent
higher search costs for housing and lenders than do whites and 5 percent
higher moving costs and that the range of surpluses is $100 per month
or $1,200 per year. This case also sets the fixed cost of housing search at
$10 and the time costs at $10 per hour. The low-discrimination case sets
the two search cost differentials at 5 percent, the moving cost differential
at zero, the range of surpluses at $50 per month, and the fixed and time
cost of housing search at $5. The high-discrimination case sets the two
search costs differentials at 25 percent, the moving cost differential at 10
percent, the range of surpluses at $150 per month, the fixed and time
costs of housing search at $25. Because of the evidence, presented in
Chapter 5, that standard measures understate discrimination in mortgage markets, the high-discrimination case also increases the differential
in mortgage denial rates from 6 to 8 percentage points.

35. To link these results to Figure 6.3, note that the base-case average range in
surplus among available houses was about $5,400 and the average starting
surplus was just below the bottom of this range. This surplus range reflects the base-case assumption that the monthly surplus range is $100
and the translation of this monthly range into a total based on each
household's time horizon. The starting surplus reflects each household's
time horizon, the change in its income between moves, and adjustments
in its starting surplus to ensure that it actually gained from moving. Note
also that with the less realistic search-rule strategy, the base-case average
cost per move is $1,354 for blacks and $1,357 for Hispanics. In general,
the costs calculated with the search-rule strategy are about 40 percent of
those calculated with the one-stop strategy, again because they rule out
the possibility that a household will see more than one unit it is willing
to buy. See Yinger (1994).

36. These figures are much higher for the search-rule strategy. With the base
case assumptions, current levels of discrimination would discourage 38
percent of moves by both black and Hispanic households. The gains from
moving are smaller with the search-rule strategy so minorities are more
easily discouraged from moving. See Yinger (1994).

37. U.S. Bureau of the Census (1992c).

38. U.S. Bureau of the Census (1992c).

**CHAPTER 7: THE IMPACT OF HOUSING DISCRIMINATION
ON HOUSING QUALITY, RACIAL SEGREGATION,
AND NEIGHBORHOOD CHANGE**

1. The information about Sherman Park in this paragraph is from Smith (1993). We will return to Sherman Park later in this chapter. The figure for Milwaukee is from Gillmore and Doig (1992, p. 50) and is repeated in Table 7.3. For other stories of failed efforts at integration, see Keating (1994), Saltman (1990), and Polikoff (1986).

2. U.S. Bureau of the Census (1993a, Tables 6, 9, and 10).

3. "Differences of over 20 percentage points in homeownership rates between white and nonwhite households as well as between Hispanic and non-Hispanic households have persisted over the past two decades" (Wachter and Megbolugbe, 1992, p. 359). Moreover, Leigh (1992, p. 24) points out that "The percentage of blacks who owned in 1980 approximated the percentage of whites who had owned in 1940. Blacks reached this 46 percent level with a 40-year lag!"

4. U.S. Bureau of the Census (1993a, Tables 6, 9, and 10). Census tables present median but not mean house values for blacks, Hispanics, and non-Hispanic whites. The black, Hispanic, and non-Hispanic white medians are $50,700, $77,200, and $80,300, respectively. The means in the text are estimated by assuming that the house value density function takes the form $Pr(V) = b[\exp(-bV)]$, where $Pr(V)$ is the probability that a house will have the value V and "exp" stands for the exponential function. With this form, which is the positive half of a normal distribution, the mean house value equals the median house value multiplied by 1.442695, regardless of the value of b. (This result can be derived with simple integration.) This assumption can be tested using data on the distribution of house values for all households, which the 1990 census does provide (U.S. Bureau of the Census, 1993a, Table 13). This test reveals that this simple form fits the data very well, explaining 98.1 percent of the variation in the cumulative house value distribution across the seventeen house-value categories given by the census (excluding the eighteenth category, for which no upper house value is given); moreover, the estimated value of b is highly significant statistically, with a t-statistic of -43.7. A less formal test of the appropriateness of this assumption comes from calculating the ratio of mean to median house value for all homeowners; this calculated ratio is 1.427, which is very close to theoretical value given above.

5. These calculations are, of course, hypothetical because we cannot observe what the world would be like without discrimination. Even if the many blacks who came to this country as slaves had migrated here of their own free will, they probably would have had lower skills and incomes than the average white American (although without slavery, many Africans would undoubtedly have brought considerable wealth to this country). This lower income probably would have had some wealth

consequences for a few generations, but without discrimination there is no reason to believe that these wealth consequences would have persisted until today. Income and housing wealth differences across American citizens with ancestors from different European ethnic groups are small relative to the differences between blacks and whites (or between Mexican Americans and whites or between Puerto Ricans and whites) despite the fact that many of the immigrants in some of these groups were very poor when they first entered the United States. See Darity and Winfrey (1994), Jencks (1992, Table 1.1), and Farley (1990). Moreover, current economic differences among racial and ethnic groups can be attributed largely to differences in the economic circumstances they encountered when they came to the United States—not to differences in their initial cultures. See Lieberson (1980) and Steinberg (1981).

6. The number of black housing units comes from U.S. Bureau of the Census (1993a, Table 6).

7. The number of Hispanic housing units come from U.S. Bureau of the Census (1993a, Table 9).

8. According to the American Housing Survey, 38.9 percent of black households, 35.6 percent of Hispanic households, and 43 percent of white households did not have any mortgages in 1989 (U.S. Bureau of the Census, 1991, Tables 2-19, 5-19, 6-19). Using the procedure described in note 4, data from the 1989 American Housing Survey also reveal that, for households with mortgages, the outstanding principal equaled 49.8 percent of value for blacks, 50.3 percent for Hispanics, and 44.9 percent for whites (U.S. Bureau of the Census, 1991, Tables 2-2, 4-3, 5-2, and 3-15).

9. Using the consumer price index may understate the growth in the net housing wealth gap; between 1990 and 1992, net housing wealth in the United States grew at an annual rate of 5.6 percent. See Council of Economic Advisers (1994, Tables B-60 and B-112).

10. The value of an asset is the present value of the stream of benefits from owning it. In the case of a long-lived flow, and discrimination surely qualifies as long-lived, the present value formula can be written as follows: the asset price equals the annual flow divided by the real interest rate, which is the observed market rate minus anticipated inflation, and the annual flow equals the asset price multiplied by the real interest rate. A reasonable value for a real interest rate is between 3 and 5 percent. In 1993, for example, the average interest rate on a 30-year Treasury bill was 6.59 and the inflation rate was 3.0 percent. See Council of Economic Advisers (1994, Tables B-62 and B-72). This inflation rate was fairly steady and probably was expected to continue, so the real rate was $6.59 - 3.0 = 3.59$ percent. A 3 percent real rate is used in the text. A higher value would raise the annual cost of past and current discrimination and decrease the share of this cost that is due to current discrimination.

11. Wachter and Megbolugbe (1992, p. 360).

12. See, for example, Horton (1992) and Bianchi, Farley, and Spain (1982).

13. One way to gain perspective on the magnitude of this housing wealth gap is to observe that it could be closed with a one-time payment of $7,732 from each of the 77.6 million white, non-Hispanic households in the United States.

14. Council of Economic Advisers (1994, Table B-112). Wealth is notoriously difficult to measure. Other data sources give a smaller share to net housing wealth. See Wolff (1994).

15. Wolff (1994, Tables 3 and 9) reports that black plus Hispanic net worth is 29 percent of white net worth and that average household in the U.S. has a net worth of $206,688. These figures imply that average white net worth is $251,476, average minority net worth is $72,928 and that the white–minority gap in net worth is $178,548. Multiplying this gap by the number of minority households in 1990, 15.977 million, yields an even larger total wealth gap than the one in the text, namely $2.853 trillion. In addition, Jaynes and Williams (1989, p. 293) report that, based on a 1984 household survey, 75 percent of blacks' wealth, compared to 53 percent of whites' wealth, was in real estate. This result suggests that the calculation in the text might underestimate the total cost of discrimination because the wealth disparity between blacks and whites appears to be much greater, in percentage terms, for nonhousing wealth than for housing wealth.

16. Previous reviews of racial differences in housing quality have included studies of racial housing price differentials. Studies based on data from around 1970 found that blacks paid more than whites for equivalent housing. See Yinger (1979) or Yinger et al. (1979). Studies based on more recent data have not found that blacks pay more than whites, and indeed several studies have concluded that blacks pay less. However, a recent, careful study of this topic by Chambers (1992) shows that these studies were biased due to inadequate controls for neighborhood quality. Using 1979 data from Chicago, Chambers finds, among other things, that black renters pay slightly more than white renters, all else equal, in the border region between black and white areas (but no more or less elsewhere); and that all homebuyers pay less when a neighborhood is undergoing, or likely to undergo, racial transition.

17. This and the following figures are from Lazere et al. (1991). Racial disparities in crowding go way back. Myrdal (1944, Table 6) reports similar racial disparities in overcrowding for 1935–1936 using the standard of the time, namely two or more people per room. In the east, overcrowding by this standard was 1.7 percent for whites and 4.7 percent for nonwhites. White overcrowding rates were higher in the central and southern regions (3.3 and 5.8 percent, respectively), but the ratio of nonwhite to white was the same, about 2.7 to 1. Finally, Leigh (1992, p. 24) points

out that "It took 20 years for black renter households to 'improve' to the level of crowdedness experienced by renter households of all races in 1950! Likewise, it was 1970 before the proportion of black owners in crowded quarters roughly equaled that proportion among owner households of all races in 1940; 30 years were required for blacks to achieve that level!"

18. U.S. Bureau of the Census (1993, Tables 6, 9, 10).

19. For a more detailed presentation of the Census/HUD definition of deficient housing, see Lazere et al. (1991, p. 22).

20. The figures in this paragraph are from Lazere et al. (1991).

21. The figures in this paragraph also are from Lazere et al. (1991).

22. Studies based on data from the 1960s and 1970s find that significant black–white differences in housing quality remain after controlling for differences in incomes and other endowments. For reviews of these studies, see Yinger (1979 and 1987).

23. For a discussion of this and other measures of segregation, see Massey and Denton (1989) or Zoloth (1976).

24. Van Valey, Roof, and Wilcox (1977).

25. See Massey and Denton (1993, Table 3.1).

26. The results in Table 7.1 are from Farley and Frey (1993), which calculates the dissimilarity index using a census block group, which typically contains 800 to 900 people, as the neighborhood scale. The indexes presented in the previous paragraph use a census tract, which is much larger, as the neighborhood scale. In general, larger neighborhood scale results in a smaller value for the dissimilarity index. The available data suggest that segregation indexes might not have dropped so much with the census tract as the neighborhood scale. In fact, comparing the census tract dissimilarity index results in Massey and Denton (1993, Table 3.1) for 1980 with the census tract dissimilarity index results in *USA Today* (1991), reveals small increases (less than 4 points) in segregation in New York, Philadelphia, Newark, Baltimore, Houston, New Orleans, and Memphis, as well as Detroit. It is not possible for me to determine, however, whether these results reflect genuine increases in segregation, subtle differences in methodology between the two studies, or changes in the definitions of urban area between the two studies. This comparison also reveals a large increase in segregation (from 41 to 77!) in Birmingham; Douglas Massey has informed me that this increase "is probably an artifact" due to his and Nancy Denton's efforts to make the Birmingham census tract groups comparable between 1970 and 1980.

27. Farley and Frey (1994, Figure 2). This study also found that declines in segregation were greatest in the south, in military communities, and in communities with a high rate of housing construction, and lower in retirement communities (Table 3).

28. These results are from Farley (1993, Table 6.3). They are based on black–white dissimilarity indexes with the block group as the neighborhood scale.

29. Farley (1993, Table 6.3). These counties include two in the Philadelphia area (one of which experienced no change in segregation), two in the Washington, D.C., area, and one each in New York, Baltimore, and Atlanta. The largest drop, 15 points, was in DeKalb County, which is next to Atlanta.

30. One way to gain perspective on these results is to look at segregation indexes for other ethnic groups. Unlike indexes for blacks, these indexes tend to decline over time and drop to the range of 20 to 30 after a couple of generations. See Lieberson (1963).

31. Among the 219 metropolitan areas examined by *USA Today* (1991), only three not in Table 7.1 (Nassau/Suffolk, Flint and Saginaw/Bay City/Midland) had black–white indexes above 80, and about 2 percent, most of them quite small, had indexes below 50. See *USA Today* (1991).

32. Farley (1993, Table 6.3). This list of counties includes four in New York City, of which the Bronx has an index of 45, and Manhattan has an index of 62.

33. Among the 21 central counties with 50,000 or more blacks not reported in Table 7.1, only one, Dayton, had a 1990 black–white segregation index of 80 or more. See Farley (1993, Table 6.3).

34. Farley and Frey (1994, Figure 2).

35. This result, along with the other results in this and the following paragraph, is from Denton and Massey (1989). The extent of segregation between black and white Hispanics appears to be growing in some cities, especially New York.

36. As Denton and Massey (1989, p. 802) put it, "race matter[s] in Hispanic segregation."

37. Denton and Massey (1989, pp. 804–805).

38. These five dimensions of segregation are described and measured in Massey and Denton (1989) and summarized in Massey and Denton (1993). The results in the following two paragraphs are from the original Massey and Denton work.

39. This isolation index for all 50 of the largest urban areas can be found in Farley (1993, Table 6.2). Farley and Frey (1993, Table 9) present an alternative isolation index for 1990, called the exposure index, for several multiethnic metropolitan areas with large black populations. This index gives the percentage white in the block group of the typical black resident. The 1990 values include 18 for New York, 19 for Newark, 13 for Chicago, 30 for Washington, D.C., 35 for Dallas, 30 for Miami, 26 for Los Angeles, 31 for Oakland, and 38 for San Francisco. Five smaller urban areas in California had indexes above 50 and one, Riverside, had

an index of 60. This source does not give comparable exposure indexes for 1980, however.

40. This study, Massey and Denton (1989), is summarized in Massey and Denton (1993).

41. The analysis of hypersegregation in 1990 is from Denton (1994). The cut-off in defining a hypersegregated city was a value of 0.6 or greater on indexes for four of the five dimensions of segregation. In 1990, two cities had three indexes above 0.6 and one just short of this cut-off; one index was 0.59 for Atlanta and one was 0.579 for Dallas.

42. The Denton (1994) study also identified ten other hypersegregated areas, but these areas were not considered in the 1980 study, Massey and Denton (1989). These other areas include Baton Rouge, Flint, Oakland, Savannah, and Trenton. In addition, Oakland, which was part of the San Francisco area in 1980, is hypersegregated in 1990. The 44 percent figure at the end of this paragraph includes all of these areas.

43. Massey and Denton (1993, p. 77).

44. The figures in this and the previous sentence come from Bullard (1992, Table 3). Two of the projects with less than 87 percent black also had 20 percent or more of their tenants from the Asian/Other category, and the maximum white percentage was 11.1.

45. See HUD (1995). According to the most recent available national evidence, which is from 1977, public housing projects, particularly family projects, are more segregated in many metropolitan areas, including some highly segregated areas, than is the private market. See Bickford and Massey (1991). This is true for both blacks and Hispanics. A survey of 47 cities in 1984 found less formal evidence of extensive racial segregation in federally assisted housing plus evidence of lower housing quality in largely black than in largely white projects. See Flournoy (1985).

46. For an insightful case history of a neighborhood turning from integrated to largely white, see Anderson (1985).

47. Smith (1991, Table 5).

48. This figure is from Lee (1985), who found 22.5 percent of tracts were racially mixed (at least 10 percent black and 10 percent white) and that only 25.5 percent of mixed tracts experienced a change in their percent black of less than 5 percent. About 16.5 percent of these tracts experienced a decline in percent black of more than 5 percent; that is, black to white transition occurred in about one tract out of twenty-seven.

49. Massey and Denton (1993, Table 3.5).

50. This consensus builds primarily on the work of Schelling (1971, 1972). Another important, but less well known contribution is by Schnare and MacRae (1978), who bring housing prices into the analysis and in the process show that stable integration is even less likely than the Schel-

ling model predicts. For more on this issue, see Yinger (1986b) or Downs (1992).

51. The results of this survey, which also was discussed in Chapter 1, are presented in Farley (1993) and Farley et al. (1993).

52. These results are all taken from Farley (1993, p. 170). Farley also indicates that the share of blacks stating an integrated neighborhood with a black majority as their first or second choice increased from 68 percent to 82 percent between 1976 and 1992. A follow-up study, Farley et al. (1994), finds that "The shift in residential preferences away from integration characterizes all components of Detroit's black population except those at the highest income and educational levels" (p. 766).

53. These figures are taken from Farley (1993, p. 173). Farley also cites Clark (1991), who found for five major cities in the 1980s that three-quarters of blacks stated a preference for a neighborhood that was 50 percent black and 50 percent white. A 1991 survey in the Cleveland area found that 82 percent of blacks prefer a racially mixed area and 55 percent of blacks would be willing to move into a neighborhood with a white majority. See Keating (1994).

54. Clark (1991, Figure 8) finds that the distribution of preferences for neighborhood ethnic composition are similar for Hispanics and blacks in Los Angeles (where preferences are expressed as the share of one's own group relative to that of non-Hispanic whites), although the Hispanic preferences are "slightly more centered on 50/50" than are black preferences (p. 15).

55. Farley (1993, Figure 6.3A). Results from a 1990 national survey by the National Opinion Research Center (NORC) find a somewhat less negative white response to integration. In particular, about 49 percent of whites said they would be somewhat or strongly opposed to living in a neighborhood where half of their neighbors were black. Farley (1993, Figure 6.5). These results are less precise than those of the Detroit survey, because they do not reveal what action the respondents would take, but they suggest that Detroit residents may exhibit more prejudice than the national average.

56. Surveys of racial attitudes were first linked to the Schelling model by Taub, Taylor, and Dunham (1984). As discussed by Yinger (1986b), the 1976 Detroit survey indicated that integration could not be maintained at 20 percent black because 24 percent of whites said they would move at that racial composition. Moreover, 7 percent black appeared to be the maximum sustainable black percentage because 7 percent of whites said they would leave if the black percentage reached that high. The logic of the Schelling model also was linked by Clark (1991) to survey results for five urban areas: Omaha, Kansas City, Milwaukee, Cincinnati, and Los Angeles. Clark concludes that stable integration is not possible in any of these areas. Clark's survey results are less appropriate for the use

in analyzing transition than the Detroit survey results, however, because they ask for "preferred" neighborhood racial or ethnic composition instead of asking whether people would be willing to stay or move into various types of neighborhood. Clark also fails to indicate the date of the surveys, all of which were conducted "as part of litigation related to desegregation cases" (p. 9).

57. Keating (1994, p. 65). In communities with a history of integration, racial attitudes may be even more tolerant. In a 1987 survey taken in the suburb of Cleveland Heights, whose story is told below, 93 percent of respondents said that the city should continue to promote racial integration. See Keating (1994, p. 134).

58. The 1990 NORC survey cited earlier (Farley, 1993, Figure 6.5) found that about 46 percent of whites said they would be somewhat or strongly opposed to living in a neighborhood where half of their neighbors were Hispanic, compared to the 49 percent figure for a half-black neighborhood. In addition, the Los Angeles survey reported by Clark (1991, Figure 8) measures whites' attitudes toward integration with Hispanics. These attitudes are similar to whites' attitudes toward integration with blacks, and Clark concludes that integration between whites and Hispanics cannot be sustained.

59. This point has been recognized for a long time. For example, the National Advisory Commission on Civil Disorders (1968, p. 245) wrote that "efforts to stop massive transition by persuading present white residents to remain will ultimately fail unless whites outside the neighborhood can be persuaded to move in."

60. Farley (1993, Figure 6.3A).

61. The link between the Detroit results and the Schelling model also is provided by Farley et al. (1993).

62. See Clark (1986, 1988, 1991). See also the responses by Galster (1988, 1989) and the reply by Clark (1989). See also Butters (1993).

63. This opinion, written by Justice Anthony Kennedy, is cited in Keating (1994, p. 11). See also Orfield (1993).

64. This point is discussed in detail by Taub, Taylor, and Dunham (1984) and Yinger (1986b).

65. Galster (1990e).

66. Galster (1990e) does not literally observe white prejudice, or "segregationist sentiment" as he calls it, for each census tract. Instead he observes the relationship between prejudice in a national survey and household characteristics, such as income, age, sex, education, and national origin, and predicts prejudice in each tract in Cleveland on the basis of this relationship and the average characteristics of whites in the tract. This strikes me as a reasonable procedure given the lack of tract level data on prejudice.

67. Orfield (1985, p. 184).

68. This evidence, which was mentioned earlier, is from Lee (1985).

69. The argument that widespread integration is an equilibrium situation (albeit an unstable one) was first expressed by Abrams (1955), and formalized by Yinger (1976).

70. Recall that this point was discussed in detail in Chapter 1.

71. The link between neighborhood preferences and racial stereotypes is explored by Farley et al. (1994). This study finds that "whites who endorse negative stereotypes were more likely to say they would flee integrated neighborhoods and were less likely to consider moving into them" (p. 777).

72. Many studies have found support for the so-called "contact hypothesis," which says that equal status contacts between groups tend to lower intergroup prejudice. For reviews of this literature, see Simpson and J. Milton Yinger (1985, Chap. 17) and Jackman and Crane (1986). Jackman and Crane (p. 461) summarize the conditions for prejudice-reducing contact as follows: "First, the contact should not take place within a competitive context. Second, the contact must be sustained rather than episodic. Third, the contact must be personal, informal, and one-to-one. Fourth, the contact should have the approval of any relevant authorities. Finally, the setting in which the contact occurs must confer equal status on both parties rather than duplicate the racial status differential." Using national data from 1975, they also give (in Table 2) a clear indication of the power of contacts: Among whites who had no black friends or acquaintances and who did not live in proximity to blacks, 87.5 percent expressed a preference for a white neighborhood, whereas among whites who had black friends and acquaintances and who lived in proximity to blacks, only 29.3 percent expressed the same preference. Finally, they find (p. 470) that to reduce white prejudice, "It seems more important to escape tokenism by establishing multiple contacts with blacks than to attain a high degree of personal intimacy with one's black contact."

73. This argument is not new. In 1944, Myrdal observed that when blacks moved into a neighborhood whites immediately moved out. He continued:

> Such a situation creates a vicious circle, in which race prejudice, economic interests, and residential segregation mutually reinforce one another. When a few Negro families do come into a white neighborhood, some more white families move away. Other Negroes hasten to take their places, because the existing Negro neighborhoods are overcrowded due to segregation. This constant movement of Negroes into white neighborhoods makes the bulk of the white residents feel that their neighborhood is doomed to be predominantly Negro, and they move out—with their attitudes against the Negro reinforced. Yet

if there were no segregation, this wholesale invasion would not have occurred. But because it does occur, segregational attitudes are increased, and the vigilant pressure to stall the Negroes at the borderline is kept up (1944, p. 623).

74. Most scholars have listed three principal causes of segregation: prejudice, discrimination, and income disparities. This list appeared as far back as Myrdal (1944, p. 619), who wrote: "Residential concentration tends to be determined by three main factors: poverty preventing individuals from paying for anything more than the cheapest housing accommodation; ethnic attachment; segregation enforced by white people." Income disparities are, of course, another aspect of the legacy of past discrimination. The impact of income disparities on segregation is not straightforward, however. For example, Massey and Denton (1993, Table 4.1) show that black–white segregation indexes are just as high within income classes as they are overall and just as high for high-income blacks as for low-income blacks. Nevertheless, Farley and Frey (1944, Table 2) find that an increase in the ratio of black to white household income leads to a significant decrease in segregation. Raising this ratio from 50 to 82 percent, for example, drops the segregation index by 12 points. Douglas Massey has pointed out to me that another cause of segregation, immigration into culturally defined areas, is important for Hispanics. Indeed, in many cities immigration may be the principal explanation for the recent increase in Hispanic–white segregation.

75. The connection between racial or ethnic and income transition is shown by the fact that at any given income or educational level, blacks live in a more disadvantaged neighborhood than do whites, with Hispanics in between. See Massey and Fong (1990). Moreover, Galster (1991) finds that a more centralized pattern of racial segregation leads to less segregation between blacks of different income levels; that is, extensive racial segregation forces blacks of different income levels to live together. However, segregation among blacks of different income levels appears to be rising. See Massey and Eggers (1990).

76. Taub, Taylor, and Dunham (1984).

77. Keating (1994, p. 65).

78. Keating (1994, p. 65) lists two other responses: "Belief racial discrimination won't take place" (48 percent); "Mortgage incentives (44 percent)." The mortgage incentive programs in Cleveland are discussed below. The survey also asked whites: "What would it take for them to accept people of another race moving into their neighborhood" (p. 65). The responses were similar, although steady property values were now mentioned by 61 percent.

79. Moreover, the detailed analysis of HDS data presented in the Appendix reveals that real estate agents are most likely to take advantage of an opportunity to discriminate against blacks in some of the cities with

the highest levels of racial segregation or racial isolation, including Birmingham, Chicago, Cincinnati, Detroit, Houston, Pittsburgh, and Washington, D.C.

80. For a detailed exposition of this argument, see Yinger et al. (1979) or Yinger (1986b).

81. Recall that this point is explored in detail in the previous chapter.

82. Farley et al. (1993, Figure 5) find that when asked about various largely white Detroit suburbs in 1992, blacks generally expect that "white residents would be upset if a black moved in." Indeed, 90 percent of blacks felt this way about some suburbs. In some cases, blacks may even anticipate a violent reception. Anyone who doubts that violent acts continue to confront blacks who move into white neighborhoods need only keep an eye on the newspaper. Several such incidents are reported in Massey and Denton (1993, p. 91) and in Orfield and Ashkinaze (1991, p. 77); many others are reported in the press. See, for example, *The New York Times* (1991, 1994b). As noted in Chapter 1, 1,689 hate crimes against blacks were reported in 1991 along with 242 against Hispanics (U.S. Department of Justice, 1992). These hate crimes include cross burnings and even house burnings. See McFadden (1990).

83. Dent (1992).

84. This study, Galster (1991), along with related work by Dr. Galster, is discussed in more detail in Chapter 8. Similar evidence is provided by Galster and Keeney (1988).

85. Many scholars have explored the links between prejudice, discrimination, and segregation. Yinger (1979) argues, for example, that even if prejudice causes an uneven distribution of blacks and whites, only discrimination, not prejudice, can explain why blacks are more centralized than whites with equal incomes and other characteristics. The work by Galster (1991) provides the first formal confirmation of this reasoning.

86. For other recent discussions of the causes of racial and ethnic segregation, see Kain (1994), Turner and Wienk (1993), Galster (1991, 1992), and Massey and Denton (1993). See also the exchange between Galster (1988, 1989) and Clark (1986, 1988, 1989). Extension of this analysis to the case of public housing can be found in Bickford and Massey (1991) and Goering and Coulibably (1989). Examples of discriminatory actions by public housing authorities also are given in Chandler (1992).

87. The information about Mattapan in this section comes from Soutner (1980) and Ginsberg (1975). Other neighborhoods that have undergone rapid, traumatic racial transition include Marquette Park (see Center for Community Change, 1980) and Austin (see Goodwin, 1979, Chap. 5 or Berry, 1979, Chap. 11), which are both in Chicago.

88. For a discussion of the BBURG line, see Soutner (1980, pp. 12–16) or Ginsberg (1975, pp. 39–42).

89. Soutner (1980, p. 11).

90. This quotation, by a former resident, is from Ginsberg (1975, p. 43). The brokers used other tactics to encourage sales, as well; "one broker sent out approximately 10,000 letters" during 1971 offering his services to households in Mattapan (Ginsberg, 1975, p. 43). Brokers sometimes have been very candid about their motives in blockbusting. One broker in the Austin neighborhood of Chicago said to an interviewer: "We don't care if the whites run all the way to Hong Kong, as long as they run. . . . I go where the money is. I'm a money-oriented guy. It's good business for us when they're frightened" (Goodwin, 1979, p. 68).

91. These quotations and figures are from Soutner (1980). Ginsberg (1975, p. 2) notes that the Jewish population of Mattapan went from 10,000 in 1968 to 2,500 in 1972.

92. Oak Park and the two Cleveland suburbs are discussed in more detail below. Park Hill, West Mt. Airy, and Park Forest are presented in Helper (1986). Butler Tarkington, the 19th Ward of Rochester, and thirteen other cases with varying degrees of success in maintaining integration are discussed in Saltman (1990). Recent developments in Park Forest are described in Hayes (1990). The early experience in Oak Park, Park Forest, and several other municipalities in the Chicago area also is presented in Berry (1979).

93. This catalog builds on the list in Polikoff (1986, pp. 44–45).

94. As Saltman (1991, p. 430) puts it,
    Affirmative marketing encourages people of the race least likely to consider moving to an area to do so. . . . Steering, in contrast, encourages those most likely to move to an area to do so. Affirmative marketing is supported by law, results in an integrative move, and expands housing choice. Steering is against the law, results in a segregative move, and restricts housing choice. The difference between the two is thus a fundamental one.

95. For a detailed discussion of the possible roles for a housing center, see Freiberg (1993).

96. We will return to this topic in Chapter 8.

97. For more on this perception, see Taub, Taylor, and Dunham (1984).

98. This is one of the oldest issues in the literature on racial transition. Property values sometimes decline when racial or ethnic transition begins because of panic selling by whites, but the literature rejects the claim that property values decline in the long run when racial or ethnic, but not income, transition occurs. See Laurenti (1960), Yinger (1979, 1987), and Chambers (1992).

99. This discussion of Oak Park draws primarily on Goodwin (1979). See also Polikoff (1986, fn. 10).

100. Goodwin (1979, pp. 157–158).

101. Saltman (1991, p. 436).

102. These and the other figures in this paragraph are from Smith (1993).

103. The story of this bombing incident is given in Keating (1994, p. 98).

104. The history of the programs in Shaker and Cleveland Heights is presented in detail by Keating (1994). See also DeMarco and Galster (1993), Husock (1989), and Cromwell (1990). The focus on encouraging whites was controversial; blacks who came to the Housing Office often were not given much assistance and in 1978 several staffers, both black and white, resigned from the Housing Office in protest. See Keating (1994, p. 101).

105. See Keating (1994, p. 116).

106. This quotation is from Saul and Farkas (1983). See also Hatton (1979). The fight against discrimination began before the filing of this suit; in fact, community groups conducted audits as early as 1970. See Keating (1994, p. 117).

107. Galster (1990e, p. 389). For a detailed discussion of the programs in these two communities, see Keating (1994).

108. Keating (1994, p. 205). Husock (1989, p. 5) reports that during the late summer of 1985, this program provided mortgages to 30 black households and 19 white households, including 16 in Shaker Heights. The effectiveness of these programs is not clear. Cromwell (1990) presents some weak evidence of their effectiveness, but three-quarters of participants say they would have made the same move even without the program (Keating, 1994, p. 207). Finally, Saltman (1991, p. 432) reports that this program "has been approved for use throughout the state of Ohio," although no information on the extent of its use is yet available.

109. The Cleveland Foundation (1988). The Fund for the Future of Shaker Heights, for example, made 75 loans in 1990, of which 66 went to white families moving into the Lomond neighborhood, which borders Cleveland and into which few whites were moving, five went to other whites and only four went to blacks. These loans averaged about $4,000. See Cromwell (1990). The Heights Fund operates a similar program in Cleveland Heights and its neighbor, University Heights. Apparently, these loan programs are all descendants of loan programs set up by community groups in Lomond and Ludlow (another Shaker Heights neighborhood) in 1961; these programs were designed to attract whites to the community when blacks started to move in. See Cromwell (1990). Keating (1994) reports that pro-integrative mortgages also have been provided by the Fund for an Open Society in Philadelphia, Washington, D.C., and a few other areas. Through 1990, this program had provided

150 mortgages, mainly for single-family houses. Moreover, as part of a court settlement, the Milwaukee Fair Housing Council has provided, since 1989, pro-integrative mortgages that are funded by the state.

110. The 1968 and 1986 figures are from Husock (1989, p. 10); the 1990 figures are from U.S. Bureau of the Census (1992a, Table 8). Keating (1994, pp. 110–111) reports that in 1990 in Shaker Heights the three neighborhoods nearest Cleveland were 68, 77, and 95 percent black, whereas the two richest tracts were less than 5 percent black. The six other tracts in the city were all between 10 and 50 percent black. In Cleveland Heights in 1990, ten tracts fell between 50 and 75 percent black, ten fell between 10 and 50 percent black, and one was 8 percent black. Keating (1994, pp. 135–137).

111. This study is Saltman (1990). See also Saltman (1991), Helper (1986), and Smith (1993).

112. The crucial role of schools also is emphasized by Orfield (1985, p. 192), who says:

Schools change racial composition before neighborhoods, and racially identifiable schools become key factors in ending the migration of white families into integrated areas. The reasons for the change in local elementary schools are simple: the new minority families tend to be younger, to have more school-age children than present residents, and to rely more strongly on public education. Very few neighborhood schools stabilize spontaneously after substantial residential desegregation begins. Unless the school district helps through policies designed to foster integration, a key element for an integrated neighborhood is very difficult to attain.

113. Smith (1993), based on a November 1991 letter from J. Saltman. George Galster also has informed me that Sherman Park "filed suit against Wisconsin's largest realtor claiming steering and advertising discrimination were responsible" for its rapid transition.

114. For more on Starrett City, see Rosenberg (1982), Goodman (1983), Morley (1984), Prial (1984), and Kifner (1988).

115. See Prial (1984). The general manager or chief operating officer of Starrett City throughout this period was Robert C. Rosenberg, who also was a senior vice president of the Starrett Housing Corporation, the parent corporation. For his story, see Rosenberg (1982).

116. See Rosenberg (1982), Goodman (1983), Morley (1984), and Prial (1984). These steps also made the project more attractive to black households, but they were designed to have a larger relative impact on whites.

117. See Morely (1984).

118. Kifner (1988).

119. A picture of this sign, the 1988 version, accompanies Finder (1988).

120. Ceiling quotas also have been used by several public housing authori-

ties. See Goering and Coulibably (1989). The legality of these quotas is discussed in Chapter 10.

121. Blair (1984).

122. Morley (1984, p. 14).

123. Blair (1984).

124. I was an expert witness for the plaintiffs. Much of the analysis in this section is taken from a statement I prepared for this suit. For more on the case, see Goodman (1983).

125. This estimate is from a study by Paul Davidoff, which is cited in Blair (1984).

126. This suit by the Justice Department was somewhat unusual because in 1980 the federal government successfully opposed an attempt by the plaintiffs to make the federal government a party to the original suit. See Fried (1984).

127. See Greenhouse (1988), who also reports that by this time Starrett City was 62 percent white, 23 percent black, 8 percent Hispanic, and 5 percent Asian.

128. After the Supreme Court decision, a statement by Robert Rosenberg said, "We are confident that Starrett City's residents will continue to show the nation that it is possible for a racially integrated housing development to thrive." Finder (1988, p. B4). See also Roberts (1992).

129. The 1988 figures are from Finder (1988) and the 1990 figures are from U.S. Bureau of the Census (1992b, Table 8, census tract 1058). Note that the share of the population classified as "other race" also increased from 2 to 7.5 percent over this period.

130. See, for example, Goodman (1983), Prial (1984), or Kifner (1988).

131. This point is emphasized in Yinger et al. (1979), Helper (1986), and Yinger (1986). It also has been made by Kenneth Clark, an expert witness on the side of the defendants in the original Starrett suit. According to Roberts (1988),

> The solution, said Dr. Kenneth B. Clark, the sociologist, must go beyond any single school or housing project. Scrapping the Starrett City quota, he warned, would perpetuate segregation if the complex became predominantly black. But pressure from black would-be tenants could be reduced as the state broadened housing opportunities by redeeming its pledge, as part of the settlement of the original Starrett City suit, to integrate other predominantly white subsidized housing projects.

132. Saltman (1990) states a similar view when she says that "the original legal decision and settlement on Starrett City was a wise and fair one" (p. 392) in part because the parties agreed to "*expand* similar area housing opportunities elsewhere" (p. 393).

133. This concise list comes from a description of Shaker Heights by Keating (1994, p. 103).

**CHAPTER 8: THE IMPACT OF HOUSING DISCRIMINATION
ON EDUCATION, EMPLOYMENT, AND POVERTY**

1. The story of Proviso West, including all the statistics, is taken from Bissinger (1994). For another detailed story about segregation in high schools, concerning Atlanta, see Orfield and Ashkinazi (1991, Chap. 5).

2. This interpretation obviously draws on analysis from earlier chapters. Chapter 3 documents dicrimination in Chicago, which was one of the HDS sites, and Chapter 7 discusses the impact of housing discrimination on neighborhood racial transition.

3. Bissinger (1994, p. 50).

4. Apparently, the attitudes of some teachers at Proviso West did little to promote racial harmony. One social studies teacher is quoted as saying, "There are some days I come in, I don't want to see anyone black. I've just had it." Bissinger (1994, p. 30).

5. Bissinger (1994, p. 56).

6. For a similar formulation of the system of discrimination, see Galster (1992b, Fig. 15.1) or Darden, Duleep, and Galster (1992).

7. For a more comprehensive treatment of the system of discrimination, see Galster (1991, 1992c, 1993b).

8. For a discussion of racial disparities in health care and in many aspects of crime and criminal justice, see Jaynes and Williams (1989, Chaps. 8 and 9). Linkages between crime and youth unemployment are discussed in Darity and Myers (1983) and Freeman (1992). Recent evidence on racial differences in health status is provided by Osei (1992). One particularly troubling health issue for minority children that is directly associated with housing (because its primary cause is eating old paint chips) is lead paint poisoning, which can lead to loss of intelligence and aggressive behavior, among other things. In 1991, 21.6 percent of black children ages 1 and 2 had dangerous levels of lead in their blood. See Blakeslee (1994). Moreover, "elevated lead levels were seven times more prevalent among black children in the inner city than among white children outside cities" (Purdy, 1994, p. B3). Other elements in the discriminatory system include attitudes and decisions about families and children. Although not formally included in my framework, this family element is discussed at several points in the chapter.

9. U.S. Bureau of the Census (1992c, Table 252). In 1987, the share of young adults aged 25–29 who had not completed high school was 15.2 percent for black males and 17.9 percent for black females, compared to 14.4 and 13.0 percent for white males and females, respectively (Hill and Rock, 1992, Table 7.8).

10. U.S. Bureau of the Census (1992c, Table 253). The dropout rate is declining for blacks and whites but increasing for Hispanics (from 30.8 percent in 1975, Table 254). This table also indicates that for young adults aged 20–24, the dropout rate is lower for blacks, 14.0 percent, than for whites, 14.4 percent, whereas the dropout rate for Hispanics reaches an astonishing 45.7 percent. Read the following sentence in the text before interpreting these results!

11. See Hill and Rock (1992) or Jaynes and Williams (1989). Both conceptual and data problems make it very difficult to count the number of high school dropouts. For a detailed discussion of this issue for Atlanta, see Orfield and Ashkinaze (1991).

12. Disparities are even larger on the S.A.T. test, which is administered by the College Board for people applying to college. The 1994 black–white disparities on the verbal portion of the S.A.T. were 21.8 percent for men and 19.7 percent for women, and the black–white disparities on the math portion (on which men outscore women by 9.3 percent) were 23.1 percent for men and 19.8 percent for women. See The New York Times (1994a). Moreover, these disparities carry over into adulthood. On a 1985 national test of prose ability for adults aged 21–25, 88 percent of whites performed above the middle possible score compared to 57.5 percent of blacks. The comparable results for a test on understanding documents were 89.9 percent for whites and 55.5 percent for blacks, and for a test on quantitative abilities they were 89.4 percent for whites and 60.4 percent for blacks. See Jaynes and Williams (1991, Table 7-4).

13. In 1994 Hispanic–white disparities in S.A.T. scores were largest for Puerto Ricans (about 17 percent for both verbal and math for both men and women). Disparities were 1–3 percentage points lower for Mexican Americans and 6 points lower for other Hispanics. See The New York Times (1994a).

14. The black–white science disparity was 12.1 percent in 1977. All these figures are from U.S. Bureau of the Census (1992c, Table 251). In many cases, minority–white disparities in S.A.T. scores also declined slightly between 1987 and 1994. However, the verbal gap for black men, for "other Hispanic" men, and for Mexican Americans of both sexes increased a bit over this period, as did the math gap for Mexican American men and for "other Hispanics" of both sexes (The New York Times, 1994a).

15. These figures also come from U.S. Bureau of the Census (1992c, Table 251). The Hispanic–white reading disparity was larger for 9-year-olds than for 17-year-olds in both 1977 and 1990, but the difference in disparities was larger in 1990 than in 1977 (5.5 percentage points versus 3.1 percentage points), which indicates that 9-year-old Hispanics have more catching up to do today than they did in 1977.

16. Jones (1994).

17. This report, from which all the material on school segregation in this section is taken, is Orfield et al. (1993). It draws on the U.S. Department of Education Common Core of Data Public School Universe, the most comprehensive data source on school segregation ever assembled.

18. For the purposes of identifying school composition, Orfield et al. (1993) define minority as black or Hispanic or Native American or Asian American. This report also presents information on the "percent of white students in school attended by typical black or Latino student" over the 1970–1991 period. This measure shows trends similar to those of the measures of segregation discussed in the text.

19. Orfield et al. (1993, p. 7). The Oklahoma case is *Board of Education* v. *Dowell* (1991). Desegregation orders also were weakened in a 1992 case in DeKalb County, which is next to Atlanta, *Freeman* v. *Pitts* (1992). See Celis (1994a) and Orfield (1993). In another case, *Missouri* v. *Jenkins,* the state of Missouri and the Kansas City school district were found liable for unconstitutional segregation (although suburban school districts were not). As a result, the state has been required to pay $800 million to improve school facilities and programs in Kansas City (and the city to raise a much smaller amount). The state believes it has done enough and has brought suit to get out of its obligations; the school district believes the state should continue its support. See Celis (1994a) and Greenhouse (1994b). I played a minor role as an expert witness in the original Kansas City case. In June 1995 the Supreme Court rejected the lower court's rationale for state involvement and returned the case for further deliberation. See Greenhouse (1995).

20. Orfield et al. (1993, p. 6).

21. The preceding figures in this paragraph are from Orfield et al. (1993, Table 13). This table also reveals that for both blacks and Hispanics, the comparable segregation measures for small central cities fall between those of large central cities and the suburbs of large central cities, and the segregation measures for towns and rural areas are about equal to those of the suburbs in small metropolitan areas.

22. Between 1980 and 1990, the black and Hispanic populations grew considerably faster in the suburbs than in the central cities. Most blacks and Hispanics still live in central cities, but the share of the minority population in central cities has declined. See DeWitt (1994).

23. For some compelling examples of the disparities between minority and white schools, see Kozol (1991).

24. These figures, which apply to 1988, are from Hill and Rock (1992), who also indicate that in the West 43.8 percent of black children live in the suburbs.

25. For further discussion of revenue-raising capacity and service responsibilities, along with an application to schools in Nebraska, see Ratcliffe, Riddell, and Yinger (1990). Also note that moving to the suburbs may

not improve the problem of high tax burdens for minority families. A recent study finds that "in many suburban areas, . . . black homeowners are paying higher property taxes than whites on homes of equal value" (Schemo, 1994b, p. A1).

26. Orfield et al. (1993, p. 22).

27. For a review of the literature on links between poverty and education, see Murnane (1994). For a recent study that clearly demonstrates the impact of poverty on educational achievement, see Ferguson (1991).

28. For a discussion of the link between poverty and school costs, and an application to Arizona, see Downes and Pogue (1994). Poverty also raises the costs of other local public services, particularly police. Ladd and Yinger (1991, pp. 85–86) estimate that "a city with a poverty rate one standard deviation above the 1982 mean must pay 36.4 percent more for police services than a city with average poverty." The comparable impact of poverty on the cost of fire services is about one third as large.

29. Orfield and Ashkinaze (1991, Figure 5.3).

30. As Orfield et al. (1993, p. 22) put it: "If poverty is systematically linked to educational inequality, as it consistently is in educational research, the very powerful link between racial and poverty segregation is a central element in perpetuating the educational inequality of minority students."

31. For a review of this literature, see Brief for NAACP (1992) or Jaynes and Williams (1989).

32. Brief for NAACP (1992, pp. 8a–8b). See also Orfield (1993).

33. Rosenbaum et al. (1993). This study, which is discussed in more detail below, also found that the suburban children did not receive lower grades despite their more demanding curriculum, and that, despite some harassment in school, particularly at first, the suburban children make friends with some white students, "have active social lives and feel they fit into their new environment" (p. 1541).

34. For a detailed discussion of this link in the case of Chicago, see Orfield (1985). A more general treatment is in Orfield (1993).

35. For a review of these studies, see Clotfelter (1979).

36. All the figures in this paragraph are from Orfield et al. (1993), which goes on to say (p. 6): "The underlying reality, of course, was a dramatic drop in the number of school age white children in the U.S., as the white birth rate fell and the white population aged."

37. This information about desegregation plans is from Orfield et al. (1993, pp. 15–16.)

38. The first four programs are described in Uchitelle (1993). The Milwau-

kee plan, which served 968 children in 1993–94, is described in Witte (1994).

39. The plans in the first four cases are discussed in Orfield et al. (1993, pp. 15–16); the St. Louis plan is discussed in Uchitelle (1993).

40. The Minnesota plan is described in Uchitelle (1993). According to Boyer (1992), 1.8 percent of school children in Minneapolis take advantage of the plan. Boyer also reports that Arkansas, Idaho, Iowa, Massachusetts, Nebraska, and Utah have some form of statewide choice program, none of which serves more than 1.2 percent of school children in the state.

41. This is not to say that such government actions did not take place. As this chapter documents, inaction by state and local officials in the form of poor enforcement of fair housing legislation and poor support for city schools has played a major role in promoting city school segregation. For more on the *Milliken* decision, see Orfield et al. (1993), Orfield (1993), or Kozol (1991).

42. In 1983, the share of whites who would have no "objection to sending your children to a school where more than half of the children are black" was 37 percent, down from 43 percent in 1972. The comparable figures for schools "where half of the children are black" are 76 percent in each of these years. See Schuman, Steeh, and Bobo (1985, Table 3.3). The only ways for parents to register these objections are to move or to send their children to private schools.

43. The link between racially identifiable schools and neighborhood transition was examined at length in Chapter 7.

44. Galster (1991). This study is discussed in more detail below.

45. For a summary of the social science evidence on these points, see Brief for NAACP (1992) and Orfield (1993).

46. The story of Oak Park is presented in detail in Chapter 7. Other examples of this positive influence come from the Cleveland suburbs discussed in Chapter 7. Shaker Heights voluntarily implemented busing and magnet schools in 1967, and Cleveland Heights did the same thing in 1976. See Keating (1994, p. 102 and 120–130).

47. This quotation is from Goodwin (1979, p. 92), which is also the source of the following information on Oak Park's school integration policies.

48. Goodwin (1979, p. 93).

49. Goodwin (1979, p. 95).

50. These figures are from Bissinger (1994, p. 31).

51. Feld (1986, p. 387).

52. Galster and Keeney (1993). According to some experts, "racial tracking," which is placing students "by race instead of test scores, grades or teacher evaluations," is a common practice, "particularly in

Southern districts where the administrators are white and at least half of the student body is black" (*The New York Times*, 1995, p. A10).

53. See Feld (1989) for an analysis of this decision and the events leading up to it.

54. These quotations are from Steinberg (1993, pp. B1 and B5); the first is taken directly from the court's decision. Yonkers was not so quick to comply with the order to disperse subsidized housing. In fact, it defied the District Court's order until September 1988 when court-imposed fines, which were upheld by the U.S. Supreme Court, reached over $1 million per day. See McFadden (1988). In 1993 the settlement in a suit brought by minority families who lived in Yonkers and received Section 8 housing certificates called for the provision of about 1,000 low-rent apartments throughout Westchester County, not just in Yonkers. See Berger (1993).

55. A detailed exploration of the link between schooling disparities and job disparities in Chicago can be found in Orfield (1992).

56. See, for example, Schiller (1989, Chap. 8), O'Neill (1990), Levy and Murnane (1992), Blank (1994), and Ferguson (1995), plus the references cited therein.

57. For a review of evidence on this point, see Brief for NAACP (1992).

58. Brief for NAACP (1992, p. 13a).

59. The influence of racial and ethnic prejudice on discrimination in housing is discussed at length in Chapter 9.

60. Recall from Chapter 1 that 19 percent of whites in 1990 believed that "blacks have worse jobs, income and housing than whites . . . because most blacks have less in-born ability to learn." See Farley (1993, Fig. 6.7). The same source also shows, however, that even more whites recognize that educational disparities play a role. Indeed, 50 percent of whites in 1990 agreed that blacks had poorer economic outcomes "because most blacks don't have the chance for the education it takes to rise out of poverty."

61. Recall from Chapter 7 that there is a large literature supporting the "contact hypothesis," which says that prejudice declines with meaningful, equal-status contact between groups.

62. School policies and actions by teachers and school staff are important to the success of integration. Schools in Montclair, New Jersey, for example, have been successfully integrated at the school level since a 1968 court desegregation order, but racial hostility recently emerged in these schools because extensive segregation remained at the classroom level. See McLarin (1994). As pointed out at the beginning of this chapter, the same problem also existed at Proviso West High School. Another sad example occurred recently in Alabama, where a high school principal's statement that a mixed-race student was a "mistake" set off a tragic se-

ries of events, culminating in the burning of the school. See Gross and Smothers (1994).

63. See Schuman, Steeh, and Bobo (1985, Fig. 2.4). Orfield (1993) cites several recent surveys in which most whites support school integration — and busing. In addition, several studies have shown that minority students who attend integrated schools are more likely than other minority students to have white friends. See Brief for NAACP (1992, p. 13a).

64. Among Hispanics the 1992 unemployment rate was highest for Puerto Ricans (14.1 percent) and Mexicans (11.7 percent) and lowest for Cubans (7.9 percent). The 1992 rate also was 6.5 percent for whites and 14.1 percent for blacks. See U.S. Bureau of the Census (1993d, Table 625).

65. These 1994 unemployment rates come from the ongoing Current Population Surveys of the U.S. Census Bureau on behalf of the U.S. Department of Labor. They were provided over the phone by Monica Castillo of the Labor Force Statistics Office, Department of Labor, on January 20, 1995.

66. Blair and Fichtenbaum (1992) show that a simple adjustment for discouraged and part-time workers doubles the unemployment rates for males and boosts the unemployment rates for females by 2½ times. Hence this adjustment increases the absolute, but not the relative, black–white unemployment gap. This source also presents evidence that higher black unemployment rates cannot be attributed to "a lower desire to work on the part of African Americans" (p. 74). The survey on which official unemployment rates are based was revised in 1994. See Cohany, Polivka, and Rothgeb (1994). These revisions are designed to pick up a wider range of work and job search activities and increase unemployment rates by a small amount. This increase is not significant for men, however.

67. These 1993 black and white employment rates come from Council of Economic Advisers (1994, Table B41).

68. The figures in this paragraph are from Blair and Fichtenbaum (1992). The adjusted unemployment rate for blacks with a college degree, 5.5 percent, was actually slightly lower than the rate for comparable whites, 6.2 percent.

69. These per capita income figures come from U.S. Bureau of the Census (1993d, Table 732).

70. U.S. Bureau of the Census (1994).

71. The study is O'Neill (1990), which also controlled for region and, in some cases, for industry and occupation. For a review of the large literature on estimating wage discrimination, see Cain (1986). Two recent studies show how discrimination can be understated by standard techniques, including those used by O'Neill (1990); these studies are Baldwin and Johnson (1993) and Gill (1994). As pointed out in Chapter 5, the

standard techniques are subject to many of the same problems that lead estimates of mortgage discrimination to be conservative. In particular, these wage studies are likely to include "control" variables that appear to be, but are not, related to worker productivity but are correlated with race or ethnicity. If so, discrimination is hidden to some degree in the coefficient of these variables. See Arvey and Foley (1988) and Gatewood and Feild (1990). The latter reference contains the federal government's guidelines for determining when hiring practices are nondiscriminatory. Note that the problem of inappropriate controls also arises in studies of discrimination in hiring or promotion.

72. Ferguson (1995), Maxwell (1994), and Neal and Johnson (1994) also find that after controlling for achievement test scores and other factors the black–white male wage gap is relatively small. These results appear to contradict the growing black–white male wage gap during the 1980s found by Bound and Freeman (1992). However, Bound and Freeman control only for years of schooling and experience. As noted earlier, the return to skill increased dramatically over this period, so excluding achievement test scores results in a greater misstatement of the black–white wage gap in 1990 than in 1980—and hence to an apparent, but in fact nonexistent, upward trend. See Ferguson (1995). Bound and Freeman also argue that lax enforcement of fair lending laws during the Reagan years increased the black–white wage gap. This claim is disputed by Smith (1993).

73. This evidence does not imply a lack of discrimination in all employment practices. Employers may still discriminate in the assignment of employees to job categories or to job training. For example, using a 1990 national sample from the Panel Study of Income Dynamics, Mason (1994) finds that black and white wages are strongly influenced by workplace segregation, with higher wages in occupations with higher white percentages. With standard control variables (but not achievement test scores) plus industry, occupation, employment stability, and employment segregation variables, white men are paid only 2.7 percent more than black men. However, this wage gap jumps to 24.6 percent when the last four categories of variables, all of which might reflect discriminatory actions, are excluded. The wage gaps (relative to non-Hispanic whites) with full controls are larger for Hispanic men: 8.1 percent for non-Mexican Latinos and 29.5 percent for Mexican Americans; 20.6 percent for white Latinos and 20.1 percent for brown Latinos; 22.3 percent for native Latinos and 25.2 percent for immigrant Latinos. However, these gaps increase proportionately less when the above industry and occupation variables are excluded. Moreover, Rodgers (1995) finds that some forms of training have a large impact on wages, and that blacks are far less likely than whites to receive this training, perhaps because of discrimination.

74. The two studies are Cross et al. (1990) for Hispanics and Turner, Fix,

and Struyk (1991) for blacks. These and other employment audit studies are reviewed in Mincy (1993), and the Hispanic audits are further analyzed in Kenney and Wissoker (1994). Another employment audit study that found discrimination against Hispanics in Washington, D.C., is described in Gaines-Carter (1992). Employment audits also have been used by enforcement officials. See Duffy (1993). Some scholars have argued that current fair employment laws and enforcement practices induce employers to stop wage discrimination and turn to hiring discrimination. See Bloch (1994, Chap. 6) or Jencks (1992, Chap. 2). Recent surveys of employers' attitudes also indicate that preconceptions about black workers, particularly black males, lead to hiring discrimination. See Kirschenman and Neckerman (1991). Finally, Bloch (1994, Chap. 3) points out that employers also may discriminate in recruitment practices.

75. These studies raise many challenging methodological issues. See Mincy (1993) and Heckman and Siegleman (1993b). See also my response to Heckman and Siegleman (Yinger 1993b) and their rejoinder (1993a).

76. For some recent evidence, see Kasarda (1985, 1989).

77. This hypothesis was first proposed by Kain (1968). Extensive reviews of the mismatch literature are provided by Jencks and Mayer (1990), Holzer (1991), Kain (1992), and Ihlanfeldt (1992). A related hypothesis is that there is a "skills mismatch" between minority workers and available jobs. See Kasarda (1989). In fact, there appears to be something of a skills mismatch for all low-skill workers, as wages for low-skill workers have fallen relative to those of high-skill workers in recent years. See Levy and Murnane (1992).

78. Figure 8.2 is adapted from Ross (1994, Fig. III-1).

79. A formal analysis of the impact of housing discrimination on household housing decisions is provided in Chapter 6.

80. See Kasarda (1989) and Jencks and Mayer (1990). Problems in interpreting these results are discussed in Jencks and Mayer (1990), Holzer (1991), and Kain (1992).

81. These sections do not provide a comprehensive review of the literature. Instead, I highlight those studies that, in my judgment, provide the clearest evidence concerning the spatial mismatch hypothesis. For comprehensive reviews, see Jencks and Mayer (1990a), Holzer (1991), Ihlanfeldt (1992), and Kain (1992).

82. Ihlanfeldt and Sjoquist (1990, 1991) and Ihlanfeldt (1992, 1993).

83. This study, Ihlanfeldt (1992), also gives results for youths aged 20–24 who do not live at home — 29 percent for blacks and 22 percent for Hispanics. These results are not as compelling because residential choices are no longer exogenous. A related study, Ihlanfeldt (1993), finds that poor accessibility explains over 30 percent of the Hispanic–white un-

employment for Puerto Rican youth but only 15–20 percent of the gap for Mexican youth.

84. Ihlanfeldt and Sjoquist (1990).

85. The results in the last four sentences are all from Ihlanfeldt (1992).

86. Some other scholars, including Ellwood (1986), conclude that racial differences in access to jobs do not help explain the black–white unemployment gap for youth. However, these studies draw on data that are far less complete than the data used by Ihlanfeldt and Sjoquist. For detailed reviews of these studies, see Ihlanfeldt (1992) or Kain (1992).

87. The willingness of households to pay more for housing in locations with better job accessibility is a central theorem of urban economics and has been supported by many empirical studies. See Coulson (1991) for a recent review. The impact of discrimination on housing outcomes is discussed in Chapters 6 and 7.

88. These studics are reviewed in Chapter 7.

89. Leonard (1987). Further discussion of the study is provided in Jencks and Mayer (1990) and Kain (1992).

90. Leonard (1987) controls for the share of blue-collar workers in the firm, but firms also might care about other unobserved dimensions of worker skill.

91. This statement is fully consistent with Leonard's own conclusion, namely: "Residential segregation not only limits where blacks can live, but it also limits where they work" (1987, p. 344).

92. Ross (1994).

93. Elements of this work can be found in previous studies. Hughes and Maddcn (1991) were the first to point out the importance of joint housing and job decisions, but their data set and their conceptual approach are too limited to fully take advantage of this insight. See Ross (1994). Zax and Kain (1991) use a unique data set drawn from the employees of a large firm that moved from Detroit to a suburb to analyze both moving and quitting decisions. They show that blacks are less likely both to move, presumably because discrimination in housing limits their options, and to quit, presumably because discrimination in labor markets limits their options. However, they do not examine joint move/quit decisions to see if housing constraints, such as discrimination, spill over into the labor market. See Ross (1994).

94. In principle, it also might indicate that racial factors from the labor market spill over into the housing market, but no plausible mechanism for such an effect has yet been identified.

95. The link between housing discrimination and the relatively high centralization of blacks and other minorities is explored in detail in Chapter 7. Stephen Ross has informed me that in analysis completed after

Ross (1994), he finds that it is clearly the centralization of the black population, not the central location for a black individual, that explains the mismatch effect.

96. For a detailed history of the Gautreaux case, see Vernarelli (1986), from which the information in this and the following paragraph is drawn. See also Davis (1993).

97. The relevant Supreme Court case is *Hills* v. *Gautreaux* (1976). For a detailed discussion of the provisions of the program, see Popkin, Rosenbaum, and Meaden (1993).

98. See DeParle (1993b) and Peterson and Williams (1994).

99. This evidence, which is from Popkin, Rosenbaum, and Meaden (1993), must be interpreted with care. Strictly speaking, neither this study nor any other study of the Gautreaux Program literally evaluates the impact of the program. Instead, they compare the outcomes for participants who move to the suburbs with those for participants who move within the central city. According to the authors, this comparison isolated the impact of suburban residence on a household's success because whether a participant ends up in the central city or suburbs is a "quasi-random" outcome (p. 558), caused by the fact that each participant is offered the next available unit, wherever it is located, and that participants accept the first housing they are offered 95 percent of the time. However, no formal test of this "randomness" interpretation has been conducted, nor has it formally been shown that post-placement counseling is the same for suburban and central city participants. Moreover, there is no indication that the real estate counselors are even aware of job accessibility when they select housing for the program. The results in this study are related to mismatch only if the suburban housing in the program has better job accessibility than the central city housing in the program (and than the public or other housing participants leave). A more appropriate test of the mismatch hypothesis would be to determine whether employment outcomes for participants are better when they are (randomly) placed in a neighborhood, city or suburban, with relatively high job accessibility. The methodological limitations of this work also are discussed in Jencks and Mayer (1990b) and Newman and Schnare (1994).

100. Rosenbaum et al. (1993). This study is subject to the caveat discussed in the previous footnote.

101. See Peterson and Williams (1994).

102. Under the original consent decree, HUD provided Section 8 certificates specifically for the program; this is no longer the case. These special certificates went to public housing residents, who made up half of the original participants. Now all the participants come from the Section 8 waiting list. See Peterson and Williams (1994).

103. This study, from which the following results are taken, is Fischer (1991).

Because it includes information on nonparticipants, this study provides a more direct test of program impacts than do the studies of the Gautreaux Program.

104. The impact of income disparities on residential segregation, which is often exaggerated, is discussed more fully in Chapter 7.

105. These studies are discussed in more detail in the later section on neighborhood effects. Also remember from earlier sections that concentrated poverty within a school undermines educational success and that poor access to jobs leads to higher dropout rates.

106. Note 60 pointed out that many whites think blacks have less ability to learn or less education than whites. In addition, 59 percent of whites in 1990 agree that relatively poor economic outcomes for blacks arise "because most blacks just don't have the motivation or willpower to pull themselves out of poverty" (Farley, 1993, Fig. 6.7).

107. The figures in this paragraph are from U.S. Bureau of the Census (1994). The poverty rate is not the same for all groups of Hispanics. In 1991, for example, the poverty rate was 39.4 percent for Puerto Ricans, 29.5 percent for Mexican Americans, 24.6 for Hispanics with Central and South American origins, and 18.0 percent for Cubans. See U.S. Bureau of the Census (1993c, Table 2).

108. In 1991 the poverty rate was 57.9 percent for Puerto Rican children and 33.3 percent for Cuban children, with the rates for other Hispanic children falling somewhere in between. See U.S. Bureau of the Census (1993c, Table 2).

109. This book is Wilson (1987).

110. There are some exceptions to this claim, including Massey and Denton (1993), which is discussed below. Mincy's (1994) review piece on this literature mentions housing discrimination and housing segregation, but only as an afterthought. However, much of this literature, including Wilson (1987), recognizes that concentrated poverty is supported by a complex system in which discrimination plays a role.

111. The concept of "sorting" by income class is well known in urban economics. See, for example, O'Sullivan (1993, Chap. 8).

112. A recent review of this literature is provided by Mincy (1994), who describes in more detail (and gives citations for) all the research discussed in this paragraph. Many of these studies are also reviewed in Jencks and Mayer (1990b) and Massey and Denton (1993, Chap. 6). As pointed out by Mincy, many of the conclusions of these studies also are supported by ethnographic research, such as Anderson (1990).

113. One study (Massey, Gross, and Eggers, 1991) found that out-of-school youth were far more likely to be unemployed if they lived in a high-poverty neighborhood. Another study found that an individual was more likely to commit a crime or use illegal drugs in a neighborhood

where such activity was common, but another study found no evidence of such a neighborhood effect. Other studies find evidence that teenage girls in distressed neighborhoods are more likely than other girls to have children out of wedlock. See Mincy (1994). The impact of a youth's surroundings also can be seen within a family: "Youth are more likely to be employed if their mothers, fathers, or siblings are employed," and "at-home youth are far more likely to work in the same industry as the mother or father, even after controlling for metropolitan-wide labor market conditions" (O'Regan and Quigley, 1993, p. 246). Moreover, as discussed below, Corcoran et al. (1992) find that a son's earnings are strongly and negatively related to receipt of welfare by his parent(s).

114. Corcoran et al. (1992).

115. Several other characteristics of zip codes prove not to affect employment outcomes. See Corcoran et al. (1992). However, the authors of this study caution that even more neighborhood effects might be seen "if community characteristics were measured in finer geographic detail" (p. 594). They also caution that their results cannot identify causal linkages between community welfare receipt and lower wage rates.

116. Corcoran et al. (1992, p. 592).

117. See Massey and Denton (1993, Chap. 5), Massey, Gross, and Shibuya (1994), and Massey, Gross, and Eggers (1991).

118. This simulation and the one in the following paragraph are taken from Massey and Denton (1993, Table 5.1). These simulations assume a fairly high degree of class segregation, as is typical in a large city.

119. The figures in this and the preceding sentence come from Massey and Eggers (1990). The figures on hypersegregated cities are repeated in Massey and Denton (1993, Table 5.2).

120. One of the great ironies of federal housing policy is that the federal government has created some of the most distressed "neighborhoods" in the country in the form of large housing projects. The history of discriminatory siting decisions is presented in Vernarelli (1986) and Gray and Tursky (1986). The level of disadvantage in public housing is discussed by Schill (1994), and the link between public housing and poverty concentration at the census tract level is explored by Massey and Kanaiaupuni (1993). Schill points out that in public housing "three-quarters of all residents have incomes below the poverty line" (p. 454), and Massey and Kanaiaupuni conclude that public housing has "greatly exacerbated the degree of poverty concentration for one group in particular—blacks" (p. 120). Massey and Kanaiaupuni also point out that "unlike poverty concentration that is created by economic restructuring or segregation, this kind of concentrated poverty is structurally permanent; no matter what the underlying trends in unemployment, wages, industrial structure, or civil rights enforcement, neighborhoods that contain housing projects will exhibit high levels of poverty concentra-

tion" (p. 118). Moreover, public housing projects with predominantly minority tenants are far more likely than those with predominantly white tenants to be located in high-poverty neighborhoods. See HUD (1995).

121. Galster (1987a, 1987b, 1991). In fact, the figures that Galster estimates (and draws) are even more complex than Figure 8.1. See also Galster and Keeney (1988). No comparable work has been done on the link between discrimination and poverty for Hispanics. However, Santiago and Wilder (1991) find that higher Hispanic–white segregation in an urban area (as measured by a dissimilarity index) is associated with a greater increase in the Hispanic poverty rate between 1970 and 1980.

122. There is a minor methodological problem with Galster's calculations: he looks at the main sources of feedback but does not fully solve his system of equations for the impact of discrimination on poverty. Alex Striker calculated the complete solutions for me and found that the full impact of sales market discrimination on poverty is virtually identical to the impact calculated by Galster but that the full impact of rental market discrimination on poverty is close to zero.

123. A similar conclusion appears in an earlier analysis of the same cities (Galster and Keeney, 1988); eliminating discrimination in housing in the average city would result in a 22 percent decline in the segregation index and a 62 percent increase in the ratio of black to white median income.

124. No formal review of Galster's work has yet appeared, but Dr. Galster discusses some of the limitations of his work himself. See Galster (1991).

CHAPTER 9: THE CAUSES OF DISCRIMINATION IN HOUSING

1. Helper (1969, p. 135). Helper also concluded that "between the broker and the people of the community there is a two-way relationship—one of interdependence. The broker wants to retain the goodwill of his clients and other property owners. To a large extent, he depends on them for his livelihood and for his standing in the community. The people in it depend on him not to introduce unwelcome neighbors" (pp. 153–154). Helper goes on to say that "The consequences for the broker who deals unrestrictedly with Negroes are drastic in proportion to the scope of such dealings and to his position in the real estate world" (p. 163).

2. Cited in Laurenti (1960, p. 269). One of the "three main reasons that impel brokers to restrict nonwhites to a special housing market," this study found, is that "to violate an established neighborhood pattern would, they believe, damage their business income and reputation" (p. 270).

3. This quotation is from Mandelbaum (1972, p. 1).

4. For other overviews of the causes of discrimination in housing, see Downs (1992) or Galster (1992c).

5. For a similar analysis of the HDS evidence on other types of housing agent behavior, see Yinger (1991a).

6. In principle, marginal discrimination applies both to the first available unit and to subsequent units, but measuring the discrimination that arises when the first unit becomes available is more complicated because it also involves a constant term. Total discrimination is $a + bA$, where a is the constant term, b is marginal discrimination (the slope), and A is the number of units available. When $A = 1$, discrimination is $a + b$. When A goes up to 2, discrimination rises to $a + 2b$; that is, the change in discrimination equals b.

7. This list does not include the possibility that the unit is not shown to either auditor. In an audit study we cannot observe a unit unless it is shown to at least one auditor.

8. For a detailed discussion of this matching procedure, see the Appendix.

9. This incentive has been developed at length by Yinger (1975, 1986a).

10. In extreme cases, a broker's property or even his life may be threatened if he sells to minority households. For example, a real estate office in Canarsie, the largely white section of Brooklyn that is next to Starrett City, was firebombed several times in 1991. The agency received phone calls indicating "that the agency would be punished for selling houses in the neighborhood to minorities" (Kurtz, 1991, p. 25). A broker in Valley Stream, an all-white section of Queens, N.Y., testified that he was threatened by other brokers and homeowners. "They have threatened to throw a bomb in the window," he said. Winerip (1987). See also Yarrow (1991).

11. A lack of cooperation was explicitly mentioned in testimony by a broker from Valley Stream. He said he "had deals ruined because I have taken clients to an all-white neighborhood. Brokers told me 'Don't ever do this again.'" Winerip (1987).

12. This evidence is reviewed in Chapter 4.

13. This incentive is discussed by Yinger (1986a) and Downs (1992).

14. The possibility of homeowner refusal to sell is discussed by Newburger (1989) and Downs (1992). One example of this behavior appears in Yarrow (1991, p. B7). A woman in Canarsie, a largely white section of Brooklyn, "had been trying to sell her home through [a real estate firm] for a year, dropping her asking price from $269,000 to $169,000, but she had gotten no offers from potential white buyers. [The firm] 'asked her what she would prefer—whites or blacks—and she said whites. Only Puerto Ricans and blacks are calling, but she doesn't want to ruin the neighborhood.'" In addition, blacks apparently believe that this type of behavior occurs. About 87 percent of blacks in the 1992 Detroit Area Study said that blacks sometimes or often miss out on housing "because white owners will not sell or rent to blacks." A similar percentage of blacks cited discrimination by real estate agents and lenders.

15. One possible exception arises in white neighborhoods with such a clear, widely known reputation for prejudice that all agents in the relevant MLS believe it would be futile to show houses to minority customers.

16. Agent perceptions may still be relevant, however, because agents also may believe that customers are unaware of the minority composition of the neighborhood surrounding an advertised unit.

17. In principle, the value of marginal discrimination for units similar to the advertised one could exceed one if an additional "similar" unit led to more discrimination in advertised units.

18. For further discussion of these incentives, see Yinger (1979).

19. Detailed evidence on this type of practice is provided by Schemo (1994a) for rental agents on Long Island, by Winerip (1988) for rental agents in Yonkers, and by Feldman (1989) for rental agents in Southern California.

20. This explanation for discrimination is presented by Simonson and Wienk (1984) and Yinger (1986a).

21. The role of anticipated difficulties in completing a transaction is discussed by Simonson and Wienk (1984).

22. This possibility is explored by Simonson and Wienk (1984) and Yinger (1986a).

23. This sentence refers to the race of the agent seen by the white auditor. Because the assignment of minority auditors to minority customers might be an agency policy, it is inappropriate to include in the analysis the difference in the race of the agents seen by audit teammates.

24. On average, men are more prejudiced than women and older people are more prejudiced than younger people. See Schuman, Steeh, and Bobo (1985). Hence a rough test for agent prejudice is to determine whether female agents discriminate less than men or older agents discriminate less than younger ones. See Yinger (1986a). These are not very precise tests, however, because female (older) agents may tend to belong to different types of firms than male (younger) agents.

25. In fact, estimated marginal discrimination is negative for the Hispanic audits in every cell (with observations) except one and it is negative and weakly significant in the first cell, that is, when both the agent's office and the advertised unit(s) are in white areas.

26. Two less likely possibilities also exist. The first is that agents not only advertise only those units they are willing to show to anyone but even practice affirmative action with these units by making extra efforts to show them to Hispanics. The second is that when several advertised units are available, the units differ in quality. If the second and third advertised units are somehow less desirable than the first one, agents may show the additional advertised units to Hispanics and show more desirable nonadvertised units to whites. No differences in quality show up in the HDS data, however.

27. Some of these "similar" units may themselves be advertised, but these advertisements are not observed by either the customer or the researcher. The key issue is whether an auditor has revealed her knowledge of the existence of a unit by referring to its advertisement.

28. Page (forthcoming) employs a fundamentally different specification of this problem in which the dependent variable is the ratio of units shown to minority and white auditors. She also finds relatively high discrimination against blacks and Hispanics in the HDS data when the advertised unit is in an integrated neighborhood.

29. Estimated marginal discrimination in the integrated unit/integrated office cell is almost as large for blacks but is not statistically significant.

30. In only three of the twenty audits in this cell was the Hispanic auditor shown units in neighborhoods with a significantly higher Hispanic concentration than those seen by her white teammate. Moreover, in three other audits in this cell, the white auditor was shown units in neighborhoods with a significantly higher Hispanic concentration.

31. For blacks, only one of the twenty-three audits in this cell involve steering (a significantly higher minority concentration for the units shown minorities), whereas four involve reverse steering. For Hispanics seven of the nineteen audits in the cell involve steering and seven involve reverse steering.

32. As indicated in the Appendix, the use of an MLS directory also lowers marginal discrimination against blacks, but the effect is small and statistically insignificant. The only significant MLS impact for blacks is the one discussed in the text.

33. In the Hispanic audits, this pattern appears in all four cells with either the units or the agent's office in white or integrated areas. The pattern is significant in both tables, however, only for the integrated/integrated cell.

34. In the case of advertised units, pro-integrative moves may be illusory. Marginal discrimination may be negative for advertised units because the minority composition of the development or building involved, unlike the minority composition of the surrounding census tract, is high. In this case agents' actions actually promote segregation at the project level by denying housing opportunities to whites.

35. Another result supports the view that agents select the best opportunity for practicing discrimination. In the sales audits, marginal discrimination in inspections is lower if discrimination in the number of units recommended is higher. See the Appendix.

36. When specific agent incentives are particularly strong, for example, when available units are in largely minority neighborhoods, marginal discrimination also might be negative for units similar to the advertised unit. We cannot test this hypothesis with HDS data, however, because so

few audits have available units concentrated in mostly minority neighborhoods.

37. The regressions in the Appendix include variables that identify some cases of multiple advertised units. In particular, this rough estimate is interacted with the type of neighborhood in which the rental agent's office is located. These variables are sometimes significant, but the roughness of the variable makes the results difficult to interpret, so the results are not presented in the text.

38. Although it is not possible to count advertised units, it is possible to determine when neither auditor inspected a unit associated with the advertisement that defined the audit.

39. Yinger (1979) and Galster (1987a) have argued that housing agents also may sometimes have an incentive to practice price discrimination; that is, to charge minorities higher prices than whites, because minorities have fewer options. Galster labels this the "ripoff hypothesis." Unfortunately, however, the HDS value and rent data often are missing or ambiguous, so price comparisons are not possible for many audits. Nevertheless, there is at least one intriguing hint that some price discrimination may be taking place, at least against blacks, as a supplement to other types of discrimination. In the black–white sales audits with both the advertised unit and other units available, 40 of the 141 audits with good price information and discrimination against blacks in number of units shown also involve a higher stated price for the advertised unit (or units) for blacks than for whites. Only 13 of these audits involve a higher price for whites. The Hispanic audits exhibit a weaker version of the same result; the Hispanic auditor was quoted a higher price in 31 of the 138 relevant audits and the white auditor was quoted a higher price in 24. These results are somewhat ambiguous, however, because it is not possible to determine whether the minority and white price quotes refer to the same set of advertised units.

40. As explained in the Appendix, the specific variable is a presence of school-aged children for blacks and a presence of any children for Hispanics. Page's (forthcoming) analysis of the HDS data finds that blacks with children can expect the relative proportion of houses they see to be reduced by 8 percent compared to those that do not have children, a result that is not quite significant at the 5 percent level.

41. The higher discrimination against single black women appears to be an example of statistical discrimination, in which a person is treated on the basis of the perceived average characteristics of her group instead of on the basis of her own characteristics. This concept is discussed in more detail in a later section on the causes of lending discrimination. The application of this concept to housing discrimination also is discussed by Downs (1992), although he does not use the term "statistical discrimination."

42. Page (forthcoming) also finds that Hispanic home buyers encounter less discrimination in housing availability from Hispanic agents than from white agents, and Yinger (1991a) obtains the same result for a wide range of agent behavior in both the sales and rental markets.

43. A similar result was found in an examination of many different types of agent behavior, not just housing availability, using the HDS data. In particular, "wives" encountered less discrimination than "husbands," but only when they encountered female agents. See Yinger (1991a).

44. Marginal discrimination also is significantly higher against single black men than against black couples. However, this result is consistent both with the view that agents do not want to deal with black men and with the view that future white neighbors prefer black females to black males.

45. In the Hispanic audits the coefficient of family income is negative and the coefficient of income relative to house value is positive. These two results are significant at the 10 percent level but are difficult to interpret.

46. Yinger (1991a) obtains similar results for many types of sales agent behavior; in particular, discrimination increases with income relative to house value for blacks and with income for Hispanics.

47. In her analysis of the HDS data, Page (forthcoming) also finds that discrimination against blacks decreases with income, holding constant price or rent. Moreover, Yinger (1991a) finds that agent discrimination against black renters declines as the income-to-rent ratio increases.

48. These results also are statistically significant. See the Appendix. These results differ from those of the 1979 Dallas audits (Hakken, 1979), which found higher discrimination against dark-skinned than against light-skinned Hispanics.

49. The relatively harsh treatment of dark-skinned Hispanics by Hispanic agents is consistent with the Denton and Massey (1989) finding that black and white Hispanics are highly segregated from each other. These results suggest that light skin is a source of status within the Hispanic community.

50. Because these results are puzzling, I experimented with a variety of different specifications for the skin color and accent variables. No other specification had nearly as much explanatory power. Moreover, these results are unaffected by alterations in the specification of the rest of the equation.

51. The one exception is Roychoudhury and Goodman (1992), which is discussed below. Another partial exception is Page (forthcoming), which is based on the HDS data and is discussed in previous footnotes. This study examines the ratio of units shown to minority auditors and units shown to majority auditors, which is an alternative way to consider the opportunity to discriminate.

52. These studies are Simonson and Wienk (1984) and Reid (1987). Less for-

mal tests based on the 1977 HMPS data also are conducted by Newburger (1989).

53. Several other coefficients are significant in Simonson and Wienk's (1984) inspections equation: female agents discriminate less, higher assigned income implies lower discrimination (holding house value fixed), discrimination is higher when the advertised unit is in a neighborhood with higher median house values and when the audit is in a metropolitan area with a lower black population. The racial composition of the advertised unit's neighborhood is not significant. They also present an equation for discrimination in inspections plus recommendations, which has far fewer significant coefficients.

54. Reid (1987) also estimates equations for discrimination in the number of units volunteered for inspection and in the number of units the auditor was invited to inspect. The invitations equation also found that black males encountered more discrimination and that older auditors and auditors with assigned children encountered less. In addition, both the oldest and youngest agents discriminated less than the middle-aged agents.

55. This study, Yinger (1986a), also presents sales and rental results for discrimination in number of units suggested as possibilities and in number of invitations to inspect. The results for these other types of discrimination are similar to those for inspections.

56. Galster (1990c).

57. Galster (1990c) and Newburger (1989) argue that agent perceptions are an unlikely explanation for audit results when both auditors request a unit in an integrated or minority neighborhood; after all, this request reveals the auditors' preferences. However, an agent may believe that the auditor was unaware of the racial composition of the neighborhood (and indeed auditors are instructed never to state neighborhood preferences explicitly) or may think that the auditor does not know what is good for her. In addition, an agent might believe that a white customer would have a hard time getting a loan in a minority neighborhood.

58. Roychoudhury and Goodman (1992). This study examines five types of agent behavior. Only the results for the number of units inspected are discussed in the text. For the most part, results for the other types of behavior are similar. One troublesome aspect of this study is that almost half of the observations were taken from complaint-driven, as opposed to randomly selected, audits. The probability of discrimination seems likely to be higher when a complaint is involved. However, Roychoudhury and Goodman state that their results are not significantly different when the complaint-driven audits are excluded.

59. Roychoudhury and Goodman (1992) use a different approach to marginal discrimination than the one presented here. Instead of finding how discrimination increases with the number of units available, they estimate how discrimination increases with the number of units shown to

the white auditor. This approach, which was originally implemented by Yinger (1991c), has the disadvantage that the number of units shown to the white auditor may be endogenous. However, Roychoudhury and Goodman argue that given their estimating technique, ordered probit, this approach leads to an underestimate of marginal discrimination. In any case, marginal discrimination has a different meaning in their study than in the work presented earlier in this chapter, so their estimate of 1.93 for marginal discrimination in number of units inspected (outside of the two neighborhoods mentioned in the text) cannot be compared to the results in Tables 9.1 to 9.5.

60. Shear and Yezer (1985) and Galster (1992c) provide brief discussions of the causes of lending discrimination.

61. Although the term "statistical discrimination" did not appear in the lending literature until the mid-1980s, the concept was discussed in Canner (1981) and Barth, Cordes, and Yezer (1983) and can be seen as an application of the theory of rational credit rationing, as developed by Stiglitz and Weiss (1980). For a more recent discussion of the concept, see Shear and Yezer (1985).

62. See the review of default studies by Quercia and Stegman (1992). Note that a scholar can control only for characteristics she observes, which may not be the same as the characteristics the lender observes. These studies do not definitively prove that minorities have a higher default rate when controlling for everything the lender observes.

63. This quotation, from ICF (1991, p. 6), is based on interviews with a large number of lenders.

64. The legal treatment of statistical and other forms of discrimination by lenders is considered in Chapter 10.

65. Recall from Chapter 5 that half of the home loans originated or purchased in 1990 were sold that year on the secondary market (Canner and Gabriel, 1992, p. 267). Adding 1990 loans sold in later years and loans sold by the small mortgage companies that were not covered in the 1990 HMDA data would bring this share to well over 50 percent.

66. As pointed out in Chapter 5, this implies that the secondary-market criteria play a crucial role in providing credit for minorities. Moreover, these criteria themselves are discriminatory if they include factors that are not related to loan returns but are correlated with minority status.

67. This quotation, from ICF (1991, p. 8), refers specifically to Fannie Mae and Freddie Mac. The information in the following sentence also comes from this report.

68. Galster (1992c) also points out that classical price discrimination could be at work in the mortgage market if lenders believe that, because of discrimination by other lenders, minority applicants have fewer options. This theory might explain why minority applicants are offered worse

terms, but it cannot explain why minorities are more likely to be denied loans.

69. Saying that prejudice is a possible cause of discrimination is not the same thing as saying that discrimination can exist only if agents are prejudiced. In my judgment, Becker's book (1971) helped economists to understand the difference between prejudice and discrimination, but ironically the literal statement in his book (repeated in 1993) defines prejudice and discrimination far more narrowly than do most subsequent scholars. To be specific, the book says

> If an individual has a "taste for discrimination" he must act *as if* he were willing to pay something either directly or in the form of a reduced income to be associated with some persons instead of others. When actual discrimination occurs, he must, in fact, either pay or forfeit income for his privilege. This simple way of looking at the matter gets to the essence of prejudice and discrimination (p. 14).

As the terms are used here (and by most scholars), however, prejudice does not necessarily lead to discrimination and people who are not prejudiced sometimes practice discrimination. Refer to the discussion in Chapter 1.

70. Shear and Yezer (1985) discuss the possibility that lenders may want to preserve their reputation with potential white customers, but they also point out that this incentive is likely to be weak because most people do not know who gave their neighbors a loan.

71. A more detailed discussion of all these linkages is provided in Chapters 7 and 8. Recall that because prejudice is endogenous, one could just as well say that segregation is caused by past discrimination in all relevant markets.

72. An enforcement auditing (or testing, as it is often called) program need not have this limit, of course, if it instructs auditors to ask about other available units.

CHAPTER 10: THE HISTORY OF FAIR HOUSING AND FAIR LENDING POLICY

1. For the history of antidiscrimination law before 1900, see Leigh (1992).

2. For a detailed discussion of the role of racial zoning, see U.S. Commission on Civil Rights (1973, p. 3), from which the figure in this paragraph is taken. Although racial zoning was outlawed by the *Buchanan* decision, some cities continued to operate in the same spirit by drawing city boundaries so as to exclude black neighborhoods. In the 1950s, for example, the city of Tuskegee "created an uncouth twenty eight sided municipal boundary that excluded all but four or five of the 400 black voters and *none* of the white voters" (Culp, 1993, p. 6). This practice was outlawed by the U.S. Supreme Court in the 1960 *Gomillion* v. *Lightfoot* decision. See Culp (1993).

3. This figure is from U.S. Commission on Civil Rights (1973, p. 3). For a detailed discussion of the history and role of race restrictive covenants, see Vose (1959).

4. For more on the *Shelly* decision, see Vose (1959).

5. Cited in Massey and Denton (1993, p. 189). Massey and Denton also describe the history of this executive order and of the regulations to implement it. Kennedy promised to issue such an order during his campaign but did not issue it until he had been in office for almost 2 years. According to Branch (1988, p. 679), the order was greatly "whittled down" from Kennedy's promise during the campaign to eliminate housing discrimination with the "stroke of a pen." It "excluded all existing housing, and all new housing except that owned or financed directly by the federal government." The early years of Kennedy's administration were marked by a dramatic struggle between the civil rights movement and the southern states. The Kennedy administration took some important steps to support civil rights, such as using the National Guard to help James Meridith enroll in the University of Mississippi, but moved with caution, in part because Kennedy needed the political support of the South. Branch gives a detailed account of this period. Kennedy's first strong public statement about civil rights, which is quoted in the Preface, was not made until June 9, 1963.

6. The passage of this law was aided by two events. The report of the National Advisory Commission on Civil Disorders (1968), which documented extensive disadvantage in the black community, was released right before the vote in the Senate, and Martin Luther King, Jr., was assassinated right before the vote in the House of Representatives. See Massey and Denton (1993).

7. Discrimination on the basis of sex was added in 1974 (Metcalf, 1988, p. 85).

8. This act, also known as Section 1982, was passed over the veto of then-President Andrew Johnson (Metcalf, 1988, p. 24).

9. In the 1975 *Zuch* v. *Hussey* case, the Supreme Court defined illegal steering as "the use of a word or phrase or action by a real estate broker or salesperson which is intended to influence the choice of a prospective buyer on a racial basis." This quotation and further analysis can be found in Lamb (1984).

10. This list of provisions draws on Massey and Denton (1993, p. 195). For a more detailed discussion of the provisions of FaHA, see Metcalf (1988, p. 86).

11. See Brown (1993, p. 6).

12. To be precise, the effects test says that if a plaintiff can show discriminatory effect, then the burden of proof shifts to the defendant to show that his actions were based on a business necessity and that alternative, non-

discriminatory actions were not available. These issues have been widely debated in fair employment law. The U.S. Supreme Court developed the effects test in fair employment law in the 1971 *Griggs* v. *Duke Power Company* and the 1975 *Albemarle Paper Company* v. *Moody* cases. The Supreme Court drastically reduced the burden of proof on defendants in the 1989 *Wards Cove Packing Co., Inc.* v. *Atonio* case, but Congress responded by passing the Civil Rights Act of 1991, which reestablishes the *Griggs* standard. For further discussion of these issues, see Bloch (1994, Chap. 4) or Cathcart et al. (1993).

13. Schwemm (1992, at 10-24, 10-25).

14. The details of the debate and the roles of Senators Dirksen and Byrd, who offered the key compromise amendments, are presented in Metcalf (1988) and Massey and Denton (1993). For a detailed discussion of the enforcement powers granted under the original FaHA, see Kushner (1989, 1992).

15. The Justice Department also can bring a suit under FaHA if the case involves a denial of rights to a group of persons and raises an issue of "general public importance." See Metcalf (1988, p. 5).

16. For a detailed discussion of the 1866 act, see Kushner (1989, 1992).

17. Kushner (1992, pp. 540–541).

18. For a review of these efforts, see Metcalf (1988).

19. These amendments actually passed the House of Representatives but did not pass the Senate before the Reagan victory. The new Republican majority in the Senate declined to follow the House's lead. See Massey and Denton (1993).

20. Cited in Kushner (1989, p. 1087).

21. The number of pattern and practice cases initiated by the Justice Department dropped precipitously when the Reagan administration took over. In fact, no cases were filed in 1981, two were filed in 1982, six were filed in 1983, and the total number of cases filed did not equal the yearly average during the Carter administration (sixteen) until 1988. Moreover, under President Reagan "most of the cases were trivial and were unlikely to establish broad precedents" (Massey and Denton, 1993, p. 207), and "President Reagan repealed long-awaited Title VIII substantive regulations promulgated in the last days of the Carter administration" (Kushner, 1989, p. 1086). The Reagan Justice Department also explicitly rejected the effects test, despite the strong support for this test in the courts. See Metcalf (1988, Chap. 2).

22. The 2-year limitation for private suits excludes the time during which a case is being investigated by HUD.

23. As discussed below, FaHAA allows judges in pattern and practice cases to impose civil penalties of up to $100,000 for repeat offenders, to award compensatory and punitive damages to aggrieved persons identified by

Justice, and to order injunctive and affirmative relief. Attorneys' fees may also be awarded if an aggrieved person hires a private attorney, intervenes into the pattern and practice suit, and becomes a plaintiff.

24. For a detailed description of the provisions of FaHAA, see Kushner (1989 or 1992). The discussion of FaHAA presented here draws heavily on the information in these two articles.

25. Failure to appear and testify and falsification or destruction of evidence are criminal offenses and are subject to a $1,000 fine or 1 year in jail.

26. In general, cases in which the region finds "no probable cause" are not reviewed by the HUD central office. Not all such cases escape scrutiny by the central office, however. Regions sometimes send such cases to HUD for review, regions sometimes make no finding in cases they send to the central office, the central office periodically reviews the performance of the regional offices, and the central office may sometimes ask to review controversial "no probable cause" cases of which it becomes aware.

27. The decision to give the OGC the authority to make a "cause" determination was included in the bill largely to satisfy the National Association of Realtors. This provision was seen as a way to moderate the impact of HUD's new enforcement role by placing the authority in the hands of an office that has broad responsibilities and no mandate to further fair housing goals, unlike FHEO. In fact, however, the secretary of HUD can instruct the general counsel to make fair housing a top priority (as Secretary Cisneros did originally) or shift to FHEO the responsibility for making "probable cause" determinations (a step taken by HUD in 1994). As a result, the long-term impact of this provision on the strength of the FaHAA is not yet clear.

28. Administrative law judges "can be removed only for cause after a hearing before another independent Federal agency, the Merit Systems Protection Board" (HUD, 1992, p. 11). Their decisions are enforced by the U.S. Court of Appeals. Administrative law judges are used by other branches of the federal government, especially the Social Security Administration.

29. For a real estate firm (but not an individual), the higher penalties are not allowed unless the second offense occurs within 5 years or the third within 7 years of the first offense. See Kushner (1989). ALJs also can provide injunctive relief.

30. See Kushner (1992).

31. This election must take place within 20 days of the time HUD finds "probable cause" and issues a charge of discrimination. Experience with the elections option is discussed in Chapter 11.

32. The election route costs defendants more because the longer time frame raises attorneys' fees. However, the Department of Justice files the suit

on behalf of the HUD complainant, who therefore has no attorneys' fees to consider unless he or she hires a private attorney.

33. Cases involving zoning or land use also must be sent to Justice.

34. For example, in the case of *Mountain Side Mobile Estate Partnership* v. *HUD* (1994), the secretary of HUD overruled an ALJ to support "disparate impact analysis," also known as the effects theory, which was discussed earlier. Justice filed a brief supporting HUD in this case. See Patrick (1994).

35. Remember that FaHA imposes a weaker burden of proof on the complainant than does the 1866 CRA, so the removal of the limit on damages broadens the circumstances in which damages can be obtained. Note that HUD does not pursue a complaint if the complainant has filed a civil suit that has gone to trial.

36. No civil penalties may be imposed in an "election" case sent to the Justice Department, but such cases have no limit on punitive damages, which ALJs cannot award.

37. Single-family houses are also covered if the seller (landlord) has three or more houses for sale (rent). Moreover, prohibitions against making statements that indicate an intention to discriminate or that indicate a preference for a non-minority buyer or renter apply to all housing units.

38. There is some evidence that this has occurred. The Assistant Attorney General for Civil Rights recently told Congress that the large number of cases based on familial status has "hindered our ability to address the problems of race and national origin discrimination" (Patrick, 1994, p. 4).

39. ECOA, like FaHA, is based on the effects test. As stated by the U.S. Senate Banking Committee in its report accompanying the 1976 ECOA amendments, "The prohibitions against discrimination on the basis of race, color, religion or national origin are unqualified. In determining the existence of discrimination on these grounds . . . , courts or agencies are free to look at the effects of a creditor's practices as well as the creditor's motives or conduct in individual transactions" (cited in Brown, 1993, p. 28).

40. Quoted in Schafer and Ladd (1981, p. 1).

41. See Bloch (1994, Ch. 4), Myers (1993), or Ashenfelter and Oaxaca (1987).

42. Interagency Task Force on Fair Lending (1994, pp. 6–7). The financial regulatory agencies are listed below.

43. This quotation is from the news release accompanying Interagency Task Force on Fair Lending (1994). According to this policy statement (pp. 7–8), in order to establish discrimination on the basis of disparate impact, an agency must show, perhaps with a "quantitative or statistical analysis," that a policy has a disparate impact on a protected group and that the policy in question cannot be justified on the grounds of

"business necessity." However, "Even if a policy or practice that has a disparate impact on a prohibited basis can be justified by business necessity, it may still be found to be discriminatory if an alternative policy or practice could serve the same purpose with less discriminatory effect." In any case, "Evidence of discriminatory intent is not necessary to establish that a policy or practice adopted or implemented by a lender that has a disparate impact is in violation of the FH Act or ECOA."

44. The Decatur consent decree is described in Turner (1993); other settlements are discussed in Chapter 11. A clear argument in support of applying fair lending laws to these lender activities can be found in Brown (1993). Additional recent cases are considered in Chapter 11. In a related development, a federal appeals court recently ruled that discrimination in home insurance is covered by FaHA. See HUD (1995).

45. As originally passed, ECOA applied only to discrimination on the basis of sex, but it was amended in 1976 to cover discrimination on the basis of race, religion, and national origin.

46. In addition, the OTS oversees 2,000 federally insured savings institutions and NCUA oversees 8,400 federally charted credit units. For additional information on the applicable laws and on the lenders supervised by each regulatory agency, see HUD (1992, 1994b).

47. Brown (1993) points out that most of the large lenders who appear to be avoiding minority neighborhoods are independent mortgage companies, including Sears Mortgage Corporation and Prudential Home Mortgage Company. For further discussion of this type of redlining, see Chapter 5. To help close this gap in the enforcement system, HUD and Justice began, in November 1993, joint investigation of some mortgage lending cases, primarily of independent mortgage companies.

48. In addition, the HUD Mortgagee Review Board can impose sanctions on lenders who violate ECOA in connection with Federal Housing Administration loans (see HUD, 1992).

49. See Riedman (1993).

50. See Lindsey (1993).

51. According to Interagency Task Force on Fair Lending (1994, p. 15), the federal banking agencies have "the authority to seek: Enforcement actions that may require both prospective and retrospective relief; and Civil money penalties . . . in varying amounts against the financial institution or any institution-affiliated party . . . , depending, among other things, on the nature of the violation and the degree of culpability." In addition, the FTC can impose "Injunctions against the violative practice; Civil penalties of up to $100,000 for each violation; and Regress to affected consumers" (p. 20).

52. Greenhouse (1993). As discussed in Chapter 11, this case also raises questions of coordination across agencies, as the Justice Department also

investigated the Shawmut Mortgage Company, a subsidiary of Shawmut National Bank. For information on other recent actions by the Fed, OCC, and FDIC, see HUD (1995).

53. See Riedman (1993) and Kushner (1992). ECOA was amended in 1991 to require referral of pattern and practice cases to the Attorney General.

54. There is some debate over who should handle mortgage discrimination cases. This issue is discussed in Chapter 11.

55. Enforcement efforts are discussed further in Chapter 11.

56. HUD (1993).

57. Reno (1993).

58. Quoted in Riedman (1993, p. 1).

59. See Ludwig (1993). The Office of the Comptroller of the Currency also set up a program of focused investigations, which investigated 20 lenders in 1993.

60. Cited in *Syracuse Herald-Journal* (1994, p. A5). An earlier speech by a member of the Fed Board of Governors made an even stronger statement. "Speaking for the Federal Reserve, no single consumer compliance issue is of greater concern to us, or to me personally, than assuring that the credit granting process in the institutions we regulate is totally free of unfair bias. Fairness in the assessment of credit applications — without regard to race, sex, or other prohibited biases — is absolutely essential to our nation's well being. Racial discrimination in particular — no matter how subtle, and whether intended or not — cannot and will not be tolerated. It harms individuals and it harms society." Lindsey (1993, p. 15).

61. Interagency Task Force on Fair Lending (1994, p. 1). The agencies that signed this statement are HUD, Justice, the five financial regulatory agencies, the Federal Trade Commission, the Federal Housing Finance Board, and the Office of Federal Housing Enterprise Oversight.

62. For a detailed discussion of the congressional debate over CRA and an analysis of congressional intent, see Fishbein (1992) or Canner (1981).

63. National League of Cities (1991, p. 8). This source also points out that twenty states have passed legislation similar to CRA.

64. For more detailed information on the anti-redlining provisions of FaHA and CRA and a discussion of the relationship between outcome-based and process-based definitions of redlining, see Barth, Cordes, and Yezer (1979) or Bradbury, Case, and Dunham (1989).

65. See Fishbein (1992) and National League of Cities (1991). In addition, supporters argued that the federal government had the right to enforce this obligation in return for providing deposit insurance.

66. As Bradbury, Case, and Dunham (1989) point out, a lack of mortgage

loans in minority neighborhoods also could be influenced by discrimination in housing markets or by actors in mortgage markets other than lenders, such as insurers or appraisers. CRA says that "even if the disparities in mortgage activity were not the fault of lenders, banks and thrifts would be expected to help correct the situation" (p. 4). This central presumption of CRA is not universally accepted. See, for example, White (1993). Other actors do not have the same affirmative responsibilities as banks and thrifts, but they are prohibited from practicing discrimination. Another justification for CRA is given by Lang and Nakamura (1993), who show that redlining may be the product of information asymmetries between lenders and borrowers and that it may be socially optimal to require both information sharing and lending in some neighborhoods.

67. This list is taken from National League of Cities (1991), which also presents the twelve specific assessment factors.

68. The text of this statement is presented in National League of Cities (1991).

69. National League of Cities (1991, p. 14). Fishbein (1992) reports that "from 1985 to 1988 only 624 (2.4 percent) of the 26,000 institutions evaluated for CRA purposes received poor grades (less than satisfactory or lower)" (p. 613).

70. According to the National League of Cities (1991, p. 15), "Most CRA observers agree that 'outstanding' ratings will be difficult to achieve." The impact of a rating below 'outstanding' on a lender's ability to act is not so clear, however.

71. The new rating system and disclosure requirements are described in detail in National League of Cities (1991).

72. Indeed, some analysts have argued that one of the strengths of CRA is that it does not alter patterns of credit allocation. See Canner (1982).

73. According to Fishbein (1992, p. 614), this merger request was turned down "partially on CRA grounds." Dreier (1991) reports that the acquisition of Continental Illinois, one of the nation's largest banks, was turned down because of "important deficiencies" in meeting CRA requirements.

74. For example, the Fed's recent rejection of an acquisition request by Shawmut National Corporation, which was discussed earlier, was based on Shawmut's possible discrimination against minorities loan applicants, not on CRA requirements. See Greenhouse (1993).

75. This phrase is from Fishbein (1992, p. 611).

76. See Fishbein (1992, p. 612) and National League of Cities (1991, p. 19). Examples of settlements can be found in Squires (1992, 1994).

77. According to Fishbein (1992, p. 612), information provided by the Center for Community Change indicates that "these agreements have resulted

in anywhere from \$7.5 billion to \$20 billion in targeted loan commitments to low- and moderate-income areas, far exceeding the conditions that would have been imposed by regulators."

78. One study of three Chicago banks cited in Fishbein (1992, p. 612) concludes that CRA loans "had resulted in almost no loan losses." Fishbein does not describe this study's methodology.

79. Cited in Polikoff (1986, p. 48).

80. Cited in Polikoff (1986, p. 48).

81. Both quotations are taken from Polikoff (1986, p. 48).

82. See, for example, Orfield (1986) or Galster (1991).

83. William Bradford Reynolds, Assistant Attorney General for Civil Rights during the Reagan administration said, "I don't think any government ought to be in the business to reorder society or neighborhoods to achieve some degree of [racial] proportionality." Cited in Polikoff (1986, p. 49).

84. The Supreme Court has taken this position in several cases in addition to *Linmark* and *Bellwood*. See Smith (1993).

85. Cited in Polikoff (1986, p. 51). The Court also ruled that the sign-banning ordinance went too far and was not permissible.

86. Cited in Polikoff (1986, p. 51). The *Bellwood* case is *Gladstone Realtors v. Village of Bellwood* (1979).

87. See Smith (1993) and Polikoff (1986).

88. The quoted phrases are from Smith (1993, p. 125).

89. This evidence was reviewed in Chapter 7.

90. This difficulty helps explain why Polikoff (1986, pp. 51–52) concludes that any integration ordinance that is "based on a determination that discrimination or its effects persist in the housing field . . . is likely to satisfy the compelling interest requirement," whereas Smith (1993, p. 125) concludes that "The most burdensome of these criteria appears to be the first."

91. This quotation, and the arguments in this paragraph, are from Polikoff (1986, pp. 52–53). The actual quotation includes the word "counseling" instead of "policy;" although Polikoff's analysis applies to any race-conscious policy, his conclusion focuses on race-conscious counseling.

92. Smith (1993, p. 126).

93. Smith (1993, p. 126).

94. Smith (1993, p. 126).

95. Starrett City is discussed at length in Chapter 7. Other cases are discussed in Smith (1993) and Goel (1990).

96. Smith (1993, p. 127). The courts have not accepted bans on for-sale signs under all circumstances, and one observer (Keating, 1994, p. 231) concludes that "These cases still leave open the circumstances under which the courts will accept or reject the legality of a total ban on 'for-sale' signs, especially if the specific or primary basis for the adoption of such a ban is racial transition rather than simple aesthetics."

97. See Smith (1993). A ban on real estate solicitation does not meet the strict scrutiny test under all circumstances. In November 1994 the Supreme Court "refused to hear New York State's appeal of a ruling that its regulations aimed at preventing blockbusting in racially mixed neighborhoods were unconstitutional"; these regulations barred "real estate agents from soliciting business in specified portions of New York City and Nassau County" (Greenhouse, 1994a, p. B5). The Court has not made clear when bans on real estate solicitation are acceptable.

98. Freiberg (1993, p. 237).

99. See Keating (1994). The case is *South-Suburban Housing Center* v. *Greater South Suburban Board of Realtors* (1991). See also Polikoff (1986), Smith (1993), and Zimmerman (1992).

100. This and the following paragraph draws on Vernarelli (1986). The case is *Hills* v. *Gautreaux* (1976).

101. Gautreaux-type programs are discussed further in Chapters 8 and 11.

CHAPTER 11: PUBLIC POLICY TO COMBAT DISCRIMINATION IN HOUSING: A COMPREHENSIVE APPROACH

1. National Advisory Commission on Civil Disorders or NACCD (1968, p. 1). This conclusion was not intended to deny that progress had been made. Instead, it was a warning that existing laws were insufficient to ensure that the position of minorities would continue to improve. A stronger interpretation is offered by Boger (1993, p. 1298), who writes "Neither *Brown* v. *Board of Education,* nor the Civil Rights Act of 1964, nor the victories of Dr. King, nor any of the hard-won accomplishments of the Second Civil Rights Revolution would suffice to heal America's racial wounds. Instead, the Commission implied, the riots were clear proof that antidiscrimination laws alone could never fully redress the residual injuries of slavery and segregation. Ironically, after a decade of achievement in court and in Congress, America faced a racial division more profound than any in its segregated past."

2. The Kerner Commission Report was not, of course, accurate in all the details of its predictions. See Boger (1993).

3. The term *white* is used to mean *non-Hispanic white.*

4. NACCD (1968, p. 395).

5. NACCD (1968, p. 396). As explained below, the integration choice also called for some ghetto enrichment.

6. This conceptualization was popularized by, but did not originate with,

the Kerner Commission Report. Indeed, the debate between development and dispersal can be traced back to the 1800s. See Peller (1990).

7. The phrase "gild the ghetto" appeared in the *Kerner Commission Report* (NAACD, 1968, p. 47): "The Negro society will be permanently relegated to its current status, possibly even if we expend great amounts of money and effort in trying to 'gild the ghetto.'" This phrase was popularized by Kain and Persky (1969).

8. In a review of his contributions to this debate, Kain (1992, p. 445) writes: "With the benefit of hindsight, our use of the term *dispersal* to describe our strategy was unfortunate, as many critics interpreted it as a call for the forced or involuntary dispersal of Afro-Americans from central-city ghettos. Nothing could have been further from our minds."

9. NACCD (1968, p. 396).

10. For an alternative effort to recast the debate, which also emphasizes the role of discrimination in housing, see Quigley (1994).

11. The impact of such programs on public support is illustrated by the fact that 58 percent of whites disagree with the statement: "Do you believe that where there has been job discrimination in the past, preference in hiring or promotion should be given to blacks today?" Only 28 percent of whites agreed with this statement. See Applebome (1993). This problem also shows up in two 1994 national surveys. In one, "a majority of whites, 51 percent, say they agree that equal rights have been pushed too far; in 1992, only 42 percent shared that view" (Berke, 1994, p. A21). In the other, "only 16 percent [of whites] endorsed preferences for blacks in hiring and promotion" (Shipler, 1995, p. E1). It must be added, however, that the strength of the negative white reaction to affirmative action policies illustrates the continuing power of our racial divisions. As deVries and Pettigrew (1993, p. 197) put it: "America's racist legacy contributes to the problems that sometimes accompany affirmative-action efforts. The irony is that it is this same legacy that requires affirmative action in the first place. Critics blame the programs for the problems, when they should point to the origin of these problems that affirmative action, properly administered and governmentally supported, could help to ameliorate." They also point out that affirmative action is popular in the Netherlands, where support for equal treatment is very high and racial and ethnic divisions are not too deep.

12. Many scholars have addressed these issues, particularly as they apply to employment. See Loury (1992) and Jencks (1992). Loury says: "Reliance on preferences to achieve minority representation in prestigious positions risks damaging the esteem of the group by encouraging the general presumption that the beneficiaries would not be able to qualify for such positions without the help of affirmative action." Steele (1994, p. 17) uses particularly strong language on this point: "Entitlements by race, sex, ethnicity and sexual orientation—categories that in no way

reflect merit—are at the root of the great social evils in American life. Aside from obvious unfairness of such entitlements, it is the distorted claims that groups must conjure to gain their benefit that absolutely require racism, sexism, anti-Semitism and all manner of collective animosities. Every such claim is backlit by the hatreds that try to make it singular and urgent." West (1994, pp. 95–99) also acknowledges that affirmative action may contribute "to the persistence of racist perceptions in the work place" but argues that it is still necessary "to confront and eliminate black poverty."

13. The application of this principle is more straightforward in some contexts than in others. It clearly is discrimination when a minority household is denied access to housing it can afford but an equally qualified white is not. As explained in Chapters 5 and 8, however, discrimination in mortgage lending and in employment are not so straightforward. It is discrimination to reject loans (or job applicants) on the basis of characteristics that are not associated with creditworthiness (or productivity) but that are correlated with race or ethnicity, but the determinants of creditworthiness (or productivity) are difficult to identify. This issue is at the heart of the current debate over affirmative action in employment and school admissions, to which we will return in Chapter 12.

14. A similar view is in Goel (1990, pp. 403–406), who argues that ceiling quotas inevitably stigmatize minorities and limit their access to housing.

15. A similar argument is made by Massey and Denton (1993, p. 227).

16. The Starrett City case is discussed at length in Chapter 7.

17. This principle cannot be implemented without deciding what is required to prove past discrimination. As explained in Chapter 10, the Civil Rights Act of 1991 reinstated the disparate impact or effects test, which says that if an employee can demonstrate that a policy has discriminatory effect, then the burden of proof is on the employer to show that the policy is nondiscriminatory and a business necessity. See Bloch (1994), Cathcart et al. (1993), and Myers (1993).

18. Some scholars have argued that the legacy of past discrimination can be very powerful and in fact that disparities between groups might not disappear over time even if all future discrimination were eliminated. See Loury (1987b).

19. Examples of employment and education policies that lessen disparities without discriminating also can be found. Some examples are presented later in this chapter.

20. As Galster (1990a) puts it, we must not confuse rejection of a particular *means* for obtaining stable residential integration with the continuing imporance of the *end* of stable residential integration. For a similar argument applied to affirmative action in employment, see Jencks (1992).

21. Similar arguments are made by Henderson (1975) and Wilson (1987, 1991). After presenting a list of social problems, Wilson (1991, p. 478) writes: "Because these problems are more concentrated in the inner cities as a result of cumulative effects of decades of racial subjugation, programs that aggressively address them will disproportionately benefit the underclass."

22. The term *disparate benefits* was suggested to me by George Galster. Another way to describe this approach is to say that it runs the "effects test" in reverse.

23. This result, from Orfield et al. (1993), is discussed in Chapter 8.

24. Several scholars have written in support of this principle in recent years. See Orfield (1986), and especially Galster (1990a, 1992a), on whom this section draws heavily. Massey and Denton (1993, p. 227) apparently disagree with this principle. They write "The most serious flaw of integration maintenance schemes . . . is that they do nothing to change the larger system of housing discrimination in the United States: they deal with the symptoms rather than the causes of residential segregation." As the following pages make clear, I believe that segregation itself is a cause and needs to be attacked directly.

25. These incentives and HDS evidence that they exist are discussed in Chapter 9.

26. Galster and Keeney (1988) show that urban areas with more segregation have a higher incidence of housing discrimination.

27. As explained in Chapter 12, the same argument applies to the labor market and to education.

28. Government support for integration has another, more technical justification. I (Yinger, 1992) show that, due to the power of the forces causing racial and ethnic transition, housing markets miss some opportunities for efficiency gains through integration. An efficiency gain is a change that benefits one group without hurting others. Efficiency gains from integration obviously are possible among minority and white families who prefer integration. As shown in Chapter 7, however, private markets may not sustain integration even in this case. Moreover, efficiency gains from integration are possible even if each white family is willing to pay more to avoid integration than each minority family is willing to pay to experience it. Consider, for example, a neighborhood containing 100 families, a set of white families each willing to pay $100 (per month, say) to avoid integration and a group of minority families each willing to pay $70 to live in an integrated neighborhood. Now compare integration at 60 percent minority with complete segregation. The aggregate benefit of integration for minorities equals the number of minority families, 60, multiplied by the benefit per family, $70, or $4,200. The aggregate cost of integration for whites equals the number of white families, 40, multiplied by the cost per family, $100, or $4,000. Thus,

minority families could fully compensate whites for living in this integrated neighborhood and still retain aggregate net benefits equal to $200. The intent of this example is to show that efficiency gains from integration are possible, not to support payments from minority families to prejudiced whites, which would be inappropriate. As discussed in Chapter 7, some communities provide subsidized mortgages or home equity insurance to give whites a financial incentive to stay in or move into integrated neighborhoods, but I do not support this type of policy at the federal level.

29. See, for example, Massey and Denton (1993) and Smith (1993).

30. See Galster (1990a). Galster writes: "Because 'equal-status' interracial residential contact is a fundamental means by which prejudices are eroded, and because prejudices of white real estate agents or their clientele are the root motivators for discriminatory acts in the housing market, attaining SRI [stable residential integration] becomes a means for attaining FOC [freedom of choice]" (p. 140). Downs (1973) was an early proponent of programs to promote integration but now (1992, p. 690) apparently believes that while policies "to promote both goals simultaneously. . . might be possible in theory. . . in practice. . . these two goals are indeed partially conflicting."

31. See Smith (1993), Kushner (1992), Lewis (1988), and Metcalf (1988).

32. This point also is made by Galster (1990a, p. 140), who writes "although certain means for achieving SRI [stable racial integration] clearly restrict FOC [freedom of choice], other means are neutral, and still others expand the range of choice." Examples of noncontradictory policies are presented later in this chapter. Goel (1990) makes a similar point by focusing on "anti-subjugation" as the overarching goal. "Subjugation" is defined by Goel as "subordinated status because of a lack of power" (p. 395), and "both color blindness and integration can either prevent or promote subjugation" (p. 397). Moreover, "Some integration measures . . . might subjugate because they stigmatize minority group members, reduce access to housing, or force integration beyond the level that minorities would otherwise choose" (p. 398). For a contrary view, see Massey and Denton (1993, p. 226), who write: "Although integration maintenance programs are consistent with the spirit of residential desegregation, ultimately they operate by restricting black residential choice and violating the letter of the Fair Housing Act. They limit black housing options either directly, by applying quotas, or indirectly through a series of tactics designed to control the rate of black entry."

33. For further discussion of this issue, see Yinger (1986b).

34. The Starrett City case is discussed in detail in Chapter 7.

35. See, for example, Kain and Persky (1969).

36. Recall that even though the Kerner Commission pushed the "integration choice," this choice as they saw it involved meeting both of these

objectives. HUD Secretary Cisneros also holds this position. He recently was quoted as saying: "Budget people, economic policy people and so forth, they just can't imagine that we could do very much along these lines of opening up surburban opportunities. They think that, well, you know, that this is hopeless. You're not going to be able to create that opportunity, so let's just focus on central-city development. But the truth of the matter is . . . you have to do both" (Montgomery, 1994).

37. As Goel (1990) points out, forcing minorities to live in integrated areas is a form of "subjugation."

38. For a detailed history of this debate in the minority community, as well as a strong argument against integration as a strategy for the minority community to follow, see Peller (1990). For a discussion of the pros and cons of integration for minority households, see Leigh and McGhee (1986).

39. Some scholars, including Downs (1992), believe that the forces causing racial transition are so powerful that any feasible actions to promote integration are doomed to failure. As this chapter makes clear, I disagree. One of the key sources of my disagreement is highlighted in the next paragraph.

40. Recall from Chapter 7 that many studies support the contact hypothesis, which says that prejudice is diminished by equal-status contact between groups.

41. Many African American and Hispanic leaders have emphasized the need for personal responsibility. Here are a few recent examples. Loury (1987a, p. 123) writes: "For too many blacks, dedication to the cause of reform has been allowed to supplant the demand for individual accountability; race, and the historic crimes associated with it, has become the single lens through which to view social experience; the infinite potential of real human beings has been surrendered on the alter [sic] of protest. In this way does the prophesy of failure, evoked by those who take the fact of racism as barring forever blacks' access to the rich possibilities of American life, fulfill itself: Emphasis on the determinative effects of the 'poisonous legacy' in the struggle to secure redress for past oppression requires the sacrifice of a primary instrument through which genuine freedom might yet be attained." In speaking about the importance of the family, Kweisi Mfume, chairman of the Congressional Black Caucus recently said: "It means taking responsibility and recognizing that the government can't and won't solve every one of our problems" (Seelye, 1994). In an afterword to the 1988 edition of her novel *The Third Life of Grange Copeland,* which was originally published in 1970, Alice Walker writes: "I believe in the soul. Furthermore, I believe it is prompt accountability for one's choices, a willing acceptance of responsibility for one's behavior and actions, that makes it powerful. The white man's oppression of me will never excuse my oppression of you, whether you are a man, woman, child, animal or tree, because the self that I prize

refuses to be owned by him. Or by anyone" (Walker, 1998, p. 345). Finally, West (1994, Chap. 1) talks about the need to combat "nihilism" among blacks by promoting "self worth and self-affirmation."

42. For other comprehensive sets of policy recommendations to deal with housing discrimination and its consequences, see Darden, Duleep, and Galster (1992) and Kain (1992, 1994).

43. For a detailed review of the Reagan record on civil rights, see Amaker (1988). Fair housing actions by the Reagan administration (and the previous three administrations) are described by Lamb (1992).

44. Support for state and local enforcement agencies was provided through the Fair Housing Assistance Program and the Fair Housing Initiatives Program, which are discussed below. The Reagan administration also greatly weakened the Voluntary Affirmative Marketing Agreement signed with the National Association of Realtors. See Metcalf (1988, pp. 20–21) and note 76 below. The Bush administration also initiated the Moving to Opportunity Program, which is discussed below. On the research front, the Housing Discrimination Study was funded by HUD during the Reagan administration, but its findings were, according to some observers, suppressed by the Bush administration. See Massey (1992). The treatment of the HDS results is somewhat puzzling given the fact that President Bush's HUD Secretary, Jack Kemp, had made fair housing one of his top five objectives and had supported fair housing in public service announcements on television.

45. President Clinton already has pledged a similar campaign against the important problem of teen-age pregnancy. See DeParle (1994).

46. Ifil (1994).

47. Quoted in DeParle (1993a, p. A16). Secretary Cisneros also supports the fifth principle when he says that policy makers must consider, in addition to racism, "other questions of behavior and individual responsibility." See also Cisneros (1994b). A statement by Reno (1993) was quoted in Chapter 5.

48. Although the message of racial healing has been fairly consistent from the Clinton administration, withdrawing the name of Lani Guinier for the position of Assistant Attorney General for Civil Rights and then waiting many months to submit another nomination, sent some mixed signals. Moreover, Republican leaders, who are often seen as being lukewarm or even hostile to civil rights, sometimes support intergroup understanding. For example, on the opening day of the 104th Congress, the new Republican Speaker of the House, Newt Gingrich, appeared to support integration when he said: "The greatest leaders in fighting for an integrated America in the 20th century were in the Democratic Party. The fact is, it was the liberal wing of the Democratic Party that ended segregation" (Gingrich, 1995, p. A19).

49. For an alternative catalog of fair housing and fair lending enforcement policies, see Downs (1992).

50. These figures are from HUD (1992, 1995). When complaints to state and local agencies are included, 54 percent of complaints are based on race and 11 percent on national origin.

51. Before the 1988 FaHAA was passed, 120 agencies were certified as "substantially equivalent" to the federal law. Many of these agencies were slow or reluctant to amend their laws to incorporate the provisions of this act. As of May 1993, for example, forty-one state and local agencies were certified as "substantially equivalent" to the federal law, and eight others were close to certification. In addition, twenty to twenty-five other agencies were in some stage of review. These figures were stated by Jackie Shelton, an official in HUD's Office of Fair Housing and Equal Opportunity, at the Home Mortgage and Lending Discrimination, Research and Enforcement Conference, Washington, D.C., May 18–19, 1993.

52. Only two of the states, Texas and North Carolina, have "full" status as substantially equivalent agencies; the other thirty-six have "interim" status. These figures come from HUD's Office of Fair Housing and Equal Opportunity, through John Goering. The share of complaints processed by state and local agencies increased between 1992 and 1993 after a 4-year decline (HUD, 1995).

53. The information in this paragraph in based primarily on interviews with several HUD officials in the fall of 1993. See also HUD (1995) and U.S. Commission on Civil Rights (1994), which includes a detailed evaluation of HUD's recent complaint processing efforts. The latter source (p. 221) emphasizes that HUD has been forced to undergo a "complete reorientation. . . from an agency devoted to resolving fair housing complaints through conciliation and voluntary compliance to one devoted to administrative enforcement. . . . HUD staff were required to learn how to make a case that could withstand scrutiny in a judicial setting." Moreover, this transformation was carried out with very limited funding.

54. These steps appear to be working. In FY1993, HUD reviewed 37 cases for prompt judicial action, conciliated 11 of them, and referred 8 of them to Justice. The courts granted relief in 7 of these 8 cases. See HUD (1995).

55. HUD (1995). Many of the conciliations and cause determinations in FY1993 apply to cases filed in earlier years.

56. Patrick (1994). According to Kushner (1992, p. 564), this high rate "may reflect the initial stern pronouncements of the administrative law court, lack of experience with the new system, or the desire for a time delay."

57. The ALJ or either party in a suit may "request a settlement judge to resolve fair housing complaints slated for administrative proceedings" HUD (1994b, p. 14).

58. The figures in this and the previous sentence are from HUD (1995). Two additional rulings in FY1993 went in favor of the defendant.

59. The 125 count is through August 23, 1994, so it leaves off over one month of the fiscal year. The figures in these two sentences are from Patrick (1994).

60. For example, 57 of the 125 elections cases are based on familial status, and, as noted in Chapter 10, "devoting such substantial resources to these cases hindered our [the Justice Department's] ability to address the problems of race and national origin discrimination" (Patrick, 1994, p. 4). The U.S. Commission on Civil Rights (1994) discusses the impact of limiting funding and of familial status cases on HUD's enforcement efforts.

61. To be declared a "substantially equivalent" agency for the purposes of FHAP, a state and local agency must not only have a law that provides equivalent rights, procedures, remedies, and judicial review to that provided by FaHAA, but must also employ practices and procedures that actually deliver substantially equivalent protection to victims of discrimination. See HUD (1994b or 1995).

62. Although this program was passed in the Reagan administration, it "continued an earlier HUD effort during the Carter administration" to help meet the Title VIII requirement that HUD turn over complaints to state and local fair housing agencies with "substantially equivalent" fair housing laws. See Metcalf (1988, p. 22).

63. This evidence is reviewed in Metcalf (1988, p. 22). For recent information on conciliation and other efforts by FHAP agencies, see HUD (1995) and U.S. Commission on Civil Rights (1994).

64. As explained in Chapter 10, FaHAA also makes a civil suit a more appealing route for a victim of discrimination.

65. HUD must either conciliate or prosecute cases with a "cause" determination. Inadequate funding would give HUD an incentive to push for weaker settlements or to make fewer cause determinations. Either step would be undesirable. Similarly, Justice must prosecute all "election" cases, but inadequate funding might result in inadequate case preparation or a push for weaker settlements.

66. In 1991, four secretary-initiated investigations were conducted, one of them jointly with the Justice Department, resulting in the filing of two secretary-initiated complaints and one pattern and practice suit. See HUD (1992, p. 8).

67. Two secretary-initiated cases were filed in FY1992 and three in FY1993. See HUD (1995).

68. These results are presented in Chapter 9. As discussed in Chapter 4, HDS also revealed how little is known about racial and ethnic steering and

about housing marketing. HUD-sponsored research on these topics would be very valuable.

69. The Justice Department also files several criminal cases each year that involve such acts of housing discrimination as arson or intimidation. See HUD (1994b, 1995).

70. All the information in this paragraph comes from Patrick (1994).

71. The testing funded under FHIP includes some pilot testing of insurance redlining. See Tisdale, Smith, and Cloud (1994). Recall that a "test" is an audit designed for enforcement purposes.

72. HUD (1995).

73. This example is from HUD (1992, p. 28), which also provides more information on FHIP. A detailed analysis of FHIP-funded testing activities is provided in Wienk, Simonson, and Smith (1994).

74. Galster (1990b).

75. Recall from Chapter 6 that the average time required for an HDS rental audit was only about 20 minutes for each auditor.

76. One voluntary connection to real estate brokers now exists. During the Ford administration, HUD and the National Association of Realtors (NAR) "signed a Voluntary Affirmative Marketing Agreement, VAMA, under which the industry, with HUD's financial backing, established a network of Community Housing Resource Boards, CHRB, to implement the law. By joining the CHRB group and promising to support fair housing, realtors could get HUD approval for FHA or any other government housing funds" Metcalf (1988, p. 20). These CHRBs were never effective, particularly after the VAMA was weakened significantly during the Reagan years, but they consumed up to 35 percent of the HUD fair housing enforcement budget. See Metcalf (1988, Chap. 2). What a poor use of resources! For recent information on the VAMA with NAR, see HUD (1995).

77. NAR, which has nearly 750,000 members, also runs programs to educate its members on their fair housing responsibilities. See HUD (1995).

78. More research on this type of broker discrimination clearly would be valuable.

79. Brokers who belong to suburban MLSs are likely to find it more economical to join up with real estate brokers who already do business in minority neighborhoods than to directly serve those neighborhoods themselves. This approach is therefore likely to expand the business opportunities of the minority and white real estate brokers who now serve minority neighborhoods.

80. As alternatives, the authority to impose fines could be given to the FTC, or the federal government could provide each state with a financial incentive to set up a CBA of its own.

81. HUD (1995).

82. As discussed in Chapter 10, these agencies are the Federal Deposit Insurance Corporation, the Federal Reserve Board, the National Credit Union Administration, the Office of the Comptroller of the Currency, and the Office of Thrift Supervision. See HUD (1995).

83. This information about enforcement efforts is from HUD (1995).

84. Greenhouse (1993).

85. According to the 1990 HMDA data, 42.9 percent of home purchase loans were made by mortgage companies. For government-backed mortgages, the figure jumps to 71.8 percent. See Canner and Gabriel (1992, Table 2). The 1990 HMDA data do not include all independent mortgage companies and therefore understate these percentages to some degree. They also do not cover department store mortgage departments, which also are regulated by FTC.

86. See HUD (1994b, pp. 24–25). In one case in FY1992, FTC obtained a consent decree against Paine Webber Mortgage Corporation, a large mortgage company, for not keeping records of rejected applicants, as required by ECOA. The decree called for a civil penalty of $10,000 and better record keeping in the future.

87. King (1994).

88. Patrick (1994, p. 7).

89. In March 1994, Justice also announced a settlement of an insurance redlining case against the American Family Insurance Group in Milwaukee. See Quint (1995). Under the terms of the settlement, this company agreed to invest $14.5 million in Milwaukee's largely black neighborhoods. This case represents a valuable broadening of Justice's enforcement efforts. Recall that evidence about insurance redlining is presented in Chapter 5.

90. The other two cases focused on discrimination in interest rates on unsecured loans; one involved discrimination against blacks by the First National Bank of Vicksburg, Mississippi, and the other involved discrimination against Native Americans by the Black Pipe State Bank in South Dakota. See Patrick (1994).

91. Patrick (1994, p. 9).

92. This quotation, as well as the following information on the Chevy Chase Federal Savings Bank case, comes from Patrick (1994, p. 8).

93. Patrick (1994, p. 10).

94. For further discussion of this issue, see Hansell (1994). The Justice Department's decision to investigate types of discrimination other than loan denial has caused complaints from some lenders and, as explained below, from some regulators. One lender is quoted (Hansell, 1994, p.

D18) as saying "The fair lending laws do not impose the obligation of being out there and establishing branches and having marketing. Justice is developing law by consent decree. There is no bank or savings and loan willing to stand up and go to court against them." As shown in Chapter 5, however, some lenders clearly discriminate in actions other than loan approval, and no lender is required to settle instead of going to court.

95. A third route for HUD participation is enforcement of compliance with HMDA data requirements. See Cisneros (1993).

96. HUD (1994b, p. 28).

97. See Reno (1993) and Cisneros (1993).

98. The Shawmut case provides one good example of the role of coordination. The Federal Reserve Board referred the Shawmut case to the Justice Department, as it is required to do for any pattern and practice case, and Justice conducted its own investigation of the Shawmut Mortgage Company, a subsidiary of Shawmut National Bank. This investigation was conducted jointly with FTC. One month after the merger was denied by the Fed, Shawmut reached a settlement with Justice in which it agreed to take corrective steps and to pay $960,000 to compensate black and Hispanic customers who had encountered discrimination. In my judgment, this case illustrates that the Fed and Justice have different enforcement tools. Other observers see a problem. As the newspaper article describing this settlement put it: "The settlement terms reflect a jarring difference between the approaches of the Justice Department and the Federal Reserve Board to the widespread complaints of lending discrimination at Shawmut" (Labaton, 1993, p. D1).

99. A third possible reason is that HUD is responsible for writing the regulations that implement FaIIA and the Fed is responsible for writing the regulations that implement ECOA.

100. See The Associated Press (1994a) and The Task Force on Fair Lending (1994), which states (on p. 21) that the participating agencies "will coordinate their enforcement actions and make every effort to eliminate unnecessarily duplicative actions." In addition, Reno (1993) describes a coordination effort between Justice and OCC. Efforts at coordination have been undercut somewhat by recent bickering, however. As described in Bradsher (1994), several regulators have complained about the aggressive enforcement efforts by Justice, and the Fed approved a bank merger in Florida despite letters from Justice about a pending discrimination investigation. The Comptroller of the Currency said "I think Justice's role, when a banking agency is doing a credible job, should be limited to accepting the referrals required by statute. Where the banking agency is doing a credible job, I don't think Justice should be a second regulator." An official from Justice replied "We have the authority to initiate cases on our own, without a referral from a regula-

tory agency." Other regulators have voiced additional complaints. A Fed official said that broadening settlements to opening branches in minority neighborhoods "is a potentially troubling matter" and an official from the OTS said that the Chevy Chase settlement "represents an application of the law that is untested in the courts." The regulators and Justice have since agreed to stop airing their disagreements in public and to hold meetings to resolve their differences.

101. Cushman (1993, p. D8).

102. A discussion of these comments, the revisions, and the latest proposal can be found in "Community Reinvestment Act Regulations" (1994).

103. "The lending test would evaluate direct lending as well as indirect lending through loan pools, subsidiaries, and the like. The service test would evaluate the bank's provision of branches in areas of low and moderate income, and the availability of credit services like counseling. An investment test would take into account investments in organizations that foster community development, small and minority ownership of business, and affordable housing." Cushman (1993, p. D8). The original twelve factors are discussed in Chapter 10. A provision that was dropped at the last minute would have required "lenders to collect and report information on the race and gender of their small business borrowers" Hershey (1995, p. A1).

104. The new rules also tried to lessen the paperwork burden by setting up expedited procedures for lenders with assets below $250 million, and by developing pre-approved plans that lenders could set up. See Cushman (1993, p. D8).

105. The ruling was made by the Justice Department's Office of Legal Counsel following a request for a ruling by the Comptroller of the Currency. See Karr and Novak (1994).

106. A story in *The New York Times* (Cushman, 1993, p. A1) claimed that "the proposal is the most important modification to equal lending enforcement since 1977." This claim was overstated, even before the sanctions in the proposal were ruled to be illegal. The proposed CRA rules may help to expand credit opportunities in minority neighborhoods, but as demonstrated by Justice's settlement in the Chevy Chase case, the recent rediscovery of mortgage lending discrimination and the 1988 amendments to the Fair Housing Act are likely to have a much greater impact on fair lending.

107. This step has been proposed to Congress. See King (1994).

108. See King (1994).

109. This approach also could be used to apply CRA-type requirements on home insurance companies and thereby to address insurance redlining.

110. Another method for rigging a study to show that there is no discrimination is to "control" for a variable that is itself contaminated by discrimi-

nation. For example, Zandi (1993) claims that the Boston Fed's finding of discrimination disappears when a variable indicating whether the applicant conforms to the lender's credit guidelines is used as a control variable. As Carr and Megbolugbe (1993) point out, however, the same discriminatory behavior that affects loan approval clearly affects the lender's own evaluation of whether an applicant meets credit guidelines! In fact, they show that blacks are far less likely to meet a lender's credit guidelines controlling for all observable credit characteristics. Hence all Zandi has done is shifted the effect of discrimination from one variable to another.

111. A similar proposal that applies to discrimination in employment is made by Jencks (1992, p. 69).

112. This program also is consistent with the line of argument in Goel (1990, pp. 400–402): it is designed to avoid placing stigma on minorities, restricting their access to housing, or forcing them to integrate.

113. An alternative approach would be to expand FHIP funding and make programs with the following characteristics eligible for FHIP. Whichever approach is taken, the program should include funds for technical assistance and evaluation, as well as for program support. Recall that the Supreme Court's tests are discussed in Chapter 10.

114. Goel (1990, pp. 406–410) distinguishes between "demand alteration" measures, which "seek to reduce minority demand or increase white demand" (p. 106) and "demand redistribution" measures, which treat all groups equally. This distinction is similar to the one drawn here, as the combination of antidiscrimination and race-conscious counseling is intended to expand, not restrict, choice. Freiberg (1993) also emphasizes that race-conscious housing programs should be "choice expanding."

115. A neighborhood should also be eligible for the maximum amount of funding if at least 27 percent of its population comes from each of three different racial or ethnic groups or if at least 20 percent of its population comes from each of four different racial or ethnic groups. For the purposes of this provision, the relevant groups are white, black, Hispanic, Asian, and Native American.

116. Recall from Chapter 7 that the Ohio pro-integrative mortgages went mainly to whites. Based on average preferences, whites are more likely than blacks to require incentives to move into an integrated neighborhood. Moreover, the effectiveness of this approach has not yet been established.

117. For a contrary view, see Galster (1990a, 1992a), Saltman (1991), or DeMarco and Galster (1993). For example, DeMarco and Galster propose federal income tax credits for people who make pro-integrative moves. Goel (1990, p. 411) argues that "Equity insurance plans stigmatize," but concludes that they are "acceptable" because "They may assist black

homeowners." I judge the costs of equity insurance to be greater than the benefits. To the best of my knowledge, no federal court has yet ruled on the legality of integration-enhancing payments to individuals.

118. In the Cleveland area, efforts to coordinate integration efforts across communities have met with limited success. See Keating (1994). Nevertheless, given the potential gains from expanding integration efforts into many communities, programs that attempt to promote coordination are worth supporting until we know more about what is needed to make coordination work.

119. Apparently the integration efforts in Shaker Heights and perhaps a few other places have benefitted from Community Development Block Grant funds. See Keating (1994, p. 169). However, no federal program has provided widespread support for these efforts.

120. A complementary argument is made by Freiberg (1993, pp. 234–5), who says that it is a "myth" that all "affirmative housing . . . programs emanate from strategies intended to 'maintain integration' or 'prevent resegregation' in areas that are racially diverse." Freiberg goes on to say that "an examination of affirmative housing programs throughout the country indicates a genuine diversity of origins and missions." The missions identified by Freiberg include supporting school integration, "promoting greater housing choice and racial diversity and improving human relations," and compensating for discrimination by local housing authorities.

121. Darden, Duleep, and Galster (1992) argue that efforts to promote integration will fail unless they are conducted in "the vast majority" of suburbs. I disagree. Efforts in a single community face serious obstacles, but a program that pushed every community toward integration is not politically feasible. I believe that the only hope for promoting integration is to give communities who want to try it the tools they need to succeed—with additional support for coordination and metropolitan programs.

122. This step also is proposed by Orfield et al. (1993).

123. This point is discussed at length in Chapter 8.

124. This quote is from Orfield et al. (1993, p. 23), who also point out that ESAA "provided billions of dollars for retraining teachers, supported early experiments in magnet schools, helped schools develop instructional materials reflecting the combinations of all parts of society, provided funds for human relations training, and funded many educational experiments."

125. Orfield et al. (1993, p. 23).

126. The Proviso West story is presented at the beginning of Chapter 8.

127. In a similar vein, Kain (1992, p. 452) calls for a program to "give gener-

ous subsidies to predominantly white school districts that agree to participate in voluntary interdistrict busing programs."

128. The connection between public housing and poverty concentration is presented in Chapter 8.

129. Recall that the link between discrimination and housing search is explored at length in Chapter 6.

130. Some early, small-scale studies found a small but significant impact of Section 8 on household mobility. See Gray and Tursky (1986), Stucker (1986). The largest and most recent study, however, finds no significant difference in the minority percentage or per capita income of origin and destination tracts for Section 8 participants. See Peterson and Williams (1994, p. 19) or HUD (1995). Peterson and Williams also point out that household mobility has been hampered by the slow speed with which new "portability" rules have been implemented. These rules allow the holder of a Section 8 certificate to use it in any jurisdiction where the public housing authority, PHA, has an agreement with the PHA granting the certificate.

131. (Davis, 1993, p. 249). Davis, who is Associate Director of the Leadership Council for Metropolitan Open Communities, which runs the Gautreaux Program, goes on to say that "the Section 8 Existing Housing Program has, at worst, contributed to increased segregation and, at best, continued the segregation status quo. Some observers feel that the conventional Section 8 Program is itself vulnerable to Gautreaux-based litigation."

132. This evidence is reviewed in Chapter 8. Additional evidence would still be valuable. Any new program of this type should include an evaluation component, preferably including random assignment of applicants to either a participant or control group.

133. Another strategy for improving employment outcomes of inner-city residents is to improve transportation links between the inner-city and suburban job sites. This type of program has met with success in a few cases (see Wartzman, 1993, and Hughes, 1993), and some analysts have argued that improving transportation is the best way to aid poor inner-city residents (again see Hughes, 1993). Although this approach appears to work when the conditions are right, I know of no evidence to support the claim that we could design a cost-effective national policy that links inner-city residential locations to typically dispersed employment sites.

134. For more on MTO, see Peterson and Williams (1994), Polikoff (1994), and Office of Policy Development and Research (1994).

135. The opposition is described in Carson (1994), Waldron (1994), and DeWitt (1995). As explained in Mariano (1994) and DeWitt (1995), the protests in Baltimore turned Senator Barbara A. Mikulski of Maryland, Chair of the Senate Appropriations Subcommittee for HUD, against the extension, and it was dropped by a Senate and House joint conference

committee on appropriations. DeWitt also points out the great irony of the events in Baltimore: The protesting communities "are too poor themselves to have been picked as destination in the program" (p. B10).

136. Bovard (1994) argues against extending MTO on the grounds that Section 8 moves "welfare recipients into affluent neighborhoods" or into luxury apartments and leads to crime and declining property values. In fact, however, Section 8 provides modest levels of support, and even in the Gautreaux program, which is by far the largest of the mobility programs tried up to now, the thousands of families that have received assistance have been scattered widely throughout the Chicago metropolitan area. Evaluations of the Gautreaux program have found no sign of trouble in suburban neighborhoods where recipients live. See Cisneros (1994a), Peterson and Williams (1994), Popkin, Rosenbaum, and Meaden (1993), and Rosenbaum et al. (1993).

137. For additional arguments in favor of expanding Gautreaux-type programs, see Massey and Denton (1993, ch. 8) or Schill (1994).

138. Brief discussions of the Choice in Residency program can be found in Peterson and Williams (1994) and Office of Policy Development and Research (1994).

139. For a discussion of this point, see Polikoff (1994).

140. The blueprint, HUD (1994a), from which all the quotations in this paragraph are taken, was offered as part of a package to trim HUD's workforce. See Gugliotta (1995). Converting public housing subsidies to household certificates was proposed by Olsen (1993). The HUD Blueprint replaces an earlier initiative to alter the way all federally assisted housing is marketed. See Peterson and Williams (1994) or Office of Policy Development and Research (1994). This initiative was built on the observation that tenant selection decisions in federally assisted housing currently are fragmented along both program and jurisdictional lines. It is not possible, therefore, for any public officials in the current system to promote integration throughout a metropolitan area. Instead, each official is limited to promoting integration in his program and jurisdiction. To eliminate this paralyzing restriction on integration policy, the initiative would have centralized tenant selection decisions for all programs in each metropolitan area. People would no longer apply to a public housing authority or to a particular Section 8 project, but would instead apply to a Metropolitan Authority for Federally Assisted Housing. This authority would tell them which units were available throughout the metropolitan area in each program. Moreover, this authority could coordinate efforts to upgrade a few " 'magnet' assisted housing developments, whose revitalization would retain and attract socioeconomic diversity and serve as the focus for broader community development initiatives" Office of Policy Development and Research (1994, p. 6). This approach also would expand resident choice and contribute to integration, but less so than the more recent initiative discussed in the text.

141. This approach also would eliminate an important catch-22 in current

public housing policy; namely, that a unit of public housing, no matter how deteriorated it is, cannot be demolished unless a replacement unit is built. See Schill (1994).

142. The extent of segregation in public and assisted housing is discussed in Chapter 7. The initiative discussed in the text is not the only way for the federal government to lessen segregation in federally funded housing. For example, HUD Secretary Henry Cisneros recently responded to a series of violent acts against the few black tenants at a public housing project in Vidor, Texas, by ordering the project to admit black tenants and to provide them with security. See *The New York Times* (1993) and Verhovek (1994). Other recent actions by HUD on this front are discussed in HUD (1995). Most of the debate about segregation in federally assisted housing has focused on site selection criteria (see Vernarelli, 1986, and Chandler, 1992), but because so little public housing is now being constructed, the site selection issue is almost moot. Chandler also discusses other methods for desegregating public housing. An initiative to lessen segregation in federally funded housing would also boost the federal government's standing to support integration in the private housing market.

143. No attempt is made to address programs to combat disparities in crime, criminal victimization, or health.

144. Follain, Ling, and McGill (1993).

145. This figure is from Follain, Ling, and McGill (1993), who also point out that switching from itemized deductions to adjustments (with no change in the maximum allowed) would cost the federal government about $8 billion.

146. See Stegman and Luger (1993), from which all the information in this paragraph is taken. The HUD Reinvention Blueprint of December, 1994 (HUD, 1994a), calls for consolidating this program with several smaller ones. This consolidation would give somewhat more flexibility to state and local governments but does not appear to represent a major change in this program. HUD (1995) points out that of the families receiving home purchase or rehabilitation assistance through this program in FY1993, 35 percent were black and 12 percent were Hispanic.

147. For a description and evaluation of existing programs to turn projects over to tenants, see Rohe and Stegman (1992).

148. For a description of the 1994 legislation, see Riddle (1994).

149. The same could be said for another well-known federal program—Head Start—and similar programs. For an evaluation of one such program, see Passell (1994).

150. Zuckman (1993). These figures apply to the version of the program that predated the 1994 legislation, which was called Chapter 1, but the allocation formula was not significantly altered.

151. The link between poverty concentration and educational costs is discussed in Chapter 8.

152. A similar argument is made by Orfield et al. (1993), who write: "It would be counterproductive to adopt a policy that has the unintended consequence of punishing schools that have managed to get poor students out of high-poverty schools and into schools with stronger educational programs" (p. 26). The general principle of avoiding grant programs based on variables that the recipient controls is discussed in Ladd and Yinger (1991).

153. This problem was widely recognized. It was highlighted, for example, by a recent U.S. Department of Education Report (1993), which says: "By prescribing the allocation of funds according to the number and needs of children to be served, the law establishes a perverse incentive: as achievement rises, funding decreases."

154. Celis (1994b). See also Riddle (1994).

155. For further discussion of this issue, see Zuckman (1993). Another feature of the old Chapter 1 that troubled many educators was that it pulled low-achieving poor students out of class for special instruction; as a result, participants often fell behind in their regular school work. Again, see Zuckman (1993). This feature has been eliminated in the new Title 1, which allows districts to try innovative teaching techniques. See Celis (1994b) or Riddle (1994).

156. For further discussion of these concepts, including methods for calculating cost indexes, see Downes and Pogue (1994), Ladd and Yinger (1991), or Ratcliffe, Riddell, and Yinger (1990).

157. For a recent review of this evidence, see Blank (1994).

158. The FY1993 budget for FHEO was $47.1 million (HUD, 1995). The following figure for FHIP also is from this source.

159. See DeWitt (1995).

160. Recall that this $4 billion figure is derived in Chapter 6.

CHAPTER 12: OPENING DOORS, OR HOW LIBERALS AND CONSERVATIVES CAN JOIN TO FIGHT DISCRIMINATION

1. National Advisory Commission on Civil Disorders (1968, p. 2).

2. See, for example, Orfield (1986) or Galster (1990a, 1992a).

3. Applebome (1993). Other, similar survey results were presented in Chapter 11.

4. This argument also applies to employment and school admissions. Segregated workforces and classrooms contribute to perpetuating racial and ethnic prejudice and discrimination. Hence, policies that promote workforce or classroom diversity clearly are warranted. I believe that affirmative action policy, which typically is viewed as a way to help individuals

who belong to a disadvantaged group, should be recast as "diversity enhancement," which treats all groups symmetrically. After all, diversity is enhanced by bringing whites into largely minority environments, just as it is enhanced by bringing minorities into largely white environments. Companies or universities that believe racial and ethnic diversity helps achieve their objectives should be allowed, and indeed encouraged, to consider diversity enhancement as a hiring or admissions criterion. Just as a company might hire applicant A instead of applicant B because her greater experience is seen to offset her lower grades, a company should be encouraged to hire candidates whose contributions to workplace diversity are seen to offset their somewhat lower qualifications on other criteria. This approach does not involve racial or ethnic preference because it is symmetrical; firms (or schools) with predominantly minority workforces (or student bodies) should be allowed to consider the extra diversity introduced by white employees (or students) when making employment (or admissions) decisions. This point on symmetry is missed by Jencks (1992, p. 60), who rejects the right of a white police force that wants more blacks to give preference to black applicants on the grounds that one would then have to allow a white police force that wants more whites to discriminate. As I see it, however, the argument is not that employers should be allowed to hire whatever racial or ethnic mix they want, it is that they should be allowed to take steps to increase the diversity of their workforce. Jenck's first example can be justified as a contribution to diversity, whereas his second example cannot.

5. Although the two policies proposed here build on the central principle of CRA, as explained in Chapter 11, they differ from CRA in that they allow the affected parties (multiple listing services and non-depository lenders) to form coalitions to help meet their CRA-type obligations.

6. Dissatisfaction with CRA extends to the Republicans in Congress, who recently submitted legislation that eliminates a community groups' standing to challenge a lender's actions if the lender has received a "satisfactory" CRA rating from a regulator. See Bradsher (1995). Since almost 98 percent of lenders receive a satisfactory rating (see Fishbein, 1992), this is a transparent attempt to scuttle CRA. This proposed legislation also exempts small lenders from CRA, which is a more drastic—and less appropriate—step than the paperwork reductions in the CRA regulations adopted in 1995. See Community Reinvestment Act Regulations (1994).

7. As explained in Chapter 11, one very promising Gautreaux-type program, called Moving to Opportunity, which was passed during the Bush administration, ran into political trouble in some Baltimore suburbs in 1994 and was killed in Congress. This outcome was particularly ironic because under the rules of the program participants were not allowed to move into the protesting suburbs. See DeWitt (1995). In any case, this experience shows that programs of this type must be accompanied by coalition building and good information.

8. See, for example, Wilson (1991).

Abariotes, Andriana, Samuel L. Myers, Jr., Lekha Subaiya, and Nathan Til-ler. 1994. "Disparities in Mortgage Lending in the Upper Midwest: Does Discrimination Exist?" Paper presented at the Western Economics Association annual meetings, July.

Abrams, Charles. 1955. *Forbidden Neighbors: A Study of Prejudice in Housing.* New York: Harper & Row.

Albemarle Paper Company v. *Moody,* 422 U.S. 405 (1975).

Allman, William F. 1994. "Why IQ Isn't Destiny." *U.S. News and World Report,* October 24, p. 73.

Amaker, Norman C. 1988. *Civil Rights and the Reagan Administration.* Washington, D.C.: The Urban Institute Press.

Anderson, Elijah. 1985. "Race and Neighborhood Transition." In *The New Urban Reality,* edited by P. E. Peterson. Washington, D.C.: The Urban Institute Press, pp. 99–127.

———. **1990.** *Streetwise: Race, Class, and Change in an Urban Community.* Chicago: University of Chicago Press.

Applebome, Peter. 1993. "Racial Divisions Persist 25 Years After King Killing." *The New York Times,* April 4, p. 16.

Arvey, Richard D., and Robert H. Foley. 1988. *Fairness in Selecting Employees,* 2nd Edition. Reading, MA: Addison-Wesley.

Arvey, Richard D., et al. 1994. "Mainstream Science on Intelligence." *The Wall Street Journal,* December 13, Op-Ed Page.

Ashenfelter, Orley, and Ronald Oaxaca. 1987. "The Economics of Discrimination: Economists Enter the Courtroom." *American Economic Review* 77 (May): 321–325.

The Associated Press. 1993. "Court Rules Fleet Loans Were Unethical, Not Illegal." *Syracuse Herald-Journal*, June 15, p. B8.

———. 1994a. "Agency Tells Banks to Quit Unintentional Bias." *Syracuse Herald-Journal*, March 9, p. B10.

———. 1994b. "Blacks Face Bias in Loans." *Syracuse Herald-Journal*, October 27, p. C8.

———. 1994c. "Insurers Bypass the Poor: Study." *Syracuse Herald-Journal*, December 23, p. B4.

———. 1995. "Banks Aren't Biased, New Study Suggests." *Syracuse Herald-Journal*, January 27, 1995, p. B5.

Avery, Robert B., Patricia E. Beeson, and Mark S. Sniderman. 1994a. "Accounting for Racial Differences in Housing Credit Markets." Working Paper Series 93-09 (Revised October 1994). Cleveland: Federal Reserve Bank of Cleveland.

———. 1994b. "Underserved Mortgage Markets: Evidence from HMDA Data." Working Paper Series 94–16. Cleveland: Federal Reserve Bank of Cleveland.

Ayers, Drummond. 1994. "New Fears for California's Undocumented Aliens." *The New York Times*, November 21, p. A10.

Ayres, Ian, and Peter Siegelman. 1992. "Race and Gender Discrimination in Bargaining for a New Car." *American Economic Review 85* (June): 304–321.

Bacon, Kenneth H. 1993. "U.S. to Use 'Testers' in New Campaign on Discrimination in Mortgage Lending." *The Wall Street Journal*, May 6, p. A2.

Baldwin, Marjorie, and William G. Johnson. 1993. "Estimating the Employment Effects of Wage Discrimination." *Review of Economics and Statistics 74* (3): 446–455.

Barrick Realty Inc. v. *City of Gary, Ind.*, 354 F. Supp. 126 (1973), appealed, 91 F. 2d 161 (7th Cir. 1974).

Barth, James R., Joseph J. Cordes, and Anthony M.J. Yezer. 1979. "Financial Institution Regulations, Redlining, and Mortgage Markets." In *The Regulation of Financial Institutions*, Conference Series No. 21, Federal Reserve Bank of Boston (October), pp. 101–143.

———. 1983. "An Analysis of Informational Restrictions on the Lending Decisions of Financial Institutions." *Economic Inquiry 21* (July): 349–359.

Becker, Gary S. 1971. *The Economics of Discrimination*, 2nd ed. Chicago: University of Chicago Press.

———. 1993. "The Evidence Against Banks Doesn't Prove Bias." *Business Week*, April 19.

Bennett, Claudette E. 1993. *The Black Population in the United States: March*

1992. U.S. Bureau of the Census, Current Population Reports, P20-471. Washington, D.C.: U.S. Government Printing Office.

Berger, Joseph. 1993. "Deal Reached in Westchester Housing Suit." *The New York Times,* September 29, p. B1.

Berke, Richard L. 1994. "U.S. Voters Focus on Selves, Poll Says." *The New York Times,* September 21, p. A16.

Berkovec, James, Glenn Canner, Stuart Gabriel, and Timothy Hannan. 1994. "Race, Redlining, and Residential Mortgage Loan Performance." *Journal of Real Estate Finance and Economics 9* (November): 263–294.

———. **1995.** "Discrimination, Default, and Loss in FHA Mortgage Lending." Paper Presented at the American Real Estate and Urban Economics Association Annual Meetings, January.

Berry, Brian J.L. 1979. *The Open Housing Question: Race and Housing in Chicago, 1966–1976.* Cambridge, MA: Ballinger.

Bianchi, Suzanne M., Reynolds Farley, and Daphne Spain, 1982. "Recent Inequalities in Housing: An Examination of Recent Trends." *Demography 19* (February): 37–51.

Bickford, Adam, and Douglas S. Massey. 1991. "Segregation in the Second Ghetto: Racial and Ethnic Segregation in American Public Housing, 1977." *Social Forces 69* (June): 1011–1036.

Bissinger, H.G. 1994. "When Whites Flee." *The New York Times Magazine,* May 29, 1994, pp. 26–33, 43, 50, 53–54, 56.

Black, Harold A., and Robert L. Schweitzer. 1985. "A Canonical Analysis of Mortgage Lending Terms: Testing for Lending Discrimination at a Commercial Bank." *Urban Studies 22:* 13–19.

Black, Harold A., Robert L. Schweitzer, and Lewis Mandell. 1978. "Discrimination in Mortgage Lending." *American Economic Review 68* (May): 186–191.

Blair, John P., and Rudy H. Fichtenbaum. 1992. "Changing Black Employment Patterns." In *The Metropolis in Black and White: Place, Power and Polarization,* edited by G. C. Galster and E. W. Hill. New Brunswick, NJ: Center for Urban Policy Research, pp. 72–92.

Blair, William G. 1984. "Accord in Minority Suit Provides for More Subsidized Apartments." *The New York Times,* May 3, p. B4.

Blakeslee, Sandra. 1994. "Concentrations of Lead in Blood Supply Drop Steeply." *The New York Times,* July 27, p. A18.

Blank, Rebecca M. 1994. "The Employment Strategy: Public Policies to Increase Work and Earnings." In *Confronting Poverty,* edited by S.H. Danziger, G. D. Sandefur, and D.H. Weinberg. Cambridge, MA: Harvard University Press, pp. 168–204.

Bloch, Farrell. 1994. *Anti-Discrimination Law and Minority Employment.* Chicago: University of Chicago Press.

Bloom, David E., and Mark R. Killingsworth. 1983. "Pay Discrimination Research and Litigation: The Use of Regression." *Industrial Relations 21* (Fall): 318–339.

Bloom, David E., Beth Preiss, and James Trussell. 1983. "Mortgage Lending Discrimination and the Decision to Apply: A Methodological Note." *AREUEA Journal 11* (1): 97–103.

Blossom, Teresa, David Everett, and John Gallagher. 1988. "Detroit Banking: The Race for Money." *The Detroit Free Press,* August 12.

Board of Education v. *Dowell,* 498 U.S. 237 (1991).

Board of Governors of the Federal Reserve System. 1993. *Report to the Congress on Community Development Lending by Depository Institutions.* Washington, D.C.: Board of Governors of the Federal Reserve System, October.

Boger, John Charles. 1993. "Race and the American City: The Kerner Commission in Retrospect—An Introduction." *North Carolina Law Review 71* (June): 1289–1349.

The Boston Globe. 1993. "Names and Numbers: Name Game a Paradox for Minorities." *Syracuse Herald American,* December 12, p. C8.

Bound, John, and Richard B. Freeman. 1992. "What Went Wrong? The Erosion of Relative Earnings and Employment Among Young Black Men in the 1980s." *Quarterly Journal of Economics 107* (February): 201–232.

Bovard, James. 1994. "Clinton's Wrecking Ball for the Suburbs." *The Wall Street Journal,* August 4, Op-Ed Page.

Boyer, Ernest. 1992. *School Choice.* Princeton, NJ: Carnegie Foundation for the Advancement of Teaching.

Bradbury, Katharine L., Karl E. Case, and Constance R. Dunham. 1989. "Geographic Patterns of Mortgage Lending in Boston, 1982–87." *New England Economic Review* (September/October): 3–30.

Bradford, Calvin. 1979. "Financing Home Ownership: The Federal Role in Neighborhood Decline." *Urban Affairs Quarterly 14* (March): 313–335.

Bradley v. *Milliken,* 418 U.S. 717 (1974).

Bradsher, Keith. 1994. "Regulators Join Banks in Protesting U.S. Discrimination Suits. *The New York Times,* October 30, p. 34.

———. 1995. "Republicans Seek a Cutback in Lending Rules for Banks." *The New York Times,* March 31, p. D1.

Branch, Taylor. 1988. *Parting the Waters: America in the King Years: 1954–1963.* New York: Simon & Schuster.

Brenner, Joel Glenn, and Liz Spayd. 1993. "A Pattern of Bias in Mortgage Loans: Statistics Show Blacks at a Disadvantage." *The Washington Post,* June 6.

Brief for NAACP. 1992. Brief for Dekalb County, Georgia, Branch of the NAACP, et al., as Amici Curiae in Support of Respondents app. at pp. 1a–33a, *Freemen* v. *Pitts,* 112 S.Ct. 1430 (1992).

Brimelow, Peter. 1993. "Racism at Work?" *National Review,* April 12, p. 42.

Brimelow, Peter, and Leslie Spencer. 1993. "The Hidden Clue." *Forbes,* January 4, p. 48.

Brown, Jonathan. 1993. *Racial Redlining: A Study of Racial Discrimination by Banks and Mortgage Companies in the United States.* Washington, D.C.: Essential Information, Inc.

Brown v. *Board of Education,* 347 U.S. 483 (1954).

Browne, Lynn E. 1993. "Boston Fed Study Shows Race Bias." *The Wall Street Journal,* Letter to the Editor, September 21, p. A23.

Browne, Lynn E., James McEneaney, and Geoffrey M.B. Tootell. 1993. "Response to *Wall Street Journal* Op-ed Article." Unpublished manuscript.

Buchanan v. *Warley,* 245 U.S. 60 (1917).

Buist, Henry, Isaac F. Megbolugbe, and Tina R. Trent. "Racial Home-ownership Patterns, the Mortgage Market, and Public Policy." *Journal of Housing Research* 5 (1): 91–116.

Bullard, Robert D. 1992. "Housing Problems and Prospects for Blacks in Houston." In *The Housing Status of Black Americans,* edited by W.A. Leigh and J.B. Stewart. New Brunswick, NJ: Transaction Publishers, pp. 175–194.

Butters, Robert D. 1993. "The Real Estate Industry's View of Audit Results: Comments." In *Clear and Convincing Evidence,* edited by M. Fix and R. J. Struyk. Washington, D.C.: The Urban Institute Press, pp. 153–163.

Byers, Kevin. 1994. *Fast Cash for Homeowners: A Study of Mortgage Lending by Consumer Finance Companies in the Richmond, VA Metropolitan Area.* Richmond: Telamon Corporation.

Cain, Glen G. 1986. "The Economic Analysis of Labor Market Discrimination: A Survey." In *Handbook of Labor Economics,* Volume I, edited by O. Ashenfelter and R. Layard. New York: Elsevier Science Publishers, pp. 693–785.

Calem, Paul S. 1993. "The Delaware Valley Mortgage Plan: Extending the Reach of Mortgage Lenders." *Journal of Housing Research* 4 (2): 337–358.

Canner, Glenn. 1981. "Redlining and Mortgage Lending Patterns." In *Research in Urban Economics,* edited by J.V. Henderson. Greenwich, CT: JAI Press, pp. 67–101.

———. **1982.** "The Community Reinvestment Act and Credit Allocation." Staff Study No. 117. Washington, D.C.: Board of Governors of the Federal Reserve System, June.

Canner, Glenn B., and Stuart A. Gabriel. 1992. "Market Segmentation and

Lender Specialization in the Primary and Secondary Mortgage Markets." *Housing Policy Debate* 3 (2): 241–329.

Canner, Glenn B., Stuart A. Gabriel, and J. Michael Woolley. 1991. "Race, Default Risk and Mortgage Lending: A Study of the FHA and Conventional Loan Markets." *Southern Economic Journal* 58 (July): 249–261.

Carr, James H., and Isaac F. Megbolugbe. 1993. "The Federal Reserve Bank of Boston Study on Mortgage Lending Revisited." *Journal of Housing Research* 4 (2): 277–313.

Carson, Larry. 1994. "Hayden Tries to Stall City Relocations." *The Baltimore Sun*, August 30.

Cathcart, David A., Leon Friedman, Marrick T. Rossein, Mark Snyderman, and Steven H. Steinglass. 1993. *The Civil Rights Act of 1991*. Philadelphia: American Law Institute—American Bar Association Committee on Continuing Professional Education.

Cavalli-Sforza, Luigi L., Paolo Menozzi, and Alberto Piazza. 1993. "Demic Expansions and Human Evolution." *Science* 259 (January): 639–646.

Celis, William, 3rd. 1994a. "Kansas City's Widely Debated Desegregation Experiment Reaches the Supreme Court." *The New York Times*, January 11, p. B7.

———. 1994b. "Schools to Get Wide License on Spending Federal Money Under New Education Law." *The New York Times*, October 19, p. B12.

Center for Community Change. 1980. *Response to Crisis: A Study of Public Policy Toward Neighborhoods and Fair Housing*. Chicago: Center for Community Change.

Chamberlain, Gary. 1980. "Analysis of Covariance with Qualitative Data." *Review of Economic Studies* 47 (January): 225–238.

Chambers, Daniel N. 1992. "The Racial Housing Price Differential and Racially Transitional Neighborhoods." *Journal of Urban Economics* 32 (September): 214–232.

Chandler, Mittie Olion. 1992. "Public Housing Desegregation: What Are the Options?" *Housing Policy Debate* 3 (2): 509–534.

Cisneros, Henry G. 1993. Testimony before the Committee on Banking, Housing, and Urban Affairs, United States Senate, November 4.

———. 1994a. "HUD Program Not Wrecking Suburbs." *The Wall Street Journal*, Letter to the Editor, August 17, p. A13.

———. 1994b. "Rights and Responsibilities: The Health of the Urban Polity." *Vital Speeches of the Day* 60 (June 15), pp. 521–524.

Clark, Kenneth B. 1965. *Dark Ghetto: Dilemmas of Social Power*. New York: Harper & Row.

Clark, William A.V. 1986. "Residential Segregation in American Cities." *Population and Policy Review* 5: 95–127.

———. 1988. "Understanding Residential Segregation in American Cities: Interpreting the Evidence: Reply to Galster." *Population and Policy Review 7*: 113–121.

———. 1989. "Residential Segregation in American Cities: Common Ground and Differences in Interpretation." *Population and Policy Review 8*: 193–197.

———. 1991. "Residential Preferences and Neighborhood Racial Segregation: A Test of the Schelling Segregation Model." *Demography 28* (February): 1–19.

The Cleveland Foundation. 1988. "Keeping the Trust: A Quarterly Report" (Fall). Cleveland: The Cleveland Foundation.

Clotfelter, Charles T. 1979. "School Desegregation as Urban Policy." In *Current Issues in Urban Economics,* edited by P. Mieszkowski and M. Straszheim. Baltimore: The Johns Hopkins University Press, pp. 359–387.

Cochran, W.G. 1977. *Sampling Techniques,* 3rd Ed. New York: Wiley.

Coe, Michael D. 1994. "The Language Within Us." *The New York Times,* Book Review, February 27, pp. 7–8.

Cohany, Sharon R., Ann E. Polivka, and Jennifer M. Rothgeb. 1994. "Revisions in the Current Population Survey Effective January 1994." *Employment and Earnings 41* (February): 13–35.

"Community Reinvestment Act Regulations." 1994. *Federal Register 59* (October 7): 51, 232–251.

Connor, Walker. 1985. "Who Are the Mexican-Americans: A Note on Comparability." In *Mexican-Americans in Comparative Perspective,* edited by W. Conner. Washington, D.C.: The Urban Institute Press, pp. 2–28.

Corcoran, Mary, Roger Gordon, Debrah McLauren, and Gary Solon. 1992. "The Association Between Men's Economic Status and Their Family and Community Origins." *Journal of Human Resources 27* (Fall): 575–601.

Coulson, N. Edward. 1991. "Tests of the Monocentric Model." *Land Economics 67* (August): 299–307.

Council of Economic Advisers. 1994. *Annual Report.* Washington, D.C.: U.S. Government Printing Office.

Courant, Paul N. 1978. "Racial Prejudice in a Search Model of the Urban Housing Market." *Journal of Urban Economics 5* (July): 329–345.

Cromwell, Brian A. 1990. "Pro-Integrative Subsidies and Their Effects on Housing Markets." Working Paper No. 9018. Cleveland: Federal Reserve Bank of Cleveland.

Cross, Harry, with Genevieve Kenney, Jane Mell, and Wendy Zimmermann. 1990. *Employer Hiring Practices: Differential Treatment of Hispanic and Anglo Job Seekers.* Urban Institute Report 90-4. Washington, D.C.: The Urban Institute Press.

Cross, Stephen. 1993. "Discrimination Studies: How Critical Are Default Rates?" Paper Presented at Home Mortgage Lending and Discrimination: Research and Enforcement Conference, sponsored by the U.S. Department of Housing and Urban Development, Washington, D.C., May.

Culp, Jerome McCristal, Jr. 1993. "Dollars Are Not Enough When Political Power Is on the Mind: The History of Legal Discrimination in Housing." Paper presented at the Colloquium on Race, Poverty, and Housing, University of Minnesota, Minneapolis, December 3.

Cushman, John H., Jr. 1993. "Clinton Proposes Tough New Rules on Bias by Banks." *The New York Times,* December 9, p. A1.

Danziger, Sheldon H., and Daniel H. Weinberg. 1994. "The Historical Record: Trends in Family Income, Inequality, and Poverty." In *Confronting Poverty,* edited by S.H. Danziger, G.D. Sandefur, and D.H. Weinberg. Cambridge, MA: Harvard University Press, pp. 18–50.

Darden, Joe T., Harriet Orcutt Duleep, and George C. Galster. 1992. "Civil Rights in Metropolitan America." *Journal of Urban Affairs 14* (3/4): 469–496.

Darity, William A., Jr., and Samuel L. Meyers, Jr. 1983. "Changes in Black Family Structure: Implications for Welfare Dependency." *American Economic Review 73* (May): 59–64.

Darity, William A., Jr., and William Winfrey. 1994. "Interethnic Disparities Across Census Divisions, 1980–90." *Cityscape: A Journal of Policy Development and Research 1* (August): 153–191.

Davis, Mary. 1993. "The Gautreaux Assisted Housing Program." In *Housing Markets and Residential Mobility,* edited by G.T. Kingsley and M.A. Turner. Washington, D.C.: The Urban Institute Press, pp. 243–253.

Dedman, B. 1988. "The Color of Money." *The Atlanta Journal and Constitution,* May 1–16.

DeMarco, Donald L., and George C. Galster. 1993. "Prointegrative Policy: Theory and Practice." *Journal of Urban Affairs 15* (2): 141–160.

Dent, David J. 1992. "The New Black Suburbs." *The New York Times Magazine,* June 14, pp. 18–25.

Denton, Nancy A. 1994. "Are African Americans Still Hypersegregated?" In *Residential Apartheid: The American Legacy,* edited by R. Bullard, J.E. Grigsby, III, and Charles Lee. Los Angeles: CAAS Publications, University of California, pp. 49–81.

Denton, Nancy A., and Douglas S. Massey. 1989. "Racial Identity Among Caribbean Hispanics: The Effect of Double Minority Status on Residential Segregation." *American Sociological Review 54* (October): 790–808.

DeParle, Jason. 1993a. "Housing Secretary Carves Out Role as a Lonely Clarion Against Racism." *The New York Times,* July 8, p. A16.

———. 1993b. "An Underground Railroad from Projects to Suburbs." *The New York Times,* December 1, p. A1.

———. 1994. "President to Campaign Against Teen-Age Pregnancy." *The New York Times,* June 10, p. A12.

DeWitt, Karen. 1994. "Wave of Suburban Growth Is Being Fed by Minorities." *The New York Times,* August 15, 1994, p. A1.

———. 1995. "Housing Voucher Test in Maryland Is Scuttled by a Political Firestorm." *The New York Times,* March 28, p. B10.

Diamond, Jared. 1994a. "How Africa Became Black." *Discover* (February): 72–81.

———. 1994b. "Race Without Color." *Discover 15* (November): 83–89.

Dobzhansky, Theodosius. 1962. *Mankind Evolving.* New Haven: Yale University Press.

Downes, Thomas A., and Thomas F. Pogue. 1994. "Adjusting School Aid Formulas for the Higher Cost of Educating Disadvantaged Students." *National Tax Journal 47* (March): 89–110.

Downs, Anthony. 1973. *Opening Up the Suburbs: An Urban Strategy for America.* New Haven, CT: Yale University Press.

———. 1992. "Policy Directions Concerning Racial Discrimination in U.S. Housing Markets." *Housing Policy Debate 3* (2): 685–745.

Dreier, Peter. 1991. "Redlining Cities: How Banks Color Community Development." *Challenge* (November/December): 15–23.

Duffy, Michael. 1993. "Covert Discrimination Uncovered by Testing." *The Wall Street Journal,* letter to the editor, June 1, p. A13.

Ellwood, David. 1986. "The Spatial Mismatch Hypothesis: Are There Jobs Missing in the Ghetto?" In *The Black Youth Employment Crisis,* edited by R.B. Freeman and H.J. Holzer. Chicago: University of Chicago Press, pp. 147–187.

Elmi, Amina, with Maris Mickelsons. 1991. *Housing Discrimination Study: Replication of 1977 Study Measures Using Current Data.* Washington, D.C.: U.S. Department of Housing and Urban Development.

Farley, Reynolds. 1990. "Blacks, Hispanics, and White Ethnic Groups: Are Blacks Uniquely Disadvantaged?" *American Economic Review 80* (May): 237–241.

———. 1993. "Neighborhood Preferences and Aspirations among Blacks and Whites." In *Housing Markets and Residential Mobility,* edited by G.T. Kingsley and M.A. Turner. Washington, D.C.: The Urban Institute Press, pp. 161–191.

Farley, Reynolds, and William H. Frey. 1993. "Latino, Asian, and Black Segregation in Multi-Ethnic Metro Areas: Findings from the 1990 Census." Population Studies Center Research Report No. 93-278. Ann Arbor: University of Michigan.

————. 1994. "Changes in the Segregation of Whites from Blacks During the 1980s: Small Steps Toward a More Integrated Society." *American Sociological Review 59* (February): 23–45.

Farley, Reynolds, Charlotte Steen, Tara Jackson, Maria Krysan, and Keith Reeves. 1993. "Continued Racial Residential Segregation in Detroit: 'Chocolate City, Vanilla Suburbs' Revisited." *Journal of Housing Research 4* (1): 1–38.

Farley, Reynolds, Charlotte Steen, Maria Krysan, Tara Jackson, and Keith Reeves. 1994. "Stereotypes and Segregation: Neighborhoods in the Detroit Area." *American Journal of Sociology 100* (November): 750–780.

Feins, Judith D., and Rachael G. Bratt. 1983. "Barred in Boston: Racial Discrimination in Housing." *Journal of the American Planning Association* (Summer): 344–355.

Feins, Judith D., Rachael G. Bratt, and Robert Hollister. 1981. *Final Report of a Study of Racial Discrimination in the Boston Housing Market.* Cambridge, Mass.: Abt Associates.

Feld, Marcia Marker. 1986. "Planners Guilty on Two Counts: The City of Yonkers Case." *Journal of the American Planning Association 52* (Autumn): 327–328.

————. 1989. "The Yonkers Case and Its Implications for the Teaching and Practice of Planning." *Journal of Planning Education and Research 8* (3): 169–175.

Feldman, Paul. 1989. "Suit Charged Large Apartment Firm with Racial Bias in Rentals." *The Los Angeles Times,* October 26.

Feldstein, Mark. 1994. "Hitting the Poor Where They Live." *The Nation* (April 4): 450–454.

Ferguson, Ronald F. 1991. "Paying for Public Education: New Evidence on How and Why Money Matters." *Harvard Journal on Legislation 28* (Summer): 465–498.

————. 1995. "Shifting Challenges: Fifty Years of Economic Change Toward Black-White Earnings Equality." *Daedalus* (Winter): 37–76.

Finder, Alan. 1988. "Starrett City Will Stop Using Quotas to Foster Integration." *The New York Times,* November 8, p. B4.

Fischer, Paul B. 1991. "Is Housing Mobility an Effective Anti-Poverty Strategy?: An Examination of the Cincinnati Experience." Unpublished Manuscript, September.

Fishbein, Allen J. 1992. "The Ongoing Experiment with 'Regulation from Below': Expanded Reporting Requirements for HMDA and CRA." *Housing Policy Debate 3* (2): 601–636.

Fix, Michael, and Raymond J. Struyk, editors. 1993. *Clear and Convincing Evidence: Testing for Discrimination in America.* Washington, D.C.: The Urban Institute Press.

Fix, Michael, George C. Galster, and Raymond J. Struyk. 1993. "Introduction." In *Clear and Convincing Evidence: Testing for Discrimination in America,* edited by M. Fix and R.J. Struyk. Washington, D.C.: The Urban Institute Press. pp. 1–68.

Flournoy, Craig. 1985. "Still Separate and Unequal." *New Perspectives* (Summer): 24, 26–30.

Follain, James R., David Ling, and Gary McGill. 1993. "The Preferential Tax Treatment of Owner-Occupied Housing: Who Really Benefits?" *Housing Policy Debate 4* (1): 1–24.

Freeman, Richard B. 1992. "Crime and the Employment of Disadvantaged Youth." In *Urban Labor Markets and Job Opportunities,* edited by G.E. Peterson and W. Vroman. Washington, D.C.: The Urban Institute Press, pp. 201–237.

Freeman v. Pitts, 118 L.Ed. 2nd 108, 137 (1992), 112 S. Ct. 1430 (1992).

Freiberg, Fred. 1993. "Promoting Residential Integration: The Role of Private Fair Housing Groups." In *Housing Markets and Residential Mobility,* edited by G.T. Kingsley and M.A. Turner. Washington, D.C.: The Urban Institute Press, pp. 219–242.

Fried, Joseph P. 1984. "U.S. Challenges Accord in Starrett City Bias Suit." *The New York Times,* June 29, p. B3.

Fritz, Richard G., and Rawi E. Abdelal. 1994. "Consortium Residential Lending and Community Reinvestment: An Analysis of the Atlanta Mortgage Consortium." Paper presented at the American Real Estate and Urban Economics Association Meetings, January.

Fullilove v. Klutznick, 448 U.S. 448 (1980).

Gabriel, Stuart A., and Stuart S. Rosenthal. 1991. "Credit Rationing, Race, and the Mortgage Market." *Journal of Urban Economics 29* (May): 371–379.

Gaines-Carter, Patrice. 1992. "Hiring Bias found by Hispanic Testers." *The Washington Post,* April 29, p. C1.

Galster, George C. 1986. "More than Skin Deep: The Effect of Housing Discrimination on the Extent and Pattern of Segregation." In *Housing Desegregation and Federal Policy,* edited by J.M. Goering. Chapel Hill: University of North Carolina Press, pp. 119–138.

———. 1987a. "The Ecology of Racial Discrimination in Housing: An Exploratory Model." *Urban Affairs Quarterly 23* (September): 84–107.

———. 1987b. "Residential Segregation and Interracial Economic Disparities: A Simultaneous-Equations Approach." *Journal of Urban Economics,* January, pp. 22–44.

———. 1988. "Residential Segregation in American Cities: A Contrary View." *Population Research and Policy Review 7:* 93–112.

————. **1989.** "Residential Segregation in American Cities: A Further Response." *Population Research and Policy Review 8:* 181–192.

————. **1990a.** "Federal Fair Housing Policy: The Great Misapprehension." In *Building Foundations,* edited by D. DiPasquale and L.C. Keyes. Philadelphia: University of Pennsylvania Press, pp. 137–156.

————. **1990b.** "Racial Discrimination in Housing Markets During the 1980s: A Review of the Audit Evidence." *Journal of Planning Education and Research 9* (3): 165–175.

————. **1990c.** "Racial Steering by Real Estate Agents: Mechanisms and Motives." *Review of Black Political Economy 19* (Summer): 39–63.

————. **1990d.** "Racial Steering in Urban Housing Markets: A Review of the Audit Evidence." *Review of Black Political Economy 18* (Winter): 105–129.

————. **1990e.** "White Flight from Racially Integrated Neighborhoods in the 1970s: The Cleveland Experience." *Urban Studies 27* (3): 385–399.

————. **1991.** "Housing Discrimination and Urban Poverty of African-Americans." *Journal of Housing Research 2* (2): 87–122.

————. **1992a.** "The Case for Racial Integration." In *The Metropolis in Black and White: Place, Power and Polarization,* edited by G.C. Galster and E.W. Hill. New Brunswick, NJ: Center for Urban Policy Research, pp. 270–285.

————. **1992b.** "A Cumulative Causation Model of the Underclass: Implications for Urban Economic Development Policy." In *The Metropolis in Black and White: Place, Power and Polarization,* edited by G.C. Galster and E.W. Hill. New Brunswick, NJ: Center for Urban Policy Research, pp. 190–215.

————. **1992c.** "Research on Discrimination in Housing and Mortgage Markets: Assessment and Future Directions." *Housing Policy Debate 3* (2): 639–683.

————. **1992d.** "A Theoretical Framework for Econometrically Analyzing Mortgage Lending Activity in Census Tracts." *Urban Affairs Quarterly 28* (September): 146–155.

————. **1993a.** "The Facts of Lending Discrimination Cannot be Argued Away by Examining Default Rates." *Housing Policy Debate 4* (1): 141–146.

————. **1993b.** "Polarization, Place, and Race." *North Carolina Law Review 71* (June): 1421–1426.

————. **1993c.** "Use of Testers in Investigating Discrimination in Mortgage Lending and Insurance." In *Clear and Convincing Evidence,* edited by M. Fix and R.J. Struyk. Washington, D.C.: The Urban Institute Press, pp. 287–334.

Galster, George C., Fred Freiberg, and Diane Houk. 1987. "Racial Differences in Real Estate Advertising Practices: An Exploratory Analysis." *Journal of Urban Affairs 9:* 199–215.

Galster, George C., and Peter Hoopes. 1993. "A Note on Aggregation Bias in Analyzing Mortgage Lending Patterns in Census Tracts." *Urban Affairs Quarterly* 29 (September): 146–153.

Galster, George C., and Heather Keeney. 1993. "Subsidized Housing and Racial Change in Yonkers, NY." *Journal of the American Planning Association 59* (Spring): 172–181.

Galster, George C., and W. Mark Keeney. 1988. "Race, Residence, Discrimination, and Economic Opportunity: Modeling the Nexus of Urban Racial Phenomena." *Urban Affairs Quarterly 24* (September): 87–117.

Garcia, Jesus M. 1993. *The Hispanic Population in the United States: March 1992.* U.S. Bureau of the Census, Current Population Reports, P20-465RV. Washington, D.C.: U.S. Government Printing Office.

Gatewood, Robert D., and Hubert S. Feild. 1990. *Human Resource Selection,* 2nd Ed. Chicago: The Dryden Press.

Gill, Andrew M. 1994. "Incorporating the Causes of Occupational Differences in Studies of Racial Wage Differentials." *Journal of Human Resources 29* (Winter): 20–41.

Gillmore, Dan, and Stephen K. Doig. 1992. "Segregation Forever?" *American Demographics* (January): 48–51.

Gingrich, Newt. 1995. "Excerpts from Gingrich's Speech on Party's Agenda for the 104th Congress." *The New York Times,* January 6, p. A19.

Ginsberg, Yona. 1975. *Jews in a Changing Neighborhood: The Study of Mattapan.* New York: The Free Press.

Gladstone, Realtors v. *Village of Bellwood,* 441 U.S. 91 (1979).

Glennon, Dennis, and Mitchell Stengel. 1994. "An Evaluation of the Federal Reserve Bank of Boston's Study of Racial Discrimination in Mortgage Lending." Economic & Policy Analysis Working Paper 94-2. Washington, D.C.: Comptroller of the Currency.

Goel, Ankur J. 1990. "Maintaining Integration Against Minority Interests: An Anti-Subjugation Theory for Equality in Housing." *The Urban Lawyer 22* (Summer): 369–416.

Goering, John M. 1992. "Anti-Discrimination Legislation in the United States: A Provisional Review of the Literature." Unpublished Manuscript, June.

Goering, John M., and Modibo Coulibably. 1989. "Investigating Public Housing Segregation: Conceptual and Methodological Issues." *Urban Affairs Quarterly 25:* 265–297.

Goldberger, Arthur S., and Charles F. Manski. 1995. "Review Article: *The*

Bell Curve by Herrnstein and Murray." *Journal of Economic Literature 33* (June): 762–776.

Goleman, Daniel. 1994. "Amid Ethnic Wars, Psychiatrists Seek Roots of Conflicts." *The New York Times,* August 2, p. C13.

Gomillion v. *Lightfoot,* 364 U.S. 399 (1960).

Gonzales, David. 1992. "What's the Problem with 'Hispanic'? Just Ask a 'Latino.'" *The New York Times,* November 15, p. E6.

Goodman, George W. 1983. "For Starrett City, an Integration Test." *The New York Times,* October 16, p. R7.

Goodwin, Carole. 1979. *The Oak Park Strategy: Community Control of Racial Change.* Chicago: The University of Chicago Press.

Gould, Stephen Jay. 1994. "Curveball." *The New Yorker,* November 28, pp. 139–149.

Gramlich, Edward, Deborah Laren, and Naomi Sealand. 1992. "Moving Into and Out of Poor Urban Areas." *Journal of Policy Analysis and Management 11* (Spring): 273–287.

Gray, Robert, and Steven Tursky. 1986. "Location and Racial/Ethnic Occupancy Patterns for HUD-Subsidized Family Housing in Ten Metropolitan Areas." In *Housing Desegregation and Federal Policy,* edited by J.M. Goering. Chapel Hill: The University of North Carolina Press, pp. 235–252.

Greenhouse, Linda. 1988. "High Court Voids Quotas on Races in Housing Units." *The New York Times,* November 8, p. A1.

———. 1994a. "Court Reopens Demotion Case at City College." *The New York Times,* November 11, p. A1.

———. 1994b. "Court Case Displays High Court Divisions on Desegregation." *The New York Times,* January 12, p. A18.

———. 1995. "Justices Say Lower Court Erred in Orders in Desegregation Case." *The New York Times,* June 13, p. A1.

Greenhouse, Steven. 1993. "Fed Stops Bank Merger Citing Bias in Lending." *The New York Times,* November 17, p. D2.

Griggs v. *Duke Power Company,* 272 U.S. 424 (1971).

Gross, Jane, and Ronald Smothers. 1994. "In Prom Dispute, a Town's Race Divisions Emerge." *The New York Times,* August 15, 1994, p. A10.

Guadalupe, Héctor Vélez. 1992. "Take Your Pick." *The New York Times,* Letter to the Editor, November 18, p. A26.

Gugliotta, Guy. 1995. "Cisneros Plans to Cut 4,400 Workers at HUD." *The Washington Post,* January 7, p. A1.

Gurr, Ted Robert. 1993. *Minorities at Risk: A Global View of Ethnopolitical Conflicts.* Washington, D.C.: United States Institute of Peace Press.

Gutin, Jo Ann C. 1994. "End of the Rainbow." *Discover 15* (November): 71–75.

Hakken, Jon. 1979. *Discrimination Against Chicanos in the Dallas Rental Housing Market: An Experimental Extension of the Housing Market Practices Survey.* Washington, D.C.: U.S. Department of Housing and Urban Development.

Hansell, Saul. 1994. "Stretching the Borders: Justice Department Redefines Lending Bias and Its Solution, Much to Banks' Concern." *The New York Times,* August 25, p. D1.

Harmon, Oskar R. 1988. "The Income Elasticity of Demand for Single-Family Owner-Occupied Housing: An Empirical Reconciliation." *Journal of Urban Economics 24* (September): 173–185.

Hatton, Katherine L. 1979. "Heights vs. Hilltop Is Parallel to Illinois Suit." *The Plain Dealer,* April 1, section 4, p. 14.

Hausman, Jerry. 1978. "Specification Tests in Econometrics." *Econometrica 46* (November): 1251–1272.

Havens v. Coleman, 455 U.S. 363 (1982).

Hayes, Arthur S. 1990. "Is Town's Housing Plan the Key to Integration or a Form of Racism?" *The Wall Street Journal,* October 4, p. A1.

Heckman, James J., and Peter Siegelman. 1993a. "Response to Comments by John Yinger." In *Clear and Convincing Evidence: Measurement of Discrimination in America,* edited by M. Fix and R.J. Struyk. Washington, D.C.: The Urban Institute Press, pp. 271–275.

———. **1993b.** "The Urban Institute Audit Studies: Their Methods and Findings." In *Clear and Convincing Evidence: Measurement of Discrimination in America,* edited by M. Fix and R.J. Struyk. Washington, D.C.: The Urban Institute Press, pp. 187–258.

Helper, Rose. 1969. *Racial Policies and Practices of Real Estate Brokers.* Minneapolis: University of Minnesota Press.

———. **1986.** "Success and Resistance Factors in the Maintenance of Racially Mixed Neighborhoods." In *Housing Desegregation and Federal Policy,* edited by J.M. Goering. Chapel Hill: The University of North Carolina Press, pp. 170–194.

Henderson, Vivian. 1975. "Race, Economics, and Public Policy." *Crisis 82* (Fall): 50–55.

Herrnstein, Richard J., and Charles Murray. 1994. *The Bell Curve: Intelligence and Class Structure in American Life.* New York: The Free Press.

Hershey, Robert D., Jr. 1995. "U.S. Regulators Drop a Proposal Aimed at Bias in Banks' Lending." *The New York Times,* April 19, p. A1.

Hill, Edward W., and Heidi Marie Rock. 1992. "Race and Inner-City Education." In *The Metropolis in Black and White: Place, Power, and Polarization,* edited by G.C. Galster and E.W. Hill. New Brunswick, N.J.: Center for Urban Policy Research, pp. 108–127.

Hill, Martha S. 1992. *The Panel Study of Income Dynamics: A User's Guide.* Newbury Park, CA: Sage Publications.

Hills v. *Gautreaux,* 425 U.S. 363 (1982).

Holmes, Steven A. 1994a. "Federal Government is Rethinking Its System of Racial Classification." *The New York Times,* July 8, p. A18.

————. 1994b. "Survey Finds Minorities Resent One Another Almost as Much as They Do Whites." *The New York Times,* March 3, p. B8.

Holshouser, William. 1984. *Final Report of a Study of Racial Discrimination in Two Boston Housing Markets.* Cambridge, MA: Abt Associates.

Holt, Jim. 1994. "Anti-Social Science?" *The New York Times,* October 19, Op-Ed Page.

Holzer, Harry J. 1991. "The Spatial Mismatch Hypothesis: What Has the Evidence Shown?" *Urban Studies 28* (February): 105–122.

Horne, David K. 1994. "Evaluating the Role of Race in Mortgage Lending." *FDIC Banking Review 7* (Spring/Summer):1–15.

Horowitz, Donald L. 1985a. "Conflict and Accommodation: Mexican-Americans in the Cosmopolis." In *Mexican-Americans in Comparative Perspective,* edited by W. Conner. Washington, D.C.: The Urban Institute Press, pp. 56–103.

————. 1985b. *Ethnic Groups in Conflict.* Berkeley: University of California Press.

Horton, Hayward D. 1992. "Race and Wealth: A Demographic Analysis of Black Homeownership." *Sociological Inquiry 62* (November): 480–489.

Hughes, Mark Alan. 1993. "Antipoverty Strategy Where the Rubber Hits the Road: Transporting Workers to Jobs." In *Housing Markets and Residential Mobility,* edited by G.T. Kingsley and M.A. Turner. Washington, D.C.: The Urban Institute Press, pp. 283–310.

Hughes, Mark Alan, and Janice Fanning Madden. 1991. "Residential Segregation and the Economic Status of Black Workers: New Evidence for an Old Debate." *Journal of Urban Economics 29* (January): 28–49.

Hula, Richard C. 1991. "Neighborhood Development and Local Credit Markets." *Urban Affairs Quarterly 27* (December): 249–267.

Husock, Howard. 1989. "Integration Incentives in Suburban Cleveland." Kennedy School of Government Case No. C16-89-877. Cambridge, MA: Kennedy School of Government, Harvard University.

ICF. 1991. *The Secondary Market and Community Lending Through Lenders' Eyes.* Report prepared for Federal Home Loan Mortgage Corporation. Fairfax, VA: ICF, Incorporated, February.

Ifil, Gwen. 1994. "Fight New Segregationism, President Urges Students." *The New York Times,* May 18, p. A20.

Ihlanfeldt, Keith R. 1992. *Job Accessibility and the Employment and School Enrollment of Teenagers.* Kalamazoo, MI: W.E. Upjohn Institute for Employment Research.

————. **1993.** "Intra-Urban Job Accessibility and Hispanic Youth Unemployment Rates." *Journal of Urban Economics 33* (March): 254–271.

Ihlanfeldt, Keith R., and David L. Sjoquist. 1990. "Job Accessibility and Racial Differences in Youth Unemployment Rates." *American Economic Review 80* (March): 267–276.

————. **1991.** "The Effect of Job Access on Black and White Youth Employment: A Cross-Sectional Analysis." *Urban Studies 28* (2): 255–265.

Interagency Task Force on Fair Lending. 1994. "Policy Statement on Discrimination in Lending." Washington, D.C.: Interagency Task Force on Fair Lending, March 8.

Jackman, Mary R., and Marie Crane. 1986. "'Some of My Best Friends Are Black . . .': Interracial Friendship and Whites' Racial Attitudes." *Public Opinion Quarterly 50:* 459–486.

James, Franklin, Betty McCummings, and Eileen Tynan. 1984. *Minorities in the Sunbelt.* New Brunswick, NJ: Rutgers University Press.

Jaynes, Gerald David, and Robin M. Williams, Jr., Eds. 1989. *A Common Destiny: Blacks in American Society.* Washington, D.C. National Academy Press.

Jencks, Christopher. 1992. *Rethinking Social Policy: Race, Poverty, and the Underclass.* New York: Harper Perennial.

Jencks, Christopher, and Susan E. Mayer. 1990a. "Residential Segregation, Job Proximity, and Black Job Opportunities." In *Inner-City Poverty in the United States,* edited by L.E. Lynn, Jr., and M.G.H. McGeary. Washington, D.C.: National Academy Press, pp. 187–222.

————. **1990b.** "The Social Consequences of Growing Up in a Poor Neighborhood." In *Inner-City Poverty in the United States,* edited by L.E. Lynn, Jr., and M.G.H. McGeary. Washington, D.C.: National Academy Press, pp. 111–127.

Johnson, Daniel A., Richard A. Porter, and Patricia L. Mateljan. 1975. "Racial Discrimination in Apartment Rentals." In *Racial Discrimination in the United States,* edited by T. F. Pettigrew. New York: Harper & Row, pp. 75–86.

Jones, Charisse. 1994. "Test Scores Show Gaps by Ethnicity." *The New York Times,* July 8, p. B1.

Jones v. *Alfred H. Mayer Co.,* 392 U.S. 409 (1968).

Kain, John F., and Joseph J. Persky. 1969. "Alternatives to the Gilded Ghetto." *The Public Interest 14* (Winter): 77–91.

Kain, John F., and John M. Quigley. 1975. *Housing Markets and Racial Dis-*

crimination: A Microeconomic Analysis. New York: National Bureau of Economic Research.

Kain, John M. 1968. "Housing Segregation, Negro Employment, and Metropolitan Decentralization." *Quarterly Journal of Economics 83* (May): 175–197.

———. **1992.** "The Spatial Mismatch Hypothesis: Three Decades Later." *Housing Policy Debate 3* (Issue 2): 371–460.

———. **1994.** "An Assessment of the Adverse Impacts of Housing Discrimination and Suggestions for Policy." In *New Beginnings Project: A First Report.* Washington, D.C.: The Center for Housing Policy, pp. 49–85.

Karr, Albert R. 1995. "Study by Fed Challenges the Contention of Minority Bias in Mortgage Lending." *The Wall Street Journal,* January 26, 1995, p. A2.

Karr, Albert R., and Viveca Novak. 1994. "Stronger Penalties for Reinvestment Act Are Ruled Illegal by Justice Department." *The Wall Street Journal,* December 16, p. A6.

Kasarda, John D. 1985. "Urban Change and Minority Opportunities." In *The New Urban Reality,* edited by P.E. Peterson. Washington, D.C.: The Brookings Institution, pp. 33–67.

———. **1989.** "Urban Industrial Transition and the Underclass." *The Annals of the American Academy of Political and Social Science 501:* 26–47.

Keating, W. Dennis. 1994. *The Suburban Racial Dilemma: Housing and Neighborhoods.* Philadelphia: Temple University Press.

Keller, Bill. 1994. "Mixed-Race South Africans Riot Over 'Favoritism' for Blacks." *The New York Times,* September 16, p. A9.

Kenney, Genevieve M., and Douglas A. Wissoker. 1994. "An Analysis of the Correlates of Discrimination Facing Young Hispanic Job-Seekers." *American Economic Review 84* (June): 674–683.

Kifner, John. 1988. "Starrett City's Nightmare: End of Quotas." *The New York Times,* November 14, p. B1.

King, Ralph T., Jr. 1994. "Some Mortgage Firms Neglect Black Areas More Than Banks Do." *The Wall Street Journal,* August 9, p. A1.

King, Thomas A. 1980. "Discrimination in Mortgage Lending: A Study of Three Cities." Working Paper No. 91. Washington, D.C.: Federal Home Loan Bank Board.

Kirschenman, Joleen, and Kathryn M. Neckerman. 1991. "'We'd Love to Hire Them, But . . .': The Meaning of Race for Employers." In *The Urban Underclass,* edited by C. Jencks and P.E. Peterson. Washington, D.C.: The Urban Institute Press, pp. 203–232.

Kohn, Ernest. 1993. "The New York State Banking Study: Research on Mortgage Discrimination." Paper presented at Home Mortgage Lending and

Discrimination: Research and Enforcement Conference, sponsored by the U.S. Department of Housing and Urban Development, Washington, D.C., May.

Kovar, Leopold J. 1974. *Auditing Real Estate Practices: A Manual.* Philadelphia: National Neighbors.

Kozol, Jonathan. 1991. *Savage Inequalities.* New York: Crown.

Krebs, Bob. 1992. "Latino? Hispanic? Quechua? No, American." *The New York Times,* Letter to the Editor, November 18, p. A26.

Kurtz, Josh. 1991. "Real Estate Agency Firebombed Again." *The New York Times,* July 28, p. 25.

Kushner, James A. 1989. "The Fair Housing Amendments Act of 1988: The Second Generation of Fair Housing." *Vanderbilt Law Review 42:* 1049–1120.

———. **1992.** "Federal Enforcement and Judicial Review of the Fair Housing Amendments Act of 1988." *Housing Policy Debate 3* (2): 537–599.

Labaton, Stephen. 1993. "U.S. Settles Bias Case with Bank." *The New York Times,* December 14, p. D1.

Ladd, Helen F., and John Yinger. 1991. *America's Ailing Cities: Fiscal Health and the Design of Urban Policy,* updated edition. Baltimore: The Johns Hopkins University Press.

Lamb, Charles M. 1984. "Equal Housing Opportunity." In *Implementation of Civil Rights Policy,* edited by C.S. Bullock III and C.M. Lamb. Monterey, CA: Brooks/Cole Publishing Co., pp. 149–183.

———. **1992.** "Fair Housing Implementation from Nixon to Reagan." Working Paper No. 11. Madison, WI: Robert M. LaFollette Institute of Public Affairs, University of Wisconsin.

Lang, William W., and Leonard I. Nakamura. 1993. "A Model of Redlining." *Journal of Urban Economics 33* (March): 223–234.

Laurenti, Luigi M. 1960. *Property Values and Race.* Berkeley: University of California Press.

Lawton, Rachel. 1993. "Pre-Application Mortgage Lending Testing Program: Lender Testing by a Local Agency." Paper Presented at Home Mortgage Lending and Discrimination: Research and Enforcement Conference, Sponsored by the U.S. Department of Housing and Urban Development, Washington, D.C., May.

Lazere, Edward B., Cusing N. Dolbeare, Paul A. Leonard, and Barry Zigas. 1991. *A Place to Call Home: The Low Income Housing Crisis Continues.* Washington, D.C.: Center on Budget and Policy Priorities.

Leadership Council for Metropolitan Open Communities. 1975. *Investigation and Auditing in Fair Housing Cases.* Chicago: Leadership Council for Metropolitan Open Communities.

Lee, Barrett A. 1985. "Racially Mixed Neighborhoods During the 1970s: Change or Stability." *Social Science Quarterly 66*: 346–364.

Leeds, Barry. 1993. "Testing for Discrimination During the Pre-Application and Post-Application Phases of Mortgage Lending." Paper presented at Home Mortgage Lending and Discrimination: Research and Enforcement Conference, sponsored by the U.S. Department of Housing and Urban Development, Washington, D.C., May.

Leigh, Wilhelmina A. 1981. "Comments." In *Do Housing Allowances Work?*, edited by K.L. Bradbury and A. Downs. Washington, D.C.: The Brookings Institution, pp. 172–183.

———. 1992. "Civil Rights and the Housing Status of Black Americans: An Overview." In *The Housing Status of Black Americans*, edited by W.A. Leigh and J.B. Stewart. New Brunswick, NJ: Transaction Publishers, pp. 5–28.

Leigh, Wilhelmina A., and James D. McGhee. 1986. "A Minority Perspective on Racial Residential Integration." In *Housing Desegregation and Federal Policy*, edited by J.M. Goering. Chapel Hill: University of North Carolina Press, pp. 31–42.

Leonard, Jonathan. 1987. "The Interaction of Residential Segregation and Employment Discrimination." *Journal of Urban Economics 21* (May): 323–346.

Levathes, Louise. 1993. "A Geneticist Maps Ancient Migrations." *The New York Times*, July 7, 1993, p. C1.

Levy, Frank, and Richard J. Murnane. 1992. "U.S. Earnings Levels and Earnings Inequality: A Review of Recent Trends and Proposed Explanations." *Journal of Economic Literature 30* (September): 1333–1381.

Lewis, Anthony. 1988. "The Danger of Rigidity." *The New York Times*, November 17, Op-ed page (A31).

Lieberson, Stanley. 1963. *Ethnic Patterns in American Cities*. New York: The Free Press.

———. 1980. *A Piece of the Pie: Black and White Immigrants Since 1880*. Berkeley: University of California Press.

Liebowitz, Stanley. 1993. "A Study that Deserves No Credit." *The Wall Street Journal*, September 1, Op-Ed Page.

Lindsey, Lawrence B. 1993. "Statement," before the Committee on Banking, Housing and Urban Affairs, U.S. Senate, November 4.

Linmark Associates Inc. v. *Township of Willingboro*, 431 U.S. 85 (1977).

Loury, Glenn C. 1987a. " 'Matters of Color' — Blacks and the Constitutional Order." *The Public Interest 86* (Winter): 109–123.

———. 1987b. "Why Should We Care About Group Inequality?" *Social Philosophy and Policy 5* (Autumn): 249–271.

————. 1992. "The Economics of Discrimination: Getting to the Core of the Problem." Public Lecture, Tsai Performance Center, Boston University, March 31.

Ludwig, Eugene A. 1993. Testimony before the Committee on Banking, Housing, and Urban Affairs, United States Senate, November 4.

McEntire, Davis. 1960. *Residence and Race.* Berkeley: University of California Press.

McFadden, Robert D. 1990. "House Sold to Blacks by a White Is Set Afire." *The New York Times,* February 9, p. B1.

McFadden, Robert D., with the assistance of James Barron, James Feron, and Wayne King. 1988. "In Its Final Days of Defiance, Yonkers Had to Pick Its Fate." *The New York Times,* September 12, p. A1.

McIntosh, Neil, and David J. Smith. 1974. *The Extent of Racial Discrimination.* London: PEP, The Social Science Institute.

McIntyre, Shelby, Dennis J. Moberg, and Barry Z. Posner. 1980. "Preferential Treatment in Preselection Decisions According to Race and Sex." *Academy of Management Journal* 23 (4): 738–749.

McLarin, Kimberly J. 1994. "The Specter of Segregation: Montclair Schools Are Troubled by Racial Imbalance Between Classrooms." *The New York Times,* August 11, 1994, p. B9.

Maddala, G.S., and Robert P. Trost. 1982. "On Measuring Discrimination in Loan Markets." *Housing Finance Review 1*: 245–266.

Mandelbaum, Joel. 1972. "Race Discrimination in Home Buying Resists Tough Laws." *The New York Times,* December 3, Section 8, p. 1.

Mariano, Ann. 1994. "Hill Panel Halts Plan to Move Poor Families." *The Washington Post,* September 3.

Mason, Patrick L. 1994. "Male Racial/Ethnic Earnings Differentials: On Culture, Human Capital, and Job Competition." Department of Economics Working Paper. Riverside, CA: University of California – Riverside, February.

Massey, Douglas S. 1992. "Shrugging Off Racism." *The Washington Post,* May 17, p. 2.

Massey, Douglas S., and Nancy A. Denton. 1989. "Hypersegregation in U.S. Metropolitan Areas: Black and Hispanic Segregation Along Five Dimensions." *Social Forces 26* (August): 373–391.

————. 1993. *American Apartheid: Segregation and the Making of the Underclass.* Cambridge, MA: Harvard University Press.

Massey, Douglas S., and Mitchell L. Eggers. 1990. "The Ecology of Inequality: Minorities and the Concentration of Poverty: 1970–1980." *American Journal of Sociology 95* (March): 1153–1188.

Massey, Douglas S., and Eric Fong. 1990. "Segregation and Neighborhood

Quality: Blacks, Hispanics, and Asians in the San Francisco Metropolitan Area." *Social Forces* 69 (September): 15–32.

Massey, Douglas S., Andrew B. Gross, and Mitchell L. Eggers. 1991. "Segregation, the Concentration of Poverty, and the Life Chances of Individuals." *Social Science Research* 20: 397–420.

Massey, Douglas S., Andrew B. Gross, and Kumiko Shibuya. 1994. "Migration, Segregation, and the Geographic Concentration of Poverty." *American Sociological Review* 59 (June): 425–445.

Massey, Douglas S., and Shawn M. Kanaiaupuni. 1993. "Public Housing and the Concentration of Poverty." *Social Science Quarterly* 74 (March): 109–122.

Maxwell, Nan L. 1994. "The Effect on Black-White Wage Differences of Differences in the Quantity and Quality of Education." *Industrial and Labor Relations Review* 47 (January): 249–264.

Mayo, Stephen K. 1981. "Theory and Estimation in the Economics of Housing Demand." *Journal of Urban Economics* 10 (July): 95–116.

Metcalf, George R. 1988. *Fair Housing Comes of Age.* New York: Greenwood.

Mills, Edwin S., and Luan' Sende Lubuele. 1994. "Performance of Residential Mortgages in Low and Moderate Income Neighborhoods." *Journal of Real Estate Finance and Economics* 9 (November): 245–260.

Mincy, Ronald B. 1993. "The Urban Institute Audit Studies: Their Research and Policy Context." In *Clear and Convincing Evidence: Measurement of Discrimination in America,* edited by M. Fix and R.J. Struyk. Washington, D.C.: The Urban Institute Press, pp. 165–186.

————. 1994. "The Underclass: Concept, Controversy, and Evidence." In *Confronting Poverty,* edited by S.H. Danziger and D.H. Weinberg. Cambridge, MA: Harvard University Press, pp. 109–146.

Missouri v. Jenkins, 495 U.S. 33 (1990), 855 F.2d 1295 (1988), 672 F. Supp. 400 (1987).

Montgomery, Lori. 1994. "HUD Chief Tries to Dismantle Nation's Segregated Ways." *The Philadelphia Inquirer,* August 30.

Montgomery, Patricia A. 1993. *The Hispanic Population in the United States: March 1993.* U.S. Bureau of the Census, Current Population Reports, P20-475. Washington, D.C.: U.S. Government Printing Office.

Moore, Joan, and Raquel Pinderhughes. 1993. *In the Barrios: Latinos and the Underclass Debate.* New York: Russell Sage Foundation.

Morley, Jefferson. 1984. "Double Reverse Discrimination." *The New Republic,* July 9, pp. 14–18.

Mountain Side Mobile Estate Partnership v. *HUD,* No. 94-9509 (10th Cir. 1994).

Munnell, Alicia H., Lynn E. Browne, James McEneaney, and Geoffrey M.B.

Tootell. 1992. "Mortgage Lending in Boston: Interpreting HMDA Data." Working Paper No. 92-7. Boston: Federal Reserve Bank of Boston. October.

Munnell, Alicia H., Geoffrey M.B. Tootell, Lynn E. Browne, and James McEneaney, 1993. "Is Discrimination Racial or Geographic?" Unpublished manuscript.

Murnane, Richard J. 1994. "Education and the Well-Being of the Next Generation." In *Confronting Poverty,* edited by S.H. Danziger, G.D. Sandefur, and D.H. Weinberg. Cambridge, MA: Harvard University Press, pp. 289–307.

Murphy, Joellyn Kapp. 1972. *Audit Handbook: Procedures for Determining the Extent of Racial Discrimination in Apartment Rentals.* Palo Alto, CA: Midpeninsula Citizens for Fair Housing.

Myers, Samuel L., Jr. 1993. "Measuring and Detecting Discrimination in the Post-Civil Rights Era." In *Race and Ethnicity in Research Methods,* edited by J. H. Stanfield II and R.M. Dennis. Newbury Park, CA: Sage Publications, pp. 172–197.

———. 1994. "Racial Disparities in Home Mortgage Refinancings." Paper presented at the Western Economic Association annual meetings, July.

Myers, Samuel L., Jr., and Tsze Chan. Forthcoming. "Racial Disparities in Housing Markets: Accounting for Credit Risk." *Social Science Quarterly.*

Myrdal, Gunnar. 1944. *An American Dilemma: The Negro Problem and Modern Democracy.* New York: Harper & Brothers.

The National Advisory Commission on Civil Disorders. 1968. *Report of the National Advisory Commission on Civil Disorders.* New York: E.P. Dutton & Co.

National Committee Against Discrimination in Housing. 1970. *Jobs and Housing: A Study of Employment and Housing Opportunities for Racial Minorities in the Suburban Areas of the New York Metropolitan Area.* Interim report. New York: National Committee Against Discrimination in Housing.

National League of Cities. 1991. *Local Officials Guide to The Community Reinvestment Act.* Washington, D.C.: By the Author.

Neal, Derek A., and William R. Johnson. 1994. "The Role of Pre-Market Factors in Black–White Wage Differences." Unpublished manuscript, University of Chicago, November.

Nelson, Kathryn P., and John G. Edwards. 1993. "Intra-Urban Mobility and Location Choice in the 1980s." In *Housing Markets and Residential Mobility,* edited by G.T. Kingsley and M.A. Turner. Washington, D.C.: The Urban Institute Press, pp. 53–95.

Newburger, Harriet. 1981. "The Nature and Extent of Racial Steering Practices in U.S. Housing Markets." U.S. Department of Housing and Urban Development Working Paper. Washington, D.C.: U.S. Department of Housing and Urban Development.

————. 1989. "Discrimination by a Profit-Maximizing Real Estate Broker in Response to White Prejudice." *Journal of Urban Economics 26* (July): 1–19.

————. 1995. "Sources of Difference in Information Used by Black and White Housing Seekers: An Exploratory Analysis." *Urban Studies 32* (April): 445–450.

Newman, Sandra, and Ann Schnare. 1994. "Back to the Future: Housing Assistance Policy for the Next Century." In *New Beginnings Project: A First Report.* Washington, D.C.: The Center for Housing Policy, pp. 2–24.

The New York Times. 1991. "Despite Vandals, Blacks Move into White L.I. Neighborhood," October 2, p. B5.

————. 1993. "Rights Violations Bring Texas Housing Seizure." September 15, p. A20.

————. 1994a. "Gender Gap Continues to Close on S.A.T.'s," August 25, p. A12.

————. 1994b. "U.S. Had More than 7,000 Hate Crimes in '93, F.B.I. Head Says," June 29, P. A16.

————. 1995. "Georgia Superintendent Battles a Subtle Racism." February 14, p. A10.

Office of Policy Development and Research, U.S. Department of Housing and Urban Development. 1994. "Residential Mobility Programs." *Urban Policy Brief* (September): 1–6.

Olsen, Ed. 1993. "Fundamental Housing Policy Reform." Unpublished Manuscript, April 2.

Ondrich, Jan, Stephen Ross, and John Yinger. 1994. "Measuring the Incidence of Discrimination." Metropolitan Studies Program Occasional Paper No. 167. Syracuse, NY: Center for Policy Research, Syracuse University.

O'Neill, June. 1990. "The Role of Human Capital in Earnings Differences Between Black and White Men." *Journal of Economic Perspectives 4* (Fall): 25–45.

O'Regan, Katherine M., and John M. Quigley. 1993. "Family Networks and Youth Access to Jobs." *Journal of Urban Economics 34* (September): 230–248.

Orfield, Gary. 1985. "Ghettoization and Its Alternatives." In *The New Urban Reality,* edited by P.E. Peterson. Washington, D.C.: The Brookings Institution, pp. 161–193.

————. 1986. "The Movement for Housing Integration: Rationale and the Nature of the Challenge." In *Housing Desegregation and Federal Policy,* edited by J.M. Goering. Chapel Hill: University of North Carolina Press, pp. 18–30.

————. 1992. "Urban Schooling and the Perpetuation of Job Inequality in Metropolitan Chicago." In *Urban Labor Markets and Job Opportunities,* edited by G.E. Peterson and W. Vroman. Washington, D.C.: The Urban Institute Press, pp. 161–199.

Orfield, Gary, with the assistance of Sara Schley, Diane Glass, and Sean Reardon. 1993. "The Growth of Segregation in American Schools: Changing Patterns of Separation and Poverty Since 1968." A Report of the Harvard Project on School Desegregation to the National School Boards Association, Cambridge, MA, December.

———. 1993. "School Desegregation after Two Generations: Race, Schools, and Opportunity in Urban Society." In *Race in America: The Struggle for Equality,* edited by H. Hill and J.E. Jones, Jr. Madison: University of Wisconsin Press, pp. 234–262.

Orfield, Gary, and Carole Ashkinaze. 1991. *The Closing Door: Conservative Policy and Black Opportunity.* Chicago: University of Chicago Press.

Osei, Awkasi. 1992. "The Persistence of Differing Trends in African-American Mortality and Morbidity Rates." In *The Metropolis in Black and White: Place, Power and Polarization,"* edited by G. C. Galster and E. W. Hill. New Brunswick, NJ: Center for Urban Policy Research, pp. 128–142.

O'Sullivan, Arthur. 1993. *Urban Economics.* 2nd ed. Homewood, IL: Irwin.

Page, Marianne. Forthcoming. "Racial and Ethnic Discrimination in Urban Housing Markets: Evidence from a Recent Audit Study." *Journal of Urban Economics.*

Passell, Peter. 1994. "'Bell Curve' Critics Say Early I.Q. Isn't Destiny." *The New York Times,* November 9, p. A25.

Patrick, Deval. 1994. "Statement" before the Subcommittee on Civil and Constitutional Rights, Committee on the Judiciary, U.S. House of Representatives, September 8.

Pearce, Diana. 1979. "Gatekeepers and Homeseekers: Institutional Patterns in Racial Steering." *Social Problems 26* (February): 325–342.

———. 1983. "A Sheltered Crisis: The State of Fair Housing Opportunity in the Eighties." In U.S. Commission on Civil Rights, *A Sheltered Crisis.* Washington, D.C., U.S. Commission on Civil Rights, pp. 143–145.

Peller, Gary. 1990. "Race Consciousness." *Duke Law Journal* (September): 758–847.

Peterson, George E., and Kale Williams. 1994. "Housing Mobility: What Has It Accomplished and What Is Its Promise?" Pre-Conference Paper for First National Conference on Housing Mobility as an Anti-Poverty Strategy, Washington, D.C.: The Urban Institute.

Peterson, Richard L. 1981. "An Investigation of Sex Discrimination in Commercial Banks' Direct Consumer Lending." *Bell Journal of Economics 12* (Autumn): 547–561.

Peterson, William, 1986. "Politics and the Measurement of Ethnicity." In

The Politics of Numbers, edited by W. Alonso and P. Starr. New York: Russell Sage Foundation, pp. 187–230.

Pettigrew, Thomas F. 1985. "New Patterns of Racism: The Different Worlds of 1984 and 1964." *Rutgers Law Review* 37 (Summer): 673–706.

Polikoff, Alexander. 1986. "Sustainable Integration or Inevitable Resegregation: The Troubling Questions." In *Housing Desegregation and Federal Policy,* edited by J. M. Goering. Chapel Hill: The University of North Carolina Press, pp. 43–71.

———. 1994. "Housing Policy and Urban Poverty." In *New Beginnings Project: A First Report.* Washington, D.C.: The Center for Housing Policy, pp. 89–124.

Popkin, Susan J., James E. Rosenbaum, and Patricia M. Meaden. 1993. "Labor Market Experiences of Low-Income Black Women in Middle-Class Suburbs: Evidence from a Survey of Gautreaux Program Participants." *Journal of Policy Analysis and Management* 12 (Summer): 556–574.

Prial, Frank J. 1984. "Starrett City: 20,000 Tenants, Few Complaints." *The New York Times,* December 10.

Purdy, Matthew. 1994. "Cost of Lead Cleanup Puts More Poor Children at Risk." *The New York Times,* August 25, p. B1.

Quercia, Roberto G., and Michael A. Stegman. 1992. "Residential Mortgage Default: A Review of the Literature." *Journal of Housing Research* 3 (2): 341–379.

Quigley, John M. 1994. "New Directions in Urban Policy." *Housing Policy Debate* 5 (1): 97–106.

Quint, Michael. 1991. "Racial Gap Found on Mortgages." *The New York Times,* October 22, p. D1.

———. 1995. "Insuror Agrees to Settlement of Milwaukee Bias Lawsuit." *The New York Times,* March 31, p. D16.

Rachlis, Mitchell B., and Anthony M.J. Yezer. 1993. "Serious Flaws in Statistical Tests for Discrimination in Mortgage Markets." *Journal of Housing Research* 4 (2): 315–336.

Ratcliffe, Kerry, Bruce Riddell, and John Yinger. 1990. "The Fiscal Condition of School Districts in Nebraska: Is Small Beautiful?" *Economics of Education Review* 9 (1): 81–99.

Reed, Veronica. 1994. "Fair Housing Enforcement: Is the Current System Adequate?" In *Residential Apartheid: The American Legacy,* edited by R.D. Bullard, J.E. Grigsby, III, and C. Lee. Los Angeles: CAAS Publications, University of California, pp. 222–236.

Reid, Clifford E. 1987. "An Analysis of Racial Discrimination in Rental Housing Markets." Unpublished manuscript, Grinnell College, July.

Reno, Janet. 1993. Testimony before the Committee on Banking, Housing, and Urban Affairs, United States Senate, November 4.

Riddle, Wayne. 1994. *Education: Reauthorization of the Elementary and Secondary Education Act.* CRS Issue Brief, October 11. Washington, D.C.: Congressional Research Service.

Riedman, Larry. 1993. "Perspectives from a Regulatory Agency." Paper Presented at Home Mortgage Lending and Discrimination: Research and Enforcement Conference, Sponsored by the U.S. Department of Housing and Urban Development, Washington, D.C., May.

Roberts, Paul Craig. 1993. "Banks on the Line of Fire." *The Washington Times,* March 12.

Roberts, Sam. 1988. "Racial Tipping: A Pivotal Issue in Fighting Bias." *The New York Times,* November 28, p. B1.

———. 1992. "White Tilt to Balance a Project in Canarsie." *The New York Times,* August 3, p. B3.

Robinson, Carla J. 1992. "Racial Disparity in the Atlanta Housing Market." In *The Housing Status of Black Americans,* edited by W.A. Leigh and J.B. Stewart. New Brunswick, NJ: Transaction Publishers, pp. 85–110.

Rodgers, William M. 1995. "How Much Can Job Training Aid in Narrowing the Black-White Wage Gap?" Paper Presented at the American Economic Association annual meetings, Washington, D.C., January.

Rogers, Rosemarie. 1985. "Migration Theory and Practice." In *Mexican-Americans in Comparative Perspective,* edited by W. Conner. Washington, D.C.: The Urban Institute Press, pp. 159–204.

Rohe, William M., and Michael A. Stegman. 1992. "Public Housing Homeownership: Will It Work and for Whom?" *Journal of the American Planning Association* 58 (Spring): 144–157.

Rosenbaum, James E., Nancy Fishman, Alison Brett, and Patricia Meaden. 1993. "Can the Kerner Commission's Housing Strategy Improve Employment, Education, and Social Integration for Low-Income Blacks?" *North Carolina Law Review* 71 (June): 1519–1556.

Rosenberg, Robert C. 1982. "Creating A Model Integrated New Community." *Real Estate Review* (Winter).

Ross, Philip E. 1991. "Hard Words." *Scientific American* (April): 139–147.

Ross, Stephen L. 1994. *Two Essays on the Interactions of Urban Labor and Housing Markets in Metropolitan Areas.* Unpublished Ph.D. dissertation, Syracuse University, July.

———. Forthcoming. "Mortgage Lending Discrimination and Racial Differences in Default." *Journal of Housing Research.*

Rossi, Peter H. 1981. "Residential Mobility." In *Do Housing Allowances*

Work?, edited by K.L. Bradbury and A. Downs. Washington, D.C.: The Brookings Institution, pp. 147–172.

Roychoudhury, Canopy, and Allen C. Goodman. 1992. "An Ordered Probit Model for Estimating Racial Discrimination Through Fair Housing Audits." *Journal of Housing Economics 2* (December 1992): 358–373.

Saltman, Juliet. 1990. *A Fragile Movement: The Struggle for Neighborhood Stabilization.* New York: Greenwood Press.

———. **1991.** "Maintaining Racially Diverse Neighborhoods." *Urban Affairs Quarterly 26* (March): 416–441.

Santiago, Anne M., and Margaret G. Wilder. 1991. "Residential Segregation and Links to Minority Poverty: The Case of Latinos in the United States." *Social Problems 38* (November): 492–515.

Saul, Stephanie, and Karen Farkas. 1983. "Hts. Suit Claims Race 'Steering'." *The Plain Dealer*, January 30, p. A-25.

Schafer, Robert, and Helen F. Ladd. 1981. *Discrimination in Mortgage Lending.* Cambridge, MA: The MIT Press.

Schelling, Thomas. 1971. "Dynamic Models of Segregation." *Journal of Mathematical Sociology 1:* 143–186.

———. **1972.** "A Process of Residential Segregation: Neighborhood Tipping." In *Racial Discrimination in Economic Life,* edited by A. Pascal. Lexington, MA: Lexington Books, pp. 157–184.

Schemo, Diana Jean. 1994a. "L.I. Apartment Service Accused of Bias in Rental Offers." *The New York Times,* February 15, 1994, p. B1.

———. **1994b.** "Suburban Taxes Are Higher for Blacks, Analysis Shows." *The New York Times,* August 17, p. A1.

Schill, Michael H. 1994. "Race, the Underclass, and Public Policy." *Law and Social Inquiry 19* (Spring): 433–456.

Schill, Michael H., and Susan M. Wachter. 1993. "A Tale of Two Cities: Racial and Ethnic Geographic Disparities in Home Mortgage Lending in Boston and Philadelphia." *Journal of Housing Research 4* (2): 245–275.

Schiller, Bradley R. 1989. *The Economics of Poverty and Discrimination,* 5th ed. Englewood Cliffs, NJ: Prentice Hall.

Schnare, Ann B. 1993. "The Role of FHA in the Provision of Credit to Minorities." Paper presented at Discrimination and Mortgage Lending: Research and Enforcement Conference, sponsored by the U.S. Department of Housing and Urban Development, Washington, D.C., May 18.

Schnare, Ann B., and C. Duncan MacRae. 1978. "The Dynamics of Neighborhood Change." *Urban Studies 15* (October): 327–331.

Schuman, Howard, Charlotte Steeh, and Lawrence Bobo. 1985. *Racial Attitudes in America.* Cambridge, Mass.: Harvard University Press.

Schwemm, Robert G. 1992. *Housing Discrimination: Law and Litigation.* Deerfield IL: Clark, Boardman, Callaghan.

———. **1993.** "Housing Discrimination and the Appraisal Industry." Paper presented at Home Mortgage Lending and Discrimination: Research and Enforcement Conference, sponsored by the U.S. Department of Housing and Urban Development, Washington, D.C., May.

Seelye, Katharine Q. 1994. "A Congressman's Personal Story Opens Session on Black Families." *The New York Times,* September 15, p. A16.

Seiberg, Jaret. 1995. "Fed Study Challenges Claims of Loan Bias." *The American Banker,* January 25, p. 1.

Sexton, Joe. 1994. "Other Banks: Check Cashers Filling a Void." *The New York Times,* April 18, p. B1.

Shear, William B., and Anthony M. J. Yezer. 1985. "Discrimination in Urban Housing Finance: An Empirical Study across Cities." *Land Economics 61* (August): 292–302.

Shelly v. Kraemer, 344 U.S. 1 (1948).

Shipler, David K. 1995. "My Equal Opportunity, Your Free Lunch." *The New York Times,* March 5, p. E1.

Shlay, Ann B. 1988. "Not in That Neighborhood: The Effects of Population and Housing on the Distribution of Mortgage Finance within the Chicago SMSA." *Social Science Research 17:* 137–163.

Shlay, Ann B., I. Goldsein, and D. Bartlett. 1992. "Racial Barriers to Credit: Comment on Hula." *Urban Affairs Quarterly 28:* 126–140.

Shreeve, James. 1994. "Terms of Estrangement." *Discover 15* (November): 57–69.

Simonson, John C., and Wienk, Ronald E. 1984. "Racial Discrimination in Housing Sales: An Empirical Test of Alternative Models of Broker Behavior." Unpublished manuscript.

Simpson, George E., and J. Milton Yinger. 1985. *Racial and Cultural Minorities: An Analysis of Prejudice and Discrimination,* 5th ed. New York: Plenum.

Siskin, Bernard R., and Leonard A. Cupingood. 1993. "Use of Statistical Models to Provide Statistical Evidence of Discrimination in the Treatment of Mortgage Loan Applicants: A Study of One Lending Institution." Paper presented at Home Mortgage Lending and Discrimination: Research and Enforcement Conference, sponsored by the U.S. Department of Housing and Urban Development, Washington, D.C., May.

Smith, James P. 1993. "Affirmative Action and the Racial Wage Gap." *American Economic Review 83* (May): 79–84.

Smith, Richard A. 1991. "The Measurement of Segregation Change Through

Integration and Deconcentration, 1979–1980." *Urban Affairs Quarterly* 26 (June): 477–496.

———. 1993. "Creating Stable Racially Integrated Communities: A Review." *Journal of Urban Affairs* 15 (2): 115–140.

Smith, Shanna, and Cathy Cloud. 1993. "The Role of Private, Non-Profit Fair Housing Enforcement Organizations in Lending Testing." Paper presented at Home Mortgage Lending and Discrimination: Research and Enforcement Conference, sponsored by the U.S. Department of Housing and Urban Development, Washington, D.C., May.

Sokal, Robert R., Neal L. Oden, and Barbara A. Thomson. 1992. "Origins of the Indo-Europeans: Genetic Evidence." *Proceedings of the National Academy of Science USA* 89 (August): 7669–7673.

Sokal, Robert R., Neal L. Oden, and Chester Wilson. 1991. "Genetic Evidence for the Spread of Agriculture in Europe by Demic Diffusion." *Nature 351* (May): 143–144.

South Suburban Housing Center v. *Greater South Suburban Board of Realtors,* **935 F. 2d 868 (7th Cir., 1991), cert. denied, 112 S. Ct. 971 (1992).**

South Suburban Housing Center v. *Greater South Suburban Board of Realtors,* **713 F. Supp. 1068 (N.D. Ill. 1988), appealed, U.S. District Court of Appeals, 7th Circuit, Nos. 89-2215, 2123, 2218, 2767, 2777, 2778, 2846 (CA-7 6-19-91).**

Soutner, Susan Blanche. 1980. "The Boston Banks Urban Renewal Group Homeownership Program." Unpublished manuscript, November.

Spain, Daphne. 1990. "The Effect of Residential Mobility and Household Composition on Housing Quality." *Urban Affairs Quarterly 25* (June): 659–683.

Spayd, Liz, and Joel Glenn Brenner. 1993. "Mortgage Companies Fill Gap—For a Price." *The Washington Post,* June 6, p. A23.

Squires, Gregory D., ed. 1992. *From Redlining to Reinvestment.* Philadelphia: Temple University Press.

———. 1994. *Capital and Communities in Black and White: The Intersections of Race, Class, and Uneven Development.* Albany: State University of New York Press.

Squires, Gregory D., and William Velez. 1988. "Insurance Redlining and the Process of Discrimination." *Review of Black Political Economy 16* (Winter): 63–75.

Steele, Shelby. 1994. "How to Grow Extremists." *The New York Times,* March 13, Op-Ed Page.

Stegman, Michael A., and Michale I. Luger. 1993. "Issues in the Design of Locally Sponsored Home Ownership Programs." *Journal of the American Planning Association 59* (Autumn): 417–432.

Steinberg, Jacques. 1993. "A Judge Calls Yonkers Slow at Integration." *The New York Times*, August 31, p. B1.

Steinberg, Stephen. 1981. *The Ethnic Myth: Race, Ethnicity, and Class in America.* New York: Atheneum Publishers.

Steptoe v. *Beverly Area Planning Association*, 647 F. Supp. 1313 (N.D. Ill. 1987).

Stiglitz, Joseph, and Andrew Weiss. 1981. "Credit Rationing in Markets with Imperfect Information." *American Economic Review 71* (June): 393–410.

Struyk, Raymond, Margery A. Turner, and John Yinger. 1991. *Housing Discrimination Study: Synthesis.* Washington, D.C.: U.S. Department of Housing and Urban Development.

Stucker, Jennifer L. 1986. "Race and Residential Mobility: The Effect of Housing Assistance Programs on Household Behavior." In *Housing Desegregation and Federal Policy*, edited by J. M. Goering. Chapel Hill: The University of North Carolina Press, pp. 253–261.

Sundiata, I.K. 1992. "Who Is Left Out." *The New York Times*, Letter to the Editor, November 18, p. A26.

Syracuse Herald-Journal. 1994. "Greenspan Speaks Out: Putting 'Redlining' in the Past." Editorial, February 12, p. A5.

Taub, Richard P., D. Garth Taylor, and Jan D. Dunham. 1984. *Paths of Neighborhood Change: Race and Crime in Urban America.* Chicago: University of Chicago Press.

Thomas, Paulette. 1991. "Mortgage Rejection Rate for Minorities is Quadruple That of Whites, Study Finds." *The Wall Street Journal*, October 21, p. A2.

———. 1992a. "Blacks Can Face a Host of Trying Conditions in Getting Mortgages." *The Wall Street Journal*, November 30, p. A1.

———. 1992b. "Federal Data Detail Pervasive Racial Gap in Mortgage Lending." *The Wall Street Journal*, March 21, p. A1.

Tisdale, William R., Shanna L. Smith, and Cathy Cloud. 1994. "Discrimination in the Homeowners Insurance Industry." Testimony of the National Fair Housing Alliance Before the Committee on Banking, Housing, and Urban Affairs, U.S. Senate, May 11.

Tootell, Geoffrey. 1993. "Defaults, Denials, and Discrimination in Mortgage Lending." *New England Economic Review* (September/October): 45–51.

Trafficante v. *Metropolitan Life Insurance Company*, 409 U.S. 205 (1972).

Turner, James P. 1993. "Statement Concerning Mortgage Lending Discrimination," Before the Committee on Banking, Housing, and Urban Affairs, United States Senate, February 24.

Turner, Margery A. 1992. "Discrimination in Urban Housing Markets: Lessons from Fair Housing Audits." *Housing Policy Debate 3* (2): 185–215.

Turner, Margery A., and Maris Mickelsons. 1992. "Patterns of Racial Steering in Four Metropolitan Areas." *Journal of Housing Economics* 2 (September): 199–234.

Turner, Margery A., Michael Fix, and Raymond J. Struyk. 1991. *Opportunities Denied, Opportunities Diminished: Racial Discrimination in Hiring.* Urban Institute Report 91-9. Washington, D.C.: The Urban Institute Press.

Turner, Margery A., Maris Mickelsons, and John G. Edwards. 1991. *Housing Discrimination Study: Analyzing Racial and Ethnic Steering.* Washington, D.C.: U.S. Department of Housing and Urban Development.

Turner, Margery A., and Ronald Wienk. 1993. "The Persistence of Segregation in Urban Areas: Contributing Causes." In *Housing Markets and Residential Mobility,* edited by G.T. Kingsley and M.A. Turner. Washington, D.C.: The Urban Institute Press, pp. 193–216.

Uchitelle, Susan. 1993. *School Choice: Issues and Answers.* Bloomington, IN: Phi Beta Kappa Educational Foundation.

U.S. Bureau of the Census. 1991. *American Housing Survey for the United States in 1989.* Washington, D.C.: U.S. Government Printing Office.

———. 1992a. *Population and Housing Characteristics for Census Tracts and Block Numbering Areas, Cleveland, OH PMSA.* 1990 Census of Population and Housing Report CPH-3-117B. Washington, D.C.: U.S. Government Printing Office.

———. 1992b. *Population and Housing Characteristics for Census Tracts and Block Numbering Areas, New York, NY PMSA.* 1990 Census of Population and Housing Report CPH-3-245H. Washington, D.C.: U.S. Government Printing Office.

———. 1992c. *Statistical Abstract of the United States: 1992.* 112th edition. Washington, D.C.: U.S. Government Printing Office.

———. 1993a. *General Housing Characteristics: Urbanized Areas.* Census Publication 1990 CH-1-1C/SEC.1. Washington, D.C.: U.S. Government Printing Office.

———. 1993b. *The Hispanic Population in the U.S.: 1992.* Washington, DC: U.S. Government Printing Office.

———. 1993c. *Poverty in the United States: 1992.* Current Population Reports, P60-185. Washington, D.C.: U.S. Government Printing Office.

———. 1993d. *Statistical Abstract of the United States: 1993.* 113th edition. Washington, D.C.: U.S. Government Printing Office.

———. 1994. "Census Bureau Announces Number of Americans in Poverty Up for Fourth Year Although Poverty Rate Unchanged; Household Income and Health Care Coverage Drop." News Release, October 6.

U.S. Commission on Civil Rights. 1973. *Understanding Fair Housing.* Clearing House Publication 42. Washington, D.C.: U.S. Government Printing Office.

————. 1994. *The Fair Housing Amendments Act of 1988: The Enforcement Report.* Washington, D.C.: U.S. Commission on Civil Rights, September.

U.S. Department of Education. 1993. *Reinventing Chapter 1.* Washington, D.C.: U.S. Government Printing Office.

U.S. Department of Housing and Urban Development. 1992. *The State of Fair Housing, 1991.* Washington, D.C.: U.S. Government Printing Office, September.

————. 1993. *Creating Communities of Opportunity: Priorities of U.S. Department of Housing and Urban Development.* Washington, D.C.: U.S. Government Printing Office, October.

————. 1994a. "Reinvention Blueprint." Washington, D.C.: By the Author, December 19.

————. 1994b. *The State of Fair Housing, 1992.* Washington, D.C.: U.S. Government Printing Office.

————. 1995. *The State of Fair Housing, 1993.* Washington, D.C.: U.S. Government Printing Office.

U. S. Department of Justice. 1992. *Hate Crime Statistics, Preliminary Release.* Washington, D.C.: By the Author.

U.S. v. Charlottesville Redevelopment and Housing Authority, **718 F. Supp. 461 (W.D. Va. 1989).**

U.S. v. Starrett City Associates, **640 F. Supp. 688 (E.D. N.Y. 1987), affirmed, 840 F.2d. 1096 (2n. Cir. 1988), cert. denied, 488 U.S. 946 (1988).**

The Urban Institute. 1991. *Housing Discrimination Study: Methodology and Data Documentation.* Washington, D.C.: U.S. Department of Housing and Urban Development.

USA Today. 1991. "Segregation: The Walls Between Us." November 11, p. 1A.

Van Order, Robert. 1993. "Discrimination and the Secondary Mortgage Market." Paper presented at Discrimination and Mortgage Lending: Research and Enforcement Conference, sponsored by the U.S. Department of Housing and Urban Development, Washington, D.C., May.

Van Valey, Thomas L., Wade Clark Roof, and Jerome E. Wilcox. 1977. "Trends in Residential Segregation: 1970–1980." *American Journal of Sociology 82* (January): 826–844.

Verhovek, Sam Howe. 1994. "Under Armed Escort, Blacks Move into White Texas Housing Project." *The New York Times,* January 14, p. A1.

Vernarelli, Michael J. 1986. "Where Should HUD Locate Assisted Housing? The Evolution of Fair Housing Policy." In *Housing Desegregation and Federal Policy,* edited by J. M. Goering. Chapel Hill: The University of North Carolina Press, pp. 214–234.

Vose, Clement E. 1959. *Caucasians Only*. Berkeley: University of California Press.

Wachter, Susan M., and Isaac F. Megbolugbe. 1992. "Racial and Ethnic Disparities in Homeownership." *Housing Policy Debate 3* (2): 333–370.

Waldron, Thomas W. 1994. "Parading Politicians Hear Critics of Housing Program." *The Baltimore Sun*, September 12.

Walker, Alice. 1988. *The Third Life of Grange Copeland*, paperback edition. New York: Pocket Books.

Wards Cove Packing Co. v. Atonia, 490 U.S. 642 (1989).

Wartzman, Rick. 1993. Good Connections: New Bus Lines Link the Inner-City Poor with Jobs in Suburbia." *The Wall Street Journal*, September 24, p. A1.

Weisbrod, G., and Avis Vidal. 1981. "Housing Search Barriers for Low-Income Renters." *Urban Affairs Quarterly 16* (June): 465–482.

West, Cornel. 1994. *Race Matters*. New York: Vintage Books.

White, Lawrence J. 1993. "The Community Reinvestment Act: Good Intentions Headed in the Wrong Direction." *Fordham Urban Law Journal 20* (Winter): 281–291.

Wienk, Ronald E. 1992. "Discrimination in Urban Credit Markets: What We Don't Know and Why We Don't Know It." *Housing Policy Debate 3* (2): 217–240.

Wienk, Ronald E., Clifford E. Reid, John C. Simonson, and Frederick J. Eggers. 1979. *Measuring Discrimination in American Housing Markets: The Housing Market Practices Survey*. Washington, D.C.: U.S. Department of Housing and Urban Development.

Wienk, Ron, John Simonson, and Robin Ross Smith, with Martha Kuhlman and Jennifer Pack. 1994. *An Evaluation of the FHIP Private Enforcement Initiative Testing Demonstration*. Washington, D.C.: U.S. Department of Housing and Urban Development, Office of Policy Development and Research, April.

Wilke, John R. 1991. "Back-Door Loans: Some Banks' Money Flows into Poor Areas—and Causes Anguish." *The Wall Street Journal*, October 21, p. A1.

Williams, Juan. 1994. "Violence, Genes, and Prejudice." *Discover 15* (November): 92–102.

Wills, Christopher. 1994. "The Skin We're In." *Discover 15* (November): 77–81.

Wilson, William Julius. 1987. *The Truly Disadvantaged: The Inner City, the Underclass, and Public Policy*. Chicago: University of Chicago Press.

————. 1991. "Public Policy Research and *The Truly Disadvantaged.*" In *The Urban Underclass,* edited by C. Jencks and P.E. Peterson. Washington, D.C.: The Urban Institute Press, pp. 460–481.

Winerip, Michael. 1987. "Steering Blacks Around an Island of White Homes." *The New York Times,* December 15, p. B1.

————. 1988. "East Side Story: The Long Trail of Housing Bias." *The New York Times,* September 9, 1988, p. B1.

Witte, John. 1994. "The Milwaukee Parental Choice Program: Third Year Report." *The La Follette Policy Report 6* (Winter): 6–7.

Wolff, Edward. 1994. "Trends in Household Wealth in the United States: 1962–1983 and 1983–1989." NIA Workshop on Cross-National Issues in Aging. Workshop Paper No. 48. Syracuse, NY: All-University Gerontology Center, Syracuse University.

Wright, Lawrence. 1994. "One Drop of Blood." *The New Yorker,* July 25, pp. 46–55.

Yarrow, Andrew L. 1991. "Realty Building in Canarsie Hit by Firecrackers." *The New York Times,* September 26, p. B7.

Yezer, Anthony M.J., Robert F. Phillips, and Robert P. Trost. 1994. "Race Redlining and Residential Mortgage Loan Performance." *Journal of Real Estate Finance and Economics 9* (November): 197–216.

Yinger, John. 1975. "An Analysis of Discrimination by Real Estate Brokers." Institute for Research on Poverty Discussion Paper No. 252-75. Madison: University of Wisconsin.

————. 1976. **"Racial Prejudice and Racial Residential Segregation in an Urban Model."** *Journal of Urban Economics 3* (October): 383–396.

————. 1979. "Prejudice and Discrimination in the Urban Housing Market." In *Current Issues in Urban Economics,* edited by P. Mieszkowski and M. Straszheim. Baltimore: The Johns Hopkins University Press, pp. 430–468.

————. 1985. "Measuring Racial and Ethnic Discrimination with Fair Housing Audits: A Review of Existing Evidence and Research Methodology." Paper presented at HUD Conference on Fair Housing Testing, Washington, D.C., December 1984 (revised February 1985).

————. 1986a. "Measuring Discrimination with Fair Housing Audits: Caught in the Act." *American Economic Review 76* (December): 881–893.

————. 1986b. "On the Possibility of Achieving Racial Integration Through Subsidized Housing." In *Housing Desegregation and Federal Policy,* edited by J.M. Goering. Chapel Hill: The University of North Carolina Press, pp. 290–312.

————. 1987. "The Racial Dimension of Urban Housing Markets in the 1980s." In *Divided Neighborhoods: Changing Patterns of Racial Segregation,* edited by G.A. Tobin. Urban Affairs Annual Reviews, vol. 32. Newbury Park, CA: Sage Publications, pp. 43–67.

———. **1991a.** "Acts of Discrimination: Evidence for the 1989 Housing Discrimination Study." *Journal of Housing Economics 1* (December): 318–346.

———. **1991b.** *Housing Discrimination Study: Incidence and Severity of Unfavorable Treatment.* Washington, D.C.: U.S. Department of Housing and Urban Development.

———. **1991c.** *Housing Discrimination Study: Incidence of Discrimination and Variation in Discriminatory Behavior.* Washington, D.C.: U.S. Department of Housing and Urban Development.

———. **1992.** "An Analysis of the Efficiency of Urban Residential Structure, with an Application to Racial Integration." *Journal of Urban Economics 31* (May): 388–407.

———. **1993a.** "Access Denied, Access Constrained: Results and Implications of the 1989 Housing Discrimination Study." In *Clear and Convincing Evidence: Testing for Discrimination in America,* edited by M. Fix and R. J. Struyk. Washington, D.C.: The Urban Institute Press, pp. 69–112.

———. **1993b.** "Audit Methodology: Comments." In *Clear and Convincing Evidence: Measurement of Discrimination in America,* edited by M. Fix and R.J. Struyk. Washington, D.C.: The Urban Institute Press, pp. 259–270.

———. **1993c.** "Discrimination in Mortgage Lending: A Literature Review." Paper presented at Discrimination and Mortgage Lending: Research and Enforcement Conference, sponsored by the U.S. Department of Housing and Urban Development, Washington, D.C., May (revised June).

———. **1994.** "Cash in Your Face: The Cost of Racial and Ethnic Discrimination in Housing." Metropolitan Studies Program Occasional Paper No. 162 (revised August 1994). Syracuse, NY: Center for Policy Research, Syracuse University.

Yinger, John, George C. Galster, Barton A. Smith, and Fred Eggers. 1979. "The Status of Research into Racial Discrimination in American Housing Markets: A Research Agenda for the Department of Housing and Urban Development." *Occasional Papers in Housing and Community Affairs 6* (December). U.S. Department of Housing and Urban Development, pp. 55–175.

Yinger, J. Milton. 1985. "Assimilation in the United States: The Mexican-Americans." In *Mexican-Americans in Comparative Perspective,* edited by W. Conner. Washington, D.C.: The Urban Institute Press, pp. 29–55.

———. **1994.** *Ethnicity: Source of Strength? Source of Conflict?* Albany: State University of New York Press.

Zandi, Mark. 1993. "Boston Fed's Bias Study Was Deeply Flawed." *American Banker,* August 19.

Zax, Jeffrey S., and John F. Kain. 1991. "Commutes, Quits, and Moves." *Journal of Urban Economics 29* (March): 153–165.

Zimmerman, M.W. 1992. "Opening the Door to Race-based Real Estate Marketing: South Suburban Housing Center v. Greater South-Suburban Board of Realtors." *DePaul Law Review 41:* 1271–1367.

Zoloth, Barbara. 1976. "Alternative Measures of School Segregation." *Land Economics 52:* 278–298.

Zuch v. *Hussey,* **394 F. Supp. 1028 (E.D. Mich. 1975), modified as to relief and aff'd** *per curiam,* **547 F. 2d 1168 (1977).**

Zuckman, Jill. 1993. "Funding Fights to Dominate in Chapter 1 Rewrite." *Congressional Quarterly 51* (May 8): 1146–1151.

NAME INDEX

Boldface numbers refer to tables and figures.

Boldface numbers refer to tables and figures.

fault rates as an indication of, 75–
78; definition of, 66–68; during
housing search, 95–96; elimination of, 210, 246; example of, 63;
laws, 196–197; in loan approval,
69–75, 95; in loan terms, 79–81; in
outreach and application procedures, 78–79; prohibitions, 194–
196; by real estate brokers, 46; rediscovery of, 64–66, 196, 204, 226,
368n; understatement of, 72, 73,
75, 298n, 308n. *See also* loans
mortgage lending, 229; cases assigned to enforcement agencies,
229; decision, 67; test, 368n
mortgage markets: actors in, 81;
consequences of discrimination
in, 81–84; current and past discrimination in, 106; direct cost of
discrimination in, **101,** 101; federal support for research of, 248;
redlining in, 84–85; role of insurers in, 82; secondary, 83–84, 183,
231; treatment of minorities in,
302n; ways to test discrimination
in, 75
mortgages: conventional, 81, 83;
FHA-insured, 123; fixed rate, 81;
government-backed, 366n; information about, 81; outstanding, 107,
312n; products marketing, 231; programs, 304n; pro-integrative, 128,
324n, 369n; qualification for, 178;
variable rate, 81. *See also* loans
mortgage terms and conditions, 72,
188, 244. *See also* loans
*Mountain Side Mobile Estate Partner-
ship* v. *HUD,* 351n
moves: discouraged by discrimination, **101,** 102; pro-integrative, 128,
250, 342n; time between, 308n–
309n
moving: costs, 92, 96, 100, **101,** 101,
306n, 310n; decisions, 151–152,
335n; discriminatory premium in
cost of, 97; gain from, 90, 100; impact of household change on surplus associated with, 99; intentions
of whites, 121; outcomes, 336n
moving business discrimination in,
96
Moving to Opportunity (MTO), 235,
240, 362n, 372n, 375n

multi-family buildings, 299n
multiple listing service/s (MLSs),
60, 91, 186, 249, 308n; access to,
58–59, 294n; coalition, 226; directory, 342n; information collected
from, 224–225; role in steering, 58,
164, 171–173, 225; use of, 58–59,
60, 180, 181, 222
multiracial category for decennial
census, 11

Nashville, **115**
Nassau County, New York, 287n,
315n, 356n
national origin, 223
Native Americans, 10, 208, 275n,
290n, 366n
Nebraska, 328n, 330n
neighborhood change, 105, 132
neighborhood choice, 215, 216, 233,
245, 246; promoting, 240, 247,
249–250
neighborhood composition, 259,
260; agent's incentives associated
with, 167, 185
neighborhood decline, 212;
blockbusting and, 122–124
neighborhood effects, 58, 155, **169,
171, 172, 175, 176,** 337n–338n,
345n
neighborhood quality, 125
neighborhood preferences, 117–120,
164, 244, 282n, 319n, 345n; factors
influencing, 121
neighborhood racial and ethnic integration, 13–14
neighborhood/s: agent behavior in
different, 180–182; definitions of,
259; denial rate patterns in different, 70; dimension on poverty,
154–156; distressed, 154, 155, 156,
250, 338n; funding eligibility for,
369n; high-poverty, 235, 240, 339n;
information about, 125, 167; low-
income, 73, 197, 198, 200, 302n;
marketing of houses in minority
and integrated, 57–60, 244, 293n;
marketing of houses in white, 57–
58; moderate-income, 200; negative comments about, 55–56, 292n;
racial composition of, 293n, 304n;
redlining in specific, 84; scale,
314n; stability, 233; steering of mi-